Constituent Power and the Law

OXFORD CONSTITUTIONAL THEORY

SERIES EDITORS

Martin Loughlin, John P. McCormick, and Neil Walker

Oxford Constitutional Theory has rapidly established itself as the primary point of reference for theoretical reflections on the growing interest in constitutions and constitutional law in domestic, regional and global contexts. The majority of the works published in the series are monographs that advance new understandings of their subject. But the series aims to provide a forum for further innovation in the field by also including well-conceived edited collections that bring a variety of perspectives and disciplinary approaches to bear on specific themes in constitutional thought and by publishing English translations of leading monographs in constitutional theory that have originally been written in languages other than English.

ALSO AVAILABLE IN THE SERIES

Euroconstitutionalism and its Discontents
Oliver Gerstenberg

Beyond the People
Social Imaginary and Constituent Imagination
Zoran Oklopcic

The Metaethics of Constitutional Adjudication
Boško Tripković

Carl Schmitt's State and Constitutional Theory
A Critical Analysis
Benjamin A. Schupmann

Law and Revolution
Legitimacy and Constitutionalism After the Arab Spring
Nimer Sultany

Constitutional and Political Theory
Selected Writings
Ernst-Wolfgang Böckenförde
Edited by Mirjam Künkler and Tine Stein

Constitutionalism
Past, Present, and Future
Dieter Grimm

Europe's Functional Constitution
A Theory of Constitutionalism Beyond the State
Turkuler Isiksel

Post Sovereign Constitution Making
Learning and Legitimacy
Andrew Arato

Popular Sovereignty in Early Modern Constitutional Though
Daniel Lee

The Cultural Defense of Nations
A Liberal Theory of Majority Rights
Liav Orgad

The Cosmopolitan Constitution
Alexander Somek

The Structure of Pluralism
Victor M. Muniz-Fraticelli

Constitutional Courts and Deliberative Democracy
Conrado Hübner Mendes

Fault Lines of Globalization
Legal Order and the Politics of A-Legality
Hans Lindahl

The Cosmopolitan State
H Patrick Glenn

After Public Law
Edited by Cormac Mac Amhlaigh, Claudio Michelon, and Neil Walker

The Three Branches
A Comparative Model of Separation of Powers
Christoph Möllers

The Global Model of Constitutional Rights
Kai Möller

The Twilight of Constitutionalism?
Edited by Petra Dobner and Martin Loughlin

Beyond Constitutionalism
The Pluralist Structure of Postnational Law
Nico Krisch

Constituting Economic and Social Rights
Katharine G. Young

Constitutional Referendums
The Theory and Practice of Republican Deliberation
Stephen Tierney

Constituent Power and the Law

JOEL COLÓN-RÍOS

OXFORD
UNIVERSITY PRESS

OXFORD
UNIVERSITY PRESS

Great Clarendon Street, Oxford, OX2 6DP,
United Kingdom

Oxford University Press is a department of the University of Oxford.
It furthers the University's objective of excellence in research, scholarship,
and education by publishing worldwide. Oxford is a registered trade mark of
Oxford University Press in the UK and in certain other countries

First Edition published in 2020

Impression: 1

Published in the United States of America by Oxford University Press
198 Madison Avenue, New York, NY 10016, United States of America

British Library Cataloguing in Publication Data
Data available

Library of Congress Control Number: 2019951596

ISBN 978–0–19–878598–9

Printed and bound by
CPI Group (UK) Ltd, Croydon, CR0 4YY

Acknowledgements

The writing of a book always is, at least at one level, a solitary endeavour. This is not merely a result of the individual nature of the act of writing, but a consequence of what takes place around it: constant thinking and rethinking of arguments, countless moments of doubt, and an absolute individual responsibility over the final result. At the same time, writing a book is an essentially social act: it is about reflecting on the acts of different individuals and groups, about engaging with the ideas of past and contemporary authors and about testing one's views against those of others. It is also made possible by the support of different institutions and the advice of friends and colleagues. In the case of this book, I would like to thank the following institutions and persons. The Royal Society of New Zealand and the Faculty of Law at Victoria University of Wellington provided me with the funding and time to carry out the necessary research and analysis that the reader will find in the pages that follow. I am very grateful to Jhonny Pabón, who assisted me with the project since the very beginning. Alec Duncan, Luna Arango, Carlos López, and Billie Haddleton provided me with excellent research assistance.

There are many colleagues whose intellectual generosity allowed me to develop certain ideas and topics in ways that would have otherwise not been possible. Many commented on draft papers or oral presentations that later became the basis of different chapters, others provided me with historical materials I had no access to, some made themselves available for face-to-face discussions, and some did all of those things. I will try to mention all of them here, knowing that the chances are there will be accidental omissions: Antoni Abat i Ninet, Richard Albert, Graeme Austin, Andrew Arato, Vicente Benitez, Mark Bennett, Rodrigo Camarena González, Claudia Geiringer, Rosalind Dixon, Eric Ghosh, Marco Goldoni, Juan Herrera, Martín Hevia, James Kierstead, Mark Hickford, Sir Kenneth Keith, Dean Knight, David Landau, Hans Lindahl, Héctor López Boffil, Martin Loughlin, Xavier Marquez, Rubén Martínez Dalmau, Campbell McLachlan, Geoff McLay, Gabriel Negretto, Zoran Oklopcic, Yaniv Roznai, Guy Sinclair, Claire Timperley, Kevin Walton, Miguel Vatter, Mariana Velasco-Rivera, and Sergio Verdugo. Finally, I would like to thank my family, both in Puerto Rico and New Zealand, for their love and support. Graciela, Lucas, and Matías, who experienced the process more closely and were more directly affected by my frequent absent-mindedness, deserve special thanks.

Contents

Table of Cases

Table of Legislation

OTHER PRIMARY SOURCES

1
Introduction

This is a book about the relationship between constituent power and the law. It examines the legal and institutional implications of the theory of constituent power, focusing on the ways in which various formulations of that relationship inform different aspects of past and current constitutional discourse. This approach will inevitably raise suspicion among some academics. After all, constituent power has been traditionally seen as an extra-legal or even pre-political force that escapes any form of institutionalization and becomes juridically irrelevant once a constitutional order is in place; although of interest to some theoretically oriented public lawyers, it should mainly be the concern of political theorists or other social scientists. But the idea that in any juridical order there is a supreme constituent authority can have important effects in actual constitutional practice. Indeed, the theory of constituent power has been, and still is, frequently used by government officials, judges, academics, and citizens to justify or challenge the legal validity of different exercises of political power.

It is true that the theory of constituent power has often been linked to naked exercises of force and that it has been deployed by dictators and military juntas to justify departures from the rule of law. In those contexts, constituent power appears as law's antithesis, as a political potency alien to the idea of legal regulation. That, however, is not what one always observes in reality. For example, constitutional courts in Latin America, Europe, and Asia have relied on the theory of constituent power to justify their jurisdiction to invalidate constitutional amendments that alter the fundamental structure of the constitution.[1] Some governments have recurred to it to defend the legality of the transformation of the constitutional order through procedures not contemplated in the constitution's amendment rule but considered participatory enough to be seen as equivalent to 'the people in action', and these attempts have sometimes been sanctioned by courts.[2] Commentators and citizens have relied on the theory of constituent power to defend (and sometimes to reject) the idea that electors

[1] Yaniv Roznai, *Unconstitutional Constitutional Amendments: The Limits of Amendment Powers* (Oxford: Oxford University Press, 2017).

[2] Joel Colón-Ríos, 'Carl Schmitt and Constituent Power in Latin American Courts: The Cases of Venezuela and Colombia', 18(3) *Constellations* 365 (2011).

Constituent Power and the Law. Joel Colón-Ríos, Oxford University Press (2020). © Joel Colón-Ríos.
DOI: 10.1093/oso/9780198785989.001.0001

have the right to instruct representatives,[3] as well as the notion that the creation of new constitutions must take place through extra-legislative entities, such as primary assemblies open to all citizens.[4] Several Latin American constitutions explicitly incorporate the theory of constituent power and allow citizens, acting through popular initiative, to trigger constitution-making episodes that may result in the replacement of the entire constitutional order.[5]

In those and other contexts, constituent power has sometimes played the functions of limiting political power, and sometimes that of enabling different types of popular and governmental action. This phenomenon, even if it remains under-theorized, has not gone unnoticed in the literature. During the last two decades, a number of articles and books have indirectly examined different aspects of the relationship between constituent power and the law. Most of these works have to do either with the doctrine of unconstitutional constitutional amendments,[6] or with analyses of contemporary constitution-making processes, frequently in the Latin American region.[7] In the former case, constituent power is mostly presented in a positive light; in the latter, as a concept that, although at one level demanding popular constitutional politics, can serve to justify different kind of abusive constitutional practices. Their contribution to the understanding of different doctrines and events notwithstanding, most of these works present little or no indication of the ways in which current approaches to constituent authority, and of its role in different contexts, are rehearsals of debates that took place decades, and in some cases, centuries ago.[8] Without revisiting those debates, one is unable to grasp the full juridical potential of the theory of constituent power for contemporary constitutional practice.

In this book, I seek to bring to the surface early understandings of the relationship between constituent power and the law, of the concept's legal and institutional implications, and explore their connections with, and relevance

[3] Joel Colón-Ríos, 'Five Conceptions of Constituent Power', 130 *Law Quarterly Review* 306.

[4] See Chapters 2 to 4 of this book. The theory of constituent power has also been deployed by judges to describe the nature of the power of the Westminster Parliament with respect to the overseas empire and by jurists to explain the (frequently limited) scope of the constitution-making power of colonial legislatures. ibid. (2014).

[5] Joel Colón-Ríos, *Weak Constitutionalism: Democratic Legitimacy and the Question of Constituent Power* (Oxon: Routledge, 2012).

[6] Roznai (n. 1).

[7] David Landau, 'Constitution-Making Gone Wrong', 64 *Alabama Law Review* 923 (2013).

[8] For a notable exception that does not focus on the legal and institutional implications of the concept, see Andrew Arato, *Adventures of the Constituent Power: Beyond Revolutions?* (Cambridge: Cambridge University Press, 2017). See also the important works by Richard S. Kay, 'Constituent Authority', 59 *American Journal of Comparative Law* 715 (2011) and Chris Thornhill, *A Sociology of Constitutions: Constitutions and State Legitimacy in Historical-Sociological Perspective* (Cambridge: Cambridge University Press, 2011).

for, current constitutional practices. Before engaging in that analysis, however, it is necessary to make some clarifications about the topic under study; to explain what is meant by 'constituent power' in contemporary constitutional discourse. In that vein, this introductory chapter begins by examining (in Parts I and II) the two main ways in which academics have understood this concept. These approaches will be presented through the work of several authors, such as Juan Donoso Cortés, Raymond Carré de Malberg, Georges Vedel, and Ernst-Wolfgang Böckenförde. The first approach identifies constituent power with revolution and extra-legality and, the second, presents it as channelled through a constitution's amendment rule.[9] Although these approaches may at first sight seem to refer to different phenomena (the first one referring to constituent power 'proper' and the second to what we may usually call the 'amending power') both are attempts of describing the nature of what is understood to be a substantively unlimited constitution-making faculty.

Both notions, it will be seen in Part III of this chapter, are not only nearly identical in the most relevant aspects but, at least potentially, present an equally dangerous 'threat' to the established constitutional order. There are, in fact, some reasons to think that the derived and the original constituent power can be understood as conceptualizations of the same constitution-making authority. And both of these conceptualizations can be deployed in ways that enable or limit the exercise of political power. However, the distinction between the derived and the original constituent power has often served as a justification of different doctrines (e.g. the doctrine of unconstitutional constitutional amendments) and procedures (e.g. the judicial sanctioning of extra-legal constituent assemblies) Ultimately, as suggested by the analysis in Chapters 9 and 10, this distinction tends to confuse constituent power and sovereignty and, as a result, miss an important aspect of the juridical nature of constituent authority.

Finally, Part IV of this introduction outlines the contents of the chapters that follow. The book begins by looking at the first theoretical formulations of the separation between the constituent and the constituted powers, and then moves to analyse different functions that the latter has played in constitutional theory and in the constitutional practice of several jurisdictions, particularly

[9] This is not to say that these are the only two approaches possible; modern and contemporary constitutional theory has always been more nuanced and sophisticated than that. My intention in this introduction is only to set the scope of the topic under analysis. The next chapters will consider its complexities. Importantly, these two approaches also reflect one of the key differences between Emmanuel Sieyès and Jean Jacques Rousseau. For the former, constituent power is always extra-legal; for the latter, it not only can, but should, be exercised through law. Indeed, Sieyès and Rousseau's thought will be present, in different ways, in all the chapters that follow.

Spain, France, Colombia, and Venezuela. Where relevant, comparisons are made with the English and American constitutional traditions. In so doing, the book seeks to capture key historical events and political/theoretical debates in the development of the relationship between constituent power and the law. The last two chapters are the most normative and engage in an analysis of the nature of constituent power, its relationship with sovereignty, and the implication of that relationship for the power of constituent assemblies. These chapters maintain that to the extent a constituent assembly acts on a commission, it can be made subject to conditions ratified through which I will call constituent referendums. In certain institutional contexts, it will be argued, those conditions would be judicially enforceable. The book ends with a conclusion that outlines what I think are its main insights and identifies future avenues of research.

I. Constituent Power as an Extra-Legal Phenomenon

There are two main ways in which the theory of constituent power has been treated by academics since it was put into practice in the great revolutions of the 18th century. Under the first approach, constituent power's extra-legal and uncontrollable character is emphasized. It is presented as a power found outside the dominion of law and therefore incapable of legal regulation. This is the way in which most legal scholars understand it, and partially explains the reason for the relative inattention to the concept in some contemporary constitutional circles. Under the second, less influential approach, constituent power is constitutionalized: it is seen as the power of altering or replacing a constitution according to certain prescribed rules. From this perspective, the fact that even the exercise of an ultimate constitution-making power is subject to law is celebrated as one of the greatest achievements of modern constitutionalism: the domestication of an apparently unruly political force. These two approaches are difficult to distinguish from each other, partly for conceptual reasons (i.e. does the constitutionalization of constituent power necessarily negate its arguably unlimited nature?), and partly for terminological ones (i.e. not all authors use the term 'constituent power' to refer to the same thing). In what follows, I will try to make the distinction as clear as possible.

The first approach was clearly exemplified in the work of Donoso Cortés. Unlike most contemporary jurists, Donoso, writing in the mid-19th century, did not see 'the people' as the bearer of constituent power and despised the idea of attributing the collective body of citizens with a sovereign ability to recreate the juridical order. Donoso thought that popular sovereignty presupposed a people with rights and no duties, a situation that could only lead to tyranny.[10] His disapproval of theories of popular sovereignty was so strong that he once described Rousseau as 'the terrible personification of the people', 'launching thunderbolts against all constituted powers and social eminences'.[11] But in Donoso's lectures at the *Ateneo de Madrid*, he not only rejected popular sovereignty, but any notion of *absolute* sovereignty altogether.[12] For him, only an entity capable of putting into practice the sovereignty of reason—an infallible entity—should be given sovereign powers, and there was no person or human institution on Earth that could meet that requirement.[13] This view led him to the democratically unpalatable conclusion that those men with a superior intelligence, that is, those who were more likely to come closer to the ideal of infallibility, were the ones to be granted (a limited) right to govern the rest.[14]

Nevertheless, Donoso believed that in exceptional circumstances, in times of disorder and insurrection, only an absolute sovereign could save society from shipwreck.[15] That true sovereign was for him the constituent power, which would act through the sole hands of 'a strong and intelligent man' charged with the task of bringing society back to order.[16] In his inimitable style, Donoso maintained that:

> the constituent power can neither be localised by the legislator nor formulated by the philosopher, because it cannot be fitted into books, and it destroys the framework of constitutions: if it ever appears, it appears like lighting that rips the bosom of a cloud, inflames the atmosphere, hurts its victim, and disappears.[17]

[10] Juan Donoso Cortés, *Obras* (Madrid: Imprenta de Tejado, 1954) 138.

[11] ibid. 135. The relationship between Rousseau's political thought and the concept of constituent power will be examined in Chapter 2.

[12] This view reflects the doctrinaire approach to sovereignty, which will be discussed in Chapter 7 of this book.

[13] Donoso (n. 10) 198.

[14] ibid. 196, 204. It was a limited right, proportional to the fallibility of those who exercised it.

[15] ibid 199. There are some obvious similarities between this aspect of Donoso's work and Carl Schmitt's views on emergency powers. These similarities will be explored in Chapter 9. For a detailed discussion, see Luis Villar Borda, *Donoso Cortés y Carl Schmitt* (Bogotá: Universidad Externado de Colombia, 2006). See also Carl Schmitt, *Dictatorship: From the Origin of the Modern Concept of Sovereignty to Proletarian Class Struggle* (Cambridge: Polity, 2014), where he refers in various instances to the works of Donoso (276 n. 11, 279 n. 22, 294 n. 38), and Carl Schmitt, *Political Theology: Four Chapters on the Theory of Sovereignty* (Chicago: University of Chicago Press, 1985), which contains one chapter dedicated to the ideas of Donoso, Joseph de Maistre, and Louis de Bonald.

[16] Donoso (n. 10) 200.

[17] ibid.

After uttering these words in an 1829 lecture, Donoso told the audience that he should better 'let [constituent power] be', rather than try to 'formulate it'[18]. Although apparently controversial, this approach is not dissimilar to the way in which constituent power is seen by authors who do not share Donoso's authoritarian ideology. For instance, in the mid-20th century, Carl Friedrich described constituent power as the '*de facto* residuary power of changing or replacing the constitution of an existing political order', the exercise of which always amounts to a revolution.[19] He attributed to the constituent subject a 'transcendental' and 'metaconstitutional' nature, and insisted in the impossibility of bringing it 'within the four corners of the constitution'.[20]

Understanding constituent power correctly, according to Friedrich, requires one to distinguish it from the amendment rules contained in typical constitutional documents. The organs authorized to alter the constitutional text are regulated by law, and this necessarily means that they do not participate in the exercise of a sovereign constitution-making faculty. Moreover, for Freidrich, the adoption of formal amendment rules 'should not be assumed to [supersede] the constituent power', which always threatens the constitutional order from the outside.[21]

The idea of constituent power as extra-legal and uncontrollable is also shared by jurists who attribute to it the function of legitimizing the existing constitutional order. A good contemporary example is provided by Ernst-Wolfgang Böckenförde. For Böckenförde, the mere fact that a constitution has been successfully brought into existence is not sufficient to guarantee its continued acceptance over time. A constitution can only be legitimate, he argued, if it rests in the (always present) constituent authority of the people. Constituent power is thus seen as an original and rudimentary potency that serves as the source of democratic legitimacy, a power that is 'capable of creating, sustaining, and cancelling the constitution'.[22] In Böckenförde's view, the question of constituent power is a juridical question because it is directly connected to the legitimacy of the legal order, but constituent power itself, he suggests, is a power that precedes the constitution and remains forever uncontrolled by its rules of change.[23]

[18] ibid.

[19] Carl J. Friedrich, *Constitutional Government and Democracy: Theory and Practice in Europe and America* (Waltham, Mass: Blaisdell Publishing Company, 1968) 138, 134.

[20] ibid. 149, 137.

[21] ibid. 149.

[22] Ersnt-Wolfgang-Böckenförde, 'El Poder Constituyente del Pueblo: Un Concepto Límite del Derecho Constitucional' in *Estudios sobre el Estado de Derecho y la Democracia* (Madrid: Editorial Trotta, 2000) 160, 163.

[23] ibid. 160, 168. It is true, Böckenförde says, that one can devise procedures that attempt to 'channel' constituent power (such as constituent assemblies). It is also correct that the exercise of constituent

Carré de Malberg, who devoted an entire chapter of his *Contribution à la Théorie Générale de l'Etat* (originally published in 1922) to an analysis of the concept, provides an excellent point of transition between the more traditional approach (exemplified here in the works of Donoso, Friedrich, and Böckenförde) and the one to be discussed in the next section.[24] For Carré, there is a clear sense in which the theory of constituent power should not even be the concern of lawyers: when used to explain the creation of a state's first constitution (the constitution that brings a new state into existence), the exercise of constituent power must be understood as purely factual, not susceptible of being governed by legal principles.[25] The same applies when a new constitution is created as a result of a legal revolution, where formal amendment rules are violated and the chain of legality between the old and the new constitutional order irreparably broken.[26] In those contexts, it is not preposterous to associate constituent power with unlawfulness, extra-legal action, and legally unregulated force.

Those exercises of constituent power are clearly outside the scope of the legal system, either because there is no positive law yet in place—as when the first constitution of a state is created—or because the existing positive law has proved unable to stop the destruction of the constitutional order. Political actions of that sort may very well raise urgent moral issues but, for Carré de Malberg, they do not present any juridical questions to be answered by a lawyer. The most a lawyer can do, he maintained in a manner reminiscent of Hans Kelsen, would be to identify the moment in which a revolutionary constitution becomes valid.[27] The details of the constitution-making process that led to its adoption are just not relevant from a juridical perspective.[28] This is why Carré de Malberg criticized the view shared by some of his contemporaries, who saw in the concept of constituent power 'the capital problem of public law'.[29] There

power is always accompanied by a certain degree of 'constitutionality', since it must always end in the production of a constitution. ibid. 169–172, 176. Nevertheless, these potential 'limits' are never enough to bring constituent power under the full reins of the constitution it precedes and legitimizes. Constituent power, he maintains, echoing Carl Schmitt (whose conception of constituent power will be discussed in Chapters 8 and 9), is always capable of manifesting itself in unanticipated ways, and even though it should act as a legitimizing force, it could very well do the opposite: ibid. 169.

[24] Raymond Carré de Malberg, *Contribución a la Teoría General del Estado* (Mexico: Fondo de Cultura Económica, 1948) 1161. Carré de Malberg's account of the place of constituent power in French constitutional theory and of what he calls the 'separation of the constituent and the constituted powers' will be discussed in Chapter 9.

[25] ibid. 1167.

[26] ibid. 1173.

[27] See Hans Kelsen, *General Theory of Law and State* (Cambridge: Harvard University Press, 1949).

[28] Carré de Malberg (n. 24) 1168.

[29] ibid. 1161, 1168.

is no role in the science of public law, he said, for the consideration of the extraordinary sovereignty of the 'great days',[30] just as there is no space in it 'for a legal theory of *coups d'état*, or of revolution and its effects'.[31]

II. Constituent Power as a Procedurally Regulated Activity

Despite Carré de Malberg's critique of those who attribute to constituent power a juridical character, he did not think it was altogether irrelevant for the student of public law. On the contrary, he maintained that in the context of an already existing constitutional order, one could speak of a 'regular and pacific' constituent power: the power to modify the existing constitution (or to replace it with a new one) according to procedures established by law. He called this the 'juridical concept' of constituent power (*la notion juridique de pouvoir constituant*), which presupposes the existence of a constitutional order and is procedurally regulated by it.[32] Modern constitutions, he maintained, have generally operated according to this view, which is why they contain carefully designed mechanisms of constitutional change. The fortunate consequence is that when a constitution is to be amended or replaced, it is neither necessary to resort to the whole body of citizens nor to engage in the exercise of an extra-legal power.[33] In such scenarios, 'the intervention of the organs that the constitution—the same constitution that will be amended or replaced—prescribes in advance for the regular and pacific exercise of the constituent power' is sufficient.[34]

Those organs (e.g. a legislative supermajority or a special assembly) are legally authorized to alter or replace the existing constitution as long as they follow the legal procedures that channel their constituent activity.[35] We thus see here the basic formulation of the second approach: constituent power as a power authorized by the constitution and capable of destroying it without breaking the law. Generally, academics who advance this approach distinguish,

[30] ibid. 1209.

[31] ibid. 1173. For a judicial attempt to regulate the legal effects of revolution, see 'Acordada de 10 de septiembre 1930', Fallos de la Corte Suprema de la Nación (10 September 1930) vol. 158. See also *Municipalidad de la Ciudad de Buenos Aires v Carlos M. Mayer*, Fallos de la Corte Suprema de la Nación (Argentina) (1945) vol. 201, and the rest in a line of cases that followed *Martinez v Otero*, Fallos de la Corte Suprema de la Nación (Argentina) (1865) vol. 2.

[32] ibid. 1175, for the French version, see *Contribution à la Théorie Générale de l'Etat* (Paris: Recuel Sirey, 1922) 500.

[33] ibid. 1174.

[34] ibid.

[35] ibid. 1173.

like Carré de Malberg, between a revolutionary constituent power and a legally regulated one. The former is sometimes identified by courts and academics as *original* constituent power and the latter as *derived* constituent power, a distinction to which I will come back shortly. Nevertheless, as we will see below, what characterizes this second approach is that both notions of constituent power (the 'original' and the 'derived' one) are seen as capable of producing the same results: the radical transformation of the constitutional regime. They are instances of the same phenomenon, moments in which the *same* power is exercised even if in different contexts and through different means.

This view, which is usually associated with (although not exclusive to) French constitutional theory, is best exemplified in the work of Vedel. Vedel operated under the standard distinction between the material and formal conceptions of a constitution.[36] From the material point of view, the constitution is equivalent to the set of rules that establish the form of government and that regulate the relationship between the state and its citizens; in short, it is the expression of the most important norms of the political system. From the formal point of view, a constitution is a legal norm that, unlike ordinary statutes, can only be enacted or modified through special, often super-majoritarian, procedures.[37] The main consequence of the formal notion of the constitution is that there must be a special (constituent) organ authorized to make use of the procedures designed to procure alterations to the constitutional text.[38] Of course, if there is no state in place, or if the constitution is being replaced by illegal means, then such organs will not exist or they will be ineffective. In such cases, Vedel, like Carré de Malberg, thought that constituent power would function as an original power (*pouvoir originaire*), not subject to any rules. However, Vedel maintained that constituent power not only manifests itself in those extra-legal contexts: it also appears whenever a constitutional text is modified or replaced, even if this occurs through organs bound by certain procedural rules.[39]

Is Vedel simply using the term 'constituent power' (or more specifically, *pouvoir constituant dérivé*) to describe the activity of ordinary constitutional reform, that is, to refer to the power of amending a constitution in accordance to its own rules? If that question is to be answered in the affirmative, then his approach is not relevant for an analysis of constituent power as such. In my view, the answer to that question must be both 'yes' and 'no'. It is true that for

[36] This distinction will be the subject of analysis in Chapter 8.
[37] Georges Vedel, *Manuel Élémentaire de Droit Constitutionnel* (Paris: Dalloz, 2002) 112.
[38] ibid. 114.
[39] ibid. 116.

Vedel, any amendment to a constitution would involve an exercise of 'constituent power'.[40] In that sense, it might be argued that I have been merely making the rather trivial point that some authors use the term 'constituent power' (or 'derived constituent power') to refer to what others would call the 'amending power'.[41] However, Vedel thought that the power exercised in revolutionary situations and the one exercised in the context of constitutional reform are identical in the most relevant sense. Both are sovereign powers that cannot be subject to substantive limits.[42] For instance, an eternity clause prohibiting the amendment of certain articles of the constitution (inserted into the document by the original constituent power) cannot ultimately bind the derived constituent power. 'The constituent [power] of today', he wrote, 'cannot bind the nation of tomorrow'. [43]

The idea is that despite being subject to certain procedures, the derived constituent power is a *constituent* power in terms of its effects.[44] As Kemal Gözler has maintained, under this view, there is an original and a derived power, but only one constituent function.[45] Another exponent of this approach is Luis Sánchez Agesta, Vedel's Spanish contemporary. Sánchez Agesta attributed to the original constituent power (which he sometimes called *poder constituyente genuino*) three defining features: first, a revolutionary nature (it is not based on a constitutional norm); second, a historical efficacy (the ability to implement its will); and third, a creative character (it does not seek to defend the constitutional order, but to transform it).[46] In this revolutionary variant, the exercise of constituent power always involves an act of juridical violence, a break in the chain of legality.[47] Nevertheless, Sánchez Agesta believed that once a juridical order is consolidated and becomes stable, the original constituent power is extinguished.[48] In such a scenario, the legal system grows capable of escaping the

[40] As we will see in Chapter 6, the idea that constituent power is exercised every time there is a change in a constitutional text was characteristic of 19th-century constitutional theory.

[41] It is telling that in a footnote to his *Constitutional Government and Democracy*, Carl Friedrich stated that: 'It is very important to keep in mind that the 'constituent power' as used here is not identical with the *pouvoir constituant* of French constitutional law, which corresponds to the amending power of American constitutional law.' Friedrich (n. 19) 629, fn 4.

[42] Georges Vedel, 'Souveraineté et Supraconstitutionalité', 67 *Pouvoirs* 79 (1993) 90.

[43] Vedel, *Manuel* (n. 37) 117.

[44] Georges Vedel, 'Schengen et Maastricht (à propos de la décision no 91-294 DC du Conseil constitutionnel du 25 julliet 1991', 8 *Revue Française de Droit Administratiff* 173 (1992) 179: 'le pouvoir constituant dérivé n'est pas un pouvoir d'une autre nature que le pouvoir constituant initial'. See also Vedel, *Manuel* (n. 37) 160, 277 and Vedel, 'Souveraineté' (n. 42).

[45] Kemal Gözler, *Pouvoir Constituant* (Bursa: Ekin Kitabevi, 2004) 15..

[46] Luis Sánchez Agesta, *Principios de Teoría Política* (Madrid: Editora Nacional, 1983) 331–332.

[47] Luis Sánchez Agesta, *Lecciones de Derecho Político* (Granada: Librería Prieto, 1959)382.

[48] ibid. 383. Sánchez Agesta briefly considers the possibility that there could always exist a residual right to rebellion, perhaps based on natural law, but does not pursue this idea further: ibid 383–384.

will of the foundational constitution-maker and of controlling the political impulses that once originated it.[49]

All that is left at that point is what Sánchez Agesta calls constituted constituent power (*poder constituyente constituido*), the power to amend the constitution according to its own rules. But like Vedel, Sánchez Agesta attributed to the 'constituted constituent power' the same sovereign faculties he assigned to the original one: 'It cannot be said that [constituted constituent power] is prior to law, since it has its origins in the constitution, but on the other hand it dominates it because it can reform or substitute it, [it can even reform] those precepts that organise its constituent competence.'[50] In the context of an established constitutional order, the original constituent power is left behind, but the constituent power that remains is a 'super-legislator' just as potent as the one that brought the regime into existence.[51]

The basic elements of this second approach (i.e. a distinction between a revolutionary and a procedurally regulated constituent power, accompanied by the attribution of sovereign features to both) clearly emerge from the work of Vedel and Sánchez Agesta. Nevertheless, one more instantiation of this view needs to be examined, which is exemplified in discussions about the nature of the Westminster Parliament's power of constitutional change.[52]

The most famous of these discussions is contained in A.V. Dicey's *Introduction to the Study of the Law and the Constitution*. Dicey saw Parliament's unlimited law-making power, which includes the ability to change 'fundamental or so-called constitutional laws . . . in the same manner as other laws', as nothing but what some (mainly foreign) commentators called 'constituent power'.[53] Not surprisingly, he largely approved of Alexis de Tocqueville's depiction of the Westminster Parliament as 'at once a legislative and a constituent assembly'.[54] When Parliament adopts ordinary laws, Dicey maintained, it acts as a legislative assembly, but when those laws 'shift the basis of the constitution' it acts in its constituent capacity.[55] As the bearer of constituent power, Parliament possesses an unrestricted ability of constitutional change, but it is always subject to certain procedural rules (the same rules that it has to follow when it acts

[49] Sánchez Agesta, *Principios* (n. 46) 332.
[50] ibid. 334.
[51] Sánchez Agesta, *Lecciones* (n. 47) 340.
[52] As we will see below and in some of the chapters that follow, there are interesting connections between the concept of constituent power and certain elements of the orthodox conception of parliamentary sovereignty.
[53] A. V. Dicey, *Introduction to the Study of the Law and the Constitution* (London: Macmillan, 1959) 37.
[54] Alexis de Tocqueville, *Democracy in America* (New York: New American Library, 1956) 74.
[55] Dicey (n. 53).

in its ordinary legislative capacity, that is to say, the joint action of the Lords, Commons, and Crown).[56] Just as in Sánchez Agesta's notion of the constituted constituent power, Parliament can always modify those rules (at least in ways that do not negate its sovereign law-making power), as the Parliament Acts of 1911 and 1949 demonstrate.[57]

By describing Parliament's power of constitutional change as capable of inserting any content into the constitution but as subject to specified procedures, Dicey was thus expounding a view that was very similar to that of proponents of the second approach identified above. However, unlike Vedel and Sánchez Agesta, Dicey did not explicitly distinguish between an original and a derived constituent power: the absence of a formal English constitution resting on an authority external to Parliament made that distinction unnecessary.[58] But Dicey's conception of legal and political sovereignty, the former attributed to Parliament and the latter to an electorate who can always revolt against parliamentary abuses, plays a very similar role.[59] The concept of political sovereignty, which meant that 'electors can in the long run enforce their will' and that their potential resistance works as an external limit to legal sovereignty, has a strong affinity with the notion of an original constituent power.[60] In this respect, there is a way of understanding Dicey's conception of parliamentary sovereignty as carrying with it a distinction between the derived constituted parliament and the original constituent people. The practical effect of that distinction in actual constitutional practice is at the moment very limited, even if this could change in the future.

[56] Carré de Malberg argued that in placing the amending power in a National Assembly comprised of both legislative chambers, the Constitution of 1875 had brought France under the English formula of parliamentary sovereignty, where there is no separation between the constituent and the legislative power. Raymond Carré de Malberg, *La Ley, Expresión de la Voluntad General: Estudio sobre el Concepto de la Ley en la Constitución de 1875* (Madrid: Marcial Pons, 2011) 115–118. I will come back to this point in Chapter 10.

[57] Parliament Act, 1911, 1 & 2 Geo.5 c.13; Parliament Act, 1949, 12, 13 & 14 Geo. 6 c. 103.

[58] This does not mean, of course, that the distinction has no applicability in a country like the United Kingdom, but that the orthodox theory of parliamentary sovereignty has no place for it. Indeed, in the 19th and early 20th centuries, the question of the constituent power of the Imperial Parliament, as well as that of the colonial legislatures, became the subject of interesting legal controversies. In this context the term 'constituent power' made frequent appearances in judicial opinions and academic writings. See Colón-Ríos, 'Five Conceptions' (n. 3). It was used to refer to the unlimited constitution-making power of Parliament with respect to the colonies and, in some cases, to the constitution-making power attributed to the colonial legislatures. This is why (and in contrast to Dicey's depiction of 'constituent power' as belonging to the political phraseology of foreign countries), Roberts-Wray wrote in *Commonwealth and Colonial Law* that the 'common law recognizes a distinct difference between the constituent power and the ordinary legislative power'. Kenneth Roberts-Wray, *Commonwealth and Colonial Law* (New York: F.A. Praeger, 1966) 158.

[59] Dicey (n. 53) 27, 30.

[60] ibid. 28, 31. In a similar way, Georges Burdeau maintained that in the United Kingdom the original constituent power rested in popular opinion, not Parliament. Georges Burdeau, *Traité de Science Politique* (Paris: LDGJ, 1983) vol. IV, 33–35.

III. The Relationship between Derived and Original Constituent Power

What is being identified by the likes of Vedel and Sánchez Agesta (and, in a certain way, by Dicey) as 'constituent power', proponents of the first approach will insist, is simply the ordinary power of constitutional reform. A power regulated by law, even if only procedurally, cannot be a constituent power. It is difficult to respond to that objection. Sieyès, who gave constituent power one of its first major theoretical formulations and distinguished it from the constituted powers of government, placed it outside of the legal order, and most contemporary analyses of the concept tend to follow Sieyès in that respect.[61] But there are at least three good reasons for not dismissing the second approach so quickly—to at least consider the possibility that 'original' and 'derived' constituent power may be conceptualizations of the same type of power. *Firstly*, as shown earlier, different authors attribute to—what they call—constituent power (even if qualified by words such as 'pacific', 'regular', 'derived', 'constituted', 'original', or 'primary') the very same substantive ability: that of introducing any content into a constitutional order. That is to say, a constituent organ (which could be, e.g., the legislature acting in a special capacity) could be understood as a juridical means for exercising the same power that once brought the constitution into existence.[62]

Moreover, both derived and original constituent power can be exercised at any time, and whether to activate the latter is harder than to exercise the former (or vice versa) is not necessarily related to their nature. The level of difficulty would normally depend on the rigidity or flexibility of the amendment rule at issue or, perhaps more accurately, in the institutional and political context in which the constitution operates, that is, in what Mariana Velasco-Rivera has recently called the 'economy of change'.[63] It is not the case, for example, that original constituent power can only be exercised in cases of near unanimous support for constitutional change, and that the exercise of derived constituent

[61] See for example Illan rua Wall, *Human Rights and Constituent Power: Without Model or Warranty* (Oxon: Routledge, 2012); Andreas Kalyvas, *Democracy and the Politics of the Extraordinary: Max Weber, Carl Schmitt and Hannah Arendt* (Cambridge: Cambridge University Press, 2008); Antonio Negri, *Insurgencies: Constituent Power and the Modern* State (University of Minnesota Press, 1999). cf. Mark Wenman, *Agonistic Democracy: Constituent Power in the Era of Globalisation* (Cambridge: Cambridge University Press, 2013) 77, 92.

[62] Some constitutions cannot be amended during certain periods—see for example Articles 7 and 89 of the Constitution of France (1958)—but, according to proponents of the second approach discussed above, those limits may also be repealed by the derived constituent power through a two-step process. The same applies to any unamendable constitutional clauses. See for example Vedel, *Manuel* (n. 37) 117.

[63] Mariana Velasco-Rivera, *Why Mexico Keeps Amending its Constitution? Secrets of a Cartel Democracy* (SJD Dissertation, Yale University, 2019).

power is merely a matter of formally complying with certain rules: amendment procedures can be designed in such a way that constitutional change is virtually impossible as long as it is opposed by a relatively small minority. The typical example here would be Article V of the US Constitution, which involves supermajority requirements at the federal and state level that are notoriously difficult to meet.[64] In that respect, both the derived and the original constituent power appear as permanent threats (and arguably as equally dangerous ones) to the existing constitution. They can always be used to replace it with a new one, even though only the latter would do it from the outside of the legal order.

A point of distinction between these two notions may be that the exercise of the original constituent power would normally take place in times of popular agitation for constitutional change and through highly participatory procedures. That is to say, the exercise of the derived constituent power merely requires the meeting of certain formalities, while that of the original constituent power requires that any formalities are accompanied by mass mobilization. But as we mentioned earlier and as we will see in the chapters that follow, on the one hand, military juntas have claimed to be the bearers of the original constituent power and, on the other, amendment processes can be designed in a way that attempts to reproduce a popular constitution-making episode. What this suggests is that, even though its sources may vary (original constituent power comes directly from the people, derived constituent power comes, in an immediate sense, from the constitution), the practical implications of this distinction may easily be overstated. This helps to explain why, in its 1992 decision on the Maastricht Treaty, the French Constitutional Council stated that 'the constituent power is sovereign; it has the power to repeal, amend, and supplement constitutional provisions in such manner it considers appropriate', without any recourse to the well-rehearsed distinction between derived and original constituent authority.[65]

Secondly, as exemplified in the earlier discussion of Dicey, under the prevailing constitutional orthodoxy of some legal systems, the distinction between an extra-legal constituent power and a legally regulated faculty of constitutional reform is of limited practical effects. The absence of a formal constitution means that there is no entity with the ability of binding the ordinary

[64] For a discussion, see Sanford Levinson, *Our Undemocratic Constitution: Where the Constitution Goes Wrong (And How We the People Can Correct It)* (Oxford University Press, 2008). Cf. Vicki Jackson, 'The (Myth of the Un) Amendability of the US Constitution and the Democratic Component of Constitutionalism', 13(3) *International Journal of Constitutional Law* 575 (2015).

[65] '. . . [L]e pouvoir constituant est souverain; qu'il lui est loisible d'abroger, de modifier ou de compléter des dispositions de valeur constitutionnelle dans la forme qu'il estime appropriée'. Decision n. 92-312 DC (2 September 1992) para. 19.

legislature and therefore no need of identifying an extra-legal source of constitutional authority. In the United Kingdom, for example, the legislature's sovereign law-making power can be understood through the lenses of the historical struggle between parliamentarians and the Crown, or simply presented as the prevailing constitutional custom. Put differently, Parliament's law-making power does not need to be seen as emerging from a fundamental decision of a constituent people. But even if one insists in attributing 'the people' with an ultimate constitution-making power in the context of such a system, that attribution will not have any legal consequences in terms of the extent of Parliament's law-making faculties; Parliament would still be considered the bearer of a *legally unlimited* power of constitutional change. To speak of certain things that only the original constituent power can do in the United Kingdom, is to speak a language radically alien to current constitutional discourse.

Thirdly, some constitutions authorize the exercise of constituent power through mechanisms that, on the one hand, seem to escape the 'legal' or 'extra-legal' categories and, on the other, lead to situations that are difficult to differentiate from revolutionary constitution-making episodes. These types of mechanisms, which only exist in a handful of national constitutions, take the form of constituent assemblies assigned with a constitution-making power not subject to substantive positive law. These assemblies can be convened by popular initiative and their existence is procedurally regulated from beginning to end, that is to say, from the convocation of the assembly to the popular ratification of its proposals.[66] From a strictly legal perspective, since they are convened according to pre-established rules, it would seem that they are no different from ordinary amendment procedures. There are nevertheless a number of strong reasons that point against that view. In particular, and unlike traditional amendment rules, these mechanisms allow for the convocation of an entity that operates separately from (and can do so even against the will of) the ordinary institutions of government.

In addition, once convened, constituent assemblies are usually not bound by substantive constitutional rules and they sometimes even intrude in the exercise of the ordinary powers of government, claiming to represent the community in its full self-governing capacity and thus able to temporarily exercise the powers of the executive, legislative, and judicial branches of government.[67] From this perspective, they truly seem as entities that, although having originated in the legal order and being subject to a number of procedural rules,

[66] This type of mechanism will be considered in more detail in Chapter 10.
[67] This type of view will be challenged in Chapter 9.

approach it from a purely political (i.e. extra-legal) terrain. They are manifestations of new legal beginnings, situations in which civil society exercises a primitive political force, coming closer than ever to a lawless state of nature. Finally, the highly participatory character of these assemblies to a great extent mimics what would be expected to happen in a democratic but revolutionary constitution-making episode. Indeed, in some cases, these mechanisms provide—at least in theory—more opportunities of mass participation in constitutional change than the most democratic of popular revolutions. In short, at least in certain contexts, the 'derived' or 'original' character of constituent power seems to have little effect on its unlimited nature.

Notwithstanding the above, there is a sense in which the conflation between the original and the derived constituent power can be seen as obscuring what may rightly be asserted to be the *question* of constituent power. That question, put crudely, is about whether the *original* constituent power can manifest after a constitution is in place. In other words, it is about whether a constitution's amendment rule excludes the possibility of its extra-legal transformation. Authors like Vedel and Carré de Malberg would probably answer that question by saying that as a matter of pure fact, constitution-making exercises that violate a constitution's rules of change can certainly occur, and that in that sense one may speak about an original constituent power always existing alongside the constitution.[68] However, that answer would continue, the ever-present possibility of revolution raises only political issues and, therefore, a jurist engaged in an analysis of the concept of constituent power has no reason to address them. But such an answer does not work, not even for lawyers.

In fact, the idea of constituent power as an extra-legal and unlimited power (and the ever-present possibility of revolution) can have multiple *legal* effects that go beyond merely placing political limits on the actions of ordinary governments and legislatures. For example, courts and jurists around the world have used the notion of original constituent power to justify the imposition of limits on the competence of the derived one. The idea is that only the people acting in a legally unmediated form can truly exercise a power capable of creating and destroying constitutions. In other words, the interplay between the notions of derived and original constituent power frequently has legal and institutional implications. As will be seen in the following chapters, it is on that interplay that the doctrine of unconstitutional constitutional amendments and

[68] A similar view is presented by Alessandro Pace, 'La Instauración de una Nueva Constitución: Perfiles de Teoría Constitucional', 97 *Revista de Estudios Políticos* 9 (1997) 24.

the justification of the right to issue legally binding instructions to representatives usually rest.

Furthermore, constitutional courts frequently explain their main responsibility as that of protecting the decisions of the constituent people, and when the actions of a constitution-making body are challenged in court, the question of whether such entity possesses a revolutionary or derived constituent power becomes the central legal issue to be answered (the commonplace idea being that only if the assembly can be characterized as a 'derived' entity, its actions are subject to judicial review). In such situations, the existence of an extra-legal constitution-making power serves as the very basis for particular legal doctrines and may result in the establishment of legal limits on political action. At the same time, the notion of an 'original' constituent power can play an enabling role: it can be used to justify the legal acceptability of different exercises of political power. For example, some courts have sanctioned popular but informal constitution-making processes (processes in which formal amendment rules are clearly violated), ruling that they amount to the exercise of the (original) constituent power and are therefore outside of the scope of the established rules of change.

In exploring these various phenomena, this book will inevitably address what was previously identified as the *question* of constituent power, although the emphasis will be on illustrating the different functions the concept has played in constitutional practice. The chapters will move from an analysis of the origins of the theory of constituent power (Chapters 2–4), to an examination of 19th-century constitutional theory and practice (Chapters 5–7), and finally consider 20th- and 21st-century developments (Chapters 8–10), always attempting to highlight the connection and disruptions in the constitutional discourse surrounding constituent power during these different epochs.

IV. Plan of the Book

The book has been organized in nine chapters, excluding this introduction and a brief conclusion. These chapters engage in a theoretical and comparative analysis that illustrates the juridical functions of the concept of constituent power at different moments in constitutional history. They draw on materials (cases, official records, academic, and popular writings) primarily from Latin American and European jurisdictions, where the theory of constituent power has been most influential. The chapters have been organized thematically (rather than by jurisdiction), and those themes (which have been selected because they illustrate circumstances in which the concept of constituent power has assumed a salient role) dictate the particular materials to be examined. The themes, which range from discussions about the imperative mandate to examinations of the notion of the material constitution, allow us to examine closely situations in which commentators, judges, and political actors treat the theory of constituent power as permitting or disallowing governmental or popular actions, as well as requiring certain types of institutional arrangements. Although the jurisdictions to be considered exhibit important differences, they are all united by the fact of having deployed—at different moments—the notion of constituent power to challenge or justify different types of political activity.

Chapter 2: Back to Rousseau

Chapter 2 provides an overview of what should be understood as one of the most sophisticated analyses of the distinction between constituent and constituted authority, that of Rousseau. The chapter engages in a close reading of Rousseau's work (focusing, but also going beyond, *The Social Contract*) and considers the ways in which it anticipated and served as the basis for Sieyès' famous theory. Rousseau, needless to say, has not generally been seen as a theorist of constituent power. This is probably a result of his apparent support for direct democracy: in a direct democracy, there is no separation between the government and the governed and, therefore, no separation between the constituted powers and the constituent subject. But Rousseau, I will show, clearly rejected direct democracy as a form of government: he only insisted in the direct intervention of the citizenry for the ratification of the 'laws'. The problem with most contemporary interpretations of Rousseau is that they attribute to his use of the term 'law' the same meaning that that term has today: an ordinary statute adopted by a representative body. There is nevertheless ample evidence in Rousseau's work that, just like Marsilius of Padua and Johannes Althusius, the Genevan was using the term 'law' to refer to the fundamental norms of the legal system, norms that only an assembly of the entire people or a multiplicity of primary assemblies could legitimately adopt.

Importantly, Rousseau's constituent power, unlike Sieyès', had a fundamental juridical nature: it had to be exercised according to established legal procedures. In this respect, it could be understood as a derived constituent power, even though exercised by the people and not subject to substantive limits. Since he insisted in the legal possibility of exercising constituent power, Rousseau was especially concerned with the kind of procedures that, from a juridical perspective, could be understood as sufficient for a constitution-making episode to count as an act of the people. At the same time, his view that constituent power could not be represented and his defence of the imperative mandate seem to be mirrored in contemporary attempts to allow electors, acting through popular initiative, to trigger episodes of fundamental constitutional change. Only by having a full grasp of these notions, will we be in a position to interrogate the theory of constituent power from a legal perspective. While Rousseau provides a conception of constituent power which sees the possibility of its future exercise through legal means as a necessary condition for the legitimacy of the constitution and as an integral part of a self-governing community, Sieyès, building on Rousseau's conception, moved constituent power to an extra-legal terrain.

Chapter 3: Sieyès *via* Rousseau

This chapter traces the gradual emergence of the distinction between the constituted and the constituent power in the work of Sieyès, using Rousseau as the main point of comparison. The focus will be on Sieyès' main three pamphlets: *Views of the Executive Means Available to the Representatives of France in 1789*, *An Essay on Privileges*, and *What is the Third Estate?* The objective will be to examine how Sieyès constructed constituent power as an extra-legal force and to explore the key juridical implications of his views. Most contemporary discussions about constituent power, both academic and judicial, see Sieyès' work as a necessary point of departure, and there are good reasons for that. Sieyès linked the concept of constituent power to political revolutions and to the notion of groups of human beings abandoning the state of nature and entering into civil society through the creation of a form of government. Such ideas, however, hide important complexities connected to the relationship between constituent power and different aspects of a constitutional order, the notion of representation, the role of the citizenry in constitution-making and constitutional reform, and the place of constituent authority once a constitution is established.

The chapter will throw light on those complexities by putting Sieyès' work into perspective, that is, by showing how he built on the work of Rousseau and considering the significance of his ideas for some of the constitutional debates that surrounded the French Revolution. In so doing, the chapter will also stress the points of divergence between Sieyès and Rousseau. For instance, it will be seen that Sieyès' conception of representation led him to defend the creation of a supreme constitution that would ensure that legislators did not act to advance their private wills. In Rousseau, since the legislative (constituent) power was to be exercised directly by the sovereign legislator (i.e. the people), it would always tend towards the general will. Under that view, it simply did not make sense to subject the 'legislature' to a supreme constitution. When Sieyès considers the subject of constitutional change, even more fundamental differences between these two authors arise. For Sieyès, a constitution that facilitates the future exercise of constituent power was no different from having no constitution at all. The exercise of constituent power was therefore always extra-legal; it could simply not be regulated by law. A constitution should of course be open to change, but through an orderly process that involves the ordinary institutions of government, and not through a direct appeal to the people, as Rousseau insisted.

Chapter 4: Between Law and Revolution

This chapter examines the practical functions that the theory of constituent power played in late 18th-century French constitutionalism, paying special attention to the speeches and interventions of Sieyès during the first stages of the revolution. The focus will be on discussions around the imperative mandate and about the role of primary assemblies in constitution-making and constitutional reform. Rousseauian defenders of these institutions often presented them as essential for the exercise of the people's constituent power, while Sieyès and like-minded politicians and commentators saw them as potentially threatening the proper functioning of the constitutional order. Although debates around primary assemblies and constituent instructions reappeared multiple times during the 19th century, they have now more or less disappeared from academic and political discourse. Nonetheless, they are important for any discussions about the relationship between constituent power and the law for two main reasons. On the one hand, they are ultimately about the legal and institutional implications of the theory of constituent power. On the other, in the process of making the concept of constituent power consistent with the abolition of the imperative mandate and certain types of primary assemblies, Sieyès and others allowed 'the nation', as opposed to 'the people', to appear as a new political (and constituent) subject.

As will be seen, Sieyès' proposals about constitution-making and constitutional reform after 1789 were often presented as antidotes to the ills of the Rousseauian conceptions defended by some radicals. In contrast to Rousseau, who argued that the imperative mandate was necessary in places where the citizenry was so numerous that constituent power had to be exercised through a representative assembly, Sieyès saw it as radically inconsistent with the very idea of representation. This conception was accepted early in the revolution and it was arguably inconsistent with the royal decree that convened the Estates General. It also played an important role in the debate about the royal veto, where deputies such as Jérôme Pétion de Villeneuve presented interesting critiques of Sieyès' position. The abolition of the imperative mandate, we will see, altered in fundamental ways the notion of what counted as an exercise of constituent power: it resulted in major changes to the main sites of direct citizen involvement, primary assemblies. In the context of constitutional change, Sieyès presented primary assemblies not as the site of the *pouvoir constituant* but of the more modest 'commissioning power', the power to elect those capable of identifying the national will. That approach contrasts with the one found in both the Constitution of 1793 and the Girondin Draft Constitution.

Chapter 5: Of Constituent Nations

This chapter focuses on three early constitution-making episodes where different aspects of the concept of constituent power and its possible legal functions are exemplified: the making of the Spanish Constitution of 1812, of the Venezuelan Constitution of 1811, and of the Colombian Constitution of 1886. The chapter begins with a theoretical discussion of the distinction between national and popular sovereignty, between the constituent nation and the constituent people. I will highlight the connections between—what I will call—the 'constituent power of the people' approach and Rousseau's constitutional thought, and argue that this approach is characterized by an attempt to realize what can be identified as the principle of participation. The 'constituent power of the nation' approach, in contrast, is fundamentally Sieyesian and therefore consistent with what can be identified as the principle of representation and the principle of exclusion. The adoption of that approach in most modern constitutional orders carried with it important legal and institutional implications. In particular, it pointed towards constitutional arrangements in which the citizenry did not need to be seen as an active decision-maker. This was clearly exemplified in the three constitution-making episodes that will be discussed in the chapter and in the debates that took place in the relevant constitution-making bodies.

For example, the embracement of the constituent power of the nation approach served to justify the adoption of constitutions through entities elected under systems that excluded important parts of the population. At the same time, these processes had important religious components: the invocation of God, as the ultimate constituent subject, was seen as fundamental for ensuring the creation of a good constitutional order, an order that would promote the national interest. What mattered was thus to facilitate the election of citizens who possessed features (virtuosity, economic independence, reputation) that armed them with the ability of identifying the national will. Constituent power, for the political actors involved in the creation of these constitutions, became an extra-ordinary constitution-making jurisdiction that could be exercised through non-participatory mechanisms. Not surprisingly, these processes were also characterized by intense discussions about the imperative mandate and by its eventual rejection. They also resulted in the adoption of constitutions largely consistent with the doctrine of parliamentary sovereignty, even if commentators generally highlighted their objective of limiting political power. In examining these topics, the chapter will put special emphasis on the thinking of certain political actors, such as Juan Germán Rocio and Miguel Antonio Caro.

Chapter 6: The Identity and Limits of the Constituent Subject

This chapter focuses on the work of a group of 19th-century authors engaged in theoretical debates about the 'true' identity of the constituent subject. These authors, most of which had recently experienced revolutions to some extent reminiscent of 1789, were interested in the same basic question: who has the authority to replace the fundamental law? Not surprisingly, they tended to defend some version of what I earlier identified as the constituent power of the nation approach. One of the main implications of recognizing the constituent power of the nation (at least at a theoretical level), was the barring of an entity attributed with both the power of making ordinary laws and of revising the constitutional text. This was particularly important at a time where it was not uncommon for constitutions to lack formal amendment rules. With some exceptions, 19th-century authors rarely insisted on the institutionalization of an extraordinary mechanism of constitutional change that facilitated the direct involvement of the citizenry. Like Sieyès, they thought that the constituent subject could be represented, even if not by legislators acting in an ordinary capacity. At the same time, however, they worried about maintaining links between citizens and representatives, and frequently reminded the latter that they were acting on a mandate from the former, even if such a mandate was not imperative.

During the 19th century, it will be seen, the concept of constituent power more often than not played the role of limiting the power of the ordinary institutions of government. The nation's power to create constitutional law was an exclusive one: no legislature, no executive entity, could assume constituent jurisdiction. The English doctrine of parliamentary sovereignty was a common object of criticism. At the same time, although some authors identified constituent power with an unlimited law-making authority (i.e. a jurisdiction to produce any legal content), they also saw the constituent subject as limited to the creation of new *constitutional* content; a constituent body could not engage in any aspects of the activity of governing. There were nonetheless authors who attributed constituent jurisdiction to parliament or to the 'constituted authority'. As we will see, those authors' embracement of the theory of constituent power came nevertheless accompanied by a natural law approach that sought to limit the type of constitution that could be legitimately created. What we will see in the works discussed in this chapter, then, is how a concept otherwise associated with revolutions and unlimited jurisdiction was strongly connected to different kinds of limits; limits on the ordinary institutions of governments and limits on the constituent authority itself.

Chapter 7: Rejecting Constituent Power

There are two related traditions of thought that reject the existence of constituent power as generally understood after the French Revolution. Their rejection of the theory of constituent power was sometimes fuelled by a desire to restore an ancient constitutional order and a fear of potentially uncontrolled exercises of political power. One of these traditions revolved around the doctrine of the *historical* or *internal* constitution. In Spain, the main exponent of this doctrine during the 19th century was Gaspar Melchor de Jovellanos. Jovellanos thought that rather than the result of an act of will, constitutions emerged through long historical processes and could not be simply created and recreated. The practical implications of this approach will be explored through an examination of the arguments of proponents of the doctrine of the historical constitution within the constitution-making body that drafted the Spanish Constitution of 1812. Theirs was a view radically inconsistent with Rousseau's and Sieyès' constitutional thought: when the nation exercised what Jovellanos called the supreme power, it was not to create a new constitutional order but to restore a previous one. Nonetheless, Jovellanos' approach came accompanied by a theory of resistance similar to that of George Lawson and John Locke.

The second tradition is found in the work of the doctrinaires (represented in France by François Guizot and, in Spain, by Donoso Cortés). For them, it was necessary to get rid of the very idea of a *human* constituent subject, of the notion that someone could ever be attributed with a right to act outside of the law. In practice, the doctrinaires defended the constitution-amending authority of the ordinary institutions of government. Although they were especially critical of Rousseau and generally hostile to popular participation, they shared with him the notion that the power to change the fundamental laws could (and should) be legally regulated. The doctrinaires nonetheless had a place for an extra-legal constituent subject whose role would be to bring society to order after a time of crisis. In those types of situations, any individual or entity able to save society from disaster could legitimately exercise an unlimited law-making faculty. The doctrinaire and the historical constitution traditions came together in the debates that took place during the adoption of the Spanish Constitution of 1845, where the concept of constituent power was sometimes abandoned and sometimes associated with the right of resistance and with states of necessity. Importantly, and in contrast to the works examined in Chapter 6, these traditions of thought not only rejected constituent power, but ended up defending the legal sovereignty of the Crown-in-Parliament.

Chapter 8: The Material Constitution

This chapter explores the notion of the material constitution in the works of Maurice Hauriou, Hans Kelsen, Carl Schmitt, Hermann Heller, and Costantino Mortati. As we saw earlier, the material constitution generally refers to the most fundamental aspects of the constitutional regime, those related to the structure of government and to the basic relations between the state and citizens. The constitution in the material sense has some important similarities with the historical constitution, but it has a very different relationship with the concept of constituent power. This chapter seeks to show how the previously mentioned authors understood that relationship, and how this understanding affected their views about the legal limits of the ordinary power of constitutional reform. I will argue that when understood from a normative perspective (the type of perspective that, I will argue below, characterizes Schmitt and, to some extent, Hauriou), the notion of the material constitution is inconsistent with the views of many of the commentators and political actors discussed in the previous two chapters. Most of the authors discussed in Chapter 6 thought that every change in the constitutional order involved the exercise of constituent power; Chapter 7 shows that for the doctrinaires and proponents of the historical constitution there was no legal power, at least not during normal times, outside of the ordinary institutions of government.

In contrast to those views, under the normative concept of the material constitution, not all constitutional rules are the same, and while some of them can certainly be amendable by the ordinary institutions of government acting through a special process, this does not apply to a constitution's truly material content. Once that idea is accepted, one important conclusion follows: if the entity authorized to amend a constitutional text is not the constituent subject, there must be limits to its power of constitutional change. Constituent power, in virtue of its relationship to the material content of the constitution, can thus serve the function of protecting certain type of constitutional norms, an idea embraced by judges who have adopted the doctrine of unconstitutional constitutional amendments. In contrast, when the notion of the material constitution does not come accompanied by the recognition of an extra-legal constituent subject, the idea of a limited power of constitutional reform becomes harder to justify. This is more clearly exemplified by Kelsen and, to lesser degrees, by Heller and Mortati. In the works of these three authors, there is no extra-legal constituent entity that can be exclusively tasked with the adoption of a constitutional order's truly material content. It is not that the possibility of the existence of a constituent an entity is negated, but that it is not attributed with any legally relevant functions.

Chapter 9: Sovereignty and Dictatorship

This chapter advances a distinction between sovereignty and constituent power. It argues that there are certain things that an assembly engaged in the exercise of constituent power cannot do. The chapter maintains that when distinguished from constituent power, sovereignty appears not as a constitution-making force, but as the ability to create any legal content without been subject to the separation of powers. The exercise of constituent power, in contrast, only involves a *constitution-making* authority. This argument is presented through a discussion of the work of Georg Jellinek, Carré de Malberg, and Schmitt. Jellinek, it will be seen, saw the constituent subject as the source of the separation of powers and, as a result, as not bound by it. Even when exercised according to established legal procedures, constituent power is ultimately subject only to limits of a moral or political nature. Carré de Malberg tried to avoid the risks of a constitution-maker attributed with the totality of political power by arguing that only the nation was sovereign, but since the nation could never directly engage in political acts, there are no instances of sovereign authority in a constitutional order. When constituent power is exercised outside the established amendment rule, however, it becomes (for Carré de Malberg) a raw political force not susceptible of legal regulation.

What Jellinek saw as the source of the separation of powers and what Carré de Malberg placed outside the realm of law, I will argue, is better understood as sovereignty plain and simple. A sovereign can produce constitutional laws and even engage in ordinary legislative or executive activity; it has an unlimited discretion to determine its own competences, it is the *Kompetenz-Kompetenz*. But when an entity, such as a constituent assembly, is authorized to adopt a new constitution, even if this occurs outside of the constitution's amendment rule, it does not become 'the sovereign'. It rather exercises a special jurisdiction which may be substantively unlimited (i.e. it can adopt any constitutional content) but is still subject to a commission: that of making a constitution. I will derive this conclusion from Schmitt's distinction between sovereignty and sovereign dictatorship, which I think has not been fully developed by constitutional theorists yet. The legal and institutional implications of this distinction are then assessed through the examination of a number of 20th- and 21st-century constitution-making instances. The confusion between sovereignty and constituent power, it will be seen, can serve to justify important departures from democratic principles. The focus of that part of the chapter will be on the way public officials and judges conceived of the powers of the Colombian Constituent Assembly of 1991, an entity that was considered sovereign *in virtue* of its constituent power. The nature of the power attributed to Francisco Franco in Spain and to the military junta in Chile will also be briefly considered, as well as that of the Venezuelan Constituent Assembly of 2017.

Chapter 10: The Juridical People

There are not many situations in which the constituent people, the flesh and blood human beings that live in a constitutional order, assume a real juridical presence. Even though we now hardly ever talk about the 'sovereign nation', the institutions associated with the constituent power of the nation have mostly stayed with us. This chapter examines instances where the constituent power of the people approach is the one having an impact on actual constitutional practice. These include situations where judicially sanctioned extra-constitutional assemblies are authorized by referendum and where constituent assemblies are legally convened through popular initiative. These practices, it will be seen, have important connections to the now mostly forgotten institution of the imperative mandate. In those cases, the relevant referendum question may be understood as involving a 'constituent mandate' establishing a set of conditions that a constituent assembly is required to abide by. This means, on the one hand, that the assembly would not be able to exercise *constituted* power (unless expressly stated in the referendum question) and that its power to draft or enact a constitution may be subject to substantive limits which, depending on the regime at issue, may be judicially enforceable.

The chapter begins by revisiting the connections between the imperative mandate and constituent power through an examination of the place of the former in early English constitutional debates and its treatment in some contemporary constitutional orders. It then considers the distinction between the people and the electorate as understood in the theoretical literature, particularly in the works of Hauriou and Carré de Malberg. Against the view that constitutionally mandated referendums are simply part of the ordinary power of constitutional reform, I develop a distinction between constitutional and constituent referendums. The latter, I will argue, take place when the purpose of the referendum is to facilitate the alteration of the material constitution. The judicial sanction of irregularly convened constituent assemblies and the notion of constituent mandates are then considered in light of the process that led to the adoption of the Venezuelan Constitution of 1999. In that process, the court recognized the possibility of convening such an entity outside of the established amendment rule, in a context where that was being done through a participatory process. At the same time, however, the mandate contained in a referendum question was arguably transgressed by the assembly. The court, relying on the theory of constituent power and in my view incorrectly, sanctioned the alleged transgression.

Chapter 11: Conclusion

The final chapter briefly outlines what I think are the main insights of the book. By exploring the development of the relationship between constituent power and the law since its first developments in the 18th century, the book aims to advance our understanding of the legal and institutional implications of the idea that in every constitutional order there is an entity that possesses an unlimited constitution-making faculty. What emerges from that idea, however, is an understanding of constituent power as a concept that, although not part of positive law, can play an important role in the assessment of the legality and illegality of different forms of political action, as well as in the types of institutions that should be present in a constitutional order whose creation is attributed to a constituent people. By focusing on the extra-legal and political features of constituent power, constitutional theory has not been able to fully understand its juridical nature and potential role as a juridical principle. There is thus a large amount of work to be done in this area. This book is an attempt to move in that direction, albeit always acknowledging that the richness of constitutional practice can never be exhausted by constitutional theory; practice is always bound to surprise us.

2
Back to Rousseau

Talk about constituent power today evokes images of popular revolutions or of a community creating its first constitution. To a large extent, those images are closely connected to Emmanuel Sieyès' notion of an extra-legal constituent power, but they hide important complexities around the relationship between political power and the law. Even in situations where a constitutional regime is created or altered in radical ways, the concept of constituent power often plays a juridical role in serving to justify the legal validity (or invalidity) of certain courses of action, as well as in placing different institutional demands on the new legal order. Those complexities can be brought to the surface by looking at one of Sieyès' main sources of inspiration: the constitutional thought of Jean Jacques Rousseau. In Rousseau's work one can find a systematic analysis of the relationship between the constitution-making people and the constituted government, as well as detailed explanations about how a legal system based on a proper understanding of that relationship should be organized. This analysis is closely connected to one of his core contributions to modern political thought: the development of the distinction between sovereignty and government.

Sovereignty, which Rousseau insisted could not be represented, was always connected to the adoption of fundamental laws. The government was a means to carry out the ordinary business of the state, including, as we will see, the adoption of statutes. As Richard Tuck has noted, the distinction between sovereignty and government allowed Rousseau to defend democratic self-rule in the modern world, where citizens, unlike ancient peoples, are unable to assemble and participate in the day-to-day decision making of their polity.[1] Once Rousseau's thought is understood in light of this fundamental distinction, an attractive constitutional theory begins to emerge and the relevance of constituent power for constitutional *law* can be better appreciated. Importantly, unlike Sieyès, whose views will be examined in the next two chapters, Rousseau

[1] Richard Tuck, *The Sleeping Sovereign: The Invention of Modern Democracy* (Cambridge University Press, 2016) 2. See also Joel Colón-Ríos, 'Rousseau, Theorist of Constituent Power', 36(4) *Oxford Journal of Legal Studies* 885 (2016), on which this chapter is partly based.

Constituent Power and the Law. Joel Colón-Ríos, Oxford University Press (2020). © Joel Colón-Ríos.
DOI: 10.1093/oso/9780198785989.001.0001

did not see constituent power as extra-legal: for him, constituent power was always to be exercised according to procedures regulated by law. These procedures would take the form of a popular assembly, or a set of primary assemblies, periodically convened according to the established constitution. Through those entities, the sovereign would express whether it wishes to maintain the established legal order, or trigger a process for the creation of a new one.

Part I argues that Rousseau rejected direct democracy as a form of government. As will be seen, he only insisted in the direct participation of the entire citizenry in the context of *law-making*. In Part II, I illustrate how Rousseau used the term 'law' (*loi*) to refer to the most fundamental rules of the political system rather than to the many rules that we would today describe interchangeably as 'laws' or 'statutes'. In Part III, I examine Rousseau's distinction between the legislative power (*puissance législative*) and the executive power (*puissance exécutive*). In Part IV, I argue that this distinction is almost indistinguishable from that between the constituent and the constituted powers and demonstrate how other aspects of Rousseau's thought support this argument. Finally, in Part V, I examine Rousseau's approach to the creation of a society's first constitution (including the role of the 'Legislator') and his institutional proposals for the future exercise of constituent power. This understanding of Rousseau, it will be seen in later chapters, was sometimes reflected in the ways that different authors and early political actors have understood his work. However, in most instances, the literature reflects the now dominant interpretation of Rousseau as a defender of directly democratic government who grudgingly accepted the need to make some concessions to representative democracy.

I. Constituent Power, Rousseau, and Direct Democracy

One of the first expressions of the idea that the people possess an ultimate political power is found in Marsilius of Padua's *Defensor Pacis* (1324). Marsilius maintained that 'the efficient power to institute or elect a principate belongs to the legislator or the universal body of the citizens . . . and any correction of the principate – or even its deposition if that is necessary for the common advantage - likewise belongs to it'.[2] Centuries later, in the 17th century,

[2] Marsilius of Padua, *The Defender of Peace: The Defensor Pacis* (Cambridge University Press, 2005) 88. Marsilius usually referred to the 'universal body of the citizens *or its prevailing part*', and there are good reasons to believe that by 'the prevailing part' he did not necessarily refer to a numerical majority: 'The prevailing part of the citizens should be identified from the honourable custom of polities, or determined according to the opinion of Aristotle, *Politics* VI chapter 2'. ibid. 68–69.

Johannes Althusius described the right of sovereignty, which God had placed in the whole body of the community, as the 'power of disposing, prescribing, ordaining, administering, and constituting everything necessary and useful for the universal association'.[3] After this initial act, what the community 'has once set in order is to be maintained and followed, unless something else pleases the common will'.[4] Around the same time in England, those opposing the divine rule of kings advanced different arguments in favour of popular sovereignty. Even if God is the remote cause of political power, it was argued, a commonwealth can only be the immediate result of human action.[5] In that vein, Samuel Rutherford contended that God 'hath given the power of government originally, not to one, but to a multitude', and Algernon Sidney maintained that 'God leaves to Man the choice of Forms of Government; and those who constitute one Form, may abrogate it'.[6]

As J. P. Sommerville has explained, supporters of monarchy, such as Marco Antonio de Dominis and Robert Filmer, contended that if those views 'were correct, communities could not lawfully alter their form of government, but would be obliged to suffer democratic rule forever'.[7] The Spanish Jesuit Francisco Suárez had already given an answer to that objection in 1613. Suárez maintained that all societies were at first democracies, but God did not prescribe any form of government, so the people were free to remain a democracy or to choose aristocracy or monarchy.[8] These theoretical antecedents to the modern notion of popular sovereignty later played an important role in

[3] Johannes Althusius, *Politica: Politics Methodically St Forth and Illustrated with Sacred and Profane Examples* (Indianapolis: Liberty Fund, 1995 [1614]) 70. An earlier, 14th-century distinction between the power to create government and the power to adopt ordinary laws can be found in the work of William of Ockham. Brian Tierney, *Religion and the Growth of Constitutional Thought 1150-1650* (Cambridge: Cambridge University Press, 1982) 51–52 and Brian Tierney, *The Idea of Natural Rights* (Scholars Press for Emory University, 1997) 174.

[4] Althusius (n. 3) 72 (emphasis added).

[5] ibid. 44. God's own power had been understood by some authors in a way that strongly resembled the constituent/constituted power distinction. Francisco Suárez, for example, distinguished between the *absolute* and the *ordinary* power of God. The former was exercised when God decided to go beyond the established laws of the universe (e.g. when a miracle took place), the latter when God acted in accordance with the laws of nature. See Francis Oakley, 'The Absolute and Ordained Power of God in Sixteenth- and Seventeenth-Century Theology', 59(3) *Journal of the History of Political Ideas* 437 (1998) 455.

[6] Samuel Rutherford, *The Due Right of Presbyteries or, A Peaceable Plea, For the Government of the Church of Scotland* (E. Griffin, 1644) 340. Algernon Sidney, *Discourses Concerning Government, Vol. 2* (Edinburgh: Hamilton & Balfour, 1750). This is not to say that this idea was first developed in the 1600s. Brian Tierney has convincingly shown that similar ideas were present as early as the 13th century. Tierney, *Religion* (n. 3) 41.

[7] J. P. Sommerville, *Royalists & Patriots, Politics and Ideology in England 1603–1640* (London and New York: Longman, 1999) 26.

[8] Francisco Suárez, *Defensa de la Fe Católica y Apostólica Contra los Errores del Anglicanismo* (Instituto de Estudios Políticos, 1970 [1613]. For a discussion, see Sommerville (n. 7) 61. See also Brian Tierney, *The Idea of Natural Rights* (Scholars Press for Emory University, 1997) 172.

arguments seeking to justify the existence of limits to the power of government, which were sometimes presented in the language of constituent power. A good example is the 1769 essay by an anonymous contributor to the *London Magazine* who wrote that 'when the delegated power assumes an authority to destroy the primitive constituting power, it cannot be expected that the people will look quietly on', for 'the whole legislative is subordinate to the end for which the power was given, namely, the preservation of liberty'.[9] Similar ideas were already present in the theories of resistance advanced by various social contract theorists, as well as by supporters of Parliament in 17th-century England.[10]

What was new in Rousseau was a definite defence of the idea that the people, even after having entered into the social contract, could re-activate their constitution-making power whenever they thought appropriate and give an already existing state a new constitution. Other social contract theorists, such as George Lawson and John Locke, restricted the exercise of such a power to instances of tyranny.[11] In that vein, Thomas Rutherford insisted in 1756 that it is one thing to say that the people have a natural right to resist a government that has broken the social compact, and quite another that the 'constitutional power of the people is necessarily superior to that of the governing body . . . merely upon account of their having been the original constituents of that body', because the latter would mean that the people can displace their governors 'at pleasure'.[12] Rousseau's theory, however, was not one of resistance. It involved someone having the power to create a constitutional order anew, a constituent subject authorized to produce any constitutional content.

Notwithstanding the above, Rousseau's political thought can be seen as having an uncertain relationship with the theory of constituent power.[13]

[9] 'An Essay on Natural Liberty', *The London Magazine or, Gentleman's Monthly Intelligencer*, Vol. XXXVIII (1769) 260. Some years earlier, Daniel Defoe expressed a similar idea when he wrote that: 'The Power vested in the Three heads of our Constitution is vested in them by the People of *England*, who were a People before there was such a thing as a Constitution.' Daniel Defoe, *The Original Power of the Collective Body of the People of England, Examined and Asserted* (London, 1702).

[10] See, for example, Henry Parker, *Observations upon Some of His Majesty's Late Answers and Expresses*, 2nd ed. (London, 1643) 1.

[11] George Lawson, *Political Sacra et Civilis* (Cambridge: Cambridge University Press, 1992); John Locke, *Two Treatises of Government: A Critical Edition with an Introduction an Apparatus Criticus* (Peter Laslett ed.) (Cambridge: Cambridge University Press, 1967). Lawson's and Locke's approaches will be considered in more detail in Chapter 7.

[12] Thomas Rutherford, *Institutes of Natural law: Being the Substance of a Course of Lectures on Grotius De Jure Belli et Pacis* (Cambridge: Printed by J. Bentham, 1756) 126–127.

[13] It is worth noting that in contemporary studies directly addressing the concept of constituent power, Rousseau's name is largely absent. See for example, the essays in Martin Loughlin and Neil Walker (eds), *The Paradox of Constitutionalism: Constituent Power and Constitutional Form* (Oxford University Press, 2007); Andreas Kalyvas, 'Popular Sovereignty, Democracy, and the Constituent Power', 12(2) Constellations 223 (2005). This also seems to be generally the case for non-English literature on constituent power. For example, see Olivier Beaud, *La Puissance de l'État* (PUF, 1994) 234–240. Claude Klein, *Théorie et Pratique du Pouvoir Constituant* (PUF, 1996). A partial exception is found in

On the one hand, his distrust of political representation and support of popular sovereignty is consistent with the idea of the people as a constituent subject. On the other hand, if Rousseau is seen as a proponent of direct democracy, then there seems to be no place in his thought for a concept that presupposes, above all, a *separation* between those who exercise a delegated authority (e.g. ordinary government officials), and those who possess an original constitution-making ability (the people). As in an absolute monarchy or in a system of parliamentary sovereignty, in a legal order in which all laws must be directly made by the people such a separation is absent: the constituent and the legislative body are one and the same. Not surprisingly, during the French Revolution, Louis-Sébastien Mercier wrote that: 'We may reproach Rousseau with not having recognised in a clear and positive way the *constituent power* as an original and necessary power.'[14]

Joan McDonald might be correct that Rousseau's influence on French revolutionaries is frequently exaggerated, that the many evocations of his name in 18th-century France were often based on misunderstandings or political calculations.[15] Yet Rousseau arguably influenced some of the main figures of the Revolution, including Sieyès, who saw himself as the originator of the distinction between the constituent and the constituted powers.[16] In what follows, I will show that Rousseau, in fact, anticipated that distinction and carefully considered its institutional implications. This analysis must begin with a discussion that is often absent from academic commentary on Rousseau: his idiosyncratic[17] use of the term *law*. Throughout Rousseau's political writings, the

Antonio Negri, *Insurgencies: Constituent Power and the Modern State* (University of Minnesota Press, 1999). According to Negri, for Rousseau 'the legislative [power] is always constituent power'. (199). Martin Loughlin has engaged in extensive and valuable discussions of Rousseau's work but has not explicitly considered him as a theorist of constituent power. See Martin Loughlin, 'The Concept of Constituent Power' 13(2) *European Journal of Political Theory* 218 (2013), at 228, 232; Martin Loughlin, *Foundations of Public Law* (Oxford University Press, 2010). In Latin America, an important exception is Carlos Sánchez Viamonte, *El Poder Constituyente* (Buenos Aires: Bibliográfica Argentina, 1957) 196.

[14] 'On pourroit reprocher à Rousseau de n'avoir pas su reconnoître d'une maniere claire et positive le *pouvoir constituant* comme un pouvoir primitif et nécessaire' (emphasis in the original). Louis-Sébastien Mercier, *De J.J. Rousseau, Considéré comme l'un des Premiers Auteurs de la Révolution* (Paris, 1791) vol. 1, 58.

[15] That is one of the main theses defended in Joan McDonald, *Rousseau and the French Revolution 1762–1791* (University of London, 1965) 6–7.

[16] See Raymond Carré de Malberg, *Teoría General del Estado* (México: Fondo de Cultura Económica, 1948) 1186, fn 7. As we will see later, Sieyès was in fact critical of several aspects of Rousseau's work. For a discussion, see Murray Forsyth, *Reason and Revolution: The Political Thought of Abbé Sieyes* (New York: Leicester University Press, 1987) 58–65.

[17] At least now, it appears idiosyncratic. Nevertheless, the distinction between law and decree that will be explained below (including the notion that 'laws' related to general matters and 'decrees' to particular ones), was already present in the 4th-century Athens concepts of *nomoi* and *psephisma*. For a discussion, see Raphael Sealey, 'On the Athenian Concept of Law', 77(4) *The Classical Journal* 289 (1982).

idea of law plays a major role. In fact, his claim that in a legitimate state every law must be directly ratified by the people is one of the best-known aspects of his constitutional thought. As Joshua Cohen has put it: '[t]he most striking feature of Rousseau's institutional views and the one that naturally draws our attention is his endorsement of a directly democratic system of law-making . . .'[18] In a similar vein, Jeremy Waldron has written that: 'People assume that Rousseau's conception of direct popular sovereignty in lawmaking is the ideal from a democratic point of view and even if we are not as scathing about representation as Rousseau was, we should nevertheless deplore representative law-making as a very distant second best.'[19]

Rousseau's support for directly democratic law-making is indeed evidenced by one of the most famous passages found in *The Social Contract*: 'Every law the people has not ratified in person is null and void - is, in fact, not a law. The people of England regard itself as free; but it is grossly mistaken; it is free only during the election of members of parliament. As soon as they are elected, slavery overtakes it, and it is nothing.'[20] For Rousseau, slavery was always illegitimate, and the purpose of *The Social Contract* was precisely to find a way out of it. Rousseau was thus looking for a form of association in which, in obeying the law, individuals would only be obeying themselves and therefore maintaining their freedom. But his solution seems alien to the theory of constituent power because it apparently requires that every single law, not only the constitution or the fundamental laws, results from a direct act of popular sovereignty. Only direct democracy, a form of government impracticable in modern states and inconsistent with the separation between the constituent people and the constituted government, would be acceptable from this perspective, and all departures from that ideal would be at best necessary evils. Rousseau, however, clearly rejected direct democracy as a form of government, and he did it more than once.

A few examples should suffice to prove this point: 'If we take the term in the strict sense, there has never been a real democracy, and there never will be. It is against the natural order for the many to govern and the few to be governed.'[21] 'It is unimaginable,' he wrote, 'that the people should remain continually assembled to devote their time to public affairs . . . Were there a people of gods, their government would be democratic. So perfect a government is not for men.'[22] Or, as he put it in the 'Discourse on Political Economy': 'Must the

[18] Joshua Cohen, *Rousseau: A Free Community of Equals* (Oxford University Press, 2010) 132.
[19] Jeremy Waldron, 'Representative Lawmaking', 89 *Boston University Law Review* 335 (2009) 345.
[20] Jean-Jacques Rousseau, *The Social Contract and The Discourses* (Everyman's Library, 1973) 263.
[21] ibid. 238–239.
[22] ibid.

whole nation be assembled together at any unforeseen event? Certainly not. It ought the less to be assembled, because it is by no means certain that its decision would be the expression of the general will; besides, the method would be impracticable in a great people, and it is hardly ever necessary where the government is well intentioned.'[23] These views were not presented with only large states in mind: '[T]hings cannot be carried on in this manner: on the contrary however small any State may be, civil societies are always too populous to be under the immediate government of all their members.'[24]

II. Law, Sovereignty, and Government

The passages quoted above, found in Rousseau's major works, can't simply be ignored. The fact that he could so casually reject direct democracy as impracticable must at least make us rethink the common place idea that that was his preferred form of government. But if Rousseau thought that direct democracy was not only impracticable but undesirable, how could he at the same time insist that direct popular ratification was a necessary condition for the validity of law? The key to understanding this apparent contradiction lies in Rousseau's conception of law. In every society, there is a multiplicity of rules that seek to regulate the behaviour of individuals. But not all of those rules, for Rousseau, were to be described as laws. What turns a particular rule into law is its object. 'The object of the laws,' he wrote 'is always general,' which means that 'law considers subjects *en masse* and actions in the abstract, and never a particular person or action . . . , no function which has a particular object belongs to the legislative power.'[25] Put differently, the laws addressed only 'the body of the nation.'[26] As many commentators have noted, these passages suggest that laws must not privilege or punish specific individuals or groups, that laws cannot be directed towards particular human beings.

That is to say, that Rousseau's conception of law comes accompanied by a strong notion of political equality. However, these passages also mean that rules that govern particular activities or public functions—rules that we normally call laws—would not count as laws under Rousseau's use of the term.

[23] ibid. 138.

[24] ibid. 153. In his 'Dedication to the Republic of Geneva' (in 'A Discourse on the Origin of Inequality'), Rousseau associated democracy with the 'rude constitution of primitive governments' and characterized it as one of 'the vices that contributed to the downfall of the Republic of Athens.' ibid. 35.

[25] Rousseau, *The Social Contract* (n. 20) 210.

[26] ibid. 206.

In fact, most contemporary legislation lacks the generality that Rousseau sees as a necessary condition for the existence of a law. Contemporary legislation does not frequently address citizens as a collective body, but rather regulates things such as the practice of particular professions, sets the standards for specific industries or economic activities, or organizes different public services. These are rules such as '[a]n Act regulating the Liquor Trade or Limited Liability Companies, an Insurance Act, a Merchant Shipping Act'.[27] In his valuable introduction to Rousseau's political writings, C. E. Vaughan maintained that the previously mentioned Acts would not be valid laws under the argument presented in *The Social Contract*.[28] For Vaughan, the reason was straightforward: these Acts sought to regulate 'particular person[s] or action[s]'[29] and were thus not addressed to the whole body of the nation.

Even though Vaughan is right that those rules would not count as valid laws according to the view presented in *The Social Contract*, he would be mistaken if he is also implying that they would be regarded by Rousseau as simple nullities. As we will see in the next section, in Rousseau's system there are other types of rules that, while perfectly valid (and therefore legally binding), are not to be described as laws. What counts as a valid *law* then? Rousseau maintained that: 'Laws are, properly speaking, only the conditions of civil association.' He also wrote that his *only* concern (in *The Social Contract*) were those rules that 'determine the structure of government', and placed special emphasis on the people's role in creating the 'constitution of the State by giving its sanction to a body of law'.[30] Statements like this suggest that Rousseau's use of the term law was limited to rules that had a fundamental character, the types of rules that we would call 'constitutional laws'. In apparent agreement with this view, G. D. H. Cole has stated that, for Rousseau, the 'laws consist not of the whole body of regulations to which the citizens are subject but only of the fundamental declarations of principle on which the entire social order rests'.[31]

Other authors have reached similar conclusions, even though, like Cole, they have not fully explored its implications for Rousseau's wider constitutional theory. For example, Frank Marini has stated that: 'Too little attention has been paid to the fact that in Rousseau's terminology', laws are something

[27] C. E. Vaughan, 'Introduction', *The Political Writings of Jean Jacques Rousseau* (Oxford: Basil Blackwell, 1962) vol. 1, 66.

[28] Rousseau, *The Social Contract* (n. 20) 210.

[29] ibid.

[30] ibid. 211 ('Les lois ne sont proprement que les conditions de l'association civile') 226, 259.

[31] Cole, 'Preface' (n. 20) 364. This led Carlos Sánchez Viamonte, the Argentinian jurist, to suggest that what Rousseau called 'laws' we simply call today 'constitution'. Sánchez Viamonte (n. 13) 196.

'close to what we would call constituent principles of the political society'.[32] More recently, Christopher Bertram has suggested that it is possible that for Rousseau laws were not equivalent to what we call legislation; that he might have reserved the term law to describe the 'constitutional framework' of society.[33] I largely agree with those interpretations. Nevertheless, in *The Social Contract*, Rousseau states that '[a]mong the different classes of laws, the political, which determine the form of government, are alone relevant to [his] subject'.[34] This suggests that in addition to laws that govern the relationship between the sovereign people and the state (which Rousseau called *political laws*), there were other kinds of laws: *civil laws* that governed the relation between citizens or between individual citizens and the state, and *criminal laws* that governed the relationship of individuals to the law. [35]

Since civil and criminal laws are not considered in any detail by Rousseau, it is not clear what type of provisions he had in mind. It is nevertheless safe to assume that those civil and criminal laws would refer only to a small number of rules that are necessary in a particular political community and would therefore be considered part of that community's basic constitutional framework.[36]

[32] Frank Marini, 'Popular Sovereignty but Representative Government', 11(4) *Midwest Journal of Political Science* 451–470 (1967) 459. For an example of an otherwise excellent analysis which nevertheless seems to miss Rousseau's conception of 'law', see John Plamenatz, 'The Sovereign People, the Law, and the Citizen' in *Machiavelli, Hobbes, and Rousseau* (John Plamenatz, Mark Philp, and Zbigniew Pelczynski eds) (Oxford University Press, 2012) 252, 259.

[33] Christopher Bertram, 'Jean Jacques Rousseau', *Stanford Encyclopaedia of Philosophy* (2010). Ethan Putterman is one of the few authors who carefully considers, and rejects, the view that Rousseau reserved the term 'law' to what we would today call 'constitution'. He maintains that although 'a number of passages in *CS* give substance to this reading by implying that sovereign responsibility is restricted to constitutional lawmaking (*loix fondamentales*) exclusively', there are other statements in Rousseau's work that he thinks point in the opposite direction. Ethan Putterman, 'Rousseau on Agenda-Setting and Majority Rule', 97(3) *American Political Science Review* 459 (2003) 464–465. Despite the many virtues of Putterman's work on Rousseau, I think that even the statements he quotes (such as those that point towards the people having a role in the creation of 'criminal laws'), are not inconsistent with the idea that for Rousseau, 'laws' were always of a constitutional nature, as will be seen shortly. In his more recent monograph on Rousseau, Putterman seems to be more agreeable to the view advanced in this chapter: 'More narrowly, the laws are a set of generalized formal rules relating to the structure of a legitimate state while executive or administrative decrees are a set of particularized commands relating to this structure's proper function.' Ethan Putterman, *Rousseau, Law and the Sovereignty of the People* (Cambridge University Press, 2010) 25–26.

[34] Rousseau, *The Social Contract* (n. 20) 226.

[35] ibid. 225–226. This view is also reflected in Jean Jacques Rousseau, 'Considerations on the Government of Poland and on its Proposed Reformation', April 1772 (ISN ETH Zurich) 30: 'You must have three codes, covering constitutional, civil and criminal law respectively; all three as clear, short and precise as possible.' He also thought that there was a fourth class of law, 'which is graven not on tablets of marble or brass, but on the hearts of citizens. This forms the real constitution of the State, takes on every day new powers when other laws decay or die out, restores them or takes their place, keeps a people in the ways in which it was meant to go, and insensibly replaces authority by the force of habit. I am speaking of morality, of custom, above all of public opinion; a power unknown to political thinkers, on which nonetheless success in everything else depends.' Rousseau, *The Social Contract* (n. 20) 226.

[36] ibid. With regards to criminal laws, Rousseau maintained that they are 'less a particular class of law than the sanction behind all the rest'. ibid.

This conclusion is consistent with the view he expressed in his *Letters Written from the Mountain,* where he maintained that he took the 'constitution' of Geneva as 'the model of political institutions'.[37] He was referring to the Act of Mediation of 1738, which in addition to 'political laws' included a series of provisions that would clearly fall under the category of 'criminal'[38] and 'civil'[39] laws.[40] In using the term law in this way, Rousseau was in fact operating under a long tradition of political thought. Under this tradition, 'law' was usually seen as something fundamental, as something that lay outside the scope of the jurisdiction of government and that was directly connected to the basic organization of political power.

This is not the place to fully explore that tradition, but the best examples are perhaps provided by Marsilius and Althusius, mentioned above. 'The authority to pass laws', for Marsilius, 'belongs solely to the universal body of the citizens or its prevailing part'.[41] It is that body, he maintained, that is called to engage in 'the determination or institution of the offices and parts of the city'.[42] For the 14th-century Italian scholar, the prince was not a law-maker. The prince only had the right to create rules to 'regulate the political or civil acts of men *according to law*'.[43] Similarly, for Althusius, 'the people first associated itself in a certain body with definite laws (*leges*), and established for it the necessary and useful rights (*jura*) of his association'.[44] The prince is authorized to administer those rights, but 'is not supreme in relation to his subject collectively, nor to law, to which he is himself subject'.[45] Likewise,

[37] Jean Jacques Rousseau, *Letter to Beaumont, Letters written from the Mountain, and Related Writings* (Christopher Kelly and Eve Grace eds) (Hanover and London: University Press of New England, 2001) 232–233. This does not mean that he agreed with the ways in which that constitution was being implemented by Genevan magistrates. See Helena Rosenblatt, *Rousseau and Geneva: From* the First Discourse *to* The Social Contract, *1749–1762* (Cambridge University Press, 1997).

[38] See, for example, Articles 55 and 33 (prohibiting acts that affect the public order and punishing the disobedience of judgments, respectively). *Règlement de L'Illustre Médiation pour la Pacification de Troubles de la République de Genève* (1738).

[39] See, for example, Article 34 of the *Règlement,* giving citizens and burghers the right to sell their own wine. *Règlement*, ibid. For the historical significance of this provision, see William C. Inness, *Social Concern in Calvin's Geneva* (Pittsburgh Theological Monographs, 1983) 189. In 'The Geneva Manuscript' (the first draft of *The Social Contract*), Rousseau described civil laws as the 'laws which regulate the respective duties and rights of citizens, . . . as far as domestic relations and the ownership of property are concerned'. Rousseau, 'The Geneva Manuscript' (n. 20) 330.

[40] The idea that for Rousseau laws were always of a constitutional or fundamental nature is also supported by the fact that he counselled against the adoption of many laws, insisting that a well-governed state 'needs very few laws', that some nations were not ready to have 'laws', and that very few nations had any laws at all. Rousseau, *The Social Contract* (n. 20) 211. See also Rousseau, 'Considerations on the Government of Poland' (n. 35); Rousseau, *The Social Contract* (n. 20) 217, 222–223, 264.

[41] Marsilius (n. 2) 68.

[42] ibid. 94.

[43] ibid. 52 (emphasis added).

[44] Althusius (n. 3) 93.

[45] ibid. 120.

Rousseau maintained that laws, because of their subject matter, must be adopted by the people and not by those who have been called to exercise ordinary political power.

That is to say, because laws regulate the conditions of civil association, their adoption requires direct popular intervention: 'The people, being subject to the laws, ought to be their author: the conditions of the society ought to be regulated solely by those who come together to form it.'[46] In saying that all laws must be authored by the people, Rousseau was also saying that the adoption of a law was an act of sovereignty. Since for Rousseau the sovereign was 'a corporate and collective body'[47] comprised of all the individuals living on a particular state, only when they came together and exercised their political power, an act of sovereignty, a law-making act, took place. He thought that a situation like this, where a sovereign people had an exclusive law-making authority, would normally be conducive to the adoption of good laws.[48] That is, being 'formed wholly of the individuals who compose it', the sovereign could be reasonably expected to act in accordance with the common good and not be blinded by private wills that would favour the interests of specific individuals or groups.[49] A collective sovereign, in short, would always tend to act in conformity with what Rousseau famously called the *general will*.

This is another way of saying that the people, and not any individual or elite, will usually be a better judge of the common good, a better judge of the constitution they should be subject to: '[W]ho can judge better than they the conditions under which they had best dwell together in the same society?'[50] Rousseau's sovereign, however, did not act every time a new legal rule needed to be adopted. In both *Letters* and *The Social Contract*, he maintained that the sovereign 'does not always show itself', that the people only made rare appearances in an already constituted commonwealth.[51] The reason for this is simple: the

[46] Rousseau, *The Social Contract* (n. 20) 271.

[47] ibid. 192. Rousseau explains the relationship between individual citizens and the sovereign in this way: 'Suppose the State is composed of ten thousand citizens . . . the Sovereign is to the subject as ten thousand to one, i.e. each member of the State has as his share only a ten-thousandth part of the sovereign authority, although he is wholly under its control.' ibid 229.

[48] The same point is made by Marsilius of Padua. The authority to adopt laws, Marsilius wrote 'belongs to that from which alone the best laws can result'. For Marsilius, it was clear that laws should be adopted by 'the universal body of citizens or its prevailing part', because from 'the universal multitude there results a greater attention to a law's common utility, since no one knowingly harms himself'. Marsilius (n. 2) 68, 69. See also Rousseau, *Émile* (Book V) (n. 20) 335.

[49] ibid 193–194.

[50] Rousseau, 'Dedication' (n. 20) 35. In a statement later paraphrased by Sieyès, Rousseau thus maintained that 'The Sovereign, merely by virtue of what it is, is always what it should be'. Rousseau, *Émile* (Book V) (n. 20) 194.

[51] Rousseau, *Letters* (n. 37) 263; Rousseau, *The Social Contract* (n. 20) 260.

sovereign had 'no force other than the legislative power'[52] and thus only appears when a body of law is created or altered. During the French Revolution, Jean Baptiste Salle expressed this idea with clarity when responding to Jean Mournier's insistence on the people's lack of capacity to govern. Explaining that the people's role was not to govern but to legislate, he maintained: '[t]he people does not know how to govern without passion! But who talks here of governing? Government is not sovereignty; to govern is not to legislate'.[53] A change in the law, like any constitutional change, would be naturally episodic and not a frequent occurrence. Moreover, since the sovereign 'cannot act save when the people is in assembly'[54] it would be impractical for it to be in a continuous session.

III. Rousseau's Executive Power

As noted earlier, for Rousseau, not all the rules that apply to a political community are created through the exercise of sovereignty. Such rules only require the intervention of the executive power. This power comprised the 'administration of civil affairs and the execution of the laws'.[55] After the sovereign has adopted a body of law, Rousseau wrote, there 'still remains an infinity of details of administration and economy, which are left to the wisdom' of the executive power.[56] The actual functions of the executive power in Rousseau's project are seldom examined in the literature, and this has unfortunately resulted in important ambiguities about the institutional arrangements he was proposing. If the executive power merely 'executes' rules, then

[52] Rousseau, *The Social Contract* (n. 20) 258. The question of how frequently the sovereign should act, however, 'depends on so many considerations that no exact rules . . . can be given'. Rousseau, *The Social Contract* (n. 20) 259–260.

[53] He added: '[T]o govern is not to legislate; when the people of Athens judged its great men, it was fulfilling the function of magistracy; it had in view a particular object; it governed, it could go wrong, and it often did so. But when the people of Athens, of Sparta, or Rome, etc., exercised sovereignty, that is, made law; when they established by themselves and for themselves, they did not go wrong, they were wise, and if their political laws were defective, since political science was in its infancy, their civil laws, as you well know, Gentlemen, are still today the wonder of the world.' *Archives Parlementaires*, vol. 8, 530–531. For a discussion, see Richard Tuck, 'Democratic Sovereignty and Democratic Government: The Sleeping Sovereign' in *Popular Sovereignty in Historical Perspective* (Richard Bourke and Quentin Skinner eds) (Cambridge University Press, 2016) 138.

[54] Rousseau, *The Social Contract* (n. 20) 258.

[55] Rousseau, 'A Discourse on the Origin of Inequality' (n. 20) 35. This conception is not dissimilar to that of other 18th-century Genevans. For example, Micheli du Crest argued that a democratic republic was 'a free state, in which the people itself exercises the acts of sovereignty, without however exercising subordinate government, but remits this government to chiefs or officers who are accountable to it and whose administration it has the right to examine'. Quoted in Rosenblatt (n. 37) 143.

[56] Rousseau, 'Discourse on Political Economy' (n. 20) 138.

the assembled people would have to regulate all sorts of aspects of social and commercial life, a situation the Genevan was at pains to avoid. Rousseau did attribute to the executive power the function of implementing the decisions of the sovereign (i.e. the laws), but this involved important rule-making activities.[57] The sovereign may have decided, for example, to adopt a political law giving all citizens the right to vote. The executive power thus has the obligation of creating an electoral system. The sovereign may have decided to adopt a criminal law that prohibits and punishes acts against the public order; the executive power thus has the obligation to define the type of conduct that amounts to an act against the public order and to punish those who commit it.

The exercise of the executive power included the issuing of decrees (*décrets* not *lois*) that relate to specific matters (such as the creation of a public education system[58]) or to particular individuals (such as sentencing someone found guilty of a crime).[59] The former type of decree would normally take the form of a statute in a contemporary legal system; the latter would take the form of a judicial determination.[60] In implementing the decisions of the sovereign, the executive power was always to be exercised in 'the spirit of the law' or, if the law was unclear or non-existent, in the way most conducive to the 'public interest' (as that interpretation would conform to the general will, which is 'the source and supplement of all laws').[61] What the executive 'executes' is thus the constitution itself. Under this approach, the legislative power 'belongs to the people, and can belong to it alone',[62] but the executive power was to be exercised by

[57] The idea of an 'executive' that creates rules is of course common in the modern administrative state.

[58] In his 'Discourse on Political Economy', Rousseau refers to public education as a matter to be regulated by government (i.e. by decree and not by law). ibid. 149.

[59] In his introduction to Rousseau's *Social Contract*, Cole explains the role of government in Rousseau's theory with clarity: 'Governments, including representative assemblies, cannot ever make laws, in Rousseau's sense of the word. They can enact only decrees, which are applications of the law to particular persons, groups or situations'. Cole (n. 20) 364. The distinction between laws and decrees was to an important extent already present in Bodin, who distinguished between 'laws' (created by the sovereign) and edicts (created by magistrates). Jean Bodin, *On Sovereignty: Four Chapters from the Six Books of the Commonwealth* (Julian Franklin ed.) (Cambridge: Cambridge University Press, 1992) Chapter 6 ('The True Attributes of Sovereignty').

[60] Like Locke, Rousseau included the judiciary as part of the executive power. See for example, Rousseau, 'A Discourse on Political Economy' (n. 20) 131; Suri Ratnapala, 'John Locke's Doctrine of the Separation of Powers: A Re-Evaluation', 38(1) *American Journal of Jurisprudence* 189 (1993) 189. As expressed by Clermont-Tonnerre during the French Revolution, 'The judicial power, or what is improperly called the judicial power, is the application of the law or general will to a particular fact. It is not, in the last instance, nothing but the execution of the law, but this execution has the particularity that it has to be preceded by a consultation, by an examination, that embraces law and fact at the same time.' *Archives Parlementaires*, vol. XV, 425 (7 May 1790).

[61] Rousseau, *The Social Contract* (n. 20) 138.

[62] ibid. 227.

a *government* who acted through an individual or entity that Rousseau interchangeably identified with the terms 'magistrate' or 'prince'.[63] Depending on the form of government, the executive power may fall in the hands of the entire citizenry (democracy), of a number of citizens (aristocracy), or of a single individual (monarchy).[64]

Rousseau, like Montesquieu before him, thought that different societies may be better served by different forms of government. However, Rousseau maintained that, generally speaking, the best form was an elected aristocracy, where 'assemblies are easily held' and 'affairs better discussed and carried out with more order and diligence'.[65] Rousseau is in fact describing here a typical system of representative democracy, where the basic constitutional framework is seen as resting in a decision of the entire people, who then elects a number of officials who are expected to carry out public acts in a manner consistent with the constitution. Frequently depicted as the severest critic of representation, Rousseau only rejected it in the context of the exercise of the legislative power. Indeed, the insistence with which commentators continue to depict Rousseau as an enemy of representative government is sometimes difficult to understand given statements like the following: '[I]t is clear that, in the exercise of the legislative power, the people cannot be represented; but in that of the executive power, which is only the force that is applied to give the law effect, it can and should be represented.'[66]

Accordingly, when Rousseau wrote that the English people lived in slavery, it was not because they were not able to ratify in person rules such as the Health and Safety at Work etc. Act 1974 or the Data Protection Act 1988.[67] Those are *decrees* that regulate particular activities and that plainly fall within the jurisdiction of the government of the day, that is, within the jurisdiction of parliament. Decrees of this type, as noted earlier, have to be consistent with the law,

[63] ibid. 228, Again, it is worth noting the similarity between Rousseau and Marsilius: 'For although the legislator . . . ought to determine which men should exercise what kinds of functions in the city, nevertheless it is the princely part that commands, and if necessary enforces, the execution of those decisions, as he does other matters of law. For it is more convenient for the execution of legal matters to take place through him than through the universal multitude of the citizens, since one or a few persons exercising the function of prince are enough for this business, in which the universal community would be unnecessarily occupied and would moreover be distracted from other necessary tasks'. Marsilius (n. 2) 90. Althusius also thought in similar terms: 'Thus the administration and government of a commonwealth is nothing other than the execution of law'. Althusius (n. 3) 139.

[64] Rousseau, *The Social Contract* (n. 20) 239.

[65] ibid. 239.

[66] ibid. 264.

[67] It is interesting to note that in 18th-century France, an anonymous commentator described as a scandal 'the praises sung to Rousseau in an Assembly [the National Assembly of 1789] whose every decree was pronounced as null by the *Social Contract*' McDonald (n. 15) 120.

but do not have to be directly ratified by the people.[68] The reason Rousseau thought the English people lived in slavery was that Parliament also had the power to adopt *laws*, rules that altered the basic legal framework of the country (the 'material' content of the constitutional system),[69] such as the Septennial Act 1716.[70] In other words, the problem was that the English Parliament routinely acted as the legislative power, that it illegitimately exercised a jurisdiction that was not susceptible of representation.[71] Put in the language of the theory of constituent power, the problem was that Parliament frequently operated as a constituent body. As a consequence, the English people were being required to live under a constitution not created by them.

In a similar vein, Maximilien Robespierre, whose speeches frequently mirrored Rousseau's ideas, complained about all those historical instances of 'magistrates oppressing the citizenry and governments devouring sovereignty'. The ills of society, he insisted, never came from the sovereign people but from government. 'How could this not be the case?', after all, '[t]he interest of the people is the public good; the interests of the man in office is a private interest'.[72] At the Constituent Assembly, Robespierre denounced the king's suggestion that he had the right to veto the declaration of rights (a suggestion that led to the debate around the question of the king's veto),[73] which he saw as 'clothed with constituent power'[74]: 'Is it for the Executive power to criticise the Constituent power? It belongs to no power on earth to subvert principles: to raise itself above the nation, and to censure it wishes.'[75] Under this openly Rousseauian approach, monarchical or parliamentary sovereignty would be nothing but a usurpation of the people's constitution-making authority, the attribution of legislative power to an executive entity that should only be engaged in ordinary governmental activities. In this sense, Rousseau was a clear precursor of the notion of constitutional supremacy under a representative form of government.

[68] Rousseau, *The Social Contract* (n. 20) 211. Even if a decree is popularly ratified, it should not be seen as an act of sovereignty: '. . . and even when the Sovereign commands with regard to a particular matter is no nearer being a law, but is a decree, an act, not of sovereignty, but of magistracy'.

[69] For the notion of the material constitution, see Chapter 8 of this book.

[70] Dicey once presented the Septennial Act as 'standing proof' of parliamentary sovereignty). A. V. Dicey, *Introduction to the Study of the Law of the Constitution* (Indianapolis: Liberty Classics, 1982) 6. Rousseau was clearly familiar with the English system of government. See, for example, Rousseau, *The Social Contract* (n. 20) 267–268.

[71] As Tuck has noted, for Rousseau, 'the English legislature was part of government'. Tuck (n. 1) 134.

[72] Maximilien Robespierre, 'Robespierre on Constitutional Principles' (10 May 1793) in *The French Revolution* (Paul H. Beik ed.) (Macmillan, 1970) 256.

[73] This debate will be briefly discussed in Chapter 3. See Eric Thompson, *Popular Sovereignty and the French Constituent Assembly 1789–91* (Manchester University Press, 1952) 37.

[74] Quoted in James Bronterre O'Brian, *The Life and Character of Maximilien Robespierre* (London, 1837) vol. 1, 232.

[75] Quoted in G. H. Lewes, *The Life of Maximilien Robespierre* (London, 1849) 112.

That was, in fact, the conclusion drawn by Robespierre: '[t]he first objective of every constitution must be to defend public and individual liberty against the government itself'.[76]

IV. Rousseau, Theorist of Constituent Power

Rousseau's distinction between the legislative and the executive power has a very close affinity (and to a large extent corresponds) to the distinction between constituent and constituted power. Carlos Sánchez Viamonte, the Argentinian jurist, was unequivocal in his support for this view, writing that what Rousseau called 'legislative power', we call today 'constituent power'.[77] If this aspect of his thought is missed, Sánchez Viamonte maintained, the interpreter would conclude that Rousseau defended the unlimited sovereignty of the state, when in fact he consistently negated the sovereignty of any entity other than the community itself.[78] Just as in contemporary societies the constituent people is usually seen as having the right to create any constitution it wants, Rousseau's legislative power involved the ability to create any body of laws, laws which content could not be limited by the positive legal system. While Rousseau's executive power, as a constituted body, could not alter the constitution, the sovereign people always had the authority to change it at will. 'There neither is nor can be', Rousseau famously wrote, 'any kind of fundamental law binding on the body of the people, not even the social contract itself'.[79]

Even though the sovereign had an unlimited legislative (constituent) power, such a power is not correctly described as arbitrary. In fact, as noted earlier, the sole function of the sovereign was to adopt laws that applied to the whole community. A sovereign who engages in functions that have a particular object (e.g. a constituent assembly that adopts ordinary laws or engages in adjudicative or executive functions) is not acting as a sovereign but as a government (a situation that would be present in a democracy and that for Rousseau was at the very least inadequate).[80] In the same way, a government that acts as a

[76] Robespierre (n. 72) 257.
[77] Sánchez Viamonte, *El Poder Constituyente* (n. 13) 196.
[78] Carlos Sánchez Viamonte, *Manual de Derecho Político: Los Problemas de la Democracia* (Editorial Bibliográfica Argentina, 1959) 86.
[79] Rousseau, *The Social Contract* (n. 20) 193. Rousseau had a somewhat similar view about God's power: 'Can God perform miracles? That is, can he depart from the Laws he has established? Seriously treated, this question would be impious if it were not absurd.' *Third Letter* (n. 37) 173.
[80] Rousseau, *The Social Contract* (n. 20) 236. In fact, he maintained that '[t]o be legitimate, the government must be, not one with the Sovereign, but its minister'. ibid. 211, fn 1. He also wrote that '[t]he right which the social compact gives the Sovereign over the subjects does not, we have seen, exceed the limits of public expediency'. Rousseau, *The Social Contract* (n. 20) 303.

sovereign is an illegitimate one: absolute monarchies were not legitimate, at least not when attributed with the power of altering the law.[81] Put in a different way, the people, in the exercise of their constituent power, can create any constitution it wants (that is to say, can establish any form of government) but can never give away its legislative power.[82] And even if, as we will see below, the original establishment of a constitution may require the intervention of an individual constitution-maker (a gifted law-giver, of which Lycurgus provided one of the best examples),[83] the constitution would not become valid 'until it has been put to the free vote of the people'.[84]

The strong connections between Rousseau's thought and the theory of constituent power are not only reflected in his conception of sovereignty, but also exemplified in some of his more practical institutional views, such as the establishment of a tribunate. As explained earlier, Rousseau thought that 'the power of the magistrates extends to everything which may maintain the constitution, without going so far as to alter it'.[85] In order to protect 'the laws and the legislative power' from the government, to protect the constituent against the constituted power, Rousseau proposed the establishment of a quasi-judicial body (*le tribunat*).[86] Akin to a contemporary constitutional court, the tribunate did not form part of the legislative or executive authorities[87] and did not have the initiative to adopt laws or decrees: it was only able to prevent them from being adopted.[88] The idea, in the last instance, was to prevent the dissolution of the state, which occurred 'when the prince ceases to administer the State in accordance with the laws, and usurps the

[81] It is important to remember that even Bodin thought that a sovereign monarch was limited by the constitutional law (i.e. the fundamental laws) of the realm. Bodin (n. 59) 13, 18. One of the changes that the idea of the constituent power of the people presupposes is that even the fundamental laws can be altered or replaced by an act of human will. This is precisely the idea rejected by 19th-century proponents of the historical constitution, as will be discussed in Chapter 7.

[82] Rousseau thought that the sovereign authority (the constituent power) is never transferred, not even in an emergency: 'If, on the other hand, the peril is of such a kind that the paraphernalia of the laws are an obstacle to their preservation, the method is to nominate a supreme ruler, who shall silence all the laws, and suspend for a moment the sovereign authority. In such a case, there is no doubt about the general will, and it is clear that the people's first intention is that the State shall not perish. Thus the suspension of the legislative authority is in no sense its abolition; the magistrate who silences it cannot make it speak; he dominates it, but cannot represent it. He can do anything; except make laws.' Rousseau, *The Social Contract* (n. 20) 290–291.

[83] ibid. 213.

[84] ibid. 214. Moreover, as we will see shortly, from then on, the constitution remains forever subject to re-constitution by an act of the sovereign.

[85] Rousseau, 'Discourse on the Origins of Inequality' (n. 20) 106.

[86] Rousseau, *The Social Contract* (n. 20) 288. Rousseau also wrote that the tribunate would protect the government from the people (as the Council of Ten in Venice, which protected the government from rebellions or insurrections) or 'maintain the balance between the two'. ibid.

[87] As noted earlier, for Rousseau, the judiciary was part of the executive power.

[88] Rousseau, *The Social Contract* (n. 20) 288.

Sovereign power'.[89] Or, in contemporary terminology, to prevent the adoption of unconstitutional laws.

Rousseau's separation of the constituent from the constituted powers becomes even clearer when one looks at his ideas about how the government is constituted and how the sovereign may protect itself from governmental abuses. He thought that a government is originally instituted through a two-step process. First, the people, acting in a sovereign capacity, determines that 'there shall be a governing body established in this or that form'.[90] Rousseau states that 'this act is clearly a law', for it involves the creation of a constitutional structure (which may take the form of a democracy, an aristocracy, or a monarchy).[91] Second, the people appoints 'the rulers who are to be entrusted with the government that has been established'.[92] Rousseau says that this second act is not a law (since it is addressed to specific individuals, i.e. those that will be in charge of the administration), but a decree, an act of magistracy. One may ask how can there be an act of magistracy (an act of the constituted power), before the government has been fully constituted; Rousseau's answer is that in this second act there is a 'sudden conversion of Sovereignty into democracy', so that the citizenry temporarily acts as a magistrate.

Rousseau nevertheless believed that the creation of a society's first constitution can seldom result from the act of an entire people: 'How can a blind multitude, which often does not know what it wills, because it rarely knows what is good for it, carry out for itself so great and difficult an enterprise as a system of legislation?'[93] 'Is it to be', he asked, 'by common agreement, by a sudden inspiration?'[94] It would be too much to ask a people that has never lived under a constitution to 'relish sound principles of political theory', 'to follow the fundamental rules of statecraft', and to exhibit the 'social spirit' that is the effect (not the cause) of a good body of laws.[95] His solution to this problem was the 'Legislator', which he described as 'the engineer who invents the machine'.[96]

[89] ibid. 255. As the reader will note, there is a clear similarity here with Locke's views about the dissolution of the state and the community's right of resistance. For a discussion, see Chapter 7 of this book.
[90] ibid. 267.
[91] ibid.
[92] ibid.
[93] ibid. 211.
[94] ibid.
[95] ibid. 215.
[96] ibid. 212. The task of the legislator is not merely to draft a code of abstract justice (that could be done, Rousseau said, by the most novice law student), but to create a constitution that would suit the community for which it is made (and this involved inquiring into variables such as the size of the population, soil and climate, national character, etc.). Jean Jacques Rousseau, *Letter à d'Alembert* (1758). The influence of Montesquieu in this aspect of Rousseau's thought is clear. See Baron De Montesquieu, *The Spirit of the Laws* (New York: Hafner Press, 1949) 221–224. Nevertheless, Althusius made a very similar point in his *Politica*. Althusius (n. 3) 149.

This aspect of Rousseau's thought is frequently interpreted as an indication of the ultimate failure of his system of popular sovereignty: in the end, no people can give laws to itself. Rousseau's Legislator has thus been described by Michael Walzer as 'simply the philosopher in heroic dress',[97] by Vaughan as a 'wonder-working magician',[98] and many others see it as a puzzle in an argument for popular sovereignty.[99]

In order to make sense of the figure of the Legislator and understand its role in a theory of constituent power, three things should be noted. Firstly, Rousseau did not present the Legislator as a necessary condition for the creation of a legitimate state, but as a practical reality in light of the fact that a society that has never lived under a constitution will normally lack the ability to create one.[100] Secondly, as noted earlier, the Legislator does not possess legislative (constituent) power: its sole faculty is that of drafting a constitution that will become valid only if ratified by the people.[101] Thirdly, although Rousseau uses the term in the singular,[102] there is no reason why the Legislator cannot take the form of a collective entity or why, in the context of a small city-state in which citizens have somehow developed the capacity to adopt a body of laws (e.g. by exposure to the constitutional system of a neighbouring state), the Legislator cannot be the people themselves. One must remember that the notion of a collective Legislator that adopts the fundamental laws is also present in earlier authors. Marsilius, for example, maintained that 'the "legislator" i.e. the primary and proper efficient cause of the law, is the people or the universal body of the citizens or else its prevailing part'.[103]

More importantly, the idea that the legislator can be a collective entity is present in *Letters*: 'In a State such as yours, where the sovereignty is in the hands of the People, the Legislator always exists, although it does not always show itself. It is assembled and speaks authentically only in the General Council [a body composed of all the citizens and burghers of Geneva].'[104] 'Outside the General Council' Rousseau continued, the Legislator 'is not annihilated; its members are scattered, but they are not dead; they cannot speak by means of Laws, but

[97] Michal Walzer, 'Philosophy and Democracy', 9(3) *Political Theory* 379–399 (1981) 384.

[98] Vaughan (n. 27) vol. 1, 31.

[99] See the discussion in Christopher Kelly, '"To Persuade without Convincing": The Language of Rousseau's Legislator' 31(2) *American Journal of Political Science* 321–335 (1987) 322.

[100] In fact, Rousseau did not mention the 'Legislator' once in the summary of *The Social Contract* included in *Letters*. Rousseau, *Letters* (n. 37) 232. He did not mention it either in the summary of *The Social Contract* contained in Book V of *Émile*. Rousseau, *Émile* (Book V) (n. 20) 332–344.

[101] Rousseau, *The Social Contract* (n. 20) 214.

[102] Rousseau also uses the terms 'Prince' or 'Magistrate' in the singular, even though they refer to 'the man or the body' entrusted with the executive power. ibid. 228.

[103] Marsilius (n. 2) 66.

[104] Rousseau, *Letters* (n. 37) 263.

they can always keep watch over the administration of the Laws . . .'[105] The Legislator, in short, is the individual or entity tasked with the responsibility of proposing a body of laws to a constituent people.[106] Evoking modern and contemporary debates about the nature of the power of a constituent assembly (entities which have, often controversially, engaged in the exercise of the ordinary powers of government even though only authorized to draft a constitution or at most to enact it),[107] Rousseau maintained that the Legislator has 'neither magistracy, nor sovereignty'.[108] That is to say, in the same way that it is not authorized to adopt a constitution (only to propose it), the Legislator cannot issue any decrees.

These ideas have to be understood in light of the fact that regardless of the identity of the drafter of a society's first constitution, Rousseau thought that each generation had the right to re-constitute the state. In this sense, Judith Shklar's view that in Rousseau 'the sovereign does very little', and that '[i]t is he [the Legislator] the sole "architect" of the edifice that the people maintains' is at best overstated.[109] True, the following passage, contained in the 'Geneva Manuscript', could be interpreted as attributing the people only with a passive role in the creation and maintenance of a body of law: 'The laws, although received, only have a lasting authority so long as the people, being free to revoke them, nevertheless does not do so.'[110] But unlike Locke and other social contract theorists, Rousseau provided an institutional mechanism for the exercise of constituent power, for the potential revocation of the laws and the re-creation of the constitutional order. Being 'not enough for the assembled people to have once fixed the constitution of the State', he maintained that 'besides the extraordinary assemblies unforeseen circumstances may demand, there must be fixed periodic assemblies which cannot be abrogated or prorogued'.[111]

[105] ibid. Rousseau here was arguing in favours of the right of remonstrance (see n. 117, below).

[106] An important problem here is how to determine who the 'constituent people' is. Rousseau's Legislator does not provide a solution to that problem: even if an individual or collective Legislator (and not the entire people) is to draft the constitution, the question of who exactly should be entitled to ratify it remains. In this respect, Rousseau's conception suffers from a problem shared by all modern theories of constituent power.

[107] For further elaboration of this point, see Chapter 9 of this book.

[108] Rousseau, *The Social Contract* (n. 20) 213.

[109] Judith N. Shklar, *Men and Citizens: A Study of Rousseau's Social Theory* (Cambridge: Harvard University Press, 1969) 181.

[110] Rousseau, 'Geneva Manuscript' (n. 20) 324.

[111] Rousseau, *The Social Contract* (n. 20) 259. These types of assemblies were also proposed by later authors, such as Thomas Jefferson. See Thomas Jefferson, *Writings* (Merrill Peterson ed.) (New York, Library of America, 1984) at 1402. When a sovereign assembly was convened, Rousseau maintained that 'the jurisdiction of government wholly lapses, the executive power is suspended, and the person of the meanest citizen is as sacred and inviolable as that of the first magistrate; for in the presence of the person represented, representatives no longer exist'. Not surprisingly, he stated that '[t]hese intervals of

A constitutional order, a form of government, always had a 'provisional form'.[112]

Crucially, both extraordinary and periodic assemblies could only be convened in accordance with established law: only a public meeting that complies with the forms posited by the entire citizenry could be taken as authorized to pronounce the general will. Although the sovereign is not bound by any substantive limits found in positive law, it can only act according to certain *procedures* recognized by law.[113] That is to say, periodic assemblies would be 'authorized by their date alone', and any other 'assembly of the people not summoned by the magistrates appointed for that purpose, and in accordance with the prescribed forms, should be regarded as unlawful'.[114] The legal possibility of an exercise of constituent power is for Rousseau an integral part of a legitimate constitutional order. His insistence in the convening of the assembly by magistrates is understandable: one could not expect the entire people to summon itself. It is nevertheless entirely possible (from a practical point of view) to place the initiative to convene the assembly in a section of the electorate (e.g. a percentage of the population), as the Rousseauian inspired Constitution of 1793 did.[115]

There is no clear indication of how frequently Rousseau thought periodic assemblies should be convened. As noted earlier, he maintained that in a well-governed state, the sovereign rarely needs to show itself. Even if it does not provide a clear indication of his views, it is worth noting that in his native Geneva it was once agreed that the General Council would meet every five years (the General Council was also convened in times of crisis).[116] Rousseau's assemblies were designed, as it where, to reproduce the two acts that take place when government is instituted for the first time. Not surprisingly, they would always put to the people two different propositions: 'The first is: "Does it please the Sovereign to preserve the present form of government?" The second is: "Does it please the people to leave its administration in the hands of those who are actually in charge of it?"'.[117] These assemblies would put the future of the entire

suspension, during which the prince recognizes or ought to recognize an actual superior, have always been viewed by him with alarm'. Rousseau, *The Social Contract* (n. 20) 261.

[112] ibid. 268.

[113] ibid. 259. This point raises issues similar to those raised by contemporary constitutional provisions authorising the convocation of 'sovereign constituent assemblies'. This question will be addressed in Chapter 9.

[114] ibid.

[115] The relevant provisions of the Constitution of 1793 will be examined in the Chapter 4.

[116] See Rosenblatt (n. 37) 109.

[117] Rousseau, *The Social Contract* (n. 20) 269. In *The Social Contract*, Rousseau maintains that although citizens always have the right to vote on any proposals related to a change in the law, the

constitutional order in the hands of the community; they would put the citizenry in a position similar to a group of individuals who decides to give themselves a body of laws after entering into the social contract.

V. Assembling the Constituent People

As noted earlier, Rousseau was well aware of the practical difficulty, outside the context of a small city-state, of convening an assembly in which all citizens sat. One must nevertheless recall that in *The Social Contract* he wrote that despite being composed of at least 400,000 citizens, the people of Rome was frequently assembled.[118] In fact, in Book IV of that work, Rousseau provided a detailed description of the ways in which citizens of the early Roman Republic were organized in different assemblies and the procedures through which their voting power was regulated.[119] But what emerges from that description is a system that seems to privilege the status of wealthy citizens, not one for the exercise of a popular constituent power. According to Rousseau, it was in the *Comitia Centuriata*, one of the three assemblies that operated in the Roman Republic, where the 'majesty of the Roman people lay'.[120] The reason was simple: unlike the other two assemblies, which excluded certain citizens (such as the rural tribes and the patricians) the *Comitia Centuriata* 'alone included all'.[121] That assembly, one could say, was the one authorized to engage in the exercise of constituent power. However, given the way in which the voting took place (where

making of proposals themselves is in the sole hands of government. *Letters* (n. 37) 263–264; Rousseau, 'Dedication to the Republic of Geneva' (n. 20) 35. Perhaps, as suggested by Cohen, Rousseau's statements against the popular initiative may be no more than an endorsement of the existing limitations in Geneva under the Act of Mediation. Cohen (n. 18) 172–173. However, the idea that individual citizens should not have the power to propose changes to the law (i.e. the constitution) was probably driven by a practical consideration: such an arrangement would allow any citizen to require, at any time, the convocation of a constitution-making assembly of all the people. On this point, see also John T. Scott, 'Rousseau's Anti-Agenda-Setting Agenda and Contemporary Democratic Theory', 99(1) *American Political Science Review* 137 (2005) 141. This does not mean that a group of citizens should not have the right to voice their opinions about constitutional matters and request government to act on them. In fact, Rousseau argued in favour of the right of remonstrance in early 18th-century Geneva. Rousseau, *Letters* (n. 37) 263–264. On this reading, Rousseau's position would also be consistent with a system in which particular formalities must be met (such as the collection of a number of signatures) before a citizen proposal can be put to the vote of the entire people.

118 Rousseau, *The Social Contract* (n. 20) 259.
119 ibid. 273–288.
120 ibid. 286.
121 ibid. It is unclear how many Roman citizens actually participated and voted in the *Comitia Centuriata* and how much space was actually available for large citizen congregations. For a discussion, see Lily Ross Taylor, *Roman Voting Assemblies: From the Hannibalic War to the Dictatorship of Caesar* (Ann Arbor: University of Michigan Press, 1966) 52, 113.

the wealthy class voted first and had a majority of the votes), this entity was hardly an 'assembly of the people'.

As Rousseau himself noted, 'in the *Comitia Centuriata*, decisions were regulated far more by depth of purses than by the number of votes'.[122] Moreover, and contrary to his early insistence in the distinction between sovereignty and government, in Book IV of *The Social Contract* Rousseau maintained that 'laws and the election of rulers were not the only questions submitted to the judgment of the comitia', but that the Roman people also exercised 'the most important functions of government'.[123] These features of the Roman Republic, as described in *The Social Contract*, seem to point away from truly popular constitution-making bodies and towards attributing certain elites with high degrees of political power. To the extent that Rousseau approves of this arrangement, this would call for an interpretation very different from the one advanced in this chapter. They also suggest that the separation between legislative and executive power does not apply in a system where the sovereign assembly is controlled by the wealthiest citizens. To my knowledge, no one has presented that argument more persuasively than John McCormick, who after a close reading of Book IV, described Rousseau as an 'anti-populist contributor [. . .] to modern constitutional thought', who 'fairly explicitly prescribes institutions that enable rather than constrain the prerogative of elites within republics and popular governments'.[124]

The exact role of Book IV in *The Social Contract* has long been a subject of debate, and this is not the place to resolve that controversy.[125] There are nevertheless good reasons to believe that Rousseau was *not* presenting Rome as an ideal example of his theory. That is to say, that even if he was sympathetic of the republic's constitutional arrangements, he was not suggesting that those arrangements were consistent with the argument in *The Social Contract*.[126] The closest Rousseau came to identifying a specific form of government as consistent with the principles of the *Social Contract* was in his *Letters*, where he wrote that in that work he had taken the Genevan Constitution, 'as the model

[122] Rousseau, *The Social Contract* (n. 20) 285.

[123] ibid. 284.

[124] John P. McCormick, 'Rousseau's Rome and the Repudiation of Populist Republicanism', 10(1) *Critical Review of International Social and Political Philosophy* 3 (2007) 22, 3.

[125] See, for example, McCormick, ibid. 9; Vaughan (n. 27) vol. 2, 109 fn 1; David Lay Williams, *Rousseau's Social Contract: An Introdution* (Cambridge University Press, 2014) 171; Chris Meckstroth, *The Struggle for Democracy: Paradoxes of Progress and the Politics of Change* (Oxford University Press, 2015) 13, fn 9.

[126] In fact, even though he describes the English constitutional system as amounting to slavery, he refers to several of its features favourably at different points in his work. See for example, Rousseau, *The Social Contract* (n. 20) 246, 267–268; *Letters* (n. 37) 246, 252, 287–291.

of political institutions' and proposed it 'as an example to Europe'.[127] In assessing Book IV, one has to take into account the three following things. Firstly, as noted earlier, one common thread through Rousseau's work is the idea that no particular form of government is suited to all peoples.[128] 'The science of government', he wrote, 'is nothing but a science of combinations, applications, and exceptions, according to times, places, circumstances'.[129] The very idea of understanding the practical implications of the argument of the *Social Contract* through Book IV is thus highly problematic. Indeed, when explaining that the Roman people was distributed into six classes, 'distinguished neither by place nor by person, but by wealth', Rousseau noted that '[w]ithout deciding now whether this third arrangement [the division of the people into six classes] was good or bad in itself, I think I may assert that it could have been made practicable' only by the character of the early Romans.[130]

Secondly, even though he maintained that the *Comitia Centuriata* exercised both sovereignty and governmental functions, it is far from clear that he actually condoned this state of affairs. In *Letters*, he actually wrote that he did 'not excuse the faults of the Roman People, I have stated them in the *Social Contract*; I blamed it for having usurped the executive power that it should have only held in check'.[131] Thirdly, and finally, after noting that the organization of the *Comitia Centuriata* into a system of classes favoured the wealthiest citizens, he described that situation as 'extreme', and quickly moved to note a number of features that 'counter-balanced the influence of the patricians in the first class'.[132] For these reasons, I don't think one should try to understand Rousseau's argument in the *Social Contract* (or even more problematically,

[127] *Letters* (n. 37) 233, 234.

[128] Chapter 8 of Book III of *The Social Contract* is thus titled 'That All Forms of Government Do not Suit All Countries', Rousseau *The Social Contract* (n. 20) 247–252.

[129] Jean-Jaques Rousseau, 'Letter to Mirabeau' in *The Social Contract and Other Latter Political Writings* (Voctor Gourevitch ed.) (Cambridge University Press, 1997) 269.

[130] Rousseau *The Social Contract* (n. 20) 282.

[131] ibid. 292. In Book III of *The Social Contract,* Rousseau notes that the Roman people 'exercised not only the rights of Sovereignty, but also a part of those of government. It dealt with certain matters, and judged certain cases, and this whole people was found in the public meeting-place hardly less often as magistrates than as citizens.' McCormick, suggests that in this passage Rousseau condones the fusion of sovereignty and government in the Roman Republic. I don't think that is the case, since the purpose of the passage is to show that even in a large capital such as Rome, it was possible for an entire people to assemble. McCormick (n. 125) 10. One can find different examples in Rousseau's work in which he praises a specific aspect of a political system, even if he considers that the political system itself suffers from a fundamental flaw. For example, when discussing mixed governments, he notes that in England (a country comprised of citizens who according to him, as noted earlier, most of the time lived in 'slavery'), the different constituent parts of government are 'in mutual dependence' an arrangement he favourably compares to that of Poland, where 'the authority of each section is independent, but imperfect'. Rousseau, *The Social Contract* (n. 20) 246.

[132] ibid. 285. For an illuminating discussion, see Williams (n. 125) 171–176.

his entire constitutional thought) through the lenses of Book IV. The issue remains, however, that in most states (and certainly in contemporary ones), the idea of convening an assembly of all the people presents an important practical difficulty.

Aware of this problem, Rousseau proposed two possible solutions. First, different groups of citizens could 'assemble by turn' in the relevant locality or region (e.g. town, city).[133] This could be interpreted as allowing each assembly, one after the other, to act as if it were a sovereign assembly of all citizens, but this was unlikely to be Rousseau's intention given that in the same passage he wrote that 'one town cannot, any more than one nation, legitimately be made subject to another'.[134] Rousseau appears to be proposing a system of primary assemblies[135] with decision-making power which, as we will see in the next two chapters, some radicals supported during the French Revolution. Under this approach, each primary assembly would participate in the exercise of the legislative (constituent) power by expressing its view on the two questions mentioned in the previous section. The votes of all the citizens participating in these assemblies, it seems, would be taken as the declaration of the general will, as an indication that the adoption of a new constitution would serve the common good in that particular society.[136] If the relevant majority answered the questions in the affirmative, a 'Legislator' (which, as noted earlier, could take the form of a collective body) would have the task of proposing to the people a new constitution to be administered by the new set of elected magistrates.

The second solution was addressed to states so large that even a system of multiple assemblies would be impractical. In those states, the people had no choice but to exercise their constituent power with the assistance of

[133] Rousseau, *The Social Contract* (n. 20) 260. See also his 'Constitutional Project for Corsica' (1765).

[134] Rousseau, *The Social Contract* (n. 20) 260.

[135] Rousseau did not use the term 'primary assemblies', but his assemblies were equivalent to the 'primary' or 'parish' assemblies that played a major role in revolutionary France (as well as in 19th-century constitution-making in Europe and Latin America). For a discussion, see Chapters 3 and 4.

[136] This is consistent with his view of assembled citizens being asked not to vote in favour or against a particular proposal, but to give their opinion as to whether a particular proposal is consistent or not with the general will. ibid. 275. For a discussion, see Cohen (n. 17) 73–82. Rousseau did not specify which rules would govern the assemblies' decision-making processes, but one can assume that decisions would be made by majority vote. It is well known that for Rousseau, the only act that required unanimity was the social contract itself, even though he accepted that particular societies may establish that only qualified majorities should have the right to decide on 'grave and important questions'. Rousseau, *The Social Contract* (n. 20) 275. In 'Considerations on the Government of Poland' he also considered this issue, arguing that between fundamental laws and mere acts of administration 'there are various intermediary cases in which the extent of agreement should be in proportion to the importance of the matter'. Rousseau, 'Considerations on the Government of Poland' (n. 35) 28. Whether those supermajority procedures could be legitimately established by a simple majority, he does not say. For an excellent analysis of Rousseau's conception of fundamental laws, see Melissa Schwartzberg, 'Rousseau on Fundamental Law', 51(1) *Political Studies* 387 (2003).

a representative body: 'One of the greatest disadvantages of large states, the one which above all makes liberty most difficult to preserve in them, is that the legislative power cannot manifest itself directly, and can act only by delegation.'[137] But in order for that situation not to amount to a form of slavery, he thought that the imperative mandate was necessary. Citizen instructions, he said, should be 'drawn up with great care', and delegates required to follow them 'exactly, and to make them render their constituents as strict account of their conduct on the diet'.[138] He thus referred to 'the negligence, the carelessness and, I would even venture to say, the stupidity of the English nation, which, after having armed its deputies with such supreme power, has added no brake to regulate the use they may make of that power through the seven years of their mandate'.[139] It is not clear how such a system would work in practice, but it should be remembered that at the time he was writing, there was a debate in Great Britain about whether communications signed by the majority of the electors of particular constituencies—instructing individual members of parliament to vote in particular ways—should be treated as legally binding.[140]

VI. Conclusion

Rousseau's distinction between sovereignty and government was not an original contribution to political thought. It is also exemplified in the work of different 17th-century (and even earlier) authors. Althusius, we saw, distinguished between the right of sovereignty and the right of administration. Other social contract theorists relied on similar distinctions. In *Letters*, Rousseau referred to Althusius, Locke, and Sidney as having views similar to the ones he expressed in the *Social Contract* ('Locke' he wrote, 'treated [these matters] exactly in the same principles as I did').[141] Bodin also distinguished between

[137] Rousseau, 'Considerations on the Government of Poland' (n. 35) 16.

[138] ibid. 17. A similar point is made in *The Social Contract* after noting that sovereignty cannot be represented: 'The deputies of the people, therefore, are not and cannot be its representatives: they are merely its stewards, and carry through no definitive acts.' Rousseau, *The Social Contract* (n. 20) 263.

[139] ibid. Rousseau's conception of citizen instructions will be discussed in more detail in Chapter 3.

[140] Citizen instructions and their relationship with constituent power will be discussed in Chapters 3 and 4, as well as in Chapter 10. For a discussion of the English tradition of citizen instructions and its relationship with the theory of constituent power, see Joel Colón-Ríos, 'Five Conceptions of Constituent Power', 130 *Law Quarterly Review* 306 (2014) and Chapter 10 of this book.

[141] Rousseau, *Letters* (n. 37) 235–236. Rousseau, like Locke, distinguished between government and the sovereign people, but there are many important differences in the work of these two authors, particularly their conceptions of the state of nature, of natural law, and the fact that the English author limited the exercise of popular sovereignty to instances of governmental abuse. For a discussion of the differences between Rousseau and Locke, see Vaughan (n. 27) vol. 1, 23, 37, and vol. 2, 184–187.

sovereignty and government, but did not think that sovereignty necessarily belonged to the people.[142] However, unlike these authors, Rousseau not only saw the community as the only legitimate sovereign, but systematically argued in favour of a formal means for the people to act independently of government. This is why his role in the development of the theory of constituent power is so crucial. As we will see in the next chapter, Sieyès followed Rousseau in many respects, even though they disagreed in important ways about the possibility of representing the constituent power. Sieyès' approach, at the same time, came accompanied by a different understanding of the relationship between constituent power and the law.

Beyond Chapter 3, Rousseau's work will be present in many ways through this book. As will be seen, he was more often than not referred to as the extreme representative of the idea that the actual human beings that comprise a nation (as opposed to 'the nation' as a separate entity), had an ultimate constitution-making faculty. At the same time, while presenting a seemingly radical conception of constituent power, Rousseau saw it as having an intimate connection with law. Not only its exercise was required every time a 'law' was adopted, but in an already instituted state it had to take place within the constitutional forms established by the sovereign. This idea encapsulates the two main legal functions that constituent power assumed in the decades that followed the publication of *The Social Contract*. Firstly, the notion that any norm inconsistent with what is considered fundamental, unless it is adopted by the constituent subject, should be treated as illegal. Secondly, the justification of the legally unlimited character of a properly constituted constitution-making entity that is authorized to speak on behalf of the constituent subject. In the chapters that follow, these and other questions will be explored in the context of different debates that took place during the French Revolution and that, to a large extent, remain unresolved today.

[142] Bodin (n. 59) 7–8. See also Loughlin, *Foundations* (n. 13) 58–59, 117.

3
Sieyès *via* Rousseau

Rousseau, we saw in the previous chapter, advanced a distinction between the constituent and the constituted powers, even though he did not use that terminology. Only the people had the authority to create fundamental laws, and any other rules created by government needed to be consistent with the decisions of the people. In adopting such rules, government was 'executing' the constitution, putting in practice the will of the constituent subject. From that conception, Rousseau reached a number of conclusions about the institutional arrangements that should be present in a legitimate state: no (fundamental) laws should be adopted without popular ratification; there should be periodic assemblies established by law in which the entire citizenry would be asked whether they wish to maintain the existing form of government or create a new one; and, in states so large that the adoption of fundamental laws needs to be put in the hands of a number of delegates, the citizenry's right to issue binding instructions should be recognized. As we will see in this chapter, although Sieyès followed Rousseau's distinction between the constitution-creating people and the ordinary law-maker, he openly rejected the institutional alternatives proposed by the Genevan. This was partly a result of Sieyès' conception of representation, and partly a consequence of a concern with what he saw as the destabilizing qualities of constituent power.

This chapter will trace the gradual emergence of the distinction between the constituted and the constituent power in the work of Sieyès. The objective will be to examine how he constructed constituent power as an extra-legal force and to consider the key juridical implications of his views. Part I briefly explores some uses of the term 'constituent power' before Sieyès or outside the context of the French Revolution. Part II examines Sieyès' early pamphlets, where he puts forward his initial understanding of the power to be exercised by the nation's representatives in the Estates-General. This approach, it will be seen in Part III, led him to propose the creation of a supreme constitution that ensured that the (representative) law-making power acted consistently with the general will. Part IV of the chapter focuses on Sieyès' main published work, *What is the Third Estate?*, which contains a more developed formulation of the distinction between constituent and constituted power, as well as about the nature of

Constituent Power and the Law. Joel Colón-Ríos, Oxford University Press (2020). © Joel Colón-Ríos.
DOI: 10.1093/oso/9780198785989.001.0001

representation. In that work, one can also see a transformation of Sieyès' conception of the legislative power, one that brought him further than ever away from Rousseau. Finally, I consider the role of extra-ordinary representatives in Sieyès' conception of constitution-making and constitutional reform.

I. Constituent Power Before Sieyès

Martin Loughlin has shown that 'the concept of constituent power was explicitly expressed during the [English] revolutionary debates of the mid-seventeenth century'.[1] He has supported this claim with an impressive analysis of early English constitutional thought, concluding that the concept of constituent power 'now serves no juristic function', having become 'entirely absorbed into the doctrine of the absolute authority of the Crown-in-Parliament to speak for the British nation'.[2] If one digs deeper into English constitutional discourse, one will find not only that the *concept* of the people's constituent power was present in mid-17th-century England, but the very term 'constituent power' was deployed by English jurists and commentators well before the French Revolution and Sieyès' *Third Estate*.[3]

For example, in 18th-century Great Britain, there was talk of 'constituent powers' in the plural,[4] to refer to the entire citizenry as a body superior to the ordinary legislative assembly. This is the case of a letter published in 1770, where 'Junius' argued that the House of Commons had the duty of interpreting the will of the people and conveying it to the Crown. However, if the interpretation was false or misleading, 'the constituent powers are called upon to deliver their own sentiments'. The voice of the constituent powers, he said, was 'rude, but intelligible; their gestures fierce, but full of explanation'.[5] Junius distinguished between the 'constituent' and the 'representative body', arguing that

[1] Martin Loughlin, 'Constituent Power Subverted: From English Constitutional Argument to British Constitutional Practice', in Martin Loughlin and Neil Walker (eds) *The Paradox of Constitutionalism* (Oxford: Oxford University Press, 2007) 28.

[2] ibid.

[3] For a fuller examination of the role of the term 'constituent power' in English constitutional discourse, see Joel Colón-Ríos, 'Five Conceptions of Constituent Power', 130 *Law Quarterly Review* 306 (2014).

[4] The use of the phrase 'constituent power' in the plural ('constituent powers') is not limited to these early references. For example, in 1984, F. M Brookfield asked whether the New Zealand General Assembly could 'in the exercise of its constituent powers, change the structure of government so as to protect constitutional legislation from repeal by the normal, simple majority-vote procedures'. F. M. Brookfield, 'Parliamentary Supremacy and Constitutional Entrenchment: A Jurisprudential Approach', 5 *Otago Law Review* 603 (1984) 605.

[5] *Junius: Stat Nominis Umbra*, vol. 2, Letter XXXII (3 April 1770) (London: Printed for Henry Sampson Woodfall, 1772) 18.

the latter did not possess an 'original power', but a power delegated to it by the constituent people.[6]

Another example is provided in a 1735 essay published in the 'Gentleman's Magazine', where it was maintained that 'the *Government* ought always be in subjection to the *legal Constitution*' and, accordingly, that 'the *legal Constitution* established by the *three Constituent Powers*, ought always to be in Subjection to the *natural Constitution* of Things established by *God himself*.'[7] Somewhat later, in 1792, when describing Parliament as vested with the power—once attributed to sovereign princes—to dispose of 'our lives and properties', Thomas Oldfield stated that the 'constituent power consists in every Englishman, from the prince to the peasant, and of whatever state, dignity, or quality, possessing the right of being present in parliament either in person or by procuration or attorney; and the consent of the parliament is understood to be every man's consent'.[8]

Around the same time, a radical conception of popular sovereignty, very close to that of Sieyès, had already been developed in North America.[9] One of the clearest formulations of this conception can be attributed to James Wilson. He told the Pennsylvania Convention called to ratify the 1787 constitution that the people possessed 'a power paramount to every constitution, inalienable in its nature, and indefinite in its extent'.[10] Expressing a similar view but having now absorbed the language of the French Revolution, Thomas Paine

[6] *The Letters of Junius*, vol. 2, Letter XXIX (not dated) (London: Printed for J. Wheble in Pater-Noster Row, 1770) 180.

[7] *The Gentleman's Magazine*, Vol. 5 (London, England, 1735) 184.

[8] Thomas Hinton Burley Oldfield, *An Entire and Complete History, Political and Personal, of the Boroughs of Great Britain* (London: Printed for G. Riley, 1792) Vol. 1, 9.

[9] In many ways, the American and French Revolutions rested in the same basic conception of the people's relationship with the constitutional order: the people are sovereign, and they have the right to live under any constitution they want. Moreover, both in France and in the territory now known as the United States, a clear theoretical distinction was made between the ordinary power of law-making and the power to create new constitutions (even if that distinction was not always fully respected in practice). It is well-known that Marquis de Lafayette saw the origins of the distinction between constituted and constituent power in North America's constitution-making practice, where the functions of legislative assemblies and constitutional conventions were mostly kept separate. But for reasons that are out of the scope of this book, it is in France and continental Europe (and later in Latin America), where most developments of the theory of constituent power have taken place. In attempting to understand the relationship between constituent power and the law, I will therefore pay special attention to the literature produced in those regions. This does not mean that the American tradition of popular sovereignty is irrelevant for my purposes in this book, but that references to US literature will be less frequent. For discussions of the US tradition, see Jason Frank, *Constituent Moments: Enacting the People in Postrevolutionary America* (Durham: Duke University Press 2010); Christian Fritz, *American Sovereigns: The People and America's Constitutional Tradition before the Civil War* (Cambridge University Press, 2001); William Partlett, 'The American Tradition of Constituent Power', 15(4) *International Journal of Constitutional Law* 955 (2017).

[10] James Wilson, 'James Wilson's Opening Address' in *Works of James Wilson* (James DeWitt Andrews ed.) (Chicago: Callaghan, 1896).

maintained that 'there ought to be, in the constitution of every country, a mode of referring back, on any extraordinary occasion, to the sovereign and original constituent power, which is the nation itself',[11] and that '[e]very age and generation must be as free to act for itself, in all cases, as the ages and generations that preceded it'.[12] Despite the existence of these and even earlier uses of the term in English,[13] it was during the French Revolution where a radical conception of the people's exclusive *constitution-making* faculty, their sovereignty over the constitutional regime, was for the first time clearly identified with the term constituent power.

This view of the relationship between constitutions and the people was in many ways influenced by the English social contract tradition, but it was Rousseau, as we saw in the previous chapter, who most explicitly made the connection between popular sovereignty and the creation of new constitutional orders. Sieyès followed Rousseau in many respects, even though he only referred to him once (and not by his full name) in his published writings. Moreover, in his unpublished notes he was more often than not critical of Rousseau's work.[14] For instance, in a manuscript titled *Bases of the Social Order*, he maintained that 'An unhappy phrase by Jean Jacques opposes this unanimous concert [about the necessity of representation]. "The will", he says, "cannot be represented". Why not? It is not a question here of the whole will of man, and there are numerous examples of private people and of powers who treat of this or that matter by way of procuration'.[15] This is an example of one of the main points of conflict between Rousseau and Sieyès. For the former, the constituent will of the people cannot be represented, and if for practical reasons it needed to be exercised indirectly, delegates must be made subject to

[11] Thomas Paine, 'Address to the Addressers', *The Political Writings of Thomas Paine*, vol. II (Charlestown: printed by George Davidson, 1824) 308. We see here an early formulation of the notion of 'original constituent power', even if unaccompanied by a reference to a derived one.

[12] Thomas Paine, 'The Rights of Man' in *Common Sense and other Writings* (The American Heritage Series, 1953) 87, 76. As is well known, this essay was not well received by many in England and was described by Horace Walpole as 'the most seditious pamphlet ever seen but in open rebellion'. See George Stead Veitch, *The Genesis of Parliamentary Reform* (Constable: London, 1913) 179.

[13] See the examples included in Part I of the previous chapter. There are also pre-French Revolution references to the concept of constituent power in other languages. For example, in a book originally written in Portuguese and translated into Spanish in 1768, Seabra da Silva maintained that the 'constituent people should be seen as superior to the constituted Emperors'. José de Seabra da Silva, *Deducción Chronológica y Analítica* (Madrid: Librería Francisco Fernandez, 1768) 134. In ancient Rome too, some variations of the term 'constituent power' were used to refer to activities that involved the alteration of the fundamental laws. For a discussion, see Andreas Kalyvas, 'Constituent Power' in *Political Concepts: A Critical Lexicon 3.1* (Political Concepts, 2013).

[14] Murray Forsyth, *Reason and Revolution: The Political Thought of the Abbé Sieyes* (Leicester University Press, 1987) at 59.

[15] Emmanuel Sieyès, 'Bases de l'Ordre Social' in Pasquale Pasquino, *Sieyes et l'Invention de la Constitution en France* (Odile Jacobs, 1998) 185.

the legally binding instructions of the citizenry. For the latter, representation was one of the greatest innovations of modern politics, and citizen instructions were a remnant of a constitutional past that needed to be left behind.

II. Sieyès' *Views*

Sieyès' conception of constituent power was to some extent inevitably influenced by the idea of God as an ultimate legislator. As Carl Schmitt maintained, during this revolutionary period 'the aftereffects of the Christian theological images of God's constituting power, despite all clarification, were still strong and vital'.[16] It is probably no coincidence that it was Sieyès, a Roman Catholic *abbé*, who famously attributed the nation with an unrestrained constituent power, the power to create an order *ex nihilo* and to recreate it at will. It is thus difficult to disagree with Heinrich Schneider when he states that 'Sieyès the theologian [gave the] nation the traditional predicates of God'.[17] But in so doing, Sieyès moved the ultimate locus of power away from both God and kings, defining the nation as 'a body of associates living under a common law, represented by the same legislature'.[18] These associates, however, would always exercise their constituent power through representatives: Sieyès rejected in no uncertain terms Rousseau's approach to the exercise of sovereign authority. This rejection is connected in important ways to Sieyès' account of the place of constituent power once a legal order has been established. Before examining this point further, we first need to look at the development of Sieyès' distinction between the *pouvoir constituant* and the *pouvoirs constitués*.

Sieyès' political views are mostly contained in three pamphlets published after it was announced that Louis XVI would summon the Estates-General in his search for a solution to the financial and political crisis of 18th-century France. Unlike some of his contemporaries, Sieyès thought that this opportunity should be used to create an entirely new constitutional order, not merely 'to obtain the redress of a bundle of grievances, or taking steps to adjust the balance of power between the three orders in the Estates-General'.[19] The latter was the position of people like Jacques Necker, Louis XVI's finance minister, who

[16] Carl Schmitt, *Constitutional Theory* (Durham: Duke University Press, 2007) 126.

[17] Heinrich Schneider, 'Patriotism and Nationalism' in *Concilium: Religion and Nationalism* (John Coleman and Miklós Tomka, eds) (London: SCM, 1995) 38.

[18] Emmanuel Sieyès, 'What is the Third Estate?' in *Political Writings* (Hackett Publishing Company, 2003) 125, 97.

[19] Forsyth (n. 14) 69.

in June 1789 presented the Estates-General with a plan of royal reform which involved a constitutional monarchy with a bicameral legislature based on the British model.[20] Such an approach, for Sieyès, was not enough to properly deal with France's problems. A new constitution, one based on the authority of the French nation and not on that of the king, was needed. The first of the pamphlets published by Sieyès during that period, 'Views' *on the Executive Means Available to the Representatives of France in 1789*, had the purpose of advancing that argument.

When Sieyès wrote 'Views', he did not know that the French parlements (the provincial high courts)[21] would eventually determine that the Estates-General would meet on the same basis as in 1614, when the representatives of the three orders of the kingdom met and voted by order.[22] This arrangement meant that the clergy and the nobility, France's privileged classes, would be easily able to outvote the commoners (i.e. the Third Estate). Against the parlements' decision, many argued that the Third Estate should have double representation in the Estates-General, and that voting should be by head and not by order.[23] In *An Essay on Privileges*, Sieyès went beyond those views and controversially argued that neither the nobility nor the clergy formed part of the French nation. Later, in *What is the Third Estate?*, he took that idea to its ultimate consequences: the constituent power he once attributed to the Estates-General could now be exercised by the Third Estate alone.[24] In this section and the rest of the

[20] For a discussion, see Alfred Cobban, *A History of Modern France—Volume 1: 1715-1799* (Penguin Books, 1963) 145–146.

[21] The parlements played a role in the legislative process and in limiting the power of the Crown. In particular, all laws needed to be registered by them before they became effective, and the parlements frequently refused to immediately register laws that they thought problematic, expressing their concerns by sending the king remonstrances often made public (the king always had the last word about the validity of law, but the parlements' failure to register a law could significantly slow down the legislative process). For a discussion, see William Doyle, *The Oxford History of the French Revolution* (Oxford University Press, 2002) 37.

[22] ibid. 134. When the parlements made this determination (when they registered the king's edict to convene the Estates-General), the form that it would take had not yet been at the centre of public debate. ibid. 88.

[23] Cobban (n. 20) 135. The Crown later decided to accept the claim for the double representation of the Third Estate but concluded that the decision about whether votes should be counted by head or by order was to be made by the Estates-General themselves. Doyle (n. 21) 93. According to the Compte de Lauraguais, this debate failed to understand the French constitutional tradition, where the number of deputies did not really matter, what was important was the trustworthiness of each deputy and the quality of the *cahiers* they carried. For a discussion, see Paul Friedland, *Political Actors: Representative Bodoes & Theatricality in the Age of the French Revolution* (Cornell University Press, 2002) 112. For a discussion of the nature of *cahiers* in France, see Chapter 4 of this book.

[24] This idea was implicit in *The Social Contract*: 'The lukewarmness of patriotism, the activity of private interest, the vastness of States, conquest, and the abuse of government suggested the method of having deputies or representatives of the people in the national assemblies. These are what, in some countries, men have presumed to call the Third Estate. Thus the individual interest of two orders is put first and second; the public interest occupies only the third place'. Jean Jacques Rousseau, 'The Social Contract', in *The Social Contract and the Discourses* (Everyman's Library, 1973) at 263.

chapter, I engage in a close reading of these three works. I will emphasize those aspects of the works that contradict, repeat, or reformulate Rousseau's constitutional thought.

The main purpose of 'Views' was to defend the idea that the Estates-General had the power to create a new constitution for France. In order to advance that argument, Sieyès first identified the Estates-General as the proper representative of the French nation and, as such, as having 'the right to make laws'.[25] As English parliamentarians had argued a century earlier, it was not in the Crown, but in the body representing the three estates of the realm, where the ultimate law-making power resided. This power was not absolute. It had the sole purpose of developing rules for the protection of the liberty of the citizens, a liberty which consisted in the assurance that each citizen was 'not being hindered or interfered with in the exercise of his *personal* property or in the use of his *real* property'.[26] Real property encompassed property over things. Personal property referred to ownership over one's own person, that is, to the liberty of doing as one wishes as long as one did not affect the liberties of others. The power of the Estates-General would 'encompass all the laws concerning the two kinds of property belonging to every citizen'.[27] If the nation could not get rid of its exclusive power to authorize new taxes, it followed that it must also have an inalienable right to adopt laws that protect personal property, that is, laws that secure the most basic liberties of individuals. [28]

In an argument highly reminiscent of Rousseau, Sieyès maintained that in order for the nation not to live in slavery, 'it had the right to consult its own interests, to deliberate, and to impose laws upon itself'.[29] The 'legislative power', in short, belonged to the nation alone.[30] A significant part of the account of the social contract included in 'Views' was directed at explaining the transformation that the exercise of the legislative power suffers as a society becomes more populous, a transformation that made it necessary for the nation to elect representatives who could act on its behalf. Like Rousseau, Sieyès thought that the transition from the state of nature to civil society was only legitimate if it was

[25] Emmanuel Sieyès, 'Views of the Executive Means Available to the Representatives of France in 1789' (n. 18) 49.
[26] ibid. (emphasis in the original).
[27] ibid. 9.
[28] ibid.
[29] ibid.
[30] ibid. Like Rousseau's sovereign, Sieyès' nation acted 'by way of general laws, never by particular acts of authority'. ibid. 31. In the same passage, echoing Bodin, Sieyès wrote that the legislative power 'cannot therefore despoil some to the benefit of others, and its mandate, however extensive it may be, cannot authorize it to crush one class of citizens to lift the tax burden from the others'. See Jean Bodin, *On Sovereignty: Four Chapters from the Six Books of the Commonwealth* (Julian Franklin ed.) (Cambridge: Cambridge University Press, 1992) 33.

based on the will of a group of individuals who became bound to each other through the act of creating a political association.[31] One of the main consequences of that transition was the possibility of groups of human beings developing a '*common* will' that could guide the actions of society.[32] Although the original act of association had to be expressed unanimously,[33] requiring that the common will is always 'the exact sum of every individual will would amount to giving up the possibility of being able to will in common and would mean the dissolution of the social union.'[34] Accordingly, in entering into the social contract, individuals unanimously agree to be bound to the will of the majority even when they find themselves in the minority.[35]

Up to this point, Sieyès seems to be operating entirely within Rousseau's system, but soon he writes: '[W]e need to press further and see how an increase in the number of associates has to give rise to new modifications in the legislative power.'[36] Rousseau would have no difficulty agreeing with this: to the same extent that a society grows, it becomes more and more difficult for all citizens to assemble and 'reconcile their differences to form a general will.'[37] Nevertheless, Sieyès' solution was very different from that proposed in *The Social Contract*. Like Rousseau, Sieyès thought that in such a growing society, the popular assembly composed of all citizens would have to be replaced by a system in which citizens living in particular districts select delegates that meet and vote according to a binding mandate. Citizens would exercise their legislative power by instructing those delegates. However, *contra* Rousseau, Sieyès believed that such a system would soon prove to be flawed: being strictly bound by those instructions, delegates will be frequently unable to find a proposition that can obtain a majority of the votes and would therefore become incapable of making laws.[38] Any rational community would thus find it necessary to give delegates the power 'to meet, to deliberate, to reconcile their views, and to come to a common will.'[39]

At this point, Sieyès says, the community would have created 'genuine representatives instead of simple vote carriers.'[40] Sieyès was of course aware of

31 Sieyès, 'Views' (n. 18) 49, 10–11.
32 ibid. 11 (emphasis in the original).
33 See Rousseau, *The Social Contract* (n. 24) 190.
34 Sieyès, 'Views' (n. 18) 11.
35 ibid. See also Rousseau, *The Social Contract* (n. 24) 190.
36 Sieyès, 'Views' (n. 18) 11.
37 ibid.
38 ibid. 12.
39 ibid.
40 ibid. For a discussion of this type of developments in England and North America, see Edmund Morgan, *Inventing the People: The Rise of Popular Sovereignty in England and America* (New York: W.W. Norton & Company, 1988) 38–54.

the dangers of a system in which a representative assembly could make decisions contrary to the people's will, a danger to which the *Social Contract* was partly a response to. This is probably why he insisted that such an arrangement should never be taken to involve 'a formal surrender of the community's original power': the law-making power exercised by representatives is 'constantly revocable' and can be limited 'both in time and in subject matter' by the community.[41] The break with the thought of Rousseau here is obvious: a rejection of the notion of constituent instructions and an embracement of the idea of representation in *law*-making, even if representation is seen as resting in an always revocable (and limitable) mandate. But there is a further transformation, one that seems to take Sieyès even further away from Rousseau. In a system such as the one described above, it would seem that each district 'ought to recognize only the work of the majority of its own representatives as the basis of law'.[42] The consequence would be that each district would have a *liberum veto* on every other, and this would prevent the legislative body from functioning properly. In the worst-case scenario, it could lead to the dissolution of the political community into smaller entities, a danger that Sieyès later associated with any type of political arrangement exhibiting federal features.[43]

To avoid such a situation, Sieyès argued that 'what has to be kept as a maxim is the principle that each deputy represents the whole association'.[44] In other words, 'since the totality of citizens either cannot, or will not, assemble together in a single place, the totality has to be divided into districts', and in nominating their representatives, all of the districts reciprocally 'authorize and entrust their affairs to one another and, by doing so, make the election the work of the whole community'.[45] This approach increases the distance between citizens

[41] Sieyès, 'Views' (n. 18) 12.

[42] ibid. It is unclear here whether Sieyès is implicitly attacking Rousseau, but in any case this was not Rousseau's approach. For him, each primary assembly would be required to follow the decision of the majority of the voters in all the primary assemblies, which would be taken as an expression of the general will. See Rousseau, *The Social Contract* (n. 24) 274–275. See also discussion in Chapter 4 of this book. There is of course a tension in this approach: individual deputies might be required to defend views that are clearly contrary to the general will (e.g. policies that would benefit a particular locality but harm the rest of the country). This tension is also expressed in Saige's defence of the imperative mandate and of Rousseau's constitutional thought. Guillaume-Joseph Saige, *Catéquisme du Citoyen ou Éléments du Droit Public Française* (France, 1788) (originally published in 1775).

[43] See Forsyth (n. 14) 139, 155.

[44] Sieyès, 'Views' (n. 18) 12.

[45] ibid. 12–13. Similar ideas were put forward in 17th-century England by authors such as Edward Coke and Algernon Sidney. For a discussion, see Morgan (n. 40) 48–51. Sidney, for example, wrote that representatives 'are not strictly and properly obliged to give account of their actions to any, unless the whole body of the Nation for which they serve, and who are equally concerned in their resolutions, could be assembled. This being impracticable, the only punishment to which they are subject, if they betray their Trust, in scorn, infamy, hatred, and an assurance of being rejected, when they shall again seek the same honour.' Algernon Sidney, *Discourses Concerning Government, Vol. 2* (Edinburgh: Hamilton & Balfour, 1750) 370.

and representatives to an extent that is radically inconsistent with Rousseau's system of popular sovereignty. But Sieyès insisted that in the context of a large society there is no other option but to nominate representatives that can execute the will on behalf of the entire people, 'and it cannot be said that the common will of these representatives does not make genuine law or law which applies to everyone'.[46] Such a representative body, he said, would be 'able to exercise the full extent of the legislative power'.[47] What Sieyès exactly means here by 'legislative power' is not clear, but to the extent that he thought that the Estates-General had the power to create a constitution, at least we know that at this point it included what he later called 'constituent power'.

III. Sieyès' Supreme Constitution

We still do not see, however, a clear separation between the constituent legislator and the administration, but we do not have to wait much longer for it to appear, even if only to fade away later. 'No one is ignorant of the fact', Sieyès wrote, that 'every political society has common needs and that to meet them several different classes of individuals have to be given a mandate and separated out from the mass of the citizenry'.[48] These individuals, he said, formed the *public establishment*, which is nothing but the means to execute the will of the nation.[49] While the representative body, the Estates-General (which in 'Views' he sometimes identified as the National Assembly)[50] was called to exercise the legislative power, the public establishment was comprised of a number

[46] Sieyès, 'Views' (n. 18). Sieyès understood the common will (which he sometimes called the 'general view' or *voue général* and sometimes, like Rousseau, *volonté général*; see, for example, Emmanuel Sieyès, *Préliminaires de la Constitution. Reconnoissance et Exposition Raisonnée des Droits de l'Homme et du Citoyen* (20–21 July 1789) (Versailles: Imprimeur ordinaire du Roi, 1789) 15) as always identified by a majority that could be 'larger or smaller according to the nature of the affair'. Sieyès, 'Views' (n. 18) 37. Like Rousseau, he thought that 'in every deliberation there is a kind of problem to be solved. This is to know, in any given case, what the general interest would prescribe', and that majorities, and not minorities, were better placed to provide the right answer. Sieyès, 'Views' (n. 18) 39. In *Third Estate* he expressed a similar view: 'Reasoned argument is pointless if for a single moment one abandons the self-evident principle that the common will is the opinion of the majority not the minority'. Emmanuel Sieyès, 'What is the Third Estate?' (n. 18) 142.

[47] Sieyès, 'Views' (n. 18) 12–13.

[48] ibid. 20. This approach can be explained through the notion of the division of labour: a professional class of politicians tasked with the role of making decisions in the interest of the nation. As Pasquale Pasquino has shown, Sieyès read Adam Smith widely. See Pasquale Pasquino, 'Emmanuel Sieyes, Benjamin Constant et le "Governement des Modernes"', 37(2) *Revue Française de Science Politique* 214–229 (1987) 220.

[49] Sieyès, 'Views' (n. 16) 20.

[50] ibid. 21. Sieyès was elected to the Estates-General (by the Third Estate of Paris) and shortly after he presented two motions that resulted in the transformation of the Estates-General into a national assembly. Forsyth (n. 14) 6.

of administrators required to implement, and act consistently with, the law. The Estates-General was thus responsible for creating the rules that would govern the public establishment. But who would adopt the rules that would regulate the exercise of the legislative power itself? Since all legislative bodies must operate according to certain rules and procedures, Sieyès thought that the Estates-General should 'use its initial sittings to give itself the organization and procedural formalities appropriate to the functions that it will be called upon to exercise'.[51]

This did not mean, he warned, that 'any ordinary legislature can be responsible for giving itself its own constitution'.[52] Such a situation would lead to a 'confusion between a constituting power [*pouvoir constituant*] and a constituted' one.[53] However, since in France's then present circumstances 'the nation has made no provision for carrying out the great task of constitution-making by way of a special deputation, it has to be supposed' that the Estates-General would combine these two powers.[54] The Estates-General, like a sovereign parliament, would thus be able to act both as an ordinary legislature and as a constituent assembly. Sieyès soon realized that in such an arrangement it would become necessary to devise a mechanism to protect the law after the Estates-General was no longer in session. That mechanism was a supreme constitution: '[D]uring the intervals between successive national assemblies, the constitution will preside over the laws that an assembly has made'.[55] A constitution, according to Sieyès, was necessary in any society so large that a number of individuals had to be attributed with the task of performing certain functions

[51] Sieyès, 'Views' (n. 18) 34.

[52] ibid.

[53] ibid; Emmanuel Sieyès, *Vues sur les moyens d'execution don't les représentans de la France pourront disposer en 1789* (1789) 80.

[54] Sieyès, 'Views' (n. 18) 34. This view was rejected by Jacques-Pierre Brissot in his 'Plan de Conduite pour les Députés du Peuple aux Etats-Généraux de 1789' (April 1789) 227–234. For Brissot, the constituent and the constituted power needed to be kept separate, which meant that the Estates-General should not be allowed to adopt a constitution. Later, in his 'Exposition Raisonnée', Sieyès maintained that a constitution adopted by an entity not specifically convened by the people for that purpose should be of a provisional nature: '[E[t portant, comme la représentation actuelle n'est pas rigoureusement conforme à ce qu'exige une telle nature de pouvoir, ils déclarent que la constitution qu'ils vont donner à la Nation, quoique provisoirement obligatoire pour tous, ne sera définitive qu'après qu'un nouveau pouvoir constituant, extraordinairement convoqué pour cet unique objet, lui aura donné un consentement que réclame la rigueur des principes'. Sieyès, *Préliminaires* (n. 46) 4.

[55] Sieyès, 'View' (n. 18) 39. Of course, even if the constitution is to be 'the guarantee of the nation's statutes', it is not clear what would guarantee the constitution itself. One would think that the expected answer to the question is 'the nation', but Sieyès gave another response: the constitution would be guaranteed by the new tax law adopted by the Estates-General, which would itself be a constitutional law. ibid. 45, 57. The idea was to give each of the 'component parts' of the constitution a function related to tax, so as to make the separation between the fiscal system and the constitution impossible. Since the only power to be feared (the executive) was unable to act without tax revenue, 'it will have to respect the constitutional laws making it possible for that tax to be levied'. ibid. 45.

that the entire citizenry is not in a position to carry out itself. Without a constitution, such individuals could become a separate class with a particular interest, a class 'that would live at the expense of the general interest'.[56]

Sieyès' constitution had two primary components. The first had the purpose of ensuring that the community is 'able to reach the goal it was created to reach . . .'.[57] Sieyès called this component the constitution of the *active* power.[58] The second component is radically alien to Rousseau's constitutional theory and brings the differences between these two authors, as well as their approach to constituent power, to their natural conclusion. This second component is the constitution of the *legislative* power.[59] Because, for Rousseau, the legislative power was exercised by the people themselves (or by delegates subject to binding instructions), it did not need to be subject to any constitutional limits. But Sieyès thought that the legislative power was to be exercised by a representative assembly, which made it necessary to find a legal means of ensuring that those representatives acted consistently with the public good: '[I]f whoever makes the law can, without having anything in common with the active power, give themselves an interest distinct from the common interest of the great body of citizens, the social order will be equally upset and soon there will be no more than despots and slaves.'[60] The legislature thus needed to be constituted in a way that prevented it from ever developing a will contrary to the 'general interest of the associates'.[61]

This approach necessarily implies a separation between the constituent and constituted powers (between the people and the ordinary legislature), and requires the establishment of a *limited* legislative authority. In addition to creating a constitution for the active and the legislative powers, Sieyès believed that the Estates-General should also adopt a number of ordinary laws; in particular a law providing for a public education system.[62] He thought that the Estates-General should 'deal with this part of the active power [i.e. public education]

[56] ibid. 49.
[57] ibid.
[58] As the reader may note, the 'active power', in Sieyès, is equivalent to what Rousseau identified as the executive power. For a discussion, see Chapter 2. ibid. 49, 50. Sieyès also thought that a strong judicial body (which as in Rousseau, was part of the executive power) was necessary to resist the political excesses of the public establishment. ibid. 51.
[59] ibid. 49. Sieyès' proposed constitutional arrangements were thus based both on norms that 'regulate the organizations and functions of the *legislative* body', and others that 'fix the organization and functions of the *active* bodies'. Sieyès, 'Third Estate' (n. 18) 136. These rules 'are said to be *fundamental*' he wrote, because 'the bodies that can exist and can act only by way of these laws cannot touch them'. ibid.
[60] Sieyès, 'Views' (n. 18).
[61] ibid.
[62] As we saw in the previous chapter, Rousseau referred to a system of public education as an example of the kind of arrangement to be adopted by decree rather than by legislation.

with the intention of connecting it to the constitution'.[63] As this example suggests, there are a number of indications that Sieyès understood the legislative power as having a task that went beyond the adoption of constitutional norms. These indications are confirmed in *Third Estate*. Indeed, unlike Rousseau's sovereign, who rarely showed itself, Sieyès' legislative body was to be 'no less *permanent* than the active bodies'. For him, '[a] legislator is made for giving life, movement, and direction to everything connected to public affairs'.[64] As a result of its frequent meetings, the French legislative body 'would be as much a part of the necessary and habitual cycle of events as it is in England'.[65] Sieyès' legislative assembly, in this sense, looked more like Rousseau's elected aristocracy and less like a popularly elected constituent power.

IV. Constructing the Constituent Subject

Sieyès thought that in order for the Estates-General to be a truly representative body, its deputies had to be drawn from the total number of parishes, whose citizens should be initially convened in what he sometimes called 'fundamental assemblies' (i.e. primary assemblies, to be discussed in more detail in Chapter 4).[66] In the context of large communities, an additional level of representation was necessary. For example, Sieyès maintained that in a society with two thousand parishes, 'the legislative body could exist only at a second level of representation, meaning that the parish deputies, instead of meeting to decide upon common affairs, would have a mandate only to nominate legislative representatives and to give them such advice as they deem to be suitable'.[67] In a more populated society, one may have to add a third level of representation, but for Sieyès it would be a mistake to add further levels: 'Every legislature has a continuous need to be refreshed by the democratic spirit. It should not therefore be placed at too great a distance from its primary constituents [*premiers*

[63] Sieyès, 'Views' (n. 18) 52.
[64] ibid. 55.
[65] ibid. 56.
[66] ibid. 53 (*assemblée fondamentale*). For a discussion, see Forsyth (n. 14) 153–155.
[67] Sieyès, 'Views' (n. 18) 39 The members of the Third Estate were in fact elected through a similar formula of indirect representation. To be eligible as a deputy for the Third Estate, one needed to be a male taxpayer over 25 years old and attend a primary assembly. Those primary assemblies chose a number of delegates (two for every hundred households) that would sit in another assembly (electoral assembly) charged with the task of electing the final Third Estate deputies. Doyle (n. 21) 96. Even though democratic by the standards of the time, this system effectively excluded peasants and artisans from the electoral assemblies. Moreover, the system allowed the electoral assemblies to elect deputies to the Third Estate who belonged to the other two orders. (97). This type of pyramidal system was also present in a number of 19th-century constitutions. See, for example, Title II of the Constitution of Ecuador of 1830.

commettans].'[68] The larger the number of intermediaries, he wrote, the more likely the general will may get lost in 'harmful aristocratism'.[69]

In *An Essay on Privileges*, Sieyès went beyond proposing an electoral system that would allow the (more numerous) commoners to elect the majority of representatives: he attempted to show that the privileged orders were not even part of the nation. Sieyès defined a privilege either as a dispensation from the law, or as an exclusive right to do something.[70] For example, in 18th-century France, members of the nobility were exempt from certain tax laws and had certain exclusive rights, such as the right to carry a sword.[71] One of the main consequences of privileges, he wrote, is that they open their beneficiaries to 'a particular interest and close [them] more or less against the common good'.[72] The result is that the privileged ends up seeing himself and his equals as a separate 'caste', 'another species of being', in short, 'a nation within the nation'.[73] Moreover, it is only possible to represent citizens with respect to interests that are common among them. Those common interests were 'the only ones by which and in whose name they can demand political rights or an active part in the formation of the social law'.[74] The particular interests of the privileged classes, he argued, were simply '*not something that can be represented*' by a national assembly.[75]

As noted in 'Views', in every large society there is a division between two classes of citizens, those who govern and those who are governed, but that was just a 'superiority of employments, not of persons'.[76] If the privileged class had an interest different to that of the nation, if it formed, for all purposes, a nation of its own, why should it play a role in the exercise of the legislative power? This is the question that Sieyès addressed in *Third Estate*, published shortly after *Privileges*. Sieyès began *Third Estate* where he had left things in his previous pamphlets: the nobility had all sorts of privileges, while all the activities that support society (e.g. the production of primary materials) were carried out by members of the Third Estate.[77] Accordingly, he provocatively asked: 'Who then

[68] Sieyès, 'Views' (n. 18) 39. See also Sieyès, 'Bases de l'Ordre Social' (n. 15) 187–188.

[69] Sieyès, 'Views' (n. 18) 39. Sieyès' proposal was by and large accepted by the Constituent Assembly. For a discussion, see Forsyth (n. 14) 166.

[70] Emmanuel Sieyès, 'Privileges' (n. 18) 69.

[71] See Malcolm Kwass, *Privilege and the Politics of Taxation in Eighteenth-Century France: Liberté, Egalité, Fiscalité* (Cambridge University Press, 2000). Nobles had the most privileges, but in 18th-century France it was not uncommon for some members of the bourgeoisie to enjoy different sorts of exclusive rights. See Doyle (n. 21) 27.

[72] Sieyès, 'Privileges' (n. 18) 75.

[73] ibid. 75, 76

[74] Sieyès, 'Third Estate' (n. 18) 156.

[75] ibid. 157 (emphasis in the original).

[76] Sieyès, 'Privileges' (n. 18) 80.

[77] Sieyès, 'Third Estate' (n. 18) 95.

would dare to say that the Third Estate does not, within itself, contain everything needed to form a complete nation?'[78] Not only did the privileged not contribute to the survival of the nation, but they weakened it. They remained 'inert in the midst of the general movement and contrive . . . to consume the better part of the product without contributing in any way to its production'.[79] Such a class, he said, is foreign to the nation 'because of its *idleness*'.[80]

The nobility[81] was just as ineligible to participate in the political life of the nation as those individuals 'whom infirmity, incapacity, incurable laziness, or the tide of moral dissolution have made strangers to all the activities involved in society'.[82] At least beggars, he wrote, have no interest contrary to that of the Third Estate, but shared with it 'a common interest against the oppression of privilege', while nobles or clerics will always be inclined to defend their own class interests.[83] Moreover, the control of the public establishment by the nobility meant that the administration now belonged to a particular class and therefore served 'the needs not of the governed, but of those who govern'.[84] A nation was nothing else but 'a body of associates living under a common law, represented by the same legislature'. The privileged class formed a separate entity, it was exempted from some laws and it even had its own set of representatives called to defend 'not the general interest, but a particular one'.[85] Only one conclusion followed: the Third Estate, 'the totality of the citizens belonging to the common order' was the true nation.[86]

[78] ibid. 96.
[79] ibid. 97.
[80] ibid.
[81] Sieyès' emphasis was on the nobility since, for him, the clergy should not even be considered an order; properly speaking it was a profession. ibid. 96, fn 3. Nevertheless, he maintained that 'Nothing can go well without the Third Estate, but everything would go a great deal better without the two others'. ibid. 96.
[82] ibid. 97.
[83] ibid. 107, 110 fn 16. This does not mean that there were no nobles or clerics who favoured the causes of the Third Estate. Forsyth (n. 14) 120.
[84] Sieyès, 'Third Estate' (n. 18) 95.
[85] ibid. 98. See also Sieyès, 'Exposition Raisonnée' (n. 54) 14. A similar idea was also expressed by Hooker in England in 1572, when arguing that the King and Commons were enough to make a Parliament since the each Lord 'doth represent but his own person, & speaketh in the behalf of him self alone'. Quoted inVernon F Snow (ed) *Parliament in Elizabethan England: John Hooker's Order and Usage* (New Haven: Yale University Press, 1977) 181–2.
[86] Sieyès, 'Third Estate' (n. 18) 99. Sieyès thought that the English Constitution was adopted by a representative body that apparently expressed the national will (the Convention of 1688). This can be inferred from the fact that, writing in 1789, he wrote that '[i]t would be wrong to decide in favour of the British Constitution simply because it has lasted for a hundred years and it looks as if it should last for centuries more'. ibid. 132). True, such a constitution could be changed by the Crown-in-Parliament, but in England, Sieyès curiously held, not only the Commons, but the king and the lords, were representatives of the nation. ibid. 138, fn. 30 That is, Sieyès did not consider the English Lords as constituting a separate order (he did not see them as belonging to a privileged groups of families); and wrote that there was 'only one order in England, and that is the nation'. ibid.

Not everyone who belonged to the common order, however, was, according to Sieyès, to be recognized as a full citizen, that is, as someone with the right to participate in the political life of the community either by electing representatives or by being one himself. Sieyès, it is well known, distinguished between passive and active citizens. The former had rights against the state (i.e. civil rights) but not political rights. These included women, foreigners, and those who had no property to contribute to the public establishment and could therefore not be trusted with the making decisions about the general interest. Political rights were reserved for active citizens, those tax paying individuals who were considered the true members of the political association.[87] Active citizens, after all, were the only ones capable of identifying the will of the nation. This national will was independent from that of the majority of individuals, even though the nation was described by Sieyès as comprised of 'the totality of citizens belonging to the common order'.[88] The legal and institutional implications of this view will be discussed in Chapters 4 and 5, but as the reader may note, it points towards a conception of the constituent subject in direct tension with that of Rousseau.

V. Sieyès' Constituent Jurisdiction

One of the main debates in the years preceding the Estates-General revolved around whether France had a constitution. There were some (particularly in the nobility) for which the answer to that question was obviously 'yes': the term 'constitution' refers to the form of government, and since France was organized as a monarchy, it necessarily had a constitution. More specifically, it had a set of fundamental laws developed through history that regulated the monarchy and prevented ministerial despotism.[89] This idea was reflected in some of the lists of grievances to be presented to the Estates-General[90] which sought the 'regeneration of the state . . . through the simple reform of abuses and reestablishment of a constitution that has existed for fourteen centuries'.[91]

[87] Sieyès, Préliminaire (n. 46) 14. In the case of women, Sieyès added the qualification 'at least in the current state of things'. The specific requirements of active citizenship are briefly discussed in Chapter 4.

[88] Sieyès, 'Third Estate' (n. 73) 99.

[89] Louis Adrien Le Paige, *Lettres Historiques sur les Fonctions Essentielles du Parlement: sur le Droit des Pairs, et sur les Loix Fondamentales du Royaume* (1753).

[90] The relationship between these lists (*cahiers*) and the concept of constituent power will be explored in Chapter 4.

[91] Keith M. Baker, 'Constitution' in *The French Revolution: Recent Debates and New Controversies* (Gary Kates ed.) 2nd ed. (New York: Routledge, 2006) 72, 69. More directly, Pierre-Suzanne Deschamps, elected by the Second Estate, maintained: 'When we were sent to the Estates General, we were not told to make a new Constitution, but to regenerate an old one, we were not told to erect our government

For Sieyès, a constitution was much more than that, it presupposed a rational system of political organization consistent with natural law.[92] Moreover, he argued that in the event of a conflict about what the constitution is, or about what it should be, the nation, the constituent power, had to be consulted.[93] 'Even if the Nation had held regular sessions of the Estates-General', Sieyès wrote, 'it would not be up to this constituted body to pronounce upon a dispute affecting its own constitution. To do so would be a petition of principle or a vicious circle'.[94]

Not surprisingly, when referring to constitutional laws as 'fundamental laws', Sieyès made clear that the adjective 'fundamental' did not place them outside the jurisdiction of the constituent nation: 'These laws are called *fundamental*, not in the sense that they could become independent of the national will, but because the bodies to which they grant existence cannot modify them.'[95] Eventually, the debate about whether France had a constitution was settled by Article 16 of the Declaration of the Rights of Man and of the Citizen of 1789: 'Any society in which no provision is made for guaranteeing rights or for the separation of powers, has no Constitution.'

For Sieyès, whenever the nation needed to settle a constitutional dispute, it had to do it through the convocation of extraordinary representatives or through the temporal attribution of extraordinary faculties to ordinary legislators. This notion is key to his alternative to Rousseau's system. Ordinary representatives, Sieyès thought, were those entrusted by the people with the power of 'exercising, according to constitutional forms, that portion of the common will that is necessary for good social administration. Their power is confined to matters of government.'[96] As the reader may note, this is a definite

within the framework of a monarchy, but to re-conform our ancient monarchy.' Eric Thompson, *Popular Sovereignty and the French Constituent Assembly 1789-91* (Manchester University Press, 1952) 41, 7. This is the kind of view that, as we will see in Chapter 7, was developed in Spain as the doctrine of the historical or internal constitution.

[92] For a discussion, see Friedland (n. 23) 106. As noted by an anonymous writer in 1776 North America, 'All countries have some form of government but few, or perhaps none, have truly a Constitution'. 'Four Letters on Interesting Subjects', quoted in Gordon S. Wood, *The Creation of the American Republic 1776-1787* (Chapel Hill: University of North Carolina Press, 1998) 267. This notion is reminiscent of Rousseau's statement that not many societies have 'laws'. For a discussion, see Chapter 2 of this book.

[93] 'It is worth emphasizing how essential it is in the civil order for citizens to find a branch of the active power readily able to exercise authority to settle their legal differences. In the same way, among a free people the various branches of the active power must have the freedom to appeal to the legislature for a decision in every unforeseen difficulty. But if the legislature itself or the various parts of this primary element of the constitution cannot agree among themselves, who is to be the supreme judge?' Sieyès, 'Third Estate' (n. 73).

[94] ibid. 139.

[95] ibid.

[96] ibid.

move towards attributing to the legislature a number of governmental functions that would be normally associated with what Sieyès elsewhere refers to as the active power and to which Rousseau would have referred to as the executive power or the administration. Unlike ordinary representatives, extraordinary ones had 'whatever new powers it pleases the Nation to give them'.[97] Those extraordinary representatives are a surrogate for an assembly of the entire nation and, as the nation, are independent from 'the constitutional forms on which they have to decide'.[98]

Sieyès maintained that the common will of extraordinary representatives had 'the same worth as that of the nation itself',[99] and there were no particular requirements as to the form in which those extraordinary representatives were to be deputed. He was aware that a body of extraordinary representatives would be seen by some as being accompanied by immense danger, by the possibility of great abuses of power. Nevertheless, he thought that it was unnecessary to establish institutional mechanisms to ensure that such abuses would not take place. He gave a number of reasons for that conclusion. Firstly, as suggested above, it is necessary to take into account that a body of extraordinary representatives does not have to be attributed with the '*plenitude* of the national will'.[100] Secondly, such a body would be called upon to deal 'with a single matter for a limited time'.[101] That is, it will have 'nothing to say about matters for which positive forms have been fixed'.[102] Thirdly, while it is true that extraordinary representatives are in a similar position as individuals in a small society that decide 'to give its government a constitution',[103] they act 'in virtue of an extraordinary commission from the people'.[104] In other words, akin to a sovereign parliament, they would be subject to important external limits: to the extent that they act inconsistently with their commission, they run the risk of being disobeyed or resisted by the nation. Finally, when the body of extraordinary representatives has been convened to settle a constitutional dispute, it would be contradictory to bind them to the very forms that are at issue.

97 ibid.

98 ibid.

99 ibid. This view was attacked by Brissot, who maintained that 'a Nation cannot be constituted by Representatives, even extraordinary ones'. Jacques-Pierre Brissot, 'Le Patriote François', 5 *Journal Libre, Impartial et National* (1789) 3.

100 Sieyès, 'Third Estate' (n. 18) 136. This is an idea reflected in the argument presented in Chapter 9.

101 ibid.

102 ibid. This view would be inconsistent with a constituent assembly that attributes itself with the jurisdiction to exercise the ordinary powers of government. This point will be further developed in Chapter 9.

103 ibid. 140

104 ibid.

For Sieyès, all this was true even if ordinary legislators, 'by virtue of special proxies', were entrusted by the nation to assemble for the purpose of exercising the constituent power.[105] If that were to happen, a situation he did not look favourably on, he insisted that efforts should be made so that both types of power (constituted and constituent) are not conflated.[106] Ideally, only an 'extraordinary' or 'constituent' representation, one separate from the ordinary legislative body, should alter or create a constitution. It must be an entity capable of representing the common interests of the nation. In France, this meant that the constitution-making body needed to be independent of any distinction of orders.[107] The Estates-General (and this is one of the main differences between 'Views' and *Third Estate*) did not constitute such a representation since it included privileged classes that sought to protect their particular interests. What was needed was for the nation to give a set of extraordinary representatives 'a special mandate to draft the constitution of an ordinary assembly'.[108] Only they would be 'true custodians of the national will' and be in a position 'to speak in the name of the whole Nation without error'.[109] From a practical perspective, this meant that the Third Estate should meet as a national assembly,[110] without the clergy and the nobility. The assembly would have the task of creating a legislative constitution; it would exercise, for the first time in French history, the nation's constituent power.[111]

[105] ibid. 139.

[106] ibid.

[107] ibid. 142

[108] ibid. 143.

[109] ibid. 150. The other two orders, at most, could only represent two hundred thousand individuals and would only be concerned with their particular interests. They were like two distinct nations, and it was 'useless to find a ratio or proportion by which each order should contribute to the formation of the general will'. At the most, these three orders 'might be able to join together to express the same wish, just as three allied nations can form the same desire. But they can never be turned into *one* nation with *one* representation and *one* common will'. ibid. 149. The privileged classes were more than welcome to abandon their exclusive rights and become entitled to be electors and deputies to the National Assembly, that is to say, to formally participate in the development of the common will. Indeed, Sieyès was elected as a deputy to the Third Estate while belonging to the first one (i.e. the clergy). Doyle (n. 21) 101, 93.

[110] In his *Reflections*, Edmund Burke distinguished the power of the National Assembly from that of the English House of Commons in the following way: 'The power, however, of the house of commons, when least diminished, is as a drop of water in the ocean, compared to that residing in a settled majority of your National Assembly. That Assembly, since the destruction of the orders, has no fundamental law, no strict convention, no respected usage to restrain it. Instead of finding themselves obliged to conform to a fixed constitution, they have a power to make a constitution which shall conform to their designs. Nothing in heaven or upon earth can serve as a control on them . . . In such a state of unbounded power, for undefined and undefinable purposes, the evil of a moral and almost physical inaptitude of the man to the function must be the greatest we can conceive to happen in the management of human affairs.' Edmund Burke, *Reflections on the Revolution of France* (Penguin Classics, 1986) 133–134, 315–316.

[111] Sieyès, 'Third Estate' (n. 18) 154. Sieyès made a number of proposals to ensure that any particular interests were isolated in the assembly, such as the renewal of a third of its membership every year and the prohibition of immediate re-election. ibid. 155.

VI. Conclusion

As Pasqual Pasquino has written, the ultimate objective of Sieyès' theory of constituent power was to limit the constituted powers, not to defend an unlimited national will.[112] To an important extent, Rousseau attempted something similar: to limit the power of government by establishing law-making as the exclusive domain of the sovereign people. Both Sieyès' nation and Rousseau's sovereign were themselves subject to substantive limits of a political character: the nation was subject to natural law, the sovereign could not engage in non-general acts. The problem, in their view, was that up to the point they were writing, the nation and the sovereign people had not been properly recognized as the bearers of the constituent power. In conceiving the nature of the constituent power, however, they differed in important ways. For Sieyès, not only constituent power could be represented, but it always remained in an extra-legal terrain to be only exercised in instances of revolution. Rousseau, in contrast, saw the possibility of the future exercise of constituent power through law as a necessary condition for the legitimacy of the juridical order. As we will see in the next chapter, this disagreement had major implications about the role of primary assemblies, about the relationship between citizens and representatives, and about the very nature of constitutional reform. In the end, Sieyès' approach prevailed.

This was dramatically exemplified in the role Sieyès had in putting an end to the revolution through the *coup d'état* he orchestrated with Napoleon Bonaparte who, ironically, identified himself as the constituent power in 1804.[113] But the fact that constituent power is seen as an extra-legal force does not necessarily mean that it will simply haunt the juridical order from the outside. The very existence of a power that remains in the hands of the community can have clear legal and institutional effects. For Sieyès, it meant that no ordinary legislature could claim to be sovereign, that legislators are not bound by the instructions of their constituents, and that even the entire citizenry meeting in multiple assemblies should not be recognized by law as the bearer of an unlimited constitution-making force. Rousseau, as we know, reached very different conclusions, and also opened the possibility of seeing the periodic exercise of

[112] Pasquino (n. 15) 65, 78.

[113] 'It is not as a general that I rule, but because the nation believes I have the civilian qualifications for governing. My system is quite simple. It has seen to me that under the circumstances the thing to do was to centralize power and increase the authority of the Government, so as to constitute the Nation. I am the constituent power.' *Distant Voices: Listening to the Leadership Lessons of the Past. Napoleon Bonaparte's Maxims, Quotes and Life in His Own Words*, 15 May 1804 (New York: iUniversity, 2005) 172.

constituent power as part of a legal order. These differences provide important insights to the understanding of the relationship between constituent power and the law. Both authors, after all, were addressing fundamental questions about law and its ability to regulate political power. I will explore the practical consequences of these approaches more closely in the next chapter.

4
Between Law and Revolution

Although the origins of the theory of constituent power are generally placed in the French Revolution, the different legal and institutional implications associated with it in late 18th-century France are seldom explored. This chapter will engage in such an exploration by focusing on two institutions that were defended by the followers of Rousseau and rejected by Sieyès: the imperative mandate and (decision-making) primary assemblies. Defenders of these institutions often presented them as essential for the exercise of the people's constituent power; detractors saw them not only as unnecessary but as potentially threatening the proper functioning of the constitutional order. During the first stages of the French Revolution, debates about the imperative mandate and primary assemblies occupied an important part of the time of commentators and political actors. Although these discussions were rehearsed multiple times during the nineteenth century, they have now more or less disappeared from academic and political discourse.[1] Nonetheless, these debates are of key importance for about the study of the relationship between constituent power and the law, for two main reasons.

Firstly, they show that the concept of constituent power, as early as in 1789, was understood as having legal and institutional implications that go beyond ascribing legitimacy to a formally illegal constitution-making entity. Secondly, in the process of making the concept of constituent power consistent with the abolition of the imperative mandate and the limiting of the functions of primary assemblies, a new constituent subject, which puts different types of demands on the legal order, was invented: the nation. The idea of the constituent power of the nation, as well as the kinds of institutions and practices that accompany it, will be discussed further in the next chapter in relation to several 19th-century constitution-making processes.

In what follows, we will see how that idea was initially developed by Sieyès and the manner in which its alternative, the constituent power of the actual human beings that comprise a nation, was rejected. Indeed, the abolition of the

[1] As we will nonetheless see in Chapter 10, discussions about the imperative mandate are still present in the form of debates about the popular initiative, the recall, and the referendum.

Constituent Power and the Law. Joel Colón-Ríos, Oxford University Press (2020). © Joel Colón-Ríos.
DOI: 10.1093/oso/9780198785989.001.0001

imperative mandate was not only facilitated by the recognition of the nation as the constituent subject but was also a key moment in the history of representative democracy. Moreover, one of the main arguments against the practice of instructing deputies was that if bound by the recorded views of particular constituencies, the members of an elected assembly would be frequently unable to defend the interests of the community as a whole or, put differently, the interests of the nation. The national interest, it was argued, would naturally be inconsistent with the particular interests of the individuals living in specific localities.

The chapter will proceed as follows. Part I focuses on Sieyès' proposals about constitution-making and constitutional reform after 1789. These proposals, it will be seen, were often presented as antidotes to the ills of the Rousseauian perspectives defended by some of Sieyès' contemporaries. For Rousseau and his followers, the possibility of the periodic recreation of constitutions was a necessary condition for the legitimacy of a juridical order and should thus be not merely tolerated but facilitated by law. In contrast, Sieyès thought that Rousseau's approach would make impossible the stability of any constitutional order, and therefore that the law should only allow for partial revisions through the specific mechanism of the constitutional jury. The idea of the periodic convocation of constituent assemblies should, according to Sieyès, be avoided at all costs. There was always the possibility for a revolutionary exercise of constituent power to take place, but unlike Rousseau, Sieyès did not attempt to channel that kind of political act through legal procedures. Importantly, in the context of that discussion, Sieyès made a distinction between sovereignty—understood as an unlimited power of producing binding norms—and constituent power—understood as an exclusive ability of creating constitutional content. This distinction, I will argue in later chapters, is fundamental for understanding the juridical nature of constituent power.

Part II will examine the role of citizen instructions during the initial stages of the Revolution. As we saw in Chapter 2, Rousseau believed that binding citizen instructions were necessary in places where the citizenry was so numerous that constituent power needed to be exercised through a representative assembly. Sieyès, in contrast, saw them as radically inconsistent with the very idea of representation. The institution of citizen instructions was abolished in 1789. In so doing, it will be shown, French revolutionaries altered in fundamental ways not only the relationship between electors and representatives, but the very nature of what counts as an exercise of constituent power. In Part III, I will focus on the role of primary assemblies during the more radical stages of the French Revolution (namely, 1792–1793). The approach to primary assemblies found in both the Constitution of 1793 as well as in the Girondin Draft Constitution reflected in important ways Rousseau's conception of those entities as a key mechanism of democratic constitutional change. This approach to constitutional change will be contrasted with that of Sieyès, who saw primary assemblies as the site for the exercise of the much more modest 'commissioning power', the power to elect those seen as capable of identifying the constituent will of the nation.

I. The Legal (Un)Authorization of Constituent Power

For both Rousseau and Sieyès, the creation of a new constitution, or the radical alteration of an existing one, was outside the scope of the jurisdiction of the entity called to adopt ordinary laws or decrees. A key difference between these two authors, which has important institutional implications, is that Rousseau thought that those fundamental changes were to take place *through law*. As we saw in Chapter 2, Rousseau maintained that the sovereign should be periodically asked whether it wishes to preserve its current constitution, and the moments in—and procedures through—which that would occur needed to be legally regulated. Constituent power, in his view, is always 'derived', in the sense its exercise takes place according to previously existing rules. Rousseau's preferred constitution, as it were, provided for its own future (legal) destruction. Sieyès, in contrast, looked at constitutional remaking as an extra-legal phenomenon. No constituted power could abandon the rules that regulate its own existence: 'Since the constituted powers were unable to constitute themselves, they are unable to change their own constitution.' Furthermore, they should not be able to 'do nothing about the constitutions of the other powers'.[2]

This view has been understood by some authors as amounting to the idea that the alteration of a constitution can *only* take place extra-legally. That is to say, that a constitution is always subject to the will of the constituent power and that it should not even contain an amendment rule, an approach that was in fact reflected in the Constitution of 1799, drafted by Sieyès.[3] Sieyès' conception

[2] Emmanuel Sieyès, 'Reasoned Exposition of the Rights of Man and Citizen' in Emmanuel Sieyès, *The Essential Political Writings* (Leiden, 2014) 126–127.

[3] For a discussion, see Kemal Gözler, *Pouvoir Constituant* (Bursa: Ekin Kitabevi, 1999) (Chapter 3). See also Georges Burdeau, *Derecho Constitucional e Instituciones Políticas* (Ramón Falcón Tello trans.) (Madrid: Editorial Nacional, 1981) 114. Burdeau maintained that in adopting an amendment formula, the National Constituent Assembly rejected Sieyès' view that a constitution could only be altered by the constituent power, which was always extra-legal. This kind of approach is also present in the 19th-century authors whose work will be discussed in Chapter 6 of this book.

can also be understood as consistent with the idea that while an ordinary legislature cannot be authorized to modify the provisions of a constitution, a specially constituted one could be authorized to do so. This would be the case, for example, of a legislature acting through an amendment rule that empowers a supermajority of legislators to introduce modifications to the constitutional text. Such an authorization, it could be argued, would nonetheless not include the jurisdiction of adopting an entirely new constitutional order, only that of potentially revising the existing one. A similar approach was eventually adopted in the Constitution of 1791, which required three legislatures, plus an augmented fourth one (an 'Assembly of Revision'), to adopt a constitutional amendment, a process that would take at least six years, and which seemed to exclude the possibility of total replacement. [4]

Nevertheless, Sieyès' comments on constitutional reform, as presented in *Préliminaire de la Constitution*, could lead one to a different conclusion, one that seems consistent with Rousseau's argument for periodic constituent assemblies convened according to law. This was the alternative defended by some delegates—including Maximilien Robespierre and Jérôme Pétion de Villeneuve—as necessary to realize the nation's right to change the constitution. It was rejected in 1791.[5] In the previously mentioned essay, read at the Constitutional Committee in July 1789, Sieyès included a draft Declaration of the Rights of Man and the Citizen. Article 32 of that draft, in an apparently Rousseauian/Jeffersonian[6] fashion, established that: 'The people always has the right to revise and reform their constitution. It is even desirable to establish fixed intervals, where such revisions considered necessary will take place.'[7] Sieyès did not make any substantive commentary on that provision, and what appeared to be an elaboration of the principle reflected in it had to wait until

[4] That is arguably the meaning of Title 7, Article 1, of the Constitution of 1791, the text of which only explicitly authorizes the reform of individual articles: 'The National Constituent Assembly declares that the nation has the imprescriptible right to change its Constitution; nevertheless, considering that it is more in conformity with the national interest to use only the right of reforming, by the means provided in the Constitution itself, those articles which experience has proven unsatisfactory, decrees that it shall be effected by an Assembly of Revision in the following form . . .'. For a discussion, see Raymond Carré de Malberg, *Teoría General del Estado* (México: Fondo de Cultura Económica, 1948) 1184, fn 6. Note, also, that in an intervention supported by the National Constituent Assembly, Jacques Guillaume Thouret argued that since the constitution was fundamentally a good one, founded on the 'immutable bases of justice and in the eternal principle of reason', it was unnecessary to provide rules for its total replacement. See *Archives Parlementaires*, vol. XXX, at 186 (3 September 1791).

[5] Eric Thompson, *Popular Sovereignty and the French Constituent Assembly 1789-91* (Manchester University Press, 1952) 106, 110.

[6] See Thomas Jefferson, *Writings* (Merrill Peterson ed.) (New York, Library of America, 1984) 1402.

[7] Emmanuel Sieyès, *Préliminaires de la Constitution. Reconnoissance et Exposition Raisonnée des Droits de l'Homme et du Citoyen* (20–21 July 1789) (Versailles: Imprimeur ordinaire du Roi, 1789) 32. For Jefferson's proposal, Jefferson (n. 6).

a speech delivered two years later, when the Revolution had already entered a different stage. In that speech, Sieyès considered the subject of constitutional reform in some detail.

By that time, he no longer held opinions as radical as those he expressed in his 1789 pamphlets. A significant part of his writings and political interventions sought to respond to views expressed by the Jacobins at the National Convention. Nevertheless, his account of constitutional reform in the Second Thermidorian Intervention is largely consistent with anything he wrote during his more radical periods. In that speech, Sieyès maintained that a constitution would be imperfect unless it provided for its own conservation through time: a constitution 'must be able to assimilate the materials needed for its proper development'.[8] That did not mean, however, that it must be subject to the type of 'periodic recreation' that some extremists seemed to look forward to.[9] Indeed, in a Madisonian fashion, Sieyès suggested that: 'Once a constitution has been placed on a reliable foundation, it should no longer be exposed to moments of complete renewal', otherwise 'it would lose all those sentiments of love and veneration that a free people devote to it'.[10] Ideally, he wrote, a constitution would have 'the terrible permanence of the laws governing the universe itself', but since human beings were imperfect, it needed to be open to piecemeal revision as opposed to entire replacement.[11]

But that was not the same as rendering 'constituent power permanent'.[12] A situation in which the constituent subject always threatens the constitutional

[8] Sieyès, 'Second Thermidorian Intervention' (n. 2) 177.

[9] ibid.

[10] ibid. Madison, it is well known, thought that Jefferson's views about constitutional change suggested to the citizenry that their current system of government was somehow defective, depriving the government of 'that veneration which time bestows on everything, and without which perhaps the wisest and freest governments would not possess the requisite stability'. See *The Federalist Papers* (Clinton Rossiter ed.) (New York: New American Library, 1961) no. 49.

[11] The distinction between revision and replacement was present in the debates of 1791 and reflected in the amendment rule proposed by Nicolas-Thérèse-Benoît Frochot, which among other things, stated: 'Section 1: The nation, in which all sovereignty resides, has the power to reform the Constitution in part, or that of changing it as a whole. When it pleases it to exercise one of these powers, it delegates it: in the first instance to a National Convention; in the second instance to a Constituent Body. Section 2: The National Convention is the Assembly of representatives having the right to revise, and the power to reform by changes, suppressions or additions, one or more determined parts of the Constitution. It cannot be called upon to touch the fundamental bases of the Constitution, nor to change the distribution of public powers . . . Section 3: The Constituent Body is the Assembly of representatives possessed of the right of revising the Constitution in its entirety, of changing the distribution of the public powers, and of creating a new Constitution'. The draft amendment rule can be found in an appendix in Thompson (n. 5) 158–160. Frochot argued that there was 'an essential difference between a partial reform and a total reconstruction of the constitution' and rhetorically asked: 'Is the power of changing the Constitution entirely separate from that of reforming it? When a partial reform is desired by the people, is it necessary that to the reformative power . . . be added the terrible power of destroying at their will?'. Thompson (n. 5) 111.

[12] ibid. Sieyès, 'Second Thermidorian Intervention' (n. 2) 177.

order was no different from having no constitution at all.[13] The constitution should instead be guided by a 'principle of unlimited perfectibility which makes it adaptable to the needs of different eras, rather than a principle of destruction by total revision, which leaves it at the mercy of contingent events'.[14] The periodic return of a constituent assembly, an entity that Sieyès described as not subject to the 'division of powers', would be a 'calamity'.[15] He thus proposed to abandon the notion of institutionalizing the periodic recreation of the constitutional order, and embraced a system in which a constitutional jury (*jury constitutionnaire*) was in charge of proposing revisions to the constitutional text. Such revisions, as in the previously mentioned Article 32 of his draft Declaration of the Rights of Man and the Citizen, would take place at fixed intervals: 'Every ten years, beginning at the end of this century, in 1800, the Constitutional Jury will publish a collection of proposals for improving the constitution.'[16] The proposals of the constitutional jury would be submitted to the legislature and disseminated publicly. Even the action of the legislature would be insufficient to approve any proposal, 'since [a legislature does not] have constituent power'.[17]

Interestingly, Sieyès maintained that primary assemblies, local entities open to all individuals with political rights, should be attributed with the task of examining the constitutional jury's proposals. Through a 'yes' or 'no' vote, they would then determine whether the legislature should be given the right to act on them. In so doing, the legislature would not be able to edit or replace the relevant proposals. It would only have the authority to adopt or reject 'some or all of them, but it will have to cite reasons for doing so'.[18] This approach, to a certain extent, brought Sieyès closer to Rousseau: for both authors, the citizenry (even if defined in a way that excluded part of the population) must be consulted before constituent power is exercised. Nonetheless, as we will see in the next section, Sieyès was not prepared to see primary assemblies as the constituent power in action. 'Constituent activity', he wrote, should be 'divided among the primary assemblies, the Constitutional Jury, and the legislature'.[19]

[13] These fears were perhaps substantiated when, in 1795, several primary assemblies refused the Convention's instruction to dissolve. See William Doyle, *The Oxford History of the French Revolution* (Oxford University Press, 2002) 320.

[14] Sieyès, 'Second Thermidorian Intervention' (n. 2) 177. This conception, it will be seen in Chapter 8, has important connections with the contemporary idea that the constitution in the material sense is outside the scope of the ordinary amendment authority.

[15] Sieyès, 'Second Thermidorian Intervention' (n. 2) 177.

[16] ibid. 178.

[17] ibid.

[18] ibid.

[19] ibid. 177.

Attributing primary assemblies with the legal faculty of exercising constituent power would be inconsistent with the conception of representation he developed in 'Views and Third Estate', and it would also be too risky. Sieyès, much more than ever before, had become increasingly concerned with the idea of unlimited political power.

'[T]he distinction between constituent and constituted power', he maintained, 'was a sensible and useful idea', but not if it was understood as justifying the right to do anything.[20] If understood in that way, it could be used to 'justify acts of folly'.[21] Even the 'French people as a whole' lacked the unlimited powers 'which flatterers attribute to it'.[22] Perhaps, he suggested, the sovereignty[23] of kings had been so 'powerful and terrible' that it was thought that the sovereignty of the people should surpass it.[24] But 'unlimited powers are a political monster and a great error of the French people, which it will not commit again in the future'.[25] What a political association acquires from its members is not the sum total of all the members' rights and powers but only the necessary minimum required 'to enforce the rights and duties of each individual'.[26] These limits should be understood as an elaboration of Sieyès' conception that all forms of political power are subject to natural law, rather than as a renunciation of the views he expressed in the pamphlets discussed earlier. It is true that for Sieyès the nation was not bound by positive law: '[t]he nation exists prior to everything; it is the origin of everything'.[27] But this does not mean that the nation was not bound *by law*. All nations existed under a law that had not been posited by men: 'Prior to the nation and above the nation there is only natural law.'[28]

The only thing that can be set above the nation, he insisted in 'Third Estate', 'is natural law that far from contradicting it, serves rather to enlighten and

[20] ibid. 159.

[21] ibid. The relevant passage reads: 'A sensible and useful idea was introduced in 1788: namely the distinction between constituent power and constituted powers. This idea belongs among the discoveries that have moved science forward, and it is owed to the French. But the intrigues that so quickly took the place of reason at the time of the Revolution rendered this idea impotent to shape a new political order. Instead, like many new ideas that quickly come to seem obvious, it was used to justify acts of folly (as is the fate of even the best instruments when placed in the hands of ignorant people). Now is the time to make better use of it'. ibid.

[22] ibid. 156.

[23] Sieyès rarely used the terms 'sovereignty', and when he used it, it was to show its dangers. See, for example, ibid. 156.

[24] ibid.

[25] ibid. 155–156.

[26] ibid. 156.

[27] Emmanuel Sieyès, 'What is the Third Estate?' in *Political Writings* (Hackett Publishing Company, 2003) 136.

[28] ibid.

guide it towards the great social union'.[29] This is an idea common to social contract theorists (as well as to some of the authors whose work will be discussed in later chapters, particularly in Chapter 6): everyone, sovereigns included, are bound by the laws of nature.[30] In light of his views about the relationship between the nation and natural law, the fact that Sieyès wrote that 'the sovereignty of the people is certainly not unlimited'[31] should not come as a surprise. At the same time, as Lucia Rubinelli has argued, such statements also support the idea that, for Sieyès, sovereignty (even popular sovereignty) and constituent power were not the same thing.[32] Sovereignty was a total power to transform any will into law; constituent power was about the adoption of new constitutions.[33] In a raw democracy (*dans la démocratie brute*), he wrote in 1795 after having criticized Rousseau's notion of representation, 'the constituent power is confused with the constituted power'.[34] In such a system, it could be argued, the people's law-making authority is as unlimited as that of absolute kings. But in a modern republic, raw democracy was not a realistic form of government.

In an apparent critique of Rousseau and his French followers, Sieyès maintained that those approaches that insist on the unlimited sovereignty of the people should be recognized as 'erroneous fancies, as defective plans for a "re-totality" [*ré-totale*] rather than a "re-public", as harmful to liberty and contrary to public and private interests'.[35] A better use of the theory of constituent power, he suggested, would be the establishment of an institution (i.e. the *jury constitutionnaire*) charged with the task of protecting and improving the constitutional order.[36] The very idea of a constitution having been adopted by a constituent power, a power different from the ordinary institutions of

[29] ibid. Elsewhere he maintains that 'There is one *supreme* law which ought to be the parent of all others, and that is, "*Do wrong to no man*". It is this great natural law which the legislature distributes, as it were, piecemeal in applying the principle case by case to the various private orders in society'. Emmanuel Sieyès, 'An Essay on Privileges' in *Political Writings* (n. 2) 70.

[30] This applies even to Hobbes' sovereign who, not being part of the social contract, remained in the state of nature: 'It is true, that Soveraigns are all subject to the Lawes of Nature, because such lawes be Divine, and cannot by any man, or Common-wealth, be abrogated. But to those Lawes which the Soveraign himselfe, that is, which the Common-wealth maketh, he is not subject.' Thomas Hobbes, *Leviathan* (Penguin Books, 1985) at 367. However, if Hobbes' sovereign breached the laws of nature, it was answerable to God, not to its subjects, who remained unable to enforce the law of nature against the sovereign. ibid. 265.

[31] Sieyès, 'First Thermidorian Intervention' (n. 2) 156.

[32] Lucia Rubinelli, 'How to Think beyond Sovereignty: On Sieyes and Constituent Power', 18(1) *European Journal of Political Theory* (2016).

[33] As will be seen in Chapter 6 of the book, during the 19th century, this distinction was largely ignored, and sovereignty and constituent power were largely presented as synonymous, or the latter as an element of the former. In Chapter 9, I develop this distinction further.

[34] Emmanuel Sieyès, 'Bases de l'Ordre Social' in Pasquale Pasquino, *Sieyes et l'Invention de la Constitution en France* (Odile Jacobs, 1998) 185.

[35] ibid.

[36] Sieyès, 'Second Thermidorian Intervention' (n. 2) 159.

government, required a means to protect the stability of the constitutional order. The establishment of a constitutional jury, and the approach to constitutional change that it would involve, did not mean that an exercise of the extra-legal constituent power that results in the adoption of a radically new constitution was rendered impossible. Such an exercise would simply have to take place outside the law. Sieyès made clear that in defending that proposal he had nothing to say about 'revolutionary upheavals, whose prevention is not the task of our jury'.[37] In defending his periodic sovereign assemblies, Rousseau had nothing to say about revolutionary upheavals either: in his system, revolutions were authorized by law.

II. Constituent Instructions and Representation

As we saw in Chapter 2, Rousseau defended the institution of citizen instructions in states so large that the exercise of the legislative (constituent) power could only take place by means of delegation.[38] In those states, he recommended to 'bind the representatives to follow [constituent] instructions exactly, and to make them render their constituents a strict account of their conduct' in the legislative body.[39] Sieyès, in contrast, unequivocally rejected the institution of citizen instructions in his famous essay on the royal veto, which will be discussed in some detail below. In a country that (like France) 'is not a democracy', he maintained, 'the people or nation . . . can only speak, can only act through its representatives'.[40] Representatives, after all, represented the whole nation: they had the task of developing a common will, not to act as deputies of particular constituencies. That view prevailed early in the French Revolution and was reflected in the official documents regulating the convocation of the Estates-General. The result, it will be seen, was the consolidation of the Sieyesian idea of the necessary extra-legal nature of the constituent power. At the same time, as we will see later, once there is no imperative mandate,

[37] ibid. 171.

[38] It is not entirely clear what Rousseau had in mind by 'large states', that is, what size and population would make the direct vote of citizens through primary assemblies unviable, but a good indication is that, according to some estimates, Poland —the place that he had in mind when developing the idea that in large states constituent power could not be exercised directly—had a population of roughly 14 million in 1772 in an area of 733,500 square metres. Irena Gieysztorowa, 'Research into the Demographic History of Poland: A Provisional Summing-Up', 18 *Acta Polonia Historica* 5 (1963) 8.

[39] Jean Jacques Rousseau, 'Considerations on the Government of Poland and on its Proposed Reformation', April 1772 (ISN ETH Zurich) 18.

[40] Sieyès, *Dire de l'abbé Sieyès, sur la question du Veto royal* (7 September 1789)

the nature of primary assemblies as the most basic sites of popular decision-making changed considerably.

At the centre of the legal framework that regulated the relationship between citizens and representatives during the first stages of the French Revolution was the royal decree that regulated the convocation of the Estates of the realm, the *Règlement*. This document invited parishes and communities 'to meet and draw up *cahiers* [lists of grievances] and nominate deputies'.[41] In practice, this meant that lower level assemblies would draw up *cahiers* to be carried by their deputies to assemblies higher in the electoral scheme.[42] Eventually, three final *cahiers*—one per order—would be presented at the Estates-General and a final compendium submitted to the king.[43] Tens of thousands of preliminary *cahiers* were drawn up by different groups in towns, villages, parishes, and guilds. Some of these were based on models distributed before the relevant assembly met, and frequently referred to issues of clear constitutional significance, such as calls for a constitutional monarchy, for representative institutions, for governmental decentralization, and for individual liberty.[44] They also referred to non-constitutional issues, but many demanded a declaration of rights and gave delegates the power to adopt a constitution and appealed to the sovereignty of the general will.[45]

Although many *cahiers* appeared to be no more than petitions, they had been treated as binding instructions in earlier meetings of the Estates-General. For instance, in the Estates-General of 1560, deputies who failed to act in accordance to their *cahiers* were subject to fines and even imprisonment.[46] In 1789, some insisted that, as before, the role of deputies was to take *cahiers* to a higher body, to work with other deputies in collating them into a form that could be presented to a higher level assembly, and to participate in the election of those

[41] Article 25, Règlement Fait par le Roi pour l'Exécution des Lettres de Convocation, 24 January 1789. See also Gilbert Shapiro and John Markoff, 'Officially Solicited Petitions: The *Cahiers de Doléances* as a Historical Source', 46 *IRSH* 79–106 (2001) 84. Doyle (n. 13) 96-97. See also Colin Jones, *The Longman Companion to the French Revolution* (Routledge, 1998) 61–63.

[42] For a discussion, see Doyle (n. 13) 96–97; Shapiro and Markoff (n. 41) 79–80.

[43] This of course never happened, given the fate of the Estates-General in the 1789 Revolution. Shapiro and Markoff (n. 41) 87.

[44] Doyle (n. 13) 134. For a detailed analysis, see Gilbert Shapiro and John Markoff, *Revolutionary Demands: A Content Analysis of the Cahiers de Doléances of 1789* (Stanford University Press, 1998). See also Melvin Edelstein, *The French Revolution and the Birth of Electoral Democracy* (Ashgate, 2014) 29. Interestingly, the *cahier* from Rennes stated that the Third Estate had been erroneously called an 'Order', and that it should be renamed the 'People' or the 'Nation'. Thompson (n. 5) 8.

[45] Thompson (n. 5) 25, 35, 99.

[46] Paul Friedland, *Political Actors: Representative Bodies & Theatricality in the Age of the French Revolution* (Cornell University Press, 2002) 34. The legal relationship between individual deputies and their electors was regulated by the ordinary civil law rules applicable to the mandate contract. Michel Fridieff, *Les Origines du Referendum dans la Constitution de 1793* (Paris: Les Presses Universitaires de France, 1932) 89, 91.

individuals that would carry the collated list of grievances further up in the hierarchy.[47] Unlike in 1560, the imperative mandate would have meant that active citizens would have the right to instruct deputies that would be drafting a new constitution. That is to say, the imperative mandate could have become a means of putting into practice a Rousseauian conception of constituent power as incapable of being represented. Of course, in the context of a monarchy like that of France, those deputies would not have been constitution-makers but 'a conduit by which the views of those below arrive at the ear of the sole legislator, the King'.[48]

This traditional conception was in fact reflected in the *Règlement*. There, deputies arguably appeared as *cahiers* carriers rather than as true representatives that could make whatever decision they thought best after a period of deliberation.[49] For example, this document referred to the 'deputies who shall be chosen by the rural parishes and communities in order to carry their *cahiers*' and described the task of high level assemblies as the 'amalgamation of the *cahiers* of the towns and communities into a single one'.[50] This approach, which as we know did not prevail, was firmly opposed by those who, like Sieyès, insisted that a representative assembly was a place for debate and compromise. 'It is not', Sieyès wrote, 'by examining separate *cahiers*, if there are any, that we can discover the will of their authors'. Such a common will could only be discovered by 'proposing, listening, consulting, changing one's opinion'.[51] This defence of assemblies as deliberative entities and of deputies not as simple *cahier* carriers also found support in the preamble of the *Règlement*, where the king ensured the three Estates of the realm that he would not 'interfere, in any way, with the freedom of their deliberations', and stated that he was persuaded that 'a representative assembly of the entire nation' should not be given any instructions that could 'halt or trouble the course of deliberations'.[52]

Jean Joseph Mounier, who thought that representatives were free to act independently of the instructions of their constituents, took that view to its natural conclusion: the very notion of a *cahier* should be abolished.[53] But that seemed to go too far for Sieyès, whose conception of representation was

[47] Shapiro and Markoff (n. 41) 87.
[48] ibid. 88
[49] ibid.
[50] Article 25, 'Règlement Fait par le Roi pour l'Exécution des Lettres de Convocation' (24 January 1789) in Jacques Cadart, *Le Régime Électoral des États Généraux de 1789 et ses Origines (1302-1614)* (Paris, 1952) 197.
[51] Sieyès, *Dire de l'abbé Sieyès, sur la question du Veto royal* (7 September 1789) 17.
[52] Preamble, 'Règlement Fait par le Roi pour l'Exécution des Lettres de Convocation' (24 January 1789) in Cadart (n. 50) 193.
[53] For a discussion, see Shapiro and Markoff (n. 41) 89.

entirely consistent with the issuing of *cahiers* that did not bind those who were elected to express the will of the French nation.[54] As he had noted in *Views*, citizen instructions would make it impossible to make laws; instead of the imperative mandate defended by Rousseau and his followers, representatives had a 'free mandate' from their constituents. From a Rousseauian perspective this approach was unacceptable. If sovereignty was shared among the many individuals who comprise the nation, how could they not be able to issue legally binding instructions? But Rousseau's thought, as many times during the French Revolution, was officially rejected. In the decree of 23 June 1789 it was thus stated: 'His Majesty declares that in subsequent sessions of the Estates General he will not permit *cahiers* or mandates ever to be considered imperative; they must be only simple instructions, entrusted to the consciences and free opinions of the deputies chosen.'[55]

Section III of the Constitution of 1791 eventually expressed this view in a more explicit manner: 'The representatives named in the departments shall not be representatives of an individual department but of the entire Nation, and they may be given no mandate.'[56] A number of assemblies had in fact ignored the royal declarations against the imperative mandate and issued instructions with the clear intention that they were understood as binding.[57] For example, the Third Estate of Charolles, which supported a constitutional monarchy, decided to 'forbid [. . .] their deputies to vote on any matter before such a constitution is granted', a decision accompanied with the threat of withdrawing 'all their powers should they contravene the above mandate'.[58] This type of behaviour had received an unequivocal response from the National Assembly. One

[54] See Sieyès, 'Views' (n. 2) 53, were he maintains that lower level assemblies could advise their elected representatives. Raymond Carré de Malberg argued that under Sieyès' conception, deliberation would take place in two stages: firstly, each of the opinions of the deputies are put forward (opinions that could very well be dominated by the content of their *cahiers*) and, secondly, those opinions are modified in order for a common will to be reached. Carré de Malberg (n. 4) s 395.

[55] 'Declaration of the King Concerning the Present Session of the Estates General', Article 6, in *The French Revolution: A Volume in The Documentary History of Western Civilization* (Paul H. Beik ed.) (The Macmillan Press, 1970) 73–74. Article 5 of the same document established: 'The King permits deputies who believe themselves to be restricted by their mandates to request new powers of their constituents; but his Majesty enjoins them to remain, meanwhile, in the Estates General, in order to be present at all deliberations on urgent affairs of state and give consultative opinions concerning them.'

[56] Indeed, the very idea of dividing electorates territorially (as opposed to, e.g., dividing them according to economic class), could be seen as having the purpose of minimizing the influences of particular wills (i.e. wills that could be defended by individual deputies and that would be different to the will of the nation). For a discussion, see Carré de Malberg (n. 4) s 395.

[57] According to Shapiro and Markoff, about three-quarters of the *cahiers* coming from the nobility, about two-fifths from the Third Estate, and about one-third from the clergy, purported to be binding. Shapiro and Markoff (n. 41) 89–90.

[58] Cited ibid. 100.

of its first resolutions had declared the invalidity of all binding instructions.[59] Despite supporting this decision, both Thouret and Sieyès, when later arguing that the assembly was the bearer of the constituent power, maintained that 'representatives have received this full power from their *commettans*' and referred to those *cahiers* that contained explicit authorizations to engage in constituent activity.[60] But that was a 'constituent mandate'[61] that authorized national representatives to create a new constitution without requiring them to adopt any particular constitutional content.

a. Representation and the Debate on the Royal Veto

The abolition of the imperative mandate facilitated some of the more radical decisions of the Constituent Assembly. This would not have been possible if deputies respected the instructions of their constituents. (And one needs to remember, for example, that it was the imperative mandate that was preventing members of the privileged orders from joining the deliberations of the National Assembly, as some *cahiers* implicitly forbade deputies from deliberating with the two other orders.)[62] Not surprisingly, the imperative mandate was most strongly defended by the most conservative elements in the assembly (even though it was also defended, to different extents, by deputies such as Robespierre and Pétion). Outside of France, Edmund Burke, who had famously rejected the notion of constituent instructions in 1774, denounced the French deputies for departing 'from the instructions of the people by whom they were sent'. For Burke, the Constituent Assembly, unlike the English Parliament, was bound by those instructions, since it did not act 'in virtue of any ancient usage or settled law'. Accordingly, those instructions 'were the sole source of their authority'.[63] At the same time, and behind those political

[59] That decision allowed them to abolish the entire juridical apparatus of the *ancient regime*, despite the contrary instructions of many *cahiers*. See Doyle (n. 13) 117–118.

[60] Carré de Malberg (n. 4) 1177.

[61] Carré de Malberg (n. 4) 1176. The notion of the 'constituent mandate' will be developed in Chapter 10.

[62] For a discussion, see Friedland (n. 46) 143.

[63] Edmund Burke, *Reflections on the Revolution of France* (Penguin Classics, 1986) 276. See also Edmund Burke 'Speech to the Electors of Bristol' (3 November 1774), *The Works of the Right Honourable Edmund Burke*. 6 vols. (London: Henry G. Bohn, 18524–1856) vol. 1, 446–448, where it is stated that Parliament 'is a *deliberative* assembly of *one* nation, with *one* interest, that of the whole . . . You choose a member, indeed; but when you have chosen him, he is not a member of Bristol, but he is a member of Parliament. If the local constituent should have an interest, or should form a hasty opinion, evidently opposite to the real good of the rest of the community, the member for that place ought to be as far, as any other, from any endeavour to give it effect.'

realities, Sieyès' rejection of binding instructions contributed to the transformation of the very notion of a 'deputy': the deputy was not called to represent the particular interest of those individuals and localities who elected him, but the common interest of the nation.

Beyond electing representatives, the electorate could not determine or limit the content of the future constitution. For Raymond Carré de Malberg, this approach amounted to the transformations of the representatives of the popular sovereign into the sovereign representatives of the people.[64] Those who at the time defended a Rousseauian conception of popular sovereignty and of the institution of the binding mandate, like the compte d'Antraigues, would insist that this was a very dangerous move. For Antraigues, liberty was necessarily tied to the *mandat impératif* because it allowed the people to conserve its sovereignty. 'Whenever sovereignty exists outside the people', he wrote, 'there is tyranny'.[65] Nonetheless, Rousseau's notion of the general will in fact served as a justification for the abolition of the institution of constituent instructions. Why should the instructions given by the neighbours of different localities, which may reflect particular interests alien to the general will, be binding on national representatives? Indeed, in the National Assembly, some deputies went as far as suggesting that by abolishing the imperative mandate, the will of the nation would be protected against 'the abuses of the constituent power'.[66] In contrast to those views and in the context of the debate around the royal veto, Pétion was not shy to inform deputies that they were mere mandataires.

It may have been true, Pétion thought, that in a situation like that in France, where 'a new order of things' needed to be introduced and prejudices uprooted, representatives needed to be given unlimited powers.[67] Nonetheless, that was not a sufficient justification for a representative system: representation was necessary because it was impossible for the whole people, the true sovereign, to assemble and deliberate about its affairs. 'The members of the legislative body' he said, 'are mandataries; the citizens who have chosen

[64] Carré de Malberg (n. 4) 1179.

[65] M. le Comte d'Antraigues, 'Mémoire sur les Etats-généraux, leurs Droits, et la Manière de les Convoquer' (1788), as cited in Friedland (n. 46) 101. The author of an anonymous pamphlet titled *La Corruption de l'Asamblée Nationale* was even more scathing: 'You have no other choice, you Frenchmen who wish to be free, than to lop the heads of all these perjuring usurpers; afterwards, assembly yourselves, not to name representatives who will be your masters & who will decree that the cahiers that contain your sovereign will shall be regarded as irrelevant, but [to name] deputies [who will be] loyal to their mandates, who will have no will other than that which these mandates will manifest, who will never violate them, & and who will remain faithful to all the affairs of the people.' Quoted in Friedland (n. 46) 162.

[66] *Archives Parlementaires* (30 June 1789) (Speech of Bertrand Barère) 205.

[67] *Archives Parliamentaires* (5 September 1789) 582.

them are the constituents [*commettans*]; therefore, the representatives are subject to the will of those from which they have received their mission and powers'.[68] Pétion saw no difference between ordinary mandataires and political ones: they were both commissioned to carry out certain tasks.[69] To be sure, Pétion's argument was not directed at the resurrection of the imperative mandate in its traditional form.[70] He was defending the idea of giving the constituent people, acting through primary assemblies, the last word about the validity of a legislative measure vetoed by the king (if he indeed were to have that power under the new constitution). It is worth briefly examining the basic contours of this debate, as it partly reveals the nature of the understanding of some deputies about the relationship between primary assemblies, the imperative mandate, and constituent power.

The debate was a reaction to the king's threat of vetoing the Declaration of Rights adopted by the Constituent Assembly. As the assembly proceeded to draft the new constitutional text, the question naturally arose about the role of the monarch in the exercise of the legislative power. The more conservative deputies favoured the royal veto both on the basis of their instructions and because it was one of the basic elements of the traditional monarchy.[71] Sieyès led the opposition against it. He maintained that such an approach would potentially allow a private will (i.e. the will of the king) to prevail over the general will.[72] In a passage reminiscent of Rousseau's distinction between the legislative and the executive power, Sieyès added that the law had to be the expression of the will of the governed, not of the government.[73] However, Sieyès did not only reject the absolute veto but also the suspensive one, that is, the alternative eventually favoured by the assembly.[74] According to that approach, the king could initially refuse his consent to a bill approved by a legislative majority, but subsequent legislatures could override that refusal and bring the law into existence. The election of a new legislature would mean,

[68] ibid.

[69] ibid.

[70] That said, Pétion had a generally positive view of the imperative mandate, understanding it as giving deputies wide discretion in deciding matters about which they had not received specific instructions. Thompson (n. 5) 49.

[71] ibid. 40–41

[72] Sieyès, 'Palabras del Abate Sieyès sobre la Cuestión del Veto Real' in *Escritos Políticos de Sieyès* (David Pantoja Morán ed.) (México: Fondo de Cultura Económica, 2013) 207–208.

[73] ibid.

[74] Chapter 3, Section 3 of the Constitution of 1791 reads in its relevant part: 'Section 3. Royal Sanction: (1) The decrees of the legislative body are presented to the King, who may refuse his consent thereto; (2) In case the King refuses his consent, such refusal shall be only suspensive. When the two legislatures following the one in which the decree was introduced have again successively presented the same decree in the same terms, the King shall be deemed to have given his sanction.'

in practice, that primary assemblies would have the opportunity to express their agreement or disagreement with the king's veto. The idea was that the king would only refuse consent when he suspected that the will of the representatives of the nation was not truly consistent with the general will, and the matter would then be settled by the people themselves, acting through primary assemblies.[75]

The suspensive veto, as Keith Baker has noted, 'reflected at once the Rousseauian's acceptance of the necessity of representation in a large state and the continuing distrust of it'.[76] In support of this view, Pétion argued that even if the whole people could not assemble and draft a new constitution, they were definitely capable of answering 'yes' or 'no' questions and should be given the opportunity to do so when possible. It was surprising, Pétion complained, that those who sat in the Constituent Assembly in virtue of being elected by lower level assemblies, now raised 'doubts concerning the wisdom' of the very people who elected them.[77] In an anti-Sieyesian fashion, he described a representative assembly freed from the actual will of the electors as a form of 'slavery'.[78] Mounier, in contrast, criticized the suspensive veto precisely on the grounds of its consistency with the notion of binding instructions, stating that 'the deputies newly elected after the veto had been used would consider themselves bound by a mandate, despite the abolition by the Constitution of the imposition of any mandate on a representative of the nation'.[79] In a similar vein, Sieyès reminded his colleagues that 'there cannot be a national will different from the will of the representatives of the nation', and that 'the nation cannot speak except through its representatives'.[80] If the national will could in fact be better expressed in the primary assemblies than in the national legislature, he asked, then why even have a permanent legislative body?[81]

[75] The king, it is important to note, had no participation in the adoption of constitutional amendments under the Constitution of 1791. That is to say, the suspensive veto only applied to ordinary legislation. For a discussion, see Maurice Fonteneau, *Du Pouvoir Constituant en France et de la Révision Constitutionnelle dans les Constitutions Françaises depuis 1789* (Caen, 1900).

[76] Keith M. Baker, 'Constitution' in *The French Revolution: Recent Debates and New Controversies* (Gary Kates ed.), 2nd ed. (New York: Routledge, 2006) 78.

[77] *Archives Parliamentaires* (5 September 1789) 583.

[78] ibid. 582.

[79] Thompson (n. 5) 43.

[80] Sieyès, 'Palabras del Abate Sieyès sobre la Cuestión del Veto Real' (n. 72) 207–209.

[81] ibid. 211. Such an approach, he warned, risked the transformation of France into a federation or a group of small republics: 'France ... cannot become a federal state comprised by a multitude of republics ... it is and must be a single whole, subject in all its parts to a common law and administration'. ibid. 211–212. He distinguished France's situation with that of England, where a royal veto was necessary since there 'was no distinction between the constituent and the legislative power', and therefore parliament could attack the royal prerogative if legislation did not require royal consent. The future legislatures of France, on the contrary, would have no power 'to touch any part of the Constitution'. ibid. 214.

III. Primary Assemblies as the Constituent Power in Action?

The emergence of mass democracy and of the notion of the modern electorate involve a particular way of conceiving the act of voting. Voting is an essentially individual act. It is done in secret, in silence, and with no need for formal deliberation. Indeed, in contemporary democracies, it is commonly prohibited to make political expressions inside polling stations. Any discussion among voters about which candidates or options should be supported will probably be seen as disrespectful and deeply inappropriate if not outright illegal. When an elector visits a voting booth, the law assumes that she has made the relevant decision beforehand; her act is merely the formal way of recording it and making it known to the state. Voting is also an individual act in the sense that it is in each voter, and not in the collection of the voters of a polling station, where political power is seen to rest. Primary assemblies, precursors to the contemporary polling station, were often seen in a very different light. Despite their undeniable democratic shortcomings (dramatically exemplified by the exclusion of women and by various types of property qualifications), they operated under an interesting conception of the act of voting. Voting was typically public and oral, and it took place in a local meeting of neighbours where it was possible to deliberate about the subject matter of the vote.[82]

Rousseau, as I argued in Chapter 2, saw in primary assemblies an appropriate means for the expression of the general will, for the exercise of

[82] For an invaluable discussion about the extent of citizen participation in primary assemblies during the French Revolution, see Patrice Gueniffey, *La Revolución Francesa y las Elecciones: Democracia y Representación a Fines del Siglo XVIII* (México: Fondo de Cultura Económica, 2001). The town meetings that played an important role in the ratification of the US Constitution (as well as of some state constitutions) were a type of primary assembly that sometimes relied in the institution of binding instructions. For a discussion, see Pauline Maier, *Ratification: The Poele Debate the Constitution, 1787-1788* (New York: Simon & Schuster, 2010) 135–153). States. For a general discussion, see Joseph Zimmerman, *New England Town Meeting: Democracy in Action* (Greenwood Publishing Group, 1999). A similar institution (which originated in medieval Spain and later migrated to colonial South America) was the *cabildo abierto*, a meeting of neighbours in the municipalities. Decisions made in this kind of meeting usually had a local character (such as the elections of municipal officials), but in some cases referred to issues of national importance, such as in the political crisis that led to declarations of independence. One of the most famours examples is the *cabildo abierto* convened in Buenos Aires in 1816. For a discussion, see José María Ramallo, 'Significado de la Revolución de Mayo', 103 *Revista Teología* 11 (2010) 24. More generally, see Silvia Cogollos Amaya and Jaime Ramírez León, 'Perspectiva Histórica del Cabildo Abierto: Una Forma de Participación Ciudadana', 8(16) *Memoria y Sociedad* 41 (2004); Francisco X. Tapia, 'Algunas Notas sobre el Cabildo Abierto en Hispanoamérica', 11(1) *Journal of Inter-American Studies* 58 (1969); William Whatley Pierson, Jr, 'Reflections on the Cabildo as an Institution', 5(4) *The Hispanic American Historical Review* 573 (1922). In some new Latin American Constitutions, the *cabildo abierto* is mentioned as a mechanism of democratic participation. In the Venezuelan Constitution of 1999, it is one of the institutions with the initiative to convene a constituent assembly (Articles 70 and 348).

constituent power. When he insisted that all laws must be ratified by the people, he meant the people assembled as a single body (as in a small society) or in primary assemblies operating in multiple localities. During the discussion of the amendment rule of the new constitution at the French National Constituent Assembly, a good number of delegates unsuccessfully argued that constitutional changes should be adopted by constituent conventions which, unlike the ordinary legislature, should be bound by the instructions of primary assemblies.[83] Only that way, it was argued, one could ensure that the true general will would be expressed. Sieyès himself, in one of his unpublished manuscripts, suggested that the nation could either *delegate* its constituent power or exercise it through primary assemblies, which he sometimes called 'the trustees of the nation'.[84] He strongly preferred the former option. The first national constitution that attempted to put into practice the latter alternative (not counting the Genevan Constitution, briefly mentioned in Chapter 2) was the French Constitution of 1793.

The Constitution of 1793 was adopted by the National Convention called after the revolutionary events of 10 August 1792 by a decree issued by the Legislative Assembly elected under the Constitution of 1791.[85] This constitution never came into effect as a result of the state of emergency decreed shortly after its adoption.[86] The Legislative Assembly's decree establishing the electoral system through which the members of the convention would be elected stated that 'primary assemblies are encouraged to invest their representatives with full authority (*confiance illimitée*)'.[87] That cautious approach, which implicitly accepted the power of primary assemblies to issue binding mandates (even if recommending against its exercise), is a reflection of the importance that these entities assumed during this new stage of the Revolution. The Legislative Assembly also abolished the distinction between active and passive citizens (described by Robespierre in 1791 as 'monstrous'):[88] all French men 21 years or older who were not servants or unemployed were allowed to vote in primary assemblies.[89] According to Robespierre, speaking in 1792, '[t]he source of all ills is the absolute independence that representatives have assumed with

[83] Thompson (n. 5) 101–102.
[84] Sieyès, 'Bases de l'Ordre Social' (n. 34) 187; Sieyès, 'Second Thermidorian Intervention' (n. 2) 174.
[85] For a discussion, see Doyle (n. 13) 174–196.
[86] For a discussion, see ibid. 246. The National Convention's decree of 10 October 1793 stated: 'Le gouvernement provisoire de la France est révolutionnaire jusqu'à la paix.'
[87] Article 6, *Décret 11-12 août 1792* (Décret relative à la formation des assemblées primaires pour le rassemblement de la convention nationale).
[88] See Maximilien Robespierre, 'Speech of 22 April 1791' in Baker, *The French Revolution* (n. 76) 144.
[89] Article 3, *Décret 11-12 août 1792* (n. 87).

respect of the Nation without consultation. They have recognized the sovereignty of the nation to, subsequently, annihilate it'.[90]

In clear contrast with the sporadic electoral function that the Constitution of 1791 attributed to primary assemblies, Robespierre insisted on their permanence and capacity for deliberation.[91] The idea was that primary assemblies allowed the people to rescue their constituent power from the national legislature: they should be seen as decision-making bodies with an authority superior to that of any representative entity. However, the main purpose of primary assemblies, according to the Constitution of 1793, was that of voting on particular proposals, a function which meant that in practice they lacked the power to issue binding mandates.[92] In a partial[93] Rousseauian fashion, the constitution returned to the language of the *Social Contract* and established that while decrees could be issued by the ordinary legislature, laws required the ratification of primary assemblies.[94] According to Marie-Jean Hérault de Séchelles, one of the main drafters of the constitution, a member of the legislature had a 'double character': it was 'a mandataire for the laws submitted to the approval of the people while it [was] a representative for the decrees'.[95]

Primary assemblies were composed of no less than 200 citizens (who resided in a particular canton) and no more than 600. They elected deputies directly (one deputy per each 39,000–41,000 citizens), a system that also made more difficult the earlier practice of issuing instructions.[96] They were held every year,

[90] Maximilien Robespierre, 'Des Maux et des Ressources de l'Etat', in *Ouvres Completes* (Boloiseay, Lefebvre and Soboul eds.) (Paris, 1958) vol. 4, 318.

[91] ibid. 350.

[92] Constitution of 1793, Articles 11–20.

[93] Partial because the constitution identifies as 'laws' a number of rules that Rousseau would have probably identified as 'decrees' (such as rules governing public education, which Rousseau explicitly used as an example of a decree related to a particular public service). See Jean-Jacques Rousseau, 'Discourse on Political Economy' in *The Social Contract and The Discourses* (Everyman's Library, 1973) 149.

[94] If forty days went by after the legislature submitted the proposed law to the departments, and at least one tenth of the primary assemblies of the majority of departments did not protest, the bill would become law. Constitution of 1793, Articles 54–61.

[95] Hérault de Séchelles, Séance du 10 juin 1793, *Archives parlementaires*, vol. 66, 258. It is interesting to note that the Constitution of 1793 attributed to the legislature a key role in the adoption of both laws and decrees. As we saw in the previous chapter, for Rousseau, the adoption of decrees could be left in the hands of a representative assembly (government), but there is no obvious reason why such an entity—as part of the administration—should play a role in the creation of laws. However, one must note that under the Constitution of 1793 the legislature (under Rousseau's conception, the administration or government) could only *propose* laws to the entire people (i.e.theoretically, it could not adopt them by itself). Rousseau left that task in the hands of the Legislator (which could take the form of an extraordinary assembly), not in the ordinary legislative body. For a critical discussion of the distinction between laws and decrees under the Constitution of 1793, see Pierre Brunet, 'Les Contraintes de la Représentation en 1793: sur la Distinction des Lois et des Décrets et sa Justification'in *Théorie des Contraints Juridiques, Sous la Dir* (M. Troper, V. Champeil-Desplats eds.) (France: Paris-Bruxelles, 2005).

[96] Constitution of 1793, Articles 11–12, 23, 116.

but could also be convened in extraordinary circumstances at the request of one-fifth of the citizenry.[97] Even though Article 10 of the 1793 constitution declared that the sovereign people 'deliberate about the laws', primary assemblies' main function, as noted earlier, was that of ratifying or rejecting particular proposals.[98] Primary assemblies also played an important role in the context of constitutional change. In particular, the constitution authorized the convocation of a National Convention by primary assemblies if, in a majority of departments, 10 per cent of the primary assemblies requested it.[99] The National Convention could be given the authority to alter particular articles of the constitution or 'revising the constitutional text'.[100]

In exercising that authority, a Convention could adopt an entirely new constitution, even though its power could be limited beforehand.[101] Although the constitutional text did not explicitly state it, it would seem natural that a newly proposed constitution would also be subject to popular ratification through primary assemblies before coming into effect[102]. Indeed, the Constitution of 1793 was ratified in a referendum: after the draft document was approved by the National Convention, it was sent to all the primary assemblies for a 'yes' or 'no' vote.[103] This approach to constitutional reform was radically different from the one found in the French constitutions of 1791 and 1795. There, the exercise of the power to create an entirely new constitution was left unregulated by law and the power of constitutional reform was, by and large, left in the hands of the ordinary institutions of government. In a relatively short period of time this radical democratic approach was abandoned. The priority became to ensure that the National Convention was able to act in accordance with the

[97] ibid. Articles 31, 34. It is unclear how the 'one-fifth of the citizenry' requirement would work in practice.

[98] Pierre Guyomar, however, saw primary assemblies as 'essentially deliberative' entities where the people exercised their sovereignty and which could subject deputies to binding instructions. Pierre Guyomar, *Le Partisan de L'égalité Politique entre les Individus, ou Problème Très-Important de Légalité en Droits etde L'inégalité en Fait* (1793) 14–15, 16.

[99] Constitution of 1793, Article 115. See also Article 28 of the Declaration of the Rights of Man and the Citizen of 1793, included in the Constitution's preamble: 'A people has always the right to revise, reform, and change its constitution. No generation can subject the future generations to its laws.'

[100] ibid.

[101] Article 117 of the Constitution of 1793 established that the National Convention could also deliberate only on the topics for which it was convened.

[102] Indeed, in a decree of 21 September 1792, the National Convention expressed that 'qu'il ne peut y avoir de Constitution que celle qui est acceptée par le peuple' The Constitution of 1795, also drafted by the National Convention, was adopted after popular ratification.

[103] Doyle (n. 13) 244. The primary assemblies favoured it 1,801,918 to 11,610 votes. According to Melvin Edelstein, primary assemblies could deliberate about the constitution and propose revisions, even though only a few hundred assemblies did. Primary assemblies were also supposed to send the minutes of their ratification meeting to the convention. Some primary assemblies decided to vote through secret ballot, others voted orally. Melvin Edelstein, *The French Revolution and the Birth of Electoral Democracy* (Ashgate, 2014) 294–296.

true interests of the people, and that involved the identification and expulsion of all those suspected of having counter-revolutionary views.[104] A sovereign National Convention, acting through its various committees, began to see itself as the people in action and those initial spaces of direct democratic participation were neutralized.[105]

The Girondin Draft Constitution (which had Nicolas de Condorcet as its main author) shared, and in a number of ways improved, some of the features of the Constitution of 1793. Condorcet was interested in finding a way of facilitating the actual participation of the people in law-making (constitution-making included), while retaining the principle of representation.[106] In his proposed constitution, primary assemblies were key to achieving that goal. For Condorcet, primary assemblies should be permanent forums for citizen discussion: their function was not to be limited to voting, they were to be sites of popular deliberation, a term he used in a very technical way.[107] Like the Constitution of 1793, the Girondin Draft Constitution attributed primary assemblies with the faculty of calling a National Convention and it also contained a provision for its periodic convocation.[108] The calling of a convention would take place through a detailed (and complex) system, in which a primary assembly would decide whether to deliberate on a citizen petition to convene

[104] See Ramón Máiz, 'Las Teorías de la Democracia en la Revolución Francesa', 6/7 *Política y Sociedad* 65, 72 (1990)

[105] See Claude Lefort, 'La Terreur Révolutionnarie' in *Essais sur le Politique* (Paris, 1986).

[106] See Máiz (n. 104) 79.

[107] Even though it is sometimes argued (e.g., see Richard Tuck, *The Sleeping Sovereign: The Invention of Modern Democracy* (Cambridge University Press, 2016) 153) that Girondins like Condorcet and Pétion rejected the notion of attributing primary assemblies with a deliberative role (limiting them to simply voting 'yes' or 'no' on particular proposals), this is not entirely the case. Condorcet, who addressed this issue directly, maintained that to be properly conducted, deliberation had to take place in a 'single assembly'. Marquis de Condorcet, 'On Consulting the People's Will via Referendum' and 'Dangers and Benefits of Consulting Assemblies of the People' in Baker, *The French Revolution* (n. 76) 239. But by 'deliberation', Condorcet had something very specific in mind: deliberation was the process through which a discussion about a particular issue was 'reduced to a certain number of more simple questions, clearly posed, on which it is possible [to vote "yes" or "no"]'. Such a process could not take place in primary assemblies (as different assemblies would come up with different sets of questions), but those entities could of course be the ones issuing the final 'yes' or 'no' vote. This is why Condorcet wrote that since primary assemblies are 'never convoked except to pronounce on questions already set, no discussion should be authorized in them'. ibid. 241. He nevertheless added: 'The citizens who compose them can, to be sure, freely discuss in the meeting place of the assembly, during the interval between the proposing of a question and the decision, the subjects that are submitted for their judgment; but at such time the officers of the assembly exercise no function'. ibid. Primary assemblies could thus be sites for 'deliberation', but in an informal way, and not for the purposes for which Condorcet reserved the term.

[108] *Plan de Constitution présenté à la Convention nationale les 15 et 16 février 1793, l'an II de la République* (Section IX). For a discussion, see Nadia Urbinati, 'Condorcet's Democratic Theory of Representative Government', 3(1) *European Journal of Political Theory* 53–75 (2004). Thomas Paine, who appears as one of the signatories of the draft constitution (even though he publicly expressed his general disagreement with its content) had views similar to Rousseau (and Jefferson) about the periodic reconstitution of the state. Thomas Paine, 'The Rights of Man' in *The Life and Major Writings of Thomas Paine* (Philip Foner ed.) (New York, Citadel, 1961) 251.

such an entity.[109] If the primary assembly decided to support the petition, it would trigger a process that could end in the convocation of all primary assemblies and in the calling of a National Convention.

Even though it never became law, the Girondin Constitutional Project provides some important clues as to the potential role of primary assemblies in the exercise of constituent power and represents a Rousseauian alternative to Sieyès' project.[110] From the perspective of Rousseau, a system of primary assemblies similar to the one conceived by the Montagnards and the Girondins would be a necessary component of a legitimate constitution of a modern state. For him, the attribution of constitution-making power to the people came accompanied by the legal possibility of its periodic exercise. Under his approach, the relationship between constituent power and the law is not one characterized by a difficult co-existence of the legal and the extra-legal: constituent power is exercised according to law and at the same time it is the condition of its legitimacy. But to the extent that constituent power is presented as a juridical faculty exercisable by a number of primary assemblies organized and activated according to established legal procedures, it seems to be deprived of part of its revolutionary potential.

This is why, at least initially, Sieyès' approach may appear more radical: the nation remains free to exercise its constituent power and to give itself an entirely new fundamental law at any time and through any procedure it considers convenient: 'The constituent power is supreme in this respect. It is not limited in advance to any specific constitution.'[111] No procedurally regulated primary assemblies, no constituted process of constitutional reform, could be taken for Sieyès as the personification of the constituent power, a view that some of his followers took to the extreme in the 19th century, as will be seen in Chapter 6. However, this approach means that the possibility of radical constitutional change would always involve a break in legal continuity. And, since in the event of a revolution, constituent power would be exercised by a representative assembly unbound by citizen instructions, such an exercise could be disconnected from the will of significant parts of the population. During a period of revolution, Sieyès' means of avoiding attributing constituent power to primary

[109] The petition needed to be signed by fifty other citizens living in the same district. *Plan de Constitution* (n. 108), Sections IX and VIII.

[110] Sieyès was a member of the committee that prepared and signed the Girondin Draft Constitution (which does not indicate his approval of the proposal). The Girondin Constitution did not require popular ratification of proposed laws. In practice, however, to the extent that under the Constitution of 1793 primary assemblies would be taken to have consented to a law unless the requisite number objected, their role in law-making would likely have been a very limited one.

[111] Emmanuel Sieyès, 'Reasoned Exposition of the Rights of Man and Citizen' (n. 2) 127.

assemblies was the notion of the 'commissioning power' (*pouvoir commettant*), that is to say, the community's right to elect representatives who would exercise constituent power on their behalf.[112]

Instead of making decisions and proposals, one of the most important functions of Sieyès' primary assemblies was to decide which active citizens were *eligibles*, that is, which were capable of sitting in assemblies higher in the hierarchy (e.g. communal, provincial, national levels).[113] Eligible active citizens, for Sieyès, were those who could be deposited with the public trust.[114] In the context of constitutional change, the consequence of this approach is that while all active citizens could vote—that is, they could exercise the *pouvoir commettant*—only a handful would be considered competent to directly engage in constituent activity. The exercise of constituent power, in short, did not require the direct participation of the community in the making of decisions about the content of the constitution. The fact that Rousseau did not explicitly distinguish between simple voters and 'eligibles' is instructive, not because it shows that he had a more inclusive idea of citizenship than Sieyès (which is debatable),[115] but because in his system, the role of an assembly of citizens was to express the general will. For Sieyès, primary assemblies were mainly called to elect those capable of speaking *on behalf* of the nation. Once a primary assembly commissioned a number of citizens with political power, each of them became a representative of *all* the primary assemblies and their decisions would count as manifestations of the national will.[116]

112 See Sieyès, 'Exposition Raisonnée' (n. 7) 36.

113 The second function was to elect those who could sit at the next level assembly. For a discussion, see Malcolm Crook, *Elections in the French Revolution: An Apprenticeship in Democracy, 1789-1799* (Cambridge University Press, 1996) 35–37.

114 In 1791, the *Comité de Constitution* divided active citizens into three categories (determined by the amount of taxes they paid): those who could vote, those who were also eligible for municipal office and departmental electoral colleges, and those who could sit in the national assembly. ibid. at 36. These qualifications, particularly those applicable to primary assemblies, were strongly criticized by Edmund Burke: 'What! A qualification on the indefeasible rights of men? Yes; but it shall be a very small qualification. Our injustice shall be very little oppressive; only the local valuation of three days labour paid to the public.' Burke (n. 63) 287–288. The distinction between active and passive citizens was present in some 19th-century constitutions. For example, Article 7 of the Constitution of Chile (1833) stated: 'Active citizens are those Chileans with the right to vote, who are 21 years or older, who can read and write, and who are enrolled in the electoral roll of their department.' Article 8 of that Constitution established the reason why someone could lose their condition of active citizenship (e.g. persons convicted of certain crimes, bankruptcy, being employed by foreign governments without Congressional authorization).

115 For an interesting take on this issue, see Catherine Larrère, 'Jean-Jacques Rousseau on Women and Citizenship', 37(2) *History of European Ideas* 218 (2011).

116 Sieyès took that idea so seriously that he argued that once a citizen was elected to an upper level assembly, he could not be recalled by those who elected him: at the moment of the election, he became a representative of all and could thus only be recalled by the entire community. Sieyès, 'Informe del Comité de Constitución' (n. 72) 228–229.

IV. Conclusion

This chapter examined some of the main legal and institutional implications of constituent power as understood in the constitutional debates that took place during the first stages of the French Revolution. It first considered the differences between Sieyès' and Rousseau's views about the types of mechanisms that should be deployed for the exercise of constituent power, that is, for the alteration of the constitutional regime. Rousseau defended the institution of periodic constituent assemblies, and Sieyès insisted in the desirability of piecemeal constitutional change and stressed the undesirability of constitutional remaking. Importantly, while for Rousseau constituent power was to be exercised through law (i.e. the law should authorize its periodic exercise), for Sieyès constituent power operated in an extra-legal terrain that would be left behind once a constitutional order is established. The chapter also examined the role of primary assemblies and the imperative mandate both in the work of these two thinkers as well as in the constitutional and political practice of the French Revolution. These two institutions were directly connected to the exercise of constituent power: they were two of the means through which the members of a large society could directly participate in the exercise of constituent power and control the decisions of the individuals sitting in a constitution-making body.

The virtual disappearance of these institutions changed the types of political practices that were understood to count as constituent activity and the kinds of demands that the concept of constituent power was thought to place upon a legal system that seeks to facilitate its future exercise. The abolition of the imperative mandate also came accompanied by a change in the identity of the constituent subject. This is best exemplified in several constitution-making episodes that took place during the 19th century in Europe and Latin America. As we will see in the next chapter, in these moments of constitutional creation, the Sieyesian attribution of constituent power to the nation, to a moral entity separate from the individuals who comprised it, assumed a central role. Rousseau's conception of popular sovereignty was generally supported at a rhetorical level but rejected in actual constitutional practice. Not surprisingly, these constitution-making processes were characterized by the early rejection of the imperative mandate and the exclusion of great majorities of the population from constituent activity, as well as by the establishment of electoral systems and institutional mechanisms designed to promote the discovery of the national will. These institutional choices, we will see, were often driven by the relevant political actors' understanding of the theory of constituent power.

5
Of Constituent Nations

This chapter examines the ways in which the debates about the nature and implications of the theory of constituent power that arose during the French Revolution reappeared in later constituent episodes. It pays particular attention to the electoral rules present in three constitution-making processes and in the types of constitutional forms that resulted from them. Those rules and institutions reflect a particular understanding of constituent power. They were adopted in constitution-making episodes characterized by a clear movement in favour of Emmanuel Sieyès' theory of constituent power (and of his conception of representation, rejection of the imperative mandate, and attribution of only the *pouvoir commettant* to primary assemblies), to the detriment of the alternative Rousseauian approach. During the discussions that took place in the different constituent bodies examined below, the tension between those approaches is reflected in interesting ways. And not surprisingly, the concept of constituent power assumed a central role in the justification of certain institutional arrangements. I will examine three constitution-making processes in the Spanish speaking world: those that led to the creation of the Constitution of Spain in 1812, the Venezuelan Constitution of 1811, and the Colombian Constitution of 1886. I will proceed as follows.

In Part I, I explore the distinction between the constituent power of the people and the constituent power of the nation. These notions have been associated with the thought of Jean Jacques Rousseau and Sieyès, respectively. The distinction between them was present during the French Revolution, but it assumed an even more explicit role during 19th-century constitutional theory. From each of these notions, different types of legal and institutional demands on the juridical order emanate. After distinguishing them, I will examine, in Part II, the ways in which they were (or not) put into practice in the constitution-making process that resulted in the creation of the Spanish Constitution of 1812. This process was a direct consequence of Napoleon's invasion of Spain in 1808 and was characterized by the embracement of the idea of the constituent power of the nation. Part III focuses on the creation of the Venezuelan Constitution of 1811, a process that was triggered by the events in Spain. Like the 1812 Spanish constituent process, the creation of the

Constituent Power and the Law. Joel Colón-Ríos, Oxford University Press (2020). © Joel Colón-Ríos.
DOI: 10.1093/oso/9780198785989.001.0001

Venezuelan Constitution of 1811 exemplifies some of the main legal and institutional implications of the idea of the constituent power of the nation. In both these processes, the nation was largely conceived as an entity with a will of its own, and what mattered was to create institutions that facilitated the identification of that will.

Finally, Part IV of the chapter examines the process that led to the adoption of the Colombian Constitution of 1886. Although taking place much later than the previously mentioned ones, it was also characterized by the adoption of the institutions associated with the constituent power of the nation. At the same time, it exhibited some unique features, such as an extraordinary body, the Council of Delegates which, in a way reminiscent of contemporary notions of post-sovereign constitution-making, was never attributed with the full power to adopt a constitution. This entity, it will be seen, was bound to draft a constitution consistent with the principles contained in a document ratified by the municipalities and which, according to some, expressed the will of the nation. The Council was comprised of delegates not bound by the instructions of their constituents, but the Council itself, it was argued, acted on an imperative mandate from the constituent nation which carried with it a number of limits in terms of the kind of constitution that could be adopted. During these three processes, constituent power became an extraordinary constitution-making jurisdiction directed at the identification of the common good, one that could be exercised through mechanisms that excluded important parts of the population.

I. Farewell to the Sovereign People?

Sieyès, as noted in the previous chapter, defined the nation as 'a body of associates living under a common law, represented by the same legislature'.[1] The nation, he maintained, was to be found in 'all the inhabitants' of the territory.[2] But that did not mean that all the human beings subject to the same constitutional system should necessarily become part of the entity called to exercise the nation's constituent power. Even though he wrote that the terms nation and people 'ought to be synonymous', Sieyès was very clear that, even if the nation can potentially (and ideally) include every person inhabiting in a particular territory, it must exclude those who did not contribute to the 'public

[1] Emmanuel Sieyès, 'What is the Third Estate' in *Political Writings: Including the Debate between Sieyès and Tom Paine in 1791* (Michael Sonenscher ed.) (Indianapolis: Hackett Publishing Company, 2003) 97.

[2] ibid. 140.

establishment'.[3] The main example is what Sieyès called the 'caste of nobles', a privileged and unproductive class—a class which he described as 'foreign to the nation'.[4] But Sieyès also thought that in every society there are individuals 'whom infirmity, incapacity, incurable laziness, or the tide of moral dissolution have made strangers to all the activities involved in society'.[5] He thus contended that only the representatives of the Third Estate, that is, those who represented the productive classes of society (and who met a number of requisites such as owning certain amounts of property), could be seen as 'true custodians of the national will'.

'They alone', he wrote, 'can speak in the name of the whole Nation without error'.[6] When assembled, these representatives would have the task of identifying a national will separate from that of the individuals who lived in the relevant territory, a sort of 'objective' will possibly contrary to the subjective preferences of the great masses of society. The electoral systems used in the constitution-making processes that will be described in Parts II to IV of this chapter were highly consistent with that approach. These systems had primary assemblies at the bottom, but their main role was to facilitate the election of those best placed to identify the will of the nation, as opposed to that of channelling popular preferences. This conception reflects what I will call the *principle of exclusion*. This principle expresses the notion that not everyone who will become subject to a constitution should necessarily be allowed to participate in its creation. All constituent episodes are to different degrees consistent with this principle: numerous groups (non-propertied individuals, women, non-citizens, indigenous peoples, minors, etc.) have been formally (e.g. through the negation of rights of political participation) or informally (e.g. through social marginalization) prevented from taking part in the exercise of constituent power.

This approach is also consistent with what can be identified as the *principle of representation*, the idea that constituent power can be exercised by representatives and that direct popular intervention is not necessary for the emergence of a legitimate constitution. Under this view, it is the *nation*, understood as a moral entity that has a will of its own, which is attributed with sovereignty or with constituent power (terms which, as we will see in Chapter 6, were often used interchangeably by 19th-century authors but that, as I will argue in

[3] ibid.

[4] ibid.; *Préliminaires de la Constitution* in *Écrits Politiques* (Roberto Zapperi ed.) (Paris 1985) 200. See also 'An Essay on Privileges' in Emmanuel Sieyès, *The Essential Political Writings* (Leiden, 2014).

[5] Sieyès, 'Third Estate' (n. 1) 97.

[6] ibid. 150.

Chapter 9, should be distinguished from each other). The citizenry at large, as in Sieyès, does not exercise the constituent power but the *pouvoir commettant*, the legally regulated function of electing those equipped with the necessary qualities to create a constitution that promotes the common good. There is a second, less dominant, but increasingly influential approach. Constituent power, under this view, must be exercised by the entire citizenry. Here, the emphasis is on finding a means for allowing individuals to become authors of their constitution. Accordingly, this second approach requires institutions that are seen as providing significant opportunities for public participation, such as referendums, popular initiatives, and extra-parliamentary constitution-making bodies. It can be generally described as the 'constituent power of the people' approach.

The people, in this context, is a juridical construct: it refers to all the citizens with political rights living in a particular jurisdiction. To find 'the will of the constituent people' means, in some way, to allow citizens to express their constitutional preferences. Inevitably, this second approach relies in an important sense on the principle of majority rule: all individuals are part of the sovereign power, and when there is no unanimity among them, the majority (or what Thomas Hobbes called 'the major part', and Marsilius of Padua the 'prevailing part')[7] has the right to issue a sovereign decision. Historically, this view has been associated with Rousseau. As we saw in Chapter 2, Rousseau thought that sovereignty was shared among individual citizens, each of them being part of a collective sovereign: 'Suppose the State is composed of ten thousand citizens . . . the Sovereign is to the subject as ten thousand to one, i.e. each member of the State has as his share only a ten-thousandth part of the sovereign authority, although he is wholly under its control.'[8] Since Rousseau believed that the sovereign power shared by those individuals could not be represented, the most an elected assembly could legitimately do was to present proposals to the popular constituent subject.

Only citizens themselves, and never a representative body, could be trusted to adopt a body of law, a phrase which, as we saw in Chapter 2, was used by Rousseau to refer to the most fundamental norms of a legal system. Moreover, since the members of the assembly are not true representatives, Rousseau thought that they should be bound by the instructions of their electors: just as each individual has a share of the sovereign power, a group of individuals

[7] Thomas Hobbes, *Leviathan* (Penguin Classics, 1985) 231; Marsilius of Padua, *The Defender of Peace* (Cambridge University Press, 2005) 68.

[8] Jean-Jacques Rousseau, *The Social Contract* (London: Everyman's Library, 1973) 229.

that elects a member of a legislative body has enough sovereignty to require that member to act in particular ways.[9] The constituent power of the people approach, in this respect, negates the principle of representation and operates under what we may call the *principle of participation*.[10] It requires a constant search for new channels of direct citizen action and, at a minimum, mandates that the entering into force of any constitution is subject to popular ratification. While the constituent power of the people approach may operate under a restrictive conception of the citizenry,[11] the principle of participation tends to push it towards high degrees of political inclusion.

Raymond Carré de Malberg provided a useful account of the distinction between these notions through an analysis of French constitutional history. In 1789, he maintained, the French Constituent Assembly rejected the idea of monarchical sovereignty: from then on, the king could only exercise power in the name of the sovereign nation.[12] This did not mean, however, that the assembly was attributing a fraction of the sovereign power to each individual with political rights.[13] Such an approach, as noted earlier, was the one defended by Rousseau, who would give citizens the original right 'to impose their discretionary will when they are a majority'.[14] For Carré de Malberg, this meant that Rousseau would have had the sovereignty that once belonged to the king simply transferred to the citizenry.[15] But the Constituent Assembly's embracement of the idea of *national* sovereignty, thus moving away from the Rousseauian system: the assembly plainly rejected the view that sovereignty could belong to an individual (i.e. a king) or to a particular group of individuals (i.e. a popular majority).[16] This was clearly exemplified in Title III of the Constitution of 1791, according to which the source of sovereignty was placed in an abstract collectivity called 'the nation', and its exercise was denied to any 'section of the people [or] individual'.[17]

[9] ibid.

[10] For further discussion of this principle, see Joel Colón-Ríos, *Weak Constitutionalism: Democratic Legitimacy and the Question of Constituent Power* (Routledge, 2012).

[11] In fact, Rousseau was not an advocate of universal suffrage (see Rosenfeld 1987). In the context of the National Convention of 1793, Maximilien Robespierre seemed to exclude certain groups from his definition of 'the people'. See Alfred Cobban, 'The Political Ideas of Maximilien Robespierre during the Period of the Convention', 61 *English Historical Review* 45–80 (1946).

[12] Raymond Carré de Malberg, *Teoría General del Estado* (México: Fondo de Cultura Económica, 1948) s 330.

[13] ibid. s 331.

[14] ibid.

[15] ibid.

[16] ibid.

[17] It was also reflected in Article 3 of the French Declaration of the Rights of Man and the Citizen of 1789: 'The source [*principe*] of all sovereignty resides essentially in the nation. No body nor individual may exercise any authority which does not proceed directly from the nation.' In an entry

II. The Constituent Nation in Action

The constituent process that took place in early 19th century Spain was naturally influenced by the French Revolution.[18] It exemplifies the practical implications of the distinction examined above and sets the stage for the discussions that grasped the attention of constitutional theorists for a good part of the 19th century. The embracement of the theory of constituent power in early 19th-century Spain was highly controversial. It was subject to strong challenges, particularly those based on the ideas of Gaspar Melchor de Jovellanos, who negated the very idea that a constitution could be *created*. Under this approach, which will be discussed in Chapter 7, a constitution is the result of history and tradition, and can only emerge through time. In this chapter, I will instead focus on the ways in which the theory of constituent power, the idea that there is someone with the power to create new constitutional orders, was put into practice in these events. This process provides interesting examples of the legal and institutional implications of the idea of the constituent power of the nation. For example, it highlights the fact that once 'the nation' is identified as the constituent subject, electoral systems based on a limited franchise appear as an acceptable option. At the same time, by seeing themselves as the depositaries of national sovereignty, constitution-making bodies become all powerful entities but, at least in theory, entities capable of creating limited governments. The analysis will focus on the debates at the assembly's sessions and emphasize the ways delegates deployed the concept of constituent power to justify or denounce certain courses of action.

in his journal, Adrien Duquesnoy, deputy for the Third Estate, maintained: 'Article 3 provides that the source of all sovereignty resides in the nation. That is not correct. It should have said: "All sovereignty resides in the nation". Indeed, it is clear that if the nation possesses only the source of sovereignty, then there is a sovereignty that is not the nation's and that only emanates from its sovereignty, which is both dangerous and false'. Perhaps more tellingly, during the debate around the royal veto, Jean Joseph Mounier noted: 'I know that the source of sovereignty resides in the nation. But to be the source of sovereignty and to exercise sovereignty are very different things.' Keith M. Baker, 'Constitution' in *The French Revolution: Recent Debates and New Controversies* (Gary Kates ed.), 2nd ed. (New York: Routledge, 2006) 74, 76. It is also present in Title III of the French Constitution of 1791: 'The nation, from which alone all powers emanate, may exercise such powers only by delegation. The French Constitution is representative; the representatives are the legislative body and the King.'

[18] The discussion of the process that led to the creation of the Constitution of Cadiz contained here is partly based on Joel Colón-Ríos, 'Constituent Power, Primary Assemblies, and the Imperative Mandate' in *Handbook on Comparative Constitution-Making* (David Landau and Hannah Lerner eds). (Edward Elgar, *forthcoming*).

a. Assembling the Constituent Nation in Spain

The creation of the Spanish Constitution of 1812 was one of the main unintended consequences of the French invasion of Spain in 1808. By that time, Napoleon had been appointed First Consul for life and crowned as emperor, asserting his right to govern as emerging from the people and not, or at least not directly, from God.[19] The French invasion allowed Joseph Bonaparte, Napoleon's brother, to assume control of the Spanish Crown, giving Spain its first written constitution, the *Estatuto de Bayona*. Bonaparte's regime was widely seen as illegitimate throughout Spanish territory. Bonaparte, defenders of the traditional monarchy insisted, may temporarily be the *de facto* sovereign, but never the *de jure* one: it was in Fernando VII, forced to abdicate by the invading army in 1808, in whom God had vested the right of sovereignty. Resistance against the French occupation of Spain initially took place through the *Juntas Supremas Provinciales* (a group of regional assemblies later renamed as *Juntas Superiores Provinciales de Observación y de Defensa*),[20] which filled the power vacuum that resulted from the displacement of ordinary authorities.[21]

In September 1803, these assemblies agreed to establish a central organ, the *Junta Suprema Central*.[22] Since they claimed to be sovereign, the *Juntas* did not see themselves subject to an imperative mandate, but claimed that the *Junta Suprema Central* would be subject to their instructions.[23] In 1809, the *Junta Suprema Central* convened the *Cortes Generales y Extraordinarias* (most commonly known as the *Cortes Constituyentes* or the Constituent Courts;[24] to avoid confusion, from now on I will call this entity the Constituent Parliament).[25] According to the Constituent Parliament's main regulation (the 'Instruction'), their task was not to create an entirely new constitutional order but to 're-establish and improve a constitution worthy of the Spanish Nation'. Those objectives, the document

[19] This conception was symbolically expressed in his decision to depart from the tradition of being physically crowned by the Pope, crowning himself instead. For a discussion, see Philip Sawyer, '"Citizen Emperor": Political Ritual, Popular Sovereignty and the Coronation of Napoleon I', 100 *History: The Journal of the Historical Association* 40 (2015).

[20] See José Ignacio Cebreiro Núñez, *La Administración Peiférica Provincial: Orígenes y Evolución al Final del Antiguo Régimen* (INAP, 2017).

[21] Quintí Casals Bergés, 'El Proceso Electoral en España y Cataluña según la Constitución de 1812', 1(1) *Rúbrica Contemporánea* 5 (2012) 5.

[22] For a discussion, see Antonio Torres del Moral, 'La Soberanía Nacional en la Constitución de Cádiz', 82 *Revista de Derecho Político* 55 (2011) 88.

[23] ibid. 89. In practice, however, they gave deputies very general instructions and authorized them to act according to their conscience. ibid. 88–89.

[24] The Spanish Parliament has been historically called *Las Cortes Generales*, that is to say, *the General Courts*. In this and other chapters, I will translate *cortes* as parliament when referring to this entity.

[25] Royal Decree (22 May 1809).

stated, could not be achieved if the particular interests of individuals were given more weight than the 'general interest' of the nation. This type of view led the *Junta Suprema Central* to develop an electoral system in which, as in Sieyès' conception, 'talentless or less than apt' individuals would be excluded.[26] Similar to the French *Règlement*, discussed in the previous chapter, the Instruction established that deputies would be selected through a system which had *asambleas parroquiales* (primary assemblies) at the bottom, and by lot.[27]

Primary assemblies could be attended by men of 25 years of age or more who had a known trade or way of sustaining themselves.[28] Criminals, debtors, 'lunatics', and the deaf-mute were excluded.[29] The electoral process had strong religious components which, at least in theory, were directed at ensuring that the best individuals would be chosen. For example, the election of deputies would take place after a mass where the priest would 'strongly encourage the people', after reminding them of 'the horrors of the unjust war unjustly imposed by the French tyrant', to vote with 'maturity and judgment'.[30] After mass, citizens would stand in line and say out loud the name of the individual they wanted to become an elector at the next level assembly (*Junta de Partido*).[31] The names of the twelve individuals who received the most votes would be read aloud, they would meet and, after a period of deliberation, select the citizen who would represent the entire *asamblea parroquial*. The elected person would march from the assembly to the church, standing between the priest and the mayor. A similar process would be followed in the *Junta de Partido*. At the next level (*Juntas de Provincia*), where most of the deputies[32] to the Constituent

[26] 'Preamble', *Instrucción que Deberá Observarse para la Elección de Diputados de Cortes* (1 January 1810).

[27] Quintí Casals Bergés, 'Proceso Electoral y Prosopografía de los Diputados de las Cortes Extraordinarias de Cádiz (1810-1813)' (2012) 13 *Historia Constitucional* 193, 202; Pilar Chavarri Sidera, *Las Elecciones de Diputados a las Cortes Generales y Extraordinarias (1810-1813)* (Centro de Estudios Constitucionales, Madrid, 1988) 10.

[28] *Instrucción* (n. 26) Chapter II, Articles 2 and 3.

[29] Additional requirements were put in place for upper level assemblies. Casals Bergés, 'Proceso Electoral y Prosopografía' (n. 27) 202. See also Antonio Torres del Moral, 'La Soberanía Nacional en la Constitución de Cádiz', 82 *Revista de Derecho Político* 55 (2011) 96.

[30] *Instrucción* (n. 26) Chapter II, Article 9. This was also the case during the first elections during the French Revolution. See Melvin Edelstein, *The French Revolution and the Birth of Electoral Democracy* (Ashgate, 2014) 13, 247, 256.

[31] *Instrucción* (n. 26) Chapter II, Article 13.

[32] Some deputies were to be elected by the *Juntas Superiores de Obvervación y de Defensa* of those cities with representation in the Parliament of 1789 (which had been abruptly cancelled once it became known that the French Estates General had been transformed into a constituent assembly), and by overseas territories. For a discussion, see Casals Bergés, 'Proceso Electoral y Propopografía' (n. 29) 209–215. Given the practical difficulties resulting from the French occupation, the electoral rules were flexibly applied in order to facilitate the formal recognition of deputies. Miguel Pino Abad 'El Consejo de Regencia y su Papel en la Convocatoria de las Cortes de Cadiz' in José Antonio Escudero (ed.) *Cortes y Constitución de Cádiz 200 años* (Espasa, Madrid, 2011) 193; Chavarri Sidera (n. 27) 22.

Parliament would be elected, a new element was added: the final deputy would be elected by drawing a name from a recipient containing the names of the three individuals who had received the highest number of votes.[33]

The Constituent Parliament first met on 24 September 1810 with 104 deputies (including 47 alternate members) from the entire Spanish territory, including the overseas empire.[34] That same day, they proclaimed themselves the depositories of national sovereignty, stating that Fernando VII's abdication was void not only because it was not freely made, but because it had been made without the nation's consent.[35] This not only involved a direct rejection of the notion of monarchical sovereignty and an indirect one of the division of society in different Estates, but also the abolition of the imperative mandate. As Pilar Chavarri Sideri has noted, if the Constituent Parliament represented the nation, it had to be seen as speaking on behalf of the whole.[36] Indeed, deputies had been elected precisely because they had qualities that were seen as necessary for the identification of the national will. Nonetheless, some deputies still considered themselves as representing not the nation but their province, and insisted in acting consistently with their instructions, but this was not a view supported by the majority of those present at the Constituent Parliament.[37] Moreover, as depositaries of national sovereignty, the Constituent Parliament felt entitled to go beyond the creation of a constitution and engage in the adoption of ordinary laws and other governmental acts, even acts of a judicial nature.[38] A constituent entity, they thought, could act *as if* it was the sovereign nation.[39]

[33] *Instrucción* (n. 26) Chapter IV, Articles 11 and 12.

[34] María Valentina Gómez Mampaso, 'La Convocatoria de las Cortes y los Diputados Presentes en la Sesión de Apertura el 24 de septiembre de 1810' in *Cortes y Constitución de Cádiz 200 años* (José Antonio Escudero ed.) (Espasa: Madrid, 2011) 204.

[35] Decree of 24 September 1810, *Cortes Generales y Extraordinarias*. For a discussion, see José Antonio Escudero 'Introducción. Las Cortes de Cádiz: Génesis, Constitución y Reformas' in *Cortes y Constitución de Cádiz 200 años* (José Antonio Escudero ed) (Espasa: Madrid, 2011) XXXII. See also Agustín de Argüelles, *Discurso Preliminar a la Constitución de 1812* (24 December 1811) (Centro de Estudios Políticos y Constitucionales, 2011) 79.

[36] Chavarri Sidera (n. 27) 29.

[37] For a discussion, see Gómez Mampaso (n. 34); Chavarri Sidera (n. 27) 29. For the role of the imperative mandate in Cádiz, see Quintí Casals Bergés, 'Los Diputados Catalanes en las Cortes de Cádiz (1810-1813): Proceso Electoral y Prosopografía)', 31 *Manuscrits* 205 (2014) 225.

[38] Joaquín Varela Suanzes-Carpegna, 'Las Cortes de Cádiz y la Constitución de 1812 (Una Visión de Conjunto)', 26 *Corts: Anuario de Derecho Parlamentario* 191 (2012) 196.

[39] The current Constitution of Spain (1978) attempts to combine the principles of national and popular sovereignty in its Article 1(2): 'National sovereignty resides in the Spanish people, from whom the powers of the State emanate' (*La soberanía nacional reside en el pueblo español, del que emanan los poderes del Estado*). Similar provisions exist in the French Constitution of 1793 and in the Girondin Draft Constitution. See also Article 5 of the Chilean Constitution (1980) which states: 'Sovereignty resides essentially in the Nation. The people exercise it through the plebiscite and through periodic elections and, also, by the authorities established by this Constitution. Neither a section of the people nor any individual may attribute themselves with their exercise.' Article 2 of the Constitution of Spain

b. Limiting the Amending Power in Cadiz

Naturally, this approach was reflected in the resulting constitution. The constitution implicitly recognized the nation's constituent power in Article 3: 'Sovereignty resides essentially in the Nation, and for that reason, it has the exclusive right to adopt its fundamental laws.'[40] It also stated that the representatives sitting in the ordinary legislature would be attributed with 'wide powers' to 'agree and decide on anything that they understand promotes the general interest.'[41] The constitution's amending procedure was regulated by Articles 373 to 382. Not surprisingly (as in the French Constitution of 1791), the monarch's participation in the process was limited: constituent power rested in the nation, and the only thing a monarch could do in the context of a constitutional amendment was to make the relevant change public.[42] The exercise of the power to reform the constitution required the convocation of a legislature whose deputies were attributed with special powers.[43] An amendment proposal needed to be supported by at least twenty deputies, and read three times (with six days in between) before it could be discussed.[44] It then needed to be approved by a two-thirds majority.[45] Once approved, the next legislature, again by a two-thirds majority, would determine if a new legislature would be convened.[46] In such a case, and in an interesting application of the imperative mandate, Article 382 stated that the provincial electoral *Juntas* would arm the elected deputies with 'a special power to make the following revision to the constitution in accordance with the decree of the Parliament: . . . '[47]

also contains an important reference to the Spanish Nation, which has become particularly relevant in the context of the Catalonian secession debate and discussions about the location of the constituent power. For example, in a case examining the constitutionality of a resolution of the Catalonian parliament proclaiming 'the opening of a citizen-led, participative, open, inclusive, and active constituent process to lay the foundations for the future Catalan constitution', the Constitutional Tribunal stated that such a document 'display[ed] an ignorance and a violation of the constitutional provisions which vest national sovereignty in the Spanish people and which, accordingly, proclaim the unity of the Spanish nation, the holder of this sovereignty . . .' and that 'the citizens of Catalonia cannot be confused with the sovereign people, conceived as the ideal unit to which constituent power can be allocated and, as such, the source of the Constitution and the legal system'. Judgment No. 259/2015, Spanish Constitutional Tribunal, Part II, paras 6, 3.

[40] Constitution of 1812, Article 3.
[41] ibid. Articles 3 and 100. As will be seen below, one interesting exception is Article 382 of the Constitution of 1812.
[42] ibid. Article 384. As opposed to having to a right to the suspensive veto as the one recognized by Articles 144, 147–149 with respect to ordinary legislation.
[43] ibid. Article 376.
[44] ibid. Articles 378–379.
[45] ibid. Article 379.
[46] ibid. Articles 380–382.
[47] ibid. Article 382.

During the debates at the Constituent Parliament, it was not that process, but the prohibition contained in Article 375, which gave rise to one of the most interesting discussions about the nature of the assembly's constituent power. That article prohibited any revisions of the constitutional text within the first eight years of the document's coming into effect. Some deputies, like Ramón Lázaro de Dou, from Catalonia, rejected that limit since, for him, there was no real difference between the assembly that was drafting the constitution and the one that would be convened under it. Accordingly, how could one attribute to future legislative assemblies a lesser power than the one being now exercised?[48] José Miguel Guridi y Alcocer, deputy from Mexico, largely agreed. For him, Article 375 would be justified 'if the Constitution were to be sanctioned by an authority superior to that of the Parliament', but that was not the case. In the same way that 'the current Parliament is Constituent, the next ones will be Revisionist . . . the Nation can restrict the power of future parliaments . . . here it is not the Nation, but a Parliament' who was adopting a temporal limit.[49] In contrast, Agustín Argüelles, one of the leading liberals present, argued that it was the nation itself, acting through the means of a Constituent Parliament, which was 'depriving itself from part of its freedom for a certain and limited time in order to ensure more and more its tranquillity and prosperity'.[50]

Another liberal deputy, José María Queipo de Llano (Conde de Toreno), who later became President of the Spanish Council of Ministers, made sure to clarify that the legislative body that would emerge from the new constitution was not the nation: the limit contained in Article 375 only applied to the former. For the Conde de Toreno, it was obvious that '[n]o one can deprive the nation of the power to alter and revise the constitution when it desires, because the contrary would be absurd in sound principles; but it is permitted to limit the authority of the ordinary Parliament which, being a delegated authority, is bound to act according to the powers it has received'.[51] The current assembly 'could legitimately act as a constituent body', he maintained, since it had been convened by the nation itself for that purpose, but future ordinary legislatures would not enjoy constituent power.[52] Joaquín Fernández de Leiva, a deputy from Chile, echoed those views: 'If it was possible for the Nation to always be

[48] *Diario de Sesiones de las Cortes Generales y Extraordinarias* (17 January 1812) no. 471, 2643.
[49] ibid. 2655.
[50] ibid. Deputies like Dou and Guridi distinguished between the constituent power and the power of constitutional revision (i.e. the amending power), even though they attributed to both the same function. That distinction was not common in 19th-century academic literature where, as we will see in Chapter 6, every change to a constitutional text was frequently seen as involving the exercise of constituent authority.
[51] ibid. 2644
[52] ibid.

assembled or represented by a Constituent Body, then the article under discussion would be of no use; but such a situation would be repugnant, violent, and even impossible'. 'Neither a nation can always be constituting itself', he maintained, 'nor can it assemble as a constituent entity outside times of revolution and disorder'.[53]

Other deputies, such as the Catalonian Felip Aner d'Esteve, one of the deputies who was not ready to leave behind his provincial instructions, reminded the assembly that their role was to 're-establish the fundamental laws', not that of creating a 'new constitution or of establishing a new social compact'.[54] Anticipating the distinction between the material and the formal constitution (which will be discussed at length in Chapter 8), Aner noted that there are 'constitutional laws that determine the rights of citizens, their religion, their form of government, etc., that should be seen as perpetually stable'. There were other 'less stable' laws, such as those that 'establish the requirements that individuals must meet in order to become deputies, the ways in which elections should be organised, and that Parliament should be convened annually', which should nevertheless be protected from change as much as possible as their alteration may negatively affect the effectiveness of the truly fundamental laws.[55] Aner thus maintained not only that a temporal limit such as the one established by Article 375 was acceptable, but that there are certain parts of any constitution that would always be outside the scope of the amending power. This kind of approach, as we will see in the next chapter, was typically championed by the royalists at the Constituent Parliament, who insisted that there was a historical constitution that transcended the momentary will of any assembly.

On 23 May 1812, the Constituent Parliament issued the convocation for the next *Cortes Ordinarias* (i.e. the ordinary parliament) through a decree that, as in France in 1789, prohibited deputies sitting at the Constituent Parliament from standing for election to the ordinary legislative assembly.[56] The legislature met in 1813. Despite the rigidity of its amendment rule and of the temporal limit established in Article 375, the constitution created in practice a system of parliamentary sovereignty: the protection of the constitution was placed in the legislature itself.[57] Indeed, the Constitution of 1812 did not

[53] ibid. 2646.
[54] ibid. 2651.
[55] ibid. 2652.
[56] In France, this motion was famously moved by Maximilien Robespierre. For a discussion, see William Doyle, *The Oxford History of the French Revolution* (Oxford University Press, 2002) 150.
[57] See Noemi García Gestoso, 'La Reforma de la Constitución de Cádiz: Algunas Consideraciones a Propósito de la Defensa de la Constitución', 29 *IRENEE* 77 (2012) 58, 74.

contain any mechanism for enforcing constitutional limits on the legislative branch. Instead, it created a Permanent Deputation of the Parliament, composed of seven individuals who had the role of 'supervising compliance with the constitution and the laws, and of notifying subsequent parliaments of any infractions'.[58] It then required new parliaments to take notice of those violations and provide any appropriate remedy.[59] In this respect, an ordinary law that violated the constitutional text, until repealed by a latter legislature, would in practice informally amend the constitution.

The constitution was abrogated in 1814 by Fernando VII, who once again became an absolute monarch. Fernando VII's actions were preceded by the publication of a document (*Manifiesto de los Persas*), signed by sixty-nine royalist members of the ordinary legislature, who denounced the Constituent Parliament for having 'introduced in Spain the subversive and impious ideas of the French Revolution, totally alien to Spain's national tradition'.[60] '[L]ike the French National Assembly', the *Manifiesto* continued, the Constituent Parliament 'proclaimed itself, against the reason for its convocation and against the express will of the King, a constituent body'.[61] Fernando VII decreed that the Constitution of 1812, as well as all decrees issued by the Constituent Parliament, were 'null and without any value or effect, neither now or at any moment, as if they had never been adopted and were removed from time'. The Constituent Parliament, the decree stated, had been convened in an unprecedented way (i.e. the orders of the realm had not been summoned) and adopted 'laws that they called fundamental, in the midst of the screams, threats, and violence' of those attending its sessions. These laws were only desired by a 'faction' but were presented as reflecting 'a colourful and deceitful *general will*'. The Constituent Parliament had thus not created 'a moderate monarchy, but a popular government headed by a chief or magistrate; a simple executor of a delegation, not a king'.[62]

[58] Constitution of 1812, Article 160. The Permanent Deputation would be made up of three deputies from Spanish Europe and three deputies from Spanish America, and one selected by lot (these individuals would be selected from the Ordinary Courts).

[59] ibid. Article 372. It also recognized, in Article 373, each citizen's right to demand the observance of the constitution. ibid. Article 373. The constitution did not contain a declaration of rights (a mode of proceeding that sought to avoid accusations of French influence), but its Article 4 stated that 'the nation is obliged to conserve and protect by wise and just laws civil freedom, property, and the rests of the legitimate rights of all individuals that comprise it'. Moreover, in Article 371, it recognized the 'freedom to write, print, or publish political ideas without previous permission (*licencia*), revision, or any form of authorisation prior to the publication'. For a discussion, see Suanzes-Carpegna, (n. 40) 202.

[60] Varela (n. 38) 203.

[61] 'Manifiesto de los Persas' (12 April 1814) para. 90.

[62] 'Decreto de Valencia' (4 May 1812).

III. The Making of the Venezuelan Constitution of 1811

In Venezuela,[63] the French invasion of Spain led to the consolidation of the independence movement and to the convocation of a constituent assembly that adopted a written constitution.[64] Like other early 19th-century Latin American constitutions, its creation was accompanied by the birth of a new independent state. The historical process that led to the adoption of the Constitution of 1811 is a long and complex one, and this is not the place to examine it in detail. Suffice to say that a key moment was the establishment, through a *cabildo abierto*,[65] of the *Junta Suprema Conservadora de los Derechos de Fernando VII* on 19 April 1810 after the Spanish governor of the *Capitanía General de Venezuela* was ousted.[66] The *Junta* worked as a provisional government that was premised on the recognition of the deposed Spanish monarch. Convened by the Province of Caracas, it could not claim to represent the entire *Capitanía*.[67] Accordingly, the *Junta* decided to call a Constituent Congress (*Congreso Constituyente*) comprised of representatives of the different provinces with the purpose of creating a new, pan-provincial, constitutional order. Along the way, the Constituent Congress issued a formal declaration of independence from the Kingdom of Spain. As in the process that resulted in the Spanish Constitution of 1812, the constituent power of the nation emerged triumphant, not only against the king but also against the people.

The Constituent Congress was convened according to an Electoral Law[68] addressed to all the 'inhabitants of Venezuela'[69]. It required the preparation of a general census by a number of commissioners assisted by the Catholic priests of the different towns' parishes, which would specify each individual's 'age, status, fatherland, neighbourhood, trade, condition, and whether he owns real or personal property'.[70] Once this census was completed, the commissioners

[63] This discussion of the process that led to the creation of the Venezuelan Constitution of 1811 is partly based on Joel Colón-Ríos, 'Constitution-Making and Constituent Power' in *Comparative Constitutional in Latin America* (Dixon and Ginsburg eds) (Edward Elgar, 2017).

[64] The constitution was adopted on 21 December 1811. The *Acta de la Confederación de las Provincias Unidas de Nueva Granada* was adopted on 27 November 1811.

[65] For a brief discussion of the *cabildo abierto*, see Chapter 4, n. 82 of this book, as well as the sources cited there.

[66] For a discussion, see Allan R. Brewer-Carías, 'Sobre el Inicio del Constitucionalismo en América Hispana en 1811, antes de la Sanción de la Constitución de Cádiz de 1812', 17 *Pensamiento Constitucional* 45–78 (2012) 49.

[67] See the opening statements of the *Reglamento para la elección y reunión de diputados que han de componer el Cuerpo Conservador de los Derechos del Sr. D. Fernando VII en las Provincias de Venezuela* (11 June 1810).

[68] ibid.

[69] ibid. Preamble.

[70] ibid. Chapter I, Article 3.

were required to prepare a list of those neighbours with the right to vote for parish electors. This list was meant to exclude a number of groups: women, men younger than 25 years of age (unless they were married), those under criminal prosecution, vagrants, foreigners, those that had public debts, and those who did not own a certain amount of property.[71] This document would then be signed by the relevant commissioners and priests, and neighbours would be notified of the number of electors that corresponded to their parish. The number was calculated on the basis of the entire population of the parish (i.e. electors also represented non-voting neighbours), according to the general formula 'one elector for each five hundred souls of any type' (*almas de todas clases*).[72] In order to be an elector, it was sufficient for an individual to live in the region to which the electing parish belonged, provided that attention was paid to the candidate's 'probity, enlightenment, and patriotism, and to other qualities contributing to the best performance of the delicate trust [that would be] deposited on him'.[73]

Those individuals selected as parish electors then elected the deputies of the Constituent Congress. The Electoral Law was very demanding in terms of the qualities that aspiring deputies should have: a 'good education, accredited conduct, talent, patriotic love, knowledge of the country, public acceptance' and other characteristics that would lead them to act with 'honour and purity'.[74] On the day of the election, the law mandated a special mass to the Holy Spirit in which 'divine intervention' would be implored as a means of aiding electors to make the correct choice.[75] These electoral rules had the explicit purpose of ensuring that not just any citizen could become a constitution-maker.[76] As Véronique Hébrard has noted, the rules operated under a 'logic of absolute representation' in which enlightened individuals 'dedicated to the exercise of reason' were to express the public opinion of the entire nation.[77]

[71] ibid. Chapter I, Article 4.

[72] ibid. Chapter I, Article 6.

[73] ibid. Chapter I, Article 12.

[74] ibid. Chapter II, Article 4.

[75] ibid. Chapter II, Article 6. In total, forty-four deputies were elected, twenty-four from the Province of Caracas. *Gazeta de Caracas* (19 February 1811).

[76] The role of the Catholic Church in the process was considered essential by some, since priests had been exposed to the 'teachings of Vitoria, Molina, and Suarez', and with those thinkers, they would be expected to reject monarchical sovereignty. S. J. Hermann González, 'Conversación sobre la Iglesia en la crisis del siglo XIX', 3 (6) Boletín CIHEV (1991) 114. Cited in Manuel Donís Ríos 'Los Diputados de la Provincia de Mérida al Supremo Congreso de Venezuela de 1811', 71 *ACTUAL Investigación* 119 (2012) 139. These ideas were also reflected in the sessions of the Constituent Congress and in the resulting constitutional text (which stated, in Article 228, to be inspired by the 'Supreme Legislator of the Universe').

[77] Véronique Hébrard, 'Opinión Pública y Representación en el Congreso Constituyente de Venezuela (1811-1812)' in *Los Espacios Públicos en Iberoamérica* (François-Xavier Guerra ed.) (Centro de Estudios Mexicanos y Centroamericanos, 2008) 31.

The Electoral Law thus reflected in important ways the constituent power of the nation approach: the nation could only speak through the voice of deputies able to identify its will and never through that of the well-intentioned but largely ignorant masses. The principle of exclusion seemed to be in full operation, as the effect of these electoral rules was that the majority of the population would not be allowed to take part in the constitution-making process.

a. National Sovereignty in Caracas

The deputies elected to the Venezuelan Constituent Congress were familiar with the views that emerged from both the French and American Revolutions.[78] Among those deputies, Juan Germán Roscio deserves special mention. An experienced jurist in Caracas, Roscio played a major role in the drafting of both the Declaration of Independence and the Constitution of 1811. Roscio's political thought is summarized in his *El Triunfo de la Libertad sobre el Despotismo*, where he narrates his 'conversion' to the ideal of the sovereignty of the people.[79] The pages of *El Triunfo* attempt to show that the Bible provides no textual support for the divine right of kings. For Roscio, 'sovereignty has always been and will always be a natural attribute, inseparable' from what he called the 'constituent people'.[80] That idea, he claimed, was 'a political and quasi-religious dogma' that was not only evident in the Bible but also reflected in books about 'natural law'.[81] Roscio did not explicitly refer to the author of any of those books, but Rousseau seems to have been one of them.[82] He made special reference to a particular book that scandalized him the first time he opened it, a book that argued that each individual is a 'little sovereign', that

[78] According to Brewer-Carías, they were particularly influenced by Thomas Paine, whose works were translated and published in Spanish as early as 1810. Allan Brewer-Carías, 'La Independencia de Venezuela y el Inicio del Constitucionalismo Hispanoamericano en 1810-1811, Como Obra de Civiles, y el Desarrollo del Militarismo a Partir de 1812 en Ausencia de Régimen Constitucional', 14 *Historia Constitucional* 405 (2013) 412–413.

[79] Juan Germán Roscio, *El Triunfo de la Libertad sobre el Despotismo: En la Confesión de un Pecador Arrepentido de sus Errores Políticos, y Dedicado a Desagraviar en esta Pate a la Religión Ofendida con el Sistema de la Tiranía* (Philadelphia, 1817).

[80] ibid. 29, 44.

[81] ibid.

[82] By 1790, the spirit of the French Revolution was already causing significant concern in Spain, and the establishment of the French Republic a few years later confirmed the worst fears of the (absolutist) Spanish Crown. A wave of repression followed, and not surprisingly, among the works that became subject to official censorship were those of Rousseau. See Cristina Gómez Álvarez and Guillermo Tovar de Teresa, *Censura y Revolución: Libros Prohibidos por la Inquisición de México* (1790–1819) (Trama Editorial y Consejo de la Crónica de la Ciudad de México, 2009) 137.

together all individuals are the sovereign, and that law is the expression of the 'general will'.[83]

However, during the debates at the Constituent Congress, Roscio qualified his enthusiasm for popular sovereignty: he seemed to have concluded that the multitude was unfit to make major political decisions. This was well exemplified during a discussion about whether the Constituent Congress had the authority to issue a declaration of independence from Spain in the absence of a popular mandate to do so. That is to say, a discussion about whether those sitting in the Constituent Congress were bound by the instructions of their constituents. Manuel Vicente de Maya, a Catholic priest and deputy for La Grita, forcefully argued in favour of the imperative mandate. Maya's opposition to the independence cause was well known. In the assembly, he argued that the deputies' instructions were limited to that of creating a new constitution while remaining loyal to Fernando VII. A declaration of independence, he insisted, required an express authorization from the people, and he not only lacked such an authorization but was instructed by his electors to vote against the separatist cause.[84] Accordingly, Maya maintained that 'being the declaration of independence a substantial mutation of the system of government adopted by the communities (*pueblos*) when they constituted their representatives, the latter need a clear and expression of the former in order . . . to give such an act the value and legitimacy it requires'.

Maya's statements where strongly denounced by other deputies, such as Francisco de Miranda, Juan Nepomuceno de Quintana and Roscio himself. The latter argued that although it was true that the deputies had sworn loyalty to the king, that action had the sole objective of appeasing the people: 'despotism had made the multitude so stupid (*embrutecida de tal manera*) that it was prudent not to clash with its beliefs'.[85] Echoing Roscio's words, another deputy stated that 'the mass believes that kings come from God, and [the king's] prestige needs to be vanquished, as Mr. Roscio has very well said'.[86] Somewhat counterintuitively, it was also suggested that the people were sovereign and that the Constituent Congress represented them, but that in virtue of that representation, the deputies 'were without a doubt sovereign themselves'.[87]

[83] ibid. 42–43, 45–46. There are good indications that Roscio had read the *Social Contract* by 1810. See, for example, his letter dated 29 June 1810 and addressed to Andrés Bello. Juan Germán Roscio, *Obras*, vol. 3 (Caracas, 1953).

[84] 'Libro de Actas del Supremo Congreso de Venezuela: 1811-1812', vol. 1 (Academia Nacional de la Historia, Caracas, Venezuela, 1959) 156.

[85] ibid. 183.

[86] ibid. 153.

[87] ibid. 149.

Any instructions contrary to what they thought beneficial to the people could thus be legitimately disregarded.[88] The idea was that the nation could be seen as the *source* of sovereignty, but that its *exercise* was a matter for its their representatives. As Joseph de Maistre wrote in the late 18th century with respect to 'the people', it is 'a sovereign who cannot exercise sovereignty'.[89] Other deputies instead engaged in a teleological interpretation of their instructions and argued that these had no other end than the common good, which would be promoted through national independence.[90]

In the end, the notion that a constituent body cannot be bound by citizen instructions (a view defended by Sieyès two decades earlier at the National Assembly and, in 1812, accepted by the constitution-making body that drafted the Constitution of Cadiz)[91] overwhelmingly prevailed. Roscio's initial rejection of monarchical sovereignty and his Rousseauian embracement of the sovereignty of the people were thus replaced, in practice, by a Sieyesian commitment to national sovereignty. As opposed to the constituent will of the people, which could only be expressed through institutions such as primary assemblies and the imperative mandate, the national will *could* be represented: what mattered was to identify the individuals who (because of their knowledge, experience, or virtue) were best placed to express it. The influence of this approach in the Constituent Congress was indeed reflected in the way this entity formally related to citizens. It is telling, for example, that although it was possible for citizens to petition the Constituent Congress, this could only be done in an individual capacity and not on behalf of any group (and much less on behalf of 'the people').[92] Only the Constituent Congress was authorized to express a general or public opinion.

This attitude was also reflected in the resulting constitutional text (which reflects the source/exercise distinction mentioned earlier). Article 144 of the new constitution stated that sovereignty lies 'essentially and originally in the general mass of [the country's] inhabitants', but that it was to be exercised only through properly elected representatives.[93] Similarly, Article 149 proudly stated that '[t]he law is the expression of the general will or [the will] of the majority of the citizens', but quickly moved to say, 'as indicated by the legally constituted

[88] ibid. 172.

[89] Joseph de Maistre, 'Etude sur la Souveraineté' in *Archives de la Révolution Française* (Oxford: Pergamon Press) 312. For the source/nation distinction, see n. 17, above.

[90] 'Libro de Actas' (n 84) 174, 155.

[91] See Chapter 4 of this book and Part II, above.

[92] Hébrard (n. 79) 11, 16. See also Constitution of 1811, Article 215.

[93] Unlike the Constitution of 1812, this Constitution contained a declaration of rights. Constitution of 1811, Article 181.

representative organ'. In giving a constituted authority operating free of the imperative mandate an exclusive power to determine the content of the general will, the constitution embraced the ideal of the constituent nation.[94]

The Constitution of 1811 was opposed by Spanish royalists, who negated its legitimacy. In 1812 the royalist threat was at its strongest and the environment of instability was increased by a strong earthquake that the Archbishop of Caracas described as God's punishment for the revolution.[95] On 4 April 1812, Congress delegated to the executive power all the necessary faculties to deal with the threat and, some days later, General Francisco de Miranda was armed with dictatorial powers. Some months later, the Spanish Constitution of 1812 was published in Caracas.[96] The identity of the constituent subject, however remained a primary subject of debate in Latin America and Europe for over century, as governments struggled to dampen the revolutionary spirit that still threatened traditional structures of power.

IV. Constituent Power and War: The Making of the Colombian Constitution of 1886

Like most countries in the region, the territory now comprising Colombia has been the site of multiple constitution-making episodes. In 1821, for example, the Constitution of the Gran Colombia (a new country comprising the territories of several current Latin American states, including Venezuela) was created, with the ensuing government having Roscio serving as Simón Bolivar's vice-president. New constitutions were later adopted in 1843, 1853, 1858, and 1863. The Constitution of 1863 reflected the ideas of a faction of the Liberal Party (radical-liberals) and established a federal country, the United States of Colombia. During the 19th century, struggles between different elites led the country towards a number of civil wars.[97] These conflicts were sometimes among states, sometimes intra-states, and sometimes had a national character.

[94] The constitution's amendment rule required proposals to be presented either by two-thirds of each chamber of Congress or of the Provincial Legislatures. They became valid once approved (again by two-thirds) by the entity (Congress or Provincial Legislatures) that did not propose it. Constitution of 1811, Articles 135–136. Despite these requirements, the legislature was presented as capable of expressing the general willwhich, by definition, could not be limited.

[95] Allan R. Brewer-Carías, *Historia Constitucional de Venezuela* (Caracas: Editorial Jurídica Venezolana, 2013) 299–300.

[96] ibid.

[97] María Teresa Uribe de Hincapié and Liliana María López Lopera, *Las Palabras de la Guerra: Un Estudio sobre las Guerras Civiles en Colombia* (Carreta Editores and Instituto de Estudios Políticos, Universidad de Antioquia, 2010).

For example, in 1876–1877, a civil war took place largely as a result of an attempt by the government of Eustorgio Salgar (1870–1872) to put in place a system of public, universal, and secular education, against the insistence by conservatives of an education system controlled by the Roman Catholic Church.[98] In 1883, Rafael Nuñez was elected President of the United States of Colombia with the support of the Conservative Party, an important milestone in the process commonly known as *Regeneración*.

A few months later, in 1884, a national civil war confronted again conservatives and radical-liberals. The latter were defeated, and President Nuñez declared that the 'Constitution of 1863 has ceased to exist'.[99] Shortly after, he issued a decree convoking a National Council of Delegates.[100] The decree stated that after a period of anarchy, 'the Nation has been saved by its own good sense and by the Divine Providence', and that it was now necessary to establish a new constitutional regime.[101] It also expressed that the 'numerous and strong manifestations' of municipalities and individual citizens evidenced wide support for constitutional change, and that it was the President's duty to formalize that support by facilitating the creation of new institutions.[102] Accordingly, Nuñez requested the governments of the nine states to appoint two delegates each, who would then meet and deliberate about the terms under which the constituent process would take place.[103] In practice, Nuñez selected the eighteen delegates, who sometimes lacked any connections with the states they represented.[104]

The Council of Delegates proceeded to draft a document titled 'Agreement on Constitutional Reform'(*Acuerdo sobre Reforma Constitucional*) that established the basis of the future constitution. It stated, for example, that the freedom of the press would be respected as long as it did not interfere with the social order, that other individual liberties would be recognized in the

[98] Jane M. Rausch, *La Educación durante el Federalismo. La Reforma Escolar de 1870* (Instituto Caro y Cuervo—Universidad Pedagógica Nacional, Santafé de Bogotá, 1993). See also Jhonny Antonio Pabón Cadavid, *De los Privilegios a la Propiedad Intelectual: La Protección en Colombia a las Obras Literarias, Artísticas y Científicas en el Siglo XIX* (Bogotá: Universidad Externado de Colombia, 2010) 103–133.

[99] Rodolfo Arango, 'La Construcción de la Nacionalidad' in *Miguel Antonio Caro y la Cultura de su Época* (Rubén Sierra Mejía ed.) (Universidad Nacional de Bogotá, Bogotá, 2002) 131. The Constitution of 1863 was thus derogated in violation of its amendment rule (Article 92), which allowed its 'total or partial reform' by the legislature (in a process that involved the unanimous vote of the Senate), or by a special convention convoked by congress at the request of the totality of the state legislatures.

[100] Decree no. 594 (10 September 1885).

[101] ibid.

[102] ibid.

[103] ibid. Article 2.

[104] Jorge Orlando Melo, 'La Constitución de 1886' in *Nueva Historia de Colombia* (Editorial Planeta, Bogotá, 1989) vol. 3.

constitution (subject to 'reasonable limitations'), and that there would be an independent judiciary.[105] Importantly, the *Acuerdo* stated that 'sovereignty resides only and exclusively in the Nation, which will be denominated *Republic of Colombia*', a statement that not only embraced the principle of national sovereignty but that was taken to amount to a rejection of federalism.[106] According to the document, the Council would 'exercise the functions of a constituent body', and the norms created by it, if approved by the Executive Power, would have 'the permanent force of a Fundamental Charter or Constitution of the Republic'.[107] Once a constitution was adopted, the *Acuerdo* continued, the Council would exercise ordinary legislative functions and would elect the President and Vice-President of the Republic for the first constitutional period.[108] The *Acuerdo* also stated that it would only become binding after being popularly ratified. The Executive Power was given the task of determining the ways in which the 'will of the Nation' would be consulted.[109]

The *Acuerdo* was presented to President Nuñez by a special commission comprised by three of the Council's delegates, with a note that stated that it had been approved unanimously and that it 'faithfully interpreted the national sentiment'.[110] In response, Nuñez expressed his confidence that the document reflected 'the necessities and desires of almost the totality of Colombians'.[111] He then issued a decree according to which the *Acuerdo* would be 'ratified by the Colombian people, as represented by the municipalities or Councils of every district of the Republic'.[112] The rules according to which the officials sitting in those entities were elected varied from state from state. A good example is provided by the State of Cundinamarca, in which the right to vote was limited to men older than 21 years of age (or younger men who were married), as long as they did not fall within some of the recognized exclusions, such as vagrancy.[113] According to the decree, the *Acuerdo* would be read aloud in the relevant assembly, and with no debate, the representatives

[105] 'Acuerdo Sobre Reforma Constitucional', *Consejo Nacional de Delegatarios* (30 November 1885), Chapter I, Articles 9, 10, 17.
[106] ibid. Chapter I, Article 1. At the same time, it suggests an identification between nation and state, later developed or challenged by some constitutional theorists (see the discussion in Chapter 9 of this book).
[107] ibid. Chapter II, Article 1.
[108] ibid. Chapter II, Article 2.
[109] ibid. Chapter II, Article 3.
[110] ibid.
[111] ibid.
[112] Article 1, Decree no. 837 (5 December 1885). Districts had one vote for each 1000 inhabitants. Article 24.
[113] Constitución del Estado de Cundinamarca (Bogotá: Imprenta de la Nación, 1857), Articles 6–8.

would be asked whether they ratify it, investing the Council with 'all the powers it requests from the Nation'.[114] Out of 619 municipalities, 605 voted 'Yes'.[115] On 16 April 1886, the Federal Supreme Court validated the election, declaring that the *Acuerdo* had been 'ratified by the national will'.[116]

The Council of Delegates discussed a draft constitution written by Miguel Antonio Caro on the request of Nuñez.[117] It is helpful to briefly discuss some of the political ideas of Caro, as well as those of another major figure in the Council, José María Samper, about the nature of constituent authority. Caro was deeply religious, and this was reflected in the way he understood political power.[118] He maintained that 'to govern men is to serve God' and that God was the 'supreme tutor and legislator of society'.[119] Even though he accepted that government should be based on the consent of the people, he was not entirely comfortable with the principle of popular sovereignty: sovereignty, as an unlimited political power, only belonged to God.[120] These ideas are reflected in the preamble of the Constitution of 1886 ('In the name of God, supreme fountain of all authority . . . '), and were also largely shared by Samper. In fact, Samper argued that one of the problems of the 1863 radical-liberal constitution was that—unlike all of the other Colombian constitutions since 1821—it had 'completely forgotten of the Divinity'.[121] The people, he argued, was the 'immediate and visible' fountain of political power, but the ultimate 'Constituent Power' lied with God.[122]

The constituent episode that took place in Colombia in 1885–1886 had some features (but of course, not the deliberative and democratic qualities) of what has been recently called a 'multi-stage' (or 'post-sovereign')

[114] Decree no. 837 (n. 112) Article 6.

[115] The Supreme Court of Justice was in charge of determining the legality of the electoral process. Decree no 837 (n. 112), Article 28. Historians have shown that during the 19th century, electoral processes in the country were characterized by many irregularities (e.g., in the election of 1875, Rafael Nuñez allegedly obtained 44,000 votes in the State of Bolivar (his opponent only receiving 7 votes), a number that was higher than the total male population of the state. David Bushnell, *Las Elecciones en Colombia: Siglo XIX* (Credencial Historia, 1994).

[116] Diario Oficial, República de Colombia, Año XXII, Bogotá, no. 6, 655 390 (21 April 1887).

[117] *Teología en América Latina, Vol. II: De las Guerras de Independencia hasta Finales del Siglo XIV (1810-1899)* (Josep-Ignasi Saranyana, dir.) (Vervuert: Iberoamericana, 2008) 424.

[118] For a discussion, see ibid. 421–428.

[119] Miguel Antonio Caro, *Escritos Políticos. Primera Serie* (Bogotá: Instituto Caro y Cuervo, 1990) 160.

[120] *Teología* (n. 117) 427.

[121] José María Samper, *Derecho Público Interno* (Biblioteca Popular de la Cultura Colombiana, Ministerio de Educación, Bogotá, 1951) 4.

[122] ibid. 6. Even though they agreed with respect to the origins of political power, Caro and Samper differed in terms of their conception of the relationship between church and state. Caro defended a confessional state while Samper, during the constituent process, rejected the idea of 'attributing to the nation' (and therefore to the state), 'the power or capacity [*facultad o aptitud*) to profess the catholic religion', because 'neither the territory, nor the institutions or the action of the government are able [*susceptibles*] to profess any religion'. Arango (n. 98) 138.

constitution-making process.[123] In explaining the reasons behind this mode of proceeding, Samper maintained that the direct ratification of a constitution by the people was seen as undesirable given that the length and novel character of the document would rule out the possibility of an informed vote. Moreover, the drafting of such a document would at the very least take four or five months, and there was an urgent need to know the basic content of the country's future fundamental law.[124] The Council therefore decided to agree on a number of fundamental principles that would form the basis for the reorganization of the republic (the *Acuerdo*), and to submit those principles to popular ratification.[125] This way, Samper argued, allowed everyone to know what would be the 'general and essential spirit of the constitutional changes', and given the fact that the principles would be 'brief and precise', the people could better appreciate their meaning.[126] Since the *Acuerdo* was in fact ratified by the municipalities and the constitution was consistent with it, Samper argued, it was no exaggeration to say that the new constitution itself had been popularly ratified.

The process that led to the creation of the Colombian Constitution of 1886 reflected in many ways the constituent power of the nation approach, even though the terms 'nation' and 'people' were often used interchangeably. The initial appointment of the delegates, as well the ratification by municipalities, were highly consistent with the principles of representation and exclusion, placing the constitution-making power on a number of representatives elected through a process in which a significant part of the population was not allowed to participate. The Council spoke on behalf of the nation, not on behalf of the inhabitants of the nation's territory. Moreover, like the previously discussed Venezuelan experience, the constitution-makers also operated under the strong influence of the earlier idea of God as an ultimate constituent power. This understanding of constituent power (and rejection of the principle of participation) is not surprising: this was a constitution born out of a civil war and created through a process led by a conservative 19th-century movement; more direct forms of popular intervention were out of the question. However, when one looks at the debates in the Council of Delegates (at one point renamed National Constituent Council), a number of interesting tensions arose.

[123] See, for example, Andrew Arato, 'Conventions, Constituent Assemblies, and Round Tables: Models, Principles and Elements of Democratic Constitution-Making', 1(1) *Global Constitutionalism* 173 (2012).

[124] Samper (n. 121) 8.

[125] ibid.

[126] ibid. 8–9.

a. Between the Nation and the People?

One of the main issues revolved around Article 6 of the *Acuerdo,* which maintained that: 'The Nation recognises that the Catholic religion is that of almost the totality of Colombians.'[127] The draft constitution, in contrast, recognized Catholicism as the religion of 'the Nation', and the question arose about whether this was consistent with Article 6 of the *Acuerdo*. Some of the delegates who thought that the answer to that question was 'no', maintaining that the powers of the Council were derived from the *Acuerdo*, so that delegates 'lacked the unlimited power of reform that is generally attributed to constituent bodies'.[128] This feature makes this process consistent with the multi-stage or post-sovereign approach to constitution-making: the Council of Delegates, at least in theory, at no moment possessed full constituent authority. It first drafted a document that would not enter into effect until ratified by the municipalities, and then approved a constitution that had to be consistent with the *Acuerdo* and ratified by the executive power. Even if one were to agree with that view, Caro argued, the true meaning of Article 6 could only be ascertained by interpretation, and since that provision had been created by the Council, no entity was better positioned to interpret it.[129] For Caro, it was entirely appropriate for the new constitution to identify a national religion, even if that religion was in fact not shared by everyone, since 'the National Constituent Council has nothing to do with minorities, majorities, or with almost totalities'.[130]

The task of the Council, according to Caro, was to represent 'a collective that is called Nation; it is in the name of the Nation, and not in the name of almost the totality of its inhabitants . . . that the entity that represents its sovereignty creates the law'.[131] This does not mean that Caro advanced the idea that the Council was free to adopt any constitution it wanted. In fact, he described the Council as acting on an 'imperative mandate' from the Nation (even if its individual members were not bound by particular instructions of their constituents), and there were certain fundamental decisions (such as the rejection of federalism) about which the Nation had spoken clearly and any disobedience (with respect to those decisions) would amount to revolution.[132] The idea, nevertheless, was that in identifying the will of the nation, the Council did not necessarily need to consult the actual human beings that comprised it. This can

[127] 'Acuerdo' (n. 105) Chapter I, Article 6.
[128] 'Informe de una Comisión', Consejo Nacional Constituyente (Bogotá: 13 May 1886) 144.
[129] ibid. 149.
[130] ibid. 159.
[131] ibid.
[132] ibid. 112.

be observed in the reasons behind the design of the new constitution's amendment rule. This rule provided that amendments were to be presented by an ordinary legislative majority, and then debated and adopted by a supermajority in the next legislature.[133] By adopting that rule, Samper explained, the Council aimed to protect the 'fundamental principles of the State' by making constitutional changes relatively difficult, but not impossible to achieve.

The latter approach was thought too dangerous, as it might result in future irregular attempts to alter the fundamental law (the Council ultimately failed to prevent that kind of event, as the adoption of the Constitution of 1991 showed).[134] Interestingly, the Council rejected a proposal for an amendment rule according to which a simple legislative majority would propose an amendment that would then be submitted to ratification by the municipalities. This process was similar to the one that led to the adoption of the *Acuerdo* and, for Samper, it was consistent 'with the principle that advises that the will of the people is consulted'. However, he explained that the Council rejected it because it was not considered convenient to involve the municipalities in 'political issues'.[135] Instead, the Council opted for an approach that avoided sudden reforms, requiring reformers to proceed in a 'calmed and correct' manner.[136] The appeal to 'the people' as represented by the municipalities was an exceptional measure required by the particular context in which the constitution was adopted, and not a necessary element in constitution-making. After all, what was essential was to adopt the constitution the nation deserved, not the constitution willed by the people.[137]

[133] Constitution of 1886, Article 206.

[134] Samper (n. 121) 498. For a discussion of the different failed attempts of reforming the Constitution of 1886 and of the 'irregular' process that led to the creation of the Constitution of 1991, see Gonzalo Ramírez Cleves, *Limites a la Reforma Constitucional en Colombia* (Bogotá: Universidad Externado de Colombia, 2005) 437–442.

[135] Samper (n. 121) 499.

[136] ibid. 500.

[137] The distinction between popular and national sovereignty (and the defence of the latter) continued to be relevant in Colombian constitutional discussions well after the 19th century. Consider, for example, one of the main arguments of the claimants in a 1957 case heard by the Supreme Court of Justice. In that case, a decree that authorized a referendum that would end in a constitutional amendment was challenged on the basis that it violated the procedure established in the amendment rule. That procedure, it was stated, was based on the principle (expressed in Articles 2 and 105 of the Constitution of 1886), that 'sovereignty resides essentially and exclusively in the Nation', that public power emanates from the nation and must be exercised according to the constitution, 'and that the representatives of the entire Nation' are the members of Congress. Judgment no. 2188-2189-2196, Supreme Court of Justice of Colombia (28 November 1957) 434. The decree, the claimants argued, would result in the replacement of the principle of the sovereignty of the nation with that of popular sovereignty: 'the Nation', the claimants argued, would be 'represented only by the men and women older than 21 years of age that wish to participate in the plebiscite'. ibid. In so doing, the decree would ultimately destroy the basis of the constitutional system, allowing future governments to depart from the constitution whenever they thought it desirable through a direct call to the electorate. ibid. 435.

V. Conclusion

The distinction between national and popular sovereignty provides a useful lens through which to understand the early constitution-making processes in Spain, Venezuela, and Colombia. The constituent power of the nation approach prevailed in these three episodes and is also reflected in most of the works that will be discussed in the next chapter. The idea of a constituent nation rested on the principles of exclusion and representation, principles that were reflected in institutions organized around a limited franchise and that facilitated elite representation. By conceiving the relevant constitution-making body as authorized to speak on behalf of the constituent power, deputies were able to develop juridical arguments directed at placing the assembly both beyond the reach of government and popular majorities. This was the kind of approach to the exercise of constituent power defended by Sieyès and rejected by Rousseau: the people as a *pouvoir commettant* who elects those called to lead constituent episodes on their behalf. It was also consistent with the rejection of the imperative mandate (an institution unacceptable from the perspective of national sovereignty), as clearly exemplified during these three processes.

As we will see in the next chapter, debates about the identity of the constituent subject continued to occupy the minds of 19th-century constitutional theorists in Europe and Latin America long after the adoption of these constitutions.[138] Nineteenth-century constitutional theorists who embraced the theory of constituent power, we will see, were particularly concerned with the legal and institutional implications that followed from it. The main debate was thus between authors who, for the most part, followed the Sieyèsian tradition and attributed constituent power to an abstract nation, and authors who attempted to give the nation a more concrete (and Rousseauian) form—a view that required a role for citizens in constitution-making. An important insight that will be underscored through the next chapter is the fact that in most of the works where the concept of constituent power was discussed, what the existence of an extra-legal constituent authority did was to justify the imposition of limits on the ordinary institutions of government (parliamentary sovereignty, e.g., was to be rejected), as well as limits on constitution-making bodies themselves (constituent assemblies, e.g., could not exercise legislative, executive, or judicial power). For some authors, those limits were not enough, and presented the constituted subject as limited by natural law.

[138] Some of these works (we will see in Chapter 7) negated the very existence of constituent power and the idea that constitutions could be properly understood as emerging from an act of will.

6
The Identity and Limits of the Constituent Subject

This chapter considers the legal and institutional implications that different 19th-century authors (who frequently doubled as politicians) derived from the theory on constituent power and that, in many cases, were reflected in actual constitutional practice. The authors whose work will be discussed wrote at a time when the struggle between national and monarchical sovereignty had not yet been resolved. Most of them had recently experienced revolutions (in their countries or in neighbouring ones) to some extent reminiscent of 1789. What unites these otherwise disparate works and allows them to be understood as a coherent body of literature is that their authors were interested in the same basic question: who has a sovereign authority to replace the fundamental law? Not surprisingly, authors who embraced the theory of constituent power normally attributed it to a moral entity usually identified as the nation (and sometimes as 'the people', but not understood in Rousseauian terms).[1] In these works, the concept of constituent power almost invariably played the role of limiting the power of the ordinary institutions of government. The nation's power to create constitutional law was an exclusive one: no legislature, no executive entity, could assume constituent jurisdiction. Every change in the constitution, these commentators usually thought, involved the exercise of constituent power. The idea of parliamentary sovereignty, in particular, was to be rejected.

At the same time, although some authors identified constituent power with an unlimited law-making ability (i.e. a jurisdiction to produce any legal content), others saw the *constituent* subject as limited to the creation of constitutional content; a constituent body could not engage in any aspects of the activity of governing. There were also commentators who, sometimes explicitly rejecting the principle of national sovereignty, attributed constituent power to parliament or to the 'constituted authority'. Those authors' embracement of the theory of constituent power, however, came accompanied by a

[1] For a discussion of Rousseau's 'constituent power of the people' approach and the prevailing idea of the Sieyèsean 'constituent power of the nation', see Chapters 2 and 5 of this book.

Constituent Power and the Law. Joel Colón-Ríos, Oxford University Press (2020). © Joel Colón-Ríos.
DOI: 10.1093/oso/9780198785989.001.0001

natural law approach that sought to limit the type of constitution that could be legitimately created. What we will see in the works discussed in this chapter, then, is how a concept otherwise associated with an unlimited jurisdiction and revolutions, was strongly linked to different kinds of limits: limits on the ordinary institutions of governments, and limits on constituent power itself. In fact, as we will see in the next chapter, it is the rejection of constituent power that facilitates the justification of unlimited governing authority. I will proceed as follows.

Part I briefly examines the general historical context in which the works discussed in the chapter were written. This was a time when the ideal of the nation's constituent power was largely accepted, although defences of constituent monarchs had not yet disappeared. The constituent power of the monarch was usually presented as an antidote to the dangers and potential excesses of national sovereignty. In Part II, I consider the constitutional theories of a group of authors who focused on the exclusive character of the nation's constituent power. Theirs were theories that largely rejected the English tradition of parliamentary sovereignty, that is, of a parliament able to engage in both constituted and constituent activity. Importantly, these conceptions were developed at a time when it was not uncommon for written constitutions to lack amendment rules. For those who rejected the theory of constituent power, that type of institutional design was understood as an implicit recognition of the legislature's power of constitutional change. For others, parliamentary sovereignty not only had to be rejected but, in the same way a legislature lacks constituent power, a constituent body lacks ordinary legislative jurisdiction. In other words, the principle of the separation of powers applied to the constituent authority itself.

In Part III, I consider the work of a group of commentators who, while largely operating under—what in the previous chapter I called—the Sieyèsian 'constituent power of the nation' approach, attempted to provide a more concrete form to 'the nation' without fully embracing Jean Jacques Rousseau's system of popular sovereignty. Some of these authors, for example, saw as illegitimate any constitution that allowed ordinary legislatures (even if acting through special thresholds) to alter the constitutional text. The legislature ultimately acted on a mandate from the constituent authority; the legislative body could not simply alter the conditions of its commission. A special jurisdiction, a constituent assembly, was needed. Others defended the convocation of periodic constituent assemblies, as well as the recognition of the right to alter the constitution through popular initiative. This type of arrangement, as we will see in

Chapter 10, is currently present in a number of national constitutions. Finally, in Part IV, I examine a number of works that reject both the idea of a constituent nation and that of a constituent monarch. From that perspective, ordinary legislatures had the power to create new constitutional norms. Placing the constituent power in the constituted authorities, under that view, was either more desirable or realistic. Nonetheless, like Emmanuel Sieyès, these authors saw constituent power as subject to natural law, and this meant that the constituent authority could only create certain type of constitutional content.

I. Of Revolutions and Constituent Monarchs

The early triumph of national over monarchical sovereignty, as exemplified in the events in France (1789) and Spain (1812) was short lived, and before the mid-19th century, most governments in Europe were again ruled by sovereign monarchs. One of the main challenges to that state of affairs came from thinkers who are usually grouped under the label of 'liberals'. Liberals supported the establishment of constitutions that guaranteed basic civil rights, and feared that both absolute monarchy and radical republicanism (usually associated with the French Jacobins of the 1790s) would supress these protections.[2] Their objective was to find a middle ground between these extremes—to develop 'a regime in which the legislative and the executive branch of government existed independently of each other, and where their actions would be mutually restrictive'. [3] This system was best exemplified in a constitutionally regulated monarchy which embraced the separation of powers. Liberals were suspicious of democratic politics, often defended a limited franchise, and sometimes distinguished the 'true majority' (the educated few who were best placed to identify the general interest), from what they frequently called the 'mere majority of numbers'.[4] Nineteenth-century conservatives, in contrast, not only defended monarchical sovereignty but thought that political institutions were the product of long historical processes and could not simply be replaced by the adoption of a written constitutional text.[5]

[2] Jonathan Sperber, *The European Revolutions, 1848–1851* Cambridge University Press 2005) 66.
[3] ibid.
[4] ibid. 67.
[5] ibid. 74. Conservatives were in this respect partisans of the *historical constitution*, a doctrine that involved the rejection of the theory of constituent power. The doctrine of the historical constitution will be discussed in Chapter 7.

Although by the 1830s some European jurisdictions adopted new constitutions that attempted to strike a balance between monarchical and national sovereignty (and that were often seen as compacts between the king and the people), by 1847 the political and economic situation in Europe, combined with popular discontent and the unwillingness of governments to make political concessions to their opponents, led the continent to a new period of revolution.[6] The events of 1848—the 'Year of Revolution'—generally culminated in the establishment of provisional governments and the convocation of constitution-making bodies. In France, for example, a new government called for the election of a Constituent Assembly that adopted the constitution of the French Second Republic in 1848. In Germany, the Frankfurt National Assembly adopted the Constitution of 1849. The assemblies received thousands of petitions from different groups and social sectors, but these were ultimately of little consequence.[7] The notion of the imperative mandate had no place in these events, even though Marx and Engels reminded readers of the *Communist Manifesto* (originally published in February 1848) that the Paris Commune (the type of republic they preferred) operated under a political system with primary assemblies at the bottom, where 'each delegate [was] at any time revocable and bound by the *mandat imperatif* (formal instructions) of his constituents'.[8]

The 1848 revolutions had relatively moderate effects: the overthrow of absolutist regimes, the establishment of parliamentary governments, the recognition of civil liberties, and the widening of the franchise.[9] The work of the authors discussed in this section must be understood in the wider pre- and post-1848 context. They generally operated at a time when the struggle between national and monarchical sovereignty was far from been resolved and they had recently witnessed political revolutions that brought back memories of 1789.

Most important to our purposes here, these authors were particularly interested in locating the ultimate source of constituent authority. As Félix Berriat-Saint-Prix noted in 1851, for them, to ask the question: 'to whom belong[s] the constituent power . . . is to ask, using different terms, who has sovereignty'?[10]

[6] For a discussion, see ibid. 109–156.

[7] ibid. 150–151.

[8] Karl Marx and Fedrerick Engels, *Manifesto of the Communist Party* (Moscow: Progress Publishers, 1969) vol. 1.

[9] Sperber (n. 2) 155.

[10] Félix Berriat-Saint-Prix, *Théorie du Droit Constitutionnel Français: Esprit des Constitutions de 1848 et de 1852 et des Sénatus-Consultes Organiques Précédé d'un Essai sur le Pouvoir Constituant* (Paris, 1851) 2.

The usual answers were the monarch or the nation.[11] Not surprisingly, those who defended the idea of a constituent monarch—a monarch with the power to alter the constitution at will—usually did so after highlighting the risks they associated with the main alternative. This was typical of 19th-century Spain, where the struggle between absolutism and liberalism following the abrogation of the Constitution of 1812 resulted in multiple acts of constitution-making in which the identity of the constituent subject was a major concern.

For example, writing in 1842, Vicente Pou criticized those who thought that the recognition of the constituent power of the nation would make the possibility of despotism less likely. By attempting to replace a constituent monarch with a constituent nation, Pou contended, liberals would end up 'creating a new power that brings together the strongest elements and incentives of tyrannical abuse'.[12] Similarly, José Lorenzo Figueroa denounced those who a few years earlier had insisted that an extraordinary constitution-making entity was called to replace the Spanish Constitution of 1837. For him, 'in times of political upheaval, nothing is more dangerous than those constituent bodies that assume all the powers of the state'. 'The establishment of that [type of] constituent power', he said, could result in 'the destruction of the constitution and of the monarchy'.[13] Those who, like Pou and Figueroa, rejected the theory of the constituent power of the nation, nonetheless thought that there were things that even a constituent monarch could not do. Even if 'the constituent power of the king of France' was described by some as an 'inviolable and sacred right', kings were, after all, God's delegates on earth.[14] As such, they were subject to divine law and, ultimately, to their subjects' right of resistance. Naturally, defences of the king's constituent power became less and less common as the century advanced.

[11] As we will see below, during the 19th century some authors did not distinguish between 'nation' and 'people', even though they were mostly committed to some version of what we identified earlier as national sovereignty.

[12] D. V. P., *España en la Presente Crisis: Examen Razonado de la Causa de los Hombres que Pueden Salvar Aquella Nación* (Monpeller, 1842) 27. For a discussion of Pou's ideas, as well as that of other 19th- and 20th- century supporters of monarchical sovereignty, see Miguel Ayuso, 'El Problema Religioso y el Problema Político en la Historia Contemporánea de España (A Propósito de Luis de Trelles)', 4 *Anales de la Fundación Francisco Elías de Tejada* 79–97 (1998).

[13] José Lorenzo Figueroa, 'Apuntes para Servir a la Historia Contemporánea: La Legislatura de 1843', 3 *Revista de Madrid* 121, 124–125 (1844).

[14] Gilibert de Merlhiac, *La France, et son Roi* (1815) 40–41. Merlhiac suggests that the idea of the constituent power of the king could be in fact understood as consistent with national sovereignty: the king of France was the constituent subject because he was recognized as such by his subjects. ibid. 41. For further discussions of the constituent power of the monarch, see, for example, Charles Cottu, *De la Nécessité d'une Dictature* (Paris 1830) 59–61; Prosper Duvergier de Hauranne, *Histoire du Gouvernement Parlementaire en France: 1814-1848* (Paris 1871) vol. 10, 355, 359–360.

II. The Exclusive Constitution-Making Power of the Nation

Defenders of the constituent power of the nation stressed the limits that its acceptance created on the legislature's law-making power. Recognizing the nation's constituent power meant, at the most basic level, that unless otherwise specified in the constitution itself, the legislature could not alter the constitutional text. This idea had already been expressed in revolutionary France, where it was frequently associated with the separation of powers. For example, Jerome Pétion de Villeneuve argued that the separation between the constituent and the legislative power was necessary, since in its absence the legislature would rule over the executive and the judiciary and the equilibrium between the different branches of government would be destroyed.[15] In the 19th century, Guillaume-François-Antoine Thouret expressed additional reasons in favour of this separation. In a speech to the French legislature in 1831 and in the midst of a debate on the amendment of the Charter of 1830, Thouret considered in some detail the separation between the constituent and the constituted power. The Charter of 1830 had been adopted after the July Revolution by the Chamber of Deputies acting in a special capacity, that is, without the Chamber of Peers. In so doing, the majority in the Chamber claimed to be following the 'imperative mandate of the circumstances and necessity' and rejected demands that the new Charter should have been ratified by the constituent power in primary assemblies.[16]

Importantly, the Charter of 1830 lacked an amendment rule (even though, in Article 68, it mandated a revision of its Article 23 in the 'session of 1831').[17] The question that Thouret addressed in 1831 was whether this meant that it could be altered as an ordinary law, that is, by the legislative chambers acting together with the king. As with other constitutions adopted during the restoration

[15] Eric Thompson, *Popular Sovereignty and the French Constituent Assembly* (Manchester University Press, 1952) 100.

[16] François Delarue, *Du Pouvoir Constituant et du Principe Souverain, d'après M. de Cormenin, au sujet de la Charte de 1830* (Paris: Levavasseur, 1831) 9; 'Declaration of the Chamber of Deputies' (August, 1830); Charter of 1830, Article 13. This constitution-making act involved the ousting of Charles X and the abolishment of the principle of hereditary monarchy. The new Charter formally limited the powers of the king in significant ways. In particular, the king's veto powers were abolished. The adoption of the Charter by the ordinary parliament was strongly criticized by some deputies, who argued that the Chamber had illegitimately appropriated the people's constituent power. For example, Delarue told his fellow deputies that '[W]ithout the participation of the people, without their sanction, you usurp the constituent power, which is inherent to their sovereignty'. Delarue, ibid 13. Delarue thus maintained that without the primary assemblies' sanction, the Charter of 1830 could not be even understood as legally binding. ibid.

[17] One of the first written constitutions ever adopted, Oliver Cromwell's 'Instrument of Government', also lacked an amendment rule. There are some more recent examples, such as the Iranian Constitution of 1978.

period in Europe, the Charter of 1830 was seen as a compact between the king and his subjects. This led some, particularly the doctrinaires (whose conception, as we will see in the next chapter, eventually prevailed), to argue that it could be altered just as any other statute. Others, notably Alexis de Tocqueville, argued that the Charter of 1830 was inconsistent with the very idea of a special constitution-making power in an even more obvious way than that of 1814, where the royal prerogative 'took its stand above and beyond the constitution' (so that in the last instance the constituent power belonged to the king).[18] But that did not mean that the Charter of 1830 could simply be changed by parliament as if it was an ordinary law. On the contrary, 'because there appears to be no legal means of changing it', it was 'immutable'.[19] Otherwise, de Tocqueville maintained, both the king and the deputies would be authorized to modify or even abrogate the very law in virtue of which they exist.[20]

Thouret, in the speech mentioned above, went beyond these ideas and told his colleagues that constituent power belonged to the nation, who had the right of establishing a form of government and of regulating the competence of the public authorities. Constituent power 'pre-existed all the other powers'.[21] Public authorities, he argued, echoing Rousseau, had no other function than to *execute* the constitution and could not in any case alter the fundamental laws.[22] Accordingly, even though it did not contain an amendment rule and lacked a prohibition on its modification by the legislative branch of government, Thouret argued that the Charter of 1830 was not subject to a general amendment power held by the legislature. A special jurisdiction, a constituent assembly, was needed.[23] For him, 'the constituted powers are never

[18] Alexis de Tocqueville, *Democracy in America* (Henry Reeve, trans.) (Penn State Electronic Classics Series Publication, 2002) vol. 2, 804. For a discussion of the notion of the constituent power of the king in the context of the Charters of 1814 and 1830, see Martin Kriele, *Introducción a la Teoría del Estado: Fundamentos Históricos de la Legitimidad del Estado Constitucional Democrático* (Eugenio Bulygin, trans.) (Buenos Aires: Ediciones Depalma, 1980) 405–406.

[19] De Tocqueville (n. 18).

[20] In the early 20th century, Joseph Barthélémy modified this approach in an interesting way (one that anticipated the ideas to be examined in Chapter 8 of the book), arguing that while the Charter could be modified by the Crown-in-Parliament, there were certain parts of it, such as the monarchical form of government and the representative legislature, that could not be the object of a reform. Joseph Barthélémy, 'La Distinction des Lois Constitutionnelles et des Lois Ordinaires sous la Monarchie de Juillet', *Revue de Droit Public* (1909).

[21] Discours de M. Thouret, 'Député du Calvados' (4 October 1831) 2.

[22] ibid. 2–3.

[23] ibid. 8. Since, as noted above, Article 68 of the Charter of 1830 itself mandated a revision in 1831 (related to the selection of the members of the Chamber of Deputies) without referring to a special assembly, Thouret agreed that the Chamber of Deputies could, by exception, assume constituent authority and proceed to alter the relevant provision. This was not the case with the reform of 1842, which was not contemplated by the constitutional text. Not surprisingly, a heated discussion between the doctrinaires and deputies like Charles Guillaume Hello later took place around this issue. It was determined that the Charter could be amended by the Crown-in-Parliament. Maurice Fonteneau, *Du Pouvoir Constituant*

the constituent power; otherwise, everything would be mixed-up, the one who mandates with the mandataires, the cause with the effect, the constitutional laws with the ordinary ones'.[24] A constitution that fails to regulate its own amendment could not be interpreted as implying a rule according to which constitutional change is a special form of law-making. Rather, it must be read as resting on a separation between the power of creating ordinary laws (a power delegated to the legislature), and the exclusive constitution-making power of the nation.

Thouret, like Sieyès, saw constituent power as extra-legal and thought that the failure to facilitate its exercise through law must not be confused with the negation of its ongoing and exclusive right to amend the fundamental laws. From this conception, one of the main limits now often associated with the theory of constituent power followed: the inadmissibility of an entity that, like a sovereign parliament, combines both the power of making ordinary laws and that of revising the constitutional text. In the cases of Venezuela, Spain, and Colombia (discussed in Chapter 5), this idea failed to be put into practice: the newly created legislatures were seen as capable of expressing the national will. As will be explained below, the same occurred in France: the attribution of constituent power to the nation did not limit an ordinary assembly seen as capable of speaking on the nation's behalf. But Thouret also derived another important limit from the separation between the constituent and the constituted powers: 'In the same way that the constituted powers can never become the constituent power', he wrote, the constituent power can never exercise constituted functions.[25] A special constitution-making assembly that attempts to exercise legislative, executive, or judicial powers, would be acting *ultra vires*. This notion involves a separation between sovereignty and constituent power, arguably already present in Sieyès and to be further developed in Chapter 9.

a. Lumbreras' Constituent Sovereign

These limiting functions of the extra-legal constituent power were also emphasized, in Spain, by Joaquín Lumbreras. Lumbreras belonged to the generation of 1812 and assumed different public offices during the liberal governments

en France et de la Révision Constitutionnelle dans les Constitutions Françaises depuis 1789 (Caen, 1900) 127–129. Hello developed this view in his academic work, as will be discussed below.

[24] Thouret (n. 21) 3.
[25] ibid. 4.

that operated before the Cadiz Constitution was definitely abrogated.[26] The validity of that constitution was briefly recognized in 1820 and 1836, but it was replaced by the Constitution of 1837. The Constitution of 1837 maintained the recognition of the principle of national sovereignty (but only in the preamble) and attributed new powers to the monarch (e.g. the power to convene, suspend, and dissolve the legislature, as well as the power to veto legislation).[27] Published in August 1837, just after the revolutionary period that forced Queen María Cristina to briefly restore the Constitution of 1812,[28] Lumbreras' *Lecciones de Doctrina Social* contains a spirited defence of the right of each generation to establish a new constitution. Lumbreras defended stable constitutional orders, warning that unless a constitution was consistent with the 'eternal principles of society' and the 'dignity of men and the liberties of citizens were respected', it would never enjoy stability. [29] However, since a constitution is based on an act of popular will, it was up to each generation to decide about its content and about its change.[30]

Like Thouret, Lumbreras thought that no institution deriving its authority from the constitution 'had the right to alter it neither totally nor partially, with the exception of reforms that can be made through the means of revision, and in the manner determined by the constitution itself'.[31] He accepted the possibility of minor amendments by a legislative supermajority, but only if such a process was constitutionally regulated. If a constitution lacked an amendment rule, then it must have been that the constituent power decided not to allow the constituted authorities to alter the constitutional text. 'There is', he wrote, 'no power superior to national sovereignty, and the legislature is a constituted, not a constituent power, which is the only one that is outside the law because it is sovereignty itself'.[32] A constitution cannot be 'replaced or modified except by the constituent power, that is to say, by the nation itself or by the body of its representatives when given a special power to do so'.[33] The nation, in the exercise of this power, must be free to act through any procedure it decides to

[26] He served, for example, as Secretary of the *Junta for the Protection of the Freedom of the Press*. José Luis Bermejo Cabrero, 'La Junta de Protección de la Libertad de Imprenta durante el Trienio Liberal' 68 *Anuario de Historia del Derecho Español* 11, 14, fn 5 (1998).

[27] In 1845, a new constitution was adopted, one which, as will be seen in Chapter 7, was based on an idea of constituent power heavily influenced by Juan Donoso Cortés and other doctrinaires.

[28] It also resulted in the derogation of the Royal Statute of 1834. 'Royal Decree' (10 April 1834). The Royal Statute of 1834 had been adopted by the constituent queen (María Cristina de Borbón) with the purpose of restoring the 'fundamental laws of the monarchy'.

[29] Joaquín Lumbreras, *Lecciones de Doctrina Social* (Madrid, 1837) 74–75.

[30] ibid. 75.

[31] ibid.

[32] ibid. 76.

[33] ibid. 110.

adopt.[34] Lumbreras' position in the debate as to who has the ability to adopt a new constitution (as opposed to amending it) was clear: only an extraordinary constitution-making body comprised of elected representatives could bring a new constitutional order into existence.

Although he thought that it was 'not necessary for the members of society to directly exercise constituent power', constitution-making representatives should not be authorized to exercise the ordinary powers of government.[35] Despite accepting Sieyès' distinction between passive and active citizens, Lumbreras maintained that no distinctions should be made among active citizens called to act as representatives.[36] That is to say, all active citizens were equal, and when authorized by the nation to exercise constituent power, they should not be subject to any property or moral qualification.[37] In this respect, Lumbreras did not fully embrace the constituent power of the nation approach and its accompanying principle of exclusion.[38] In fact, he maintained that like all political representatives, the individuals called to draft a constitution should be guided by public opinion.[39] Moreover, he referred to the people's right to assemble and 'instruct their representatives' as well as the right to petition public officials.[40] To be sure, Lumbreras did not defend the institution of binding instructions, but rather insisted that while 'no portion of the people is authorized to exercise the whole of the popular power, each section of the sovereign people assembled should enjoy the right to express their will with absolute liberty'.[41]

b. Hello's Rejection of Formal Constitutional Change

Some years later, in France, Charles Guillaume Hello stressed the limits posed by the existence of an extra-legal constituent subject and developed in important ways the previously mentioned view that the Charter of 1830 could not be amended by the ordinary legislature.[42] In the third edition of his main

[34] ibid. 152.
[35] ibid. 152.
[36] ibid. 152–153.
[37] ibid. 84.
[38] ibid. 154. Despite usually referring to the nation as the constituent subject, Lumbreras thought that nation and people were synonymous: 'All public power without distinction emerges from the general will; it emerges from the people, that is to say, from the nation. These two terms should be understood as equivalent.'
[39] ibid. 84.
[40] ibid. 59, 69.
[41] ibid. 60.
[42] The Charter of 1830 was eventually replaced after the Revolution of 1848 by a republican constitution drafted by a popularly elected National Constituent Assembly.

work, *Du Régime Constitutionnel*, he examined the question of what happens once 'the constituent power has fulfilled its function, that is, when it has proclaimed the rights that will be guaranteed and has organised that guarantee'.[43] One view, he said, would see the constituent subject returning to nothingness after creating a constitution. But he thought that constituent power continued to exist, either as an abstraction that permanently waits for the opportunity to become real, or as a special jurisdiction that can be exercised through one of the constituted powers. In the context of the French Charter, Hello maintained that if the latter were true, then the only constituted power that could have been endowed with such faculties would be the legislature, since the Charter explicitly forbids the executive power to suspend or disapply any law.[44] His position on these issues was introduced through a comparison between French and English constitutional thought.

The English constitution, he wrote, is characterized by an experimental method in which, 'without a plan, and without a theory', new statutes and precedents are chronologically added to existing ones.[45] Under that approach, the English Parliament is free to adopt any law it considers desirable, and the only hierarchy applicable to those laws is that of time (i.e. express or implied repeal). France, in contrast, had opted for what Hello called a rational method: in 1789, the French nation adopted a set of constitutional laws which aspired to provide a rational basis for a government but that had not been tested by history. One of the consequences of this approach was to bring to the surface the separation between the constituent and the legislative power. The basic implication of this separation was exemplified during the French Revolution when the Constitution of 1791 was adopted by a Constituent Assembly, and this entity proceeded to create another assembly only attributed with the power to create ordinary laws.[46] The French nation, however, did not stop at creating a new constitution, but attempted to find a place for itself in the new constitutional order.[47] It did so through an amendment process according to which three consecutive legislatures could insert changes into the constitutional text.

This, for Hello, had been a mistake: a constitution should not deal in advance with its own alteration, it should not attempt to regularize a power that is by nature accidental and sometimes violent.[48] The idea of a constituent

[43] C. G. Hello, *Du Régime Constitutionnel* (Paris, 1848) vol. 2, 16.
[44] ibid.
[45] ibid. 18.
[46] ibid. 18–19
[47] ibid. 20.
[48] ibid. 21.

power surviving in a constitutional provision, he maintained, had since then been correctly discredited: 'constituent power is a useless power when inert, and a dangerous one when it becomes active'.[49] Even Sieyès understood this well when, late in the Revolution, he insisted upon the creation of institutions designed not to alter, but to protect the continuous existence of the Constitution. This was the role of the *Sénat Conservateur* under the Constitution of 1799, which was attributed with the power of invalidating public acts (when asked to do so by the other two chambers of the legislature) found unconstitutional.[50] Since under the Charter of 1830 parliament was the higher law-making authority, it is understandable that some concluded that it was there where the constituent power lay. But that view failed to consider the development of French constitutional thought, which had now reached a consensus about the error committed in 1791. One of the means to correct that error was precisely to refrain from adopting amendment rules at all, as in 1799 and 1830.

It would be very strange, Hello suggested, that the consequence of protecting the constitution by omitting a formal amendment process was to be the attribution to the ordinary legislature of the power to alter the constitution in the same way it can alter ordinary laws.[51] This would mean that the Charter could be easily destroyed at any moment, or at least at any time that the legislature is in session.[52] 'Under a regime which places the guarantee of rights in the division of powers', he maintained, one cannot 'unite in the same hands that which constitutes the State and that which governs it by laws'.[53] Put differently, one should not deprive society of the idea that there is a supreme and inviolable rule which, even if it is not eternal, is 'fixed and stable'.[54] Hello recognized that the English had endured great stability without a fixed constitution, but this had been for their 'superstitious respect for precedents', which protects them against the worst consequences of confusing the constituted and the constituent authority.[55] However, the problem was that the fortunate rejection of the idea 'of a permanent personification of the constituent power' in France had led to the unfortunate one of the exercise of constituent power 'as a right inherent to the nation'.[56]

[49] ibid.
[50] ibid. Constitution of 1799, Article 21.
[51] ibid. 22.
[52] ibid.
[53] ibid. 23.
[54] ibid.
[55] ibid. 24.
[56] Ibid. 25.

Hello thought that this view, which as we will see in the next chapter was brought to its ultimate consequences by the doctrinaires, was understandable but misguided. It failed to understand constituent power's role 'as a limit, as a veto', on the actions of the constituted institutions.[57] The text of the Charter implied a separation between the constituent and the constituted powers that could not simply be ignored. For example, when Article 7 stated: 'Censorship can never be re-established', it sought to limit the power of the institution authorized to adopt ordinary laws. This must mean, he argued, that the Charter was adopted by an entity that enjoyed a power different from that now held by the legislature. Otherwise, the legislature could simply ignore that provision and proceed to re-establish censorship, as it had done at different times earlier in the 19th century.[58] The constituent power of 1830, unlike that of 1791, had not established a mechanism for its future exercise, but that was not the same as saying that it had ceased to exist. And its existence was important, because it was precisely what limited the jurisdiction of the constituted authorities. What the lack of an amendment rule meant was that constituent power could not be exercised by the ordinary institutions of government. Its exercise would normally require the extra-legal convocation of a constituent assembly.

c. Laboulaye's Critique

If an extra-legal constituent assembly was convened, how could one ensure that it would only draft a constitution and would not engage in the exercise of the ordinary powers of government? In the Third French Republic, an influential essay by Édouard Laboulaye addressed this question. Laboulaye thought that the theory of constituent power that had emerged from the French Revolution was destined to cause disorder and ruin. He maintained that the French had failed to properly institutionalize an otherwise revolutionary power.[59] Despite the distinction between the constituent and the constituted powers, under the traditional Sieyèsian approach the extra-legal nation always ended up abdicating its sovereignty to those individuals sitting in a constituent assembly

[57] ibid. 27.
[58] ibid. 28.
[59] Édouard Laboulaye, *Del Poder Constituyente* (Guatemala, 1872) 6. For Laboulaye, the main purpose of a constitution was to establish limits on the three branches of government and to list the rights that government must guarantee (a constitution, he said, might include many other types of provisions, but those do not have a truly constitutional character). ibid. 9. Put in a different way, only the provisions that limit the competences of the constituted powers and that guarantee rights, for Laboulaye, had a 'material' character even if other types of rules could in fact be included in the 'formal' constitution. The notions of the material constitution will be discussed in Chapter 8 of this book.

or in an ordinary legislature.[60] On the one hand, extraordinary representatives sitting in a constitution-making assembly became 'masters of the country', able to operate free from the limits imposed by the separation of powers and go well beyond the task of creating or revising a constitution.[61] On the other, since the legislative chambers created by these entities were then seen as the 'voice of the nation', and since the national will could not be limited, the ordinary legislature's power was also understood as unlimited.[62]

Reminiscent of Pétion's complaint to his colleagues at the National Constituent Assembly in 1789, Laboulaye believed that such a view identified the mandataires with the mandating citizens.[63] He contrasted this situation to that of the United States, where the legislative power clearly was a 'subaltern or derived' power, and only constitutional conventions called by the legislature according to a set of pre-established rules were recognized as the constituent authority.[64] According to Laboulaye, in the US constitutional tradition, constitutional conventions had an 'original character' that decisively distinguished them from the ordinary legislative assembly.[65] The members of these conventions were not genuine representatives, but delegates: they co-existed with the legislature that convened them and lacked any decision-making faculties. A convention was thus 'a simple committee attributed with the task of submitting to the people a draft constitution'.[66] Laboulaye's reading of the US system is nonetheless characterized by a sleight of hand. He maintained that all amendments to the Federal Constitution had to be ratified by the 'entire nation' because 'the right to organise government, the constituent power, only belongs to it'.[67] But ratification by 'the entire nation' could only refer to ratification by the representatives sitting in state legislatures.[68]

[60] ibid. 26.
[61] ibid. 7–8, 26.
[62] ibid. 14.
[63] ibid.. For a discussion of Pétion's views on this issue, see Chapter 4 of this book.
[64] ibid. 18–19.
[65] ibid. 20.
[66] ibid. In practice, however, constitutional conventions in US states did not work as mere committees with the only power of drafting constitutions subject to popular ratification, but often engaged in the exercise of the ordinary powers of government. For a discussion, see Roger Sherman Hoar, *Constitutional Conventions: Their Nature, Power, and Limitations* (Kessinger Publishing, 1917).
[67] Laboulaye (n. 59) 23, 25. For a positive reception of Laboulaye's account by US author of the epoch, see John A. Jameson, 'Constitutional Conventions' in *Cyclopaedia of Political Science, Political Economy, and of the Political History of the United States* (John J. Lalor ed.) (New York: Charles E. Meeril & Co., 1899) vol. 1, 626.
[68] Only the 21st Amendment (adopted long after Laboulaye was writing) to the Federal Constitution was ratified by state conventions (which, in any case, can hardly be understood as equivalent to an act of the 'entire nation'). The situation was different in some state constitutions, which contained amendment formulas that required ratificatory referendums.

Be that as it may, Laboulaye rejected what he identified as Sieyès' model and, in so doing, came closer to seeing constituent power as a faculty of constitutional change to be exercised through law, a view that in Chapter 2 I associated with Rousseau. Only by institutionalizing the separation between the constituent and the constituted powers could one ensure that the former's unlimited character not only effectively limited the ordinary legislature but also any 'constituent' entity called to act on its behalf. The objective was thus to avoid the full transfer of sovereignty to an ordinary or extraordinary state organ: sovereignty, as in Rousseau, 'could not be delegated'.[69] That is why the power exercised by a constituent assembly was described by Laboulaye as 'regular, legal, and limited', a notion that suggested a separation between sovereignty and constituent power.[70] The assembly could draft a new constitution on behalf of the nation, but that did not mean it was sovereign. 'Before and after an election', he maintained in his essay on sovereignty, 'there is only one sovereign in France: the Nation', forever unable to delegate its sovereignty.[71] Since a constituent assembly was not the true sovereign, its draft constitution needed to be subject to popular ratification, even though, as we saw earlier, Laboulaye treated ratification by US state legislators as ratification by the 'entire nation'.[72]

In this section, we have seen the ways in which a number of19th-century authors associated constituent power with the establishment of limits on the ordinary institutions of government and, in particular, with the rejection of parliamentary sovereignty. For them, not even a constitution without an amendment rule, that is, a constitution that did not explicitly prohibit a legislative majority to alter it, could be amended as if it was an ordinary law. Moreover, in the same way that a legislature cannot amend a constitution, it cannot adopt statutes inconsistent with it. Like Laboulaye, many of the authors writing about constituent power during this period were also concerned about making sure constitution-making bodies were subject to limits and, at the same time, they largely followed Sieyès' conception of constituent power. This was the case of Thouret, Lumbreras, and Hello. Theirs was a constitution-making faculty that, unlike Rousseau's, could be exercised by representatives and did not require the direct involvement of the citizenry. It was also consistent with a limited

[69] Laboulaye (n. 59) 25–26. While Laboulaye saw Sieyès as the main culprit for the confusion of constituent and constituted power, he also associated it with the French doctrinaires, whose ideas will be considered in the next chapter. ibid. 10, 12. For a response to Laboulaye's essay that rests on the writings of François Guizot, Pierre Royer-Collard, and other doctrinaires, see Charles-Alfred Bertauld, *Du Pouvoir Constituant de L'Assemblée Nationale* (Paris, 1871).

[70] Laboulaye (59) 18. This distinction will be further developed in Chapter 9.

[71] Édouard Laboulaye, 'De la Souveraineté' in *Questions Constitutionnelles* (Paris, 1872) 414.

[72] Laboulaye (n. 59) 17–18, 23, 27.

franchise, a system that (as the one used at the constitution-making processes examined in the previous chapter) would only attribute political rights to those citizens who were seen as capable of contributing to the public establishment. Under this approach, the citizenry becomes an 'electorate' that is called to play a particular function: that of electing representatives, some of which would exercise ordinary powers, others who would exercise constituent ones.[73]

III. Concretizing the Constituent Nation

In 1869, Paul Pradier-Foderé defined constituent power in the following way: 'The right to make a constitution is called the constituent power. It belongs to the nation, which is sovereign [and which] can only exercise it through mandataires'.[74] The authors discussed above would largely agree with that definition but would have probably made a number of qualifications. First, note that Pradier-Foderé refers to constituent power as the right to *make* a constitution. For most of the previous authors, the making of a new constitution certainly counted as an exercise of constituent power, but also its piecemeal change. Second, he saw a constitution as 'a revocable mandate',[75] and the references to *mandataires* might have created some discomfort. Nevertheless, some of the commentators discussed in this section insisted that while representatives were free to make the decisions they thought consistent with the national interest even if contradicting the preferences of their constituents, they were still mandataires: in adopting a constitution, the nation had issued a general (binding) mandate about the limits of the law-making authority and about the ways in which political power could be exercised. This was the case of Jacques Berriat-Saint-Prix, who maintained that according to the theory of the mandate, representatives were bound to respect the decisions contained in the constitution. A mandataire simply had no power to alter the limits under which he is authorized to act.[76]

[73] For an analysis of the concept of the electorate and its relation to constituent power, see Chapter 10 of this book.

[74] Paul Pradier-Fodéré, *Principes Généraux de Droit, de Politique et de Legislation* (Paris, 1869) 209.

[75] ibid. 210.

[76] Jacques Berriat-Saint-Prix (n. 10) 45. See also Paul Pradier-Fodéré, *De Droit, De Politique et de Législation* (Paris, 1869) 229. A similar notion is contained in the Federalist Papers: 'There is no position which depends on clearer principles, than that every act of a delegated authority, contrary to the tenor of the commission under which it is exercised, is void. No legislative act, therefore, contrary to the Constitution, can be valid. To deny this, would be to affirm, that the deputy is greater than his principal; that the servant is above his master; that the representatives of the people are superior to the people themselves; that men acting by virtue of powers, may do not only what their powers do not authorize, but what they forbid.' *Federalist no. 78* (Alexander Hamilton) (28 May 1788).

Despite that kind of view, which seems directed at reducing the distance between representatives and citizens, the idea of the constituent nation, of a moral entity with a will separate from that of the individuals who comprise it, was still dominant. However, as the 19th century advanced, constitutional theorists began to think about 'the nation' in more concrete ways, in some cases approaching what in the previous chapter I called the 'constituent power of the people' approach. An interesting example is that of Cerbeleón Pinzón, a prominent Colombian jurist who served in a number of official capacities, including as President of the Supreme Court in 1863.[77] For Pinzón, 'the constituent power, or the electoral power, has the task of constituting the representatives of the Nation for the exercise of public authority'.[78] At first sight, this approach is reminiscent of Sieyès' *pouvoir commettant*—it is about citizens authorizing a number of individuals to act on behalf of the nation, not about a multitude attributed with a power of constitutional change. But Pinzón also claimed that 'once it is recognised that sovereignty resides in all the members of the association', it must be concluded that the right to exercise constituent power can only take place with the authorization of the entire community.[79] Any other approach would end up attributing constituent power to a faction, and would therefore be inconsistent with the idea of popular government.[80]

These views seem highly consistent with those of Rousseau, but it must be noted that Pinzón explicitly rejected the notion of the social contract.[81] For him, the power to create a government was independent of any compact: human societies, by the very fact of existing, had a sovereign power to organize themselves.[82] Nevertheless, like Rousseau's, Pinzón's thought is in direct tension with the constituent power of the nation approach. He believed that for a political act to count as a true exercise of constituent power it needed to involve the entire community, which in practice meant that it needed to respect the principle of universal suffrage.[83] At the same time, Pinzón maintained that

[77] Patricia Cardona and Carolina Céspedes, 'Cerbeleón Pinzón y la Paz Pública', 14 *Revista Coherencia* 13, 15 (2017).

[78] Cerbeleón Pinzón, *Tratado de Ciencia Constitucional*, 2nd ed. (Bogotá, 1852) 186.

[79] ibid.

[80] ibid. 186, 187.

[81] A similar conception had already been advanced by Adam Ferguson, who maintained that men always existed in society and that the idea of the state of nature, and by implication that of the social contract, were fictions. Adam Ferguson, *An Essay on the History of Civil Society* (Philadelphia, 1819) 3.

[82] ibid. 3. Sovereign power, he said, is born out of the intelligence and strength of all of the individuals that comprise society, and when these individuals disagree with each other, 'sovereignty moves to the majority, as it must be supposed that where there is a higher number of individuals there are more intelligences and strengths together'. ibid.

[83] Pinzón (n. 78) 189–190.

an absolute and non-accountable freedom of speech and print was necessary, as this allowed citizens to freely speak the language of the 'general interest'.[84] When the general interest was spoken, he wrote, 'particular interests will fail to find intelligible words and, humiliated before popular dignity, would have to silently allow the interests of everyone to prevail'.[85] Naturally, in the context of constitution-making, the entire people would elect a number of individuals tasked with the drafting of a constitutional text. And such an election, he stated, must be direct: 'Only direct election faithfully channels the people's views and is capable of expressing the true popular will'.[86] Direct election also made difficult the manipulation of voters that he argued could prevail in primary assemblies.[87]

Once a constitution has been ratified 'by duly authorised delegates, strictly speaking no additional step is needed for it to be binding', but Pinzón noted that it would be highly convenient to submit it to a referendum where it can be 'accepted or rejected *in its totality*'.[88] Moreover, once a constitution is adopted, the legislative power should not be seen as sovereign: the legislature 'is the representative of the Nation for the purpose of adopting ordinary laws, and nothing else . . . [I]t must act within the limits prescribed in the Constitution'.[89] Although Pinzón argued that a constitution should contain an amendment rule, he limited himself to stress the notion that it should not allow for ill-considered reforms, and did not engage in a discussion of which entity should be attributed with the power of formal constitutional change.[90] To a large extent, what makes Pinzón's approach interesting is his realism. His identification of the 'constituent' and the 'electoral' power points towards the fact that, at least at the time he was writing, the most a people could do in the context of constitution-making, was to vote. The constituted powers originate from that vote, and this meant that they were subject to the limits and conditions stated in the -ideally popularly ratified-, constitution. Moreover, for the very idea of constituent power to be respected, everyone, and not only enlightened or propertied individuals, should be granted the right to vote, the right to directly participate in the election of a constitution-making body and in the potential ratification of the proposed constitutional text.

[84] ibid. 10, 188.
[85] ibid. 188.
[86] ibid. 190.
[87] ibid.
[88] ibid. 14 (emphasis in the original).
[89] ibid. 28. For Pinzón, any questions about the constitutionality of a law should be settled by the judicial power. ibid.
[90] ibid. 171.

a. Fernández Concha's Original Sovereign Subject

Unlike Pinzón, Rafael Fernández Concha, the Chilean jurist and theologian, engaged directly with questions of constitutional reform. Writing in the late 19th century, Concha rejected what he called Rousseau's 'constitutive social pact' as an unnecessary fiction that, even if true, could only bind the individuals who actually entered into the contract.[91] Rousseau's ideas, he maintained, would lead to a system in which the only right of citizens was that of contributing, 'to form the general will where sovereignty, that despotic monster imagined by the misanthropist sophist from Geneva, is located'.[92] Like Pinzón, Fernández Concha maintained that one must find the origins of sovereignty in nature itself. Society and sovereignty are 'co-created'.[93] Whenever there is a society, there is a right to constitute the means necessary for its protection and development which would allow the nation to find 'its own destiny'.[94] Sovereignty always exists, the question is who has it. The main alternatives were a particular individual (or a particular group) or the entire community. The former had to be rejected: as 'nature itself does not make anyone superior to the others and there is no human act in virtue of which nature directly conferred an individual with civil jurisdiction'.[95] Accordingly, he maintained, 'sovereignty originally resides in the collective being of the entire community'.[96]

In light of that original sovereignty, the community not only has the right to elect the person or persons who will later exercise political power, but also to constitute the form of government itself.[97] Fernández Concha knew that that conclusion was reminiscent of Rousseau, and he made sure to highlight three important differences between their views. Firstly, for Rousseau, sovereignty was a human creation, for him (i.e. Fernández Concha), it existed by nature in every society.[98] Secondly, for the former, sovereignty was the expression of the general will and therefore was not subject to any form of law; for him, given its origins, sovereignty was subject to natural law.[99] Thirdly, and finally, for Rousseau 'sovereignty is distributed among all associates, each of them having part of it'.[100] For Fernández Concha, (who here clearly exemplifies the

[91] Rafael Fernández Concha, *Filosofía del Derecho, o Derecho Natural Dispuesto para Servir de Introducción a las Ciencias Legales*, vol. 2 (Barcelona, 1888) 173.
[92] ibid. 175.
[93] ibid. 177.
[94] ibid.
[95] ibid. 190.
[96] ibid.
[97] ibid. 189.
[98] ibid. 191.
[99] ibid. 191.
[100] ibid. 192.

constituent power of the nation approach) sovereignty is not divided among individuals, but belongs to 'a moral entity comprised by them . . . sovereignty resides in the nation and not in the citizens'.[101] Once Fernández Concha reched a conclusion about the ultimate location of sovereignty, his theory of constituent power began to emerge. He defined the constituent subject as the one who 'establishes the fundamental organism of the State, determining the form of government, the division and relationship between the public powers, their hierarchy, the primary laws through which the exercise of public power is regulated, etc.'[102]

An important question was what happens to constituent power after a form of government has been established. Does the nation merely delegate it, or does it abdicate it completely? If the former, Fernández Concha wrote, 'the people [he uses people and nation interchangeably] remains sovereign by law and fact: the magistrates constituted by it are mere mandataires, subject to any instructions and to recall *ad nutum*'.[103] Interestingly, he did think that this could be the case: 'to negate to the people the faculty to constitute itself in this way, one would have to demonstrate that natural law (in virtue of which the people is originally sovereign) requires it to abdicate all its sovereign power'.[104] But the people, in the exercise of the constituent power, could also fully deprive itself of sovereignty, attributing it to the constituted authorities.[105] Such an arrangement, he wrote, was not only useful but necessary in large communities. Otherwise, one would end up with a system in which government is always subject to the will and instructions of informally convened popular assemblies, which could at any point attempt to change the form of government itself.[106] This is why those constitutions that adopt the principle that sovereignty resides in the nation and that the constituted powers exercise it through delegation (as the constitution then in place in Chile did),[107] 'relegate that principle to the world of theory, negating in practice all its natural and necessary consequences', and declaring 'seditious any act, by the people or by someone claiming to represent it, inconsistent with the established order'.[108]

[101] ibid. 192.
[102] ibid. 202.
[103] ibid. 194.
[104] ibid.
[105] ibid.
[106] ibid. 195.
[107] ibid. 196. The Chilean Constitution of 1833, Article 149, stated: 'No person or assembly of persons may claim to be or to represent the people, attribute itself with the rights of the people, or make petitions in the people's name. The violation of this article constitutes sedition'. Similar provisions can be found in other Latin American constitutions.
[108] ibid. 196

This same logic informed Fernández Concha's approach to constitution-making and constitutional reform. He maintained that 'in dictating the Constitution which will regulate the State, the people has the right to impose conditions and limits to the constituted government'.[109] Indeed, he noted that he was not aware of any country where governors have 'the plenitude of the constituent power:they either cannot alter the form of government or can only do so through established mechanisms'.[110] If there is no such mechanism and the public good requires a new form of government, such a change 'can only be made by the people or through its votes'.[111] That is to say, unless otherwise stated, it must be assumed that only the constituent subject can change the constitution. But in the same way that the constituent authority could decide to abdicate the totality of its political power, it could attribute to the constituted institutions the power of constitutional change. 'The Constitution of the State', he wrote, 'cannot be changed without popular authorisation, unless it establishes the authority and the means through which the changes or reforms that the public good of the nation requires can be obtained'.[112] However, even in the latter case, the power to change the constitution according to its own rules is 'founded on the primitive will of the people',[113] that is, in the original decision of the constituent power of establishing an organized means of constitutional reform.

Fernández Concha's views about the alteration of the form of government and his notion that constitutional reform according to an established amendment rule ultimately rests on the people's constituent power, qualified in important ways the possibility of a total abdication of sovereignty at the time a constitution is adopted. Indeed, he maintained that despite his previous comments, 'the people can never radically deprive itself of sovereignty, so that it cannot even provide for its conservation in cases of extreme necessity'.[114] The exercise of this kind of resistance would be triggered, for example, in cases where 'the constituted powers become tyrannical . . . or create an imminent danger to the integrity or independence of the nation'.[115] In those situations, the original abdication of sovereignty would become void. As in John Locke and George Lawson's right of resistance,[116] the nation could recover its constituent power

[109] ibid.
[110] ibid.
[111] ibid. 196.
[112] ibid. 201–202.
[113] ibid. 193.
[114] ibid. 196.
[115] ibid. 197.
[116] Locke and Lawson's theories of resistance will be discussed in Chapter 7.

and create a new form of government. Fernández Concha's conception of constituent power implicitly admitted both the possibility of parliamentary sovereignty, as well as that of a system of constitutional supremacy.[117] Nonetheless, he also accepted the potential legitimacy of a system of popular government in which sovereignty was not abdicated, but only delegated, by the community. In both cases, attributing constituent power to the people (or the nation), would have important legal or institutional consequences: the continuing existence of a right of resistance, the existence of legal limits to the exercise of ordinary political power, and the potential validity of binding instructions and the right to recall elected officials.[118]

b. Quimper and Orban: Approaching the Constituent People

Even though Fernández Concha implicitly admitted the possibility that constituent power is exercised through law (i.e. through an amendment process in which even the form of government can be altered), he saw the constituent subject inhabiting an extra-legal terrain. It was a force that acted as a limit on the constituted institutions, legitimated constitutional reform, and re-appeared in cases of extreme necessity. Writing around the same time, José María Quimper, a Peruvian lawyer who served as President of the Peruvian Constituent Congress of 1867, went well beyond Fernández Concha and insisted that a constitution could *only* be amended by the constituent people (as Fernández Concha, Quimper also used the terms nation and people interchangeably).[119] Quimper maintained that 'the constituent power always belongs to the Nation and cannot be alienated, exhausted, or delegated. It is the national will in action, it is the almighty issuing its laws among thunder and strikes . . . *vox populi vox Dei*'.[120] Even though, like the previous authors, Quimper rejected

[117] Some aspects of Fernández Concha's thought seem to be implicit in a declaration signed by more than fifty professors from the Faculty of Law of the *Pontificia Universidad Católica de Chile* in 1980 that sought to justify the legitimacy of the referendum for the ratification of a constitution adopted by a military junta, as well as the power claimed by the latter. According to the declaration, the original constituent power exercised by the junta was the result of 'society's need of giving itself an institutional form that provides support to a juridical order that allows for a collective life', and its existence was ultimately founded on 'human nature itself, which spiritual and material dimensions requires men to live together in society'. The constitution adopted by the junta, the document argued, exhibited 'a perfect consistency with the Natural Law' and with 'the democratic tradition that has historically characterised the national being'. 'Declaración de los Profesores de la Facultad de Derecho de la Pontificia Universidad Católica de Chile Respecto a la Convocatoria a Plebiscito para Ratificar la Constitución' (1980).

[118] For a discussion of the relationship between the imperative mandate and the recall, see Chapter 10 of this book.

[119] J. M. Quimper, *Derecho Político General* (Lima, 1887) vol. 2.

[120] ibid. 122.

Rousseau's theory of the social contract,[121] he explicitly relied on Rousseau when claiming that 'the constituent power always remains active [*permanece siempre en acción*] and the constituted powers, which only exist in a precarious manner, can only be modified or altered' by it.[122]

In fact, Quimper denounced those constitutions that, while recognizing the principle of popular sovereignty, contained an amendment formula that allowed ordinary legislatures—even if subject to special thresholds—to alter the constitution.[123] The recognition of the people's constituent power was simply inconsistent with legislatures with amending authority.[124] In the same way that 'no mandataire can modify his mandate',[125] no constituted power could alter the constitutional text. Quimper knew that this was not true of the English Parliament, 'but that is because England lacks a true constitution'.[126] Since a people cannot change a constitution directly, it had to 'appoint commissaries with a special mandate . . . , commissaries that could only represent the opinion of those who commissioned them, being their only duty to express it even if it is different from theirs'.[127] Those commissaries would not sit on ordinary legislatures but in constituent assemblies that could not exercise any other power than that of adopting new constitutional rules.[128] Like Rousseau (and Jefferson), Quimper favoured a system according to which constituent assemblies would be periodically convened by law. He suggested that this should happen every nine years, as such a period would allow each generation to be free from the previous one.

'Without a constituent power that is exercised periodically by *ad hoc* congresses', he wrote, 'the true bases of a democratic system and the foundation of its legitimacy would be absent'.[129] This does not mean that Quimper favoured a constantly amended constitution: the constitution should be fully respected (and, it seemed, untouched) during the period between constituent assemblies.[130] Anticipating the notion of the material constitution, he even maintained that every constitution contained an invariable part and a variable one: the former included the basic rights of individuals and the second the

[121] ibid. 128. He thought that the notion of a social contract had no historical basis (no society was founded on a pact), and that its undesirability was exemplified by the fact that it had led Rousseau to defend freedom and Thomas Hobbes to defend despotism. ibid. 101.
[122] ibid. 122.
[123] ibid. 123–124.
[124] ibid. 126.
[125] ibid. 137.
[126] ibid.
[127] ibid.
[128] ibid.
[129] ibid. 140.
[130] ibid. 138.

organization of the institutions of government which desirability depended on the circumstances. Not even the constituent power could alter the invariable content: no one can legitimately deprive citizens of rights that they have by the very fact of existing.[131] Moreover, he maintained that just as an individual cannot voluntarily become a slave, the nation could not deprive itself of its sovereign authority.[132]

Like some of the authors discussed earlier, Quimper thought that any changes to the constitutional text required an exercise of constituent power and were therefore outside the scope of the legislature's jurisdiction. He thus placed particular importance on the mechanism that should be available for extra-parliamentary constitutional change: the legitimacy of the constitutional order depended on the possibility of its potential re-creation of by periodically elected constituent assemblies. And although he came very close to defending the notion of the imperative mandate in the context of constitution-making, he did not insist in direct popular participation. His periodic constituent assemblies could adopt a new or radically transformed constitution without popular ratification.[133] That is to say, Quimper, like all of the authors discussed in the previous sections of this chapter, thought that the direct intervention of the citizenry—other than in the context of electing a constitution-making body—was not a necessary component of an exercise of constituent power. This view is, perhaps, a reflection of the strength that the constituent power of the nation approach enjoyed during the 19th century.

Oscar Orban, Professor of Public Law in Liège during the late 19th century, provides an interesting exception to this tendency. He suggested that the '"dismemberment" of sovereignty into constituent and constituted power' was an ineffective limit if the exercise of the former did not include opportunities for direct popular intervention.[134] Since constituent power, almost by definition, was exercised *against* the constituted institutions (in order to alter them or to override an executive, legislative, or judicial decision), it was necessary to ensure that citizens, acting outside of the ordinary institutions of government, had a means of triggering its exercise. A solution, he said, was the recognition of the right to change the constitution through popular initiative.[135] This solution was not presented as a means of facilitating participatory democracy (as

[131] ibid. 129. This idea puts Quimper in the same camp as some of the authors that will be discussed in the next section.
[132] ibid.
[133] ibid. 139.
[134] Oscar Orban, 'Des Immunités Constitutionnelles' 3 *Revue du Droit Public et de la Science Politique en France et a L'étranger* 193, 209 (1895).
[135] ibid. 213–214.

is arguably the case for some of the constitutional arrangements considered in Chapter 10), but as one of controlling the power of the three branches of government. It is, nonetheless, more consistent to what in the previous chapter I identified as the principle of participation than any other of the works discussed above. Orban's approach, as well as the ones presented by many of the authors discussed earlier, was mostly about the legal implications of constituent power, implications that were most clearly manifested in the limits applicable to ordinary government and in those applicable to constitution-making entities.

IV. Constituent Power, Natural Law, and the Common Good

As we saw in the previous sections, during the 19th century, authors who embraced the theory of constituent power usually sought to limit governments and legislatures by appealing to an extra-parliamentary constituent subject attributed with an exclusive constitution-making jurisdiction. And they also insisted that, in instances of constitutional change, the extra-parliamentary entity authorized to exercise constitution-making faculties should not be allowed to exercise the ordinary powers of government. However, the question about whether constituent power itself was subject to substantive limits (that is, whether there was a type of constitutional content it could not create) was not directly addressed, and when it was, the response usually appealed to constituent power's allegedly absolute nature. Sometimes relying openly on a natural law approach (one that, as seen in Chapter 3, was already present in Sieyès), those concerned with the potential abuses of a constituent subject attempted to deal both with the dangers of a sovereign parliament and of an unlimited constitution-maker. A good point of departure for this discussion is the work of Manuel Durán y Bas, a Catalonian jurist who served as Minister of Justice of Spain in 1899 and was generally associated with the Spanish doctrinaires.[136]

a. Durán y Bas' Constituted Sovereigns

In 1856, Durán y Bas published his *Estudios Políticos y Económicos*, where he advanced an argument that, in some ways, serves as a point of transition

[136] The constitutional thought of the doctrinaires will be discussed in Chapter 7.

between the authors discussed in the previous section and the natural law approach that more clearly characterizes the works discussed in this part of the chapter.[137] The first part of Durán y Bas' book dealt with the question of where the 'original, or constituent, sovereignty' resides.[138] Like other 19th-century commentators, he argued that government (or simply 'Power', as he called it) was an inevitable feature of human societies. If that is the case, he maintained, the question of where the original constituent power resides seems beside the point: 'if one recognises . . . the existence of a government wherever there is a society, why look at its origin, at its cause, at its principles, at its foundation and reason of existence?'[139] The question is nevertheless important since its answer determines the identity of the entity authorized to alter the constitutional order. If one thinks that governments are the result of an act of will, that they are based on a social contract, one will end up defending the constituent power of the people; if one concludes that government has divine origins, a defence of the constituent power of the monarch would follow.[140]

For Durán y Bas, the latter notion was far from convincing. Just as it could be argued that God delegated its ultimate constituent power to a monarch, it could be argued with the same force (as Marsilius of Padua and Francisco Suarez did) that he delegated it to the world's peoples.[141] But the other option, that constituent power belongs to the people, could not be true either. The idea of the constituent power of the people was for Durán y Bas directly connected to the theory of the social contract. Social contract theorists, he believed, implausibly claimed that society could exist in the absence of government; that there could be a pre-political moment in which a society comes together and decides to create a set of public institutions.[142] The social contract theory was now 'profoundly discredited',[143] and thus the alleged constituent power of the people was frequently defended by appealing to the notion that since governing pertains to everyone, 'the universality of the associates has the power to give itself the laws that are more consistent with their rights and common interests' (*que más convengan al derecho y al interés común*).[144] But no society had ever operated in this way: history has indeed shown that government can only be

[137] Manuel Durán y Bas, *Estudios Políticos y Económicos* (Barcelona: Imprenta de Antonio Brusi, 1856).
[138] ibid. 2
[139] ibid.
[140] ibid. 3.
[141] ibid. 5.
[142] ibid. 4.
[143] ibid. 5.
[144] ibid.

put in the hands of those who are 'intelligent and foresighted' (*inteligentes y previsores*).[145]

Moreover, the impracticability of the notion of the constituent power of the people, Durán y Bas maintained, raised serious doubts about its plausibility. It would require that every single human being, 'every man or woman, young or old, wise or foolish, adult or child' is given the right to participate in the making of the fundamental laws, a system that has never been, and should never be, put into practice. Durán y Bas rejected this approach, preferring instead to attribute constituent power to 'the nation'. He thus maintained, mostly relying on Pellegrino Rossi, that constituent authority rests in the nation, but understood as an entity independent of the universality of citizens, as having a 'political individuality' and a 'legal personality'.[146] Like a human being, a nation has a 'moral end to fulfil', an end different from the sum of the moral ends of the multiplicity of individuals who comprise it.[147] In particular, each nation had the end of conserving itself through time, of protecting its independence, moral dignity, its growth through the development of its strengths, and the freedom of governing itself according to the law of nature and morality (*las eternas reglas del Derecho y la moral*).[148]

In order to achieve those ends, the nation assumes a political existence, an existence consistent with what Durán y Bas, relying on the work of Friedrich Karl von Savigny, called the 'national spirit'.[149] In that sense, he wrote, one could say that the nation exercises a 'constituent sovereignty'.[150] From the idea that the nation is the constituent authority it did not follow, however, that the adoption of a constitution has to take place through a particular type of procedure, that only the entire citizenry could legitimately exercise constituent power, or that only 'an assembly that calls itself "constituent"' has the right to alter the fundamental laws.[151] Any entity that, in each country and in each epoch is guided by the national spirit and acts according to the laws of nature and morality (and here this thought is at odds with Savigny's rejection of natural law)[152] could legitimately exercise the ultimate constitution-making authority. For him, no one, not even the people, could 'pretend to be the exclusive possessor of the constituent sovereignty'.[153] Indeed, he maintained that

[145] ibid. 6.
[146] ibid. 8. See Pellegrino Rossi, *Cours d'Economie Politique* (Paris, 1843).
[147] Durán y Bas (n 137) 9.
[148] ibid.
[149] ibid. 9–10, 12–13.
[150] ibid. 13–14.
[151] ibid. 15.
[152] For a discussion, see Frederick C. Beiser, *The German Historicist Tradition* (Oxford University Press, 2011) 13, 217.
[153] ibid. 15. As will be seen in Chapter 7, this idea was advanced by the doctrinaires.

constituent power would normally be exercised by the constituted authorities. And in times of emergency, the constituent power may be temporarily placed in whatever hands would move society towards its moral ends.[154]

Whoever exercises constituent power, and in this Durán y Bas was very clear, was subject to the previously mentioned 'eternal rules of law and morality'.[155] This conception of constituent power, and of its functions and limits, in Durán y Bas' view, in the end, served to protect the constituted institutions of government. The insistence on an extra-legal constituent power that could act at any moment (expressed, e.g., in constitutional provisions that ambiguously referred to the sovereignty of the nation), acts as a permanent threat to the constituted authorities, signalling that there is a mysterious extra-legal power that may annihilate them at any moment.[156] This, he maintained, puts the constituted powers in a condition of inferiority, risking their 'authority, force, and dignity'.[157] In terms of its institutional implications, this approach is consistent the notion that the law can channel the power of altering the constitution through a set of procedures. Nonetheless, Durán y Bas saw the power of altering or replacing a constitution as always subject to limits of a moral nature. His emphasis was not on vanishing constituent power from juridical discourse or relegating it to moments of crisis or emergency, but on impressing in it a substantive duty so that not every act of constitutional creation would count as legitimate constituent activity.

b. Taparelli's Common Good

This distinction becomes clearer in the work of Luigi Taparelli d'Azeglio, the Italian Catholic scholar. According to Taparelli, human beings 'are born with a right to constitute, that is, a right that brings individuals together, in an organised way, for the joint creation of society'.[158] Following the Thomist tradition, Taparelli maintained that since God had implanted in all individuals a

[154] ibid. 20, 23, 73. This view is also reflected in the letter from the Chilean professors quoted in n. 117, above: 'In establishing a juridical order', the declaration stated, the original constituent power concretises the 'Natural Law, which is the very basis of the state.' Despite not been subject to positive law, the original constituent power could not violate neither 'the limits imposed by the Natural Law, derived from human nature', nor the 'characteristics that historically configure the true identity (*sana identidad*) and the normal being of the social body that is to be regulated'. 'Declaración de los Profesores de la Facultad de Derecho' (n. 117).

[155] Durán y Bas (n 137) 15.

[156] ibid. 20.

[157] ibid. 20.

[158] Luigi Taparelli d'Azeglio, *Curso Elemental de Derecho Natural* (México, 1875) 199.

natural tendency towards the common good, the exercise of the 'right to constitute' will tend towards the creation of orderly political communities.[159] Far from being free 'to organise society on a whim'[160] and give it any constitution, the constituent subject was charged with the responsibility of recognizing pre-existing natural rights.[161] In fact, to engage in the exercise of constituent power meant 'to clarify through constitutional law what justice and convenience'[162] require about how public authority should be organized and exercised. The goal was to produce constitutional content that promoted the common good by respecting certain principles, such as the natural right to property but also the right to the 'absolutely necessary means of subsistence'.[163] In promoting the protection of the common good, Taparelli found it necessary to conclude, with Durán y Bas, that constituent power did not need to be exercised by all those who would be subject to the future constitutional order. On the contrary, only some men were *capable* of directing others towards the common good, and it is that individual (or those individuals) who ought to have the actual power to create (or recreate) society. [164]

Taparelli's intention was to prove that if the exercise of an otherwise sovereign power failed to respect the principles of natural law (and by so doing failed to promote the common good), the constitutional forms that result from it would be dangerously incomplete: natural law principles would continually demand their inclusion into the legal order.[165] At the same time, human beings, who have a natural tendency towards those principles, would feel the moral necessity to move in their direction. As a result, they could be left with no other option than to violate the constitution in order to improve it.[166] If a stable constitutional order was to emerge, the constituent subject thus needed to respect those principles. Moreover, if the constitution was ever to be changed, it was not enough that the established constitutional forms are respected, but that the rights that promote the common good are protected 'as if one was adopting a constitution for the first time'.[167] Taparelli's was thus a defence of a substantive conception of constituent power, one in which

[159] ibid. 257.
[160] ibid. 285–286.
[161] ibid. 285, 287.
[162] ibid. 287.
[163] ibid. 134–135.
[164] ibid. 151–152.
[165] ibid. 285.
[166] ibid. 285.
[167] ibid. 287–288, 222–223. See also Luis Taparelli, *Ensayo Teórico Apoyado en los Hechos* (Madrid, 1867) 386–387.

no institution has the ability to change the constitution at will. For the previous authors, a constituent body that adopts a constitution inconsistent with justice and reason would be exercising its constituent power irresponsibly; for Taparelli and Durán y Bas, it would not be exercising constituent power at all, even if, from a juridical perspective, there may be no means for invalidating the norms it has created.

c. Mellado's Physical and Moral Rules

Writing some decades later, Francisco Mellado developed the natural law approach to constituent power in more detailed ways. Like Taparelli, Mellado argued that—what he called—'originary sovereignty'[168] emanated from God, and that the fact that human beings have a natural tendency to live in society is a direct result of God's sovereignty.[169] The *raison d'être* of constituent power (for Mellado, the type of sovereignty that is exercised when a constitution is created) is to create the rules and structures that make the existence of a political community possible.[170] Attributing the constituent power to the people[171] was no option: that would only lead to anarchy and to the arbitrary decisions of numerical majorities.[172] The very nature of the will of the people rules out the desirability of a popular constituent subject: 'the will of the multitude is variable and transient', while the constituent power is destined to create something permanent.[173] Only the representatives of the nation, acting on behalf and in the interests of all social forces, and not the will of any individual or multitude, would be able to fulfil the main mission of the constituent power.[174] The easiest way of achieving that end, Mellado maintained, was to recognize the 'constituted sovereignty' (i.e. the Crown-in-Parliament), [175] as the entity best placed

[168] Fernando Mellado, *Tratado Elemental de Derecho Político* (Madrid, 1891) 329.
[169] ibid.
[170] Like Durán y Bas, Mellado maintained that constituent power was 'a means for a people to achieve its ends' (*un medio para que cada pueblo alcance su fin*) and, like Taparelli he saw natural law as a code that 'God has impressed in our consciences' and that the constituent power must follow. ibid. 352, 329, 331.
[171] Unlike some of his contemporaries, Mellado distinguished between popular and national sovereignty. He thought that popular sovereignty was of interest to political science (as a factor that affects the way in which political power is exercised), and that only national sovereignty was strictly relevant for 'political law' (*derecho politico*). ibid. National sovereignty, as expressed by a representative assembly, should always be seen as the source of all positive law. ibid. 334.
[172] ibid. 350–351.
[173] ibid. 351.
[174] ibid. 333.
[175] ibid. 368.

to speak for the nation and to engage in constituent activity.[176] But that entity would be limited by a number of rules.[177]

Mellado classified those rules into physical and moral ones. Their violation could result in the very dissolution of the political community and would therefore be *ultra vires* the constituent subject. Firstly, there are 'physical laws' related to things such as climate, topography, and culture that, as Montesquieu famously noted, influence the constitution of every country. These elements posed 'physical' limits on the type of constitution a parliament would ever adopt.[178] Secondly, Mellado enumerated a series of moral laws which apply in every state and that establish substantive limitations on the exercise of constituent power. Among those norms, he included the idea that 'the constituent power must direct and organise social forces towards the common good', that it 'must respect religion as a bonding knot and as a means to achieve the end of each people', that it 'must respect justice as the norm and basis of any social organisation of Nations'; that it 'must aim at the harmony of social and political order'; and that it must 'coordinate the individual with the collective, the state with the social forces or entities'.[179] When the constituent subject respects those moral norms, what Taparelli called the internal constitution of the people (i.e. its character, its social mode of being)[180] and the external one (the set of rules that govern the relationship between citizens and the state and that establish the structure of the latter) would likely coincide with each other.[181]If the constituent power creates an external constitution inconsistent with the internal one, 'a struggle between the ideal and the real, between theory and practice'[182] would be produced. And that struggle could result in the destruction of the state.

Two main things follow from the approaches discussed in this section. First, constituent power must result in the creation of a constitution that fulfils some end that benefits the society at issue, that is, a moral destiny or the common good. Second, while the exercise of constituent power can be channelled through law, it is always limited by principles of natural law that lie outside,

[176] ibid. 354. Not surprisingly, he rejected the idea that a referendum was needed in order to legitimate constitutional change. For him, since the constituted powers acted on behalf of the nation, 'they have full authority to decide on any constitutional matter'. ibid. 373.

[177] ibid. 352.

[178] ibid. 352.

[179] ibid. 353.

[180] This notion is closely connected to the doctrine of the historical (or internal) constitution, examined in Chapter 7.

[181] Mellado also wrote that there are some institutions 'that are founded on justice; those are inalterable. There are others that are founded on the will and can be modified.' ibid. 352.

[182] ibid. 360.

or above, the positive legal system. These ideas are of course inter-related; for example, the common good can only be achieved if the constitution-maker respects natural law. By insisting in the constituent subject's compliance with natural law principles, these authors were, in the last instance, defending the idea that whoever has the authority to create the fundamental laws must do so in the general interest. For Rousseau, the best way of guaranteeing that result (to ensure that a new constitution reflects the general will) was by attributing the constitution-making power to a popular assembly or a set of primary assemblies; for the authors discussed in this section, achieving that goal required identifing those individuals and institutions most capable of promoting justice, reason, or the nation's moral destiny. The idea that even the constituent subject is accountable to natural law limits was not left behind in the 19th century. It has reappeared in contemporary academic and judicial proceedings, even if human rights, human dignity, or fundamental common law principles now assume the place of natural law.[183]

[183] For example, in a 1957 judgment where the Colombian Supreme Court of Justice rejected the doctrine of unconstitutional constitutional amendments, the Attorney General referred to constituent power as the 'power or faculty of society to organise or constitute itself, in virtue of its own nature and within the norms of natural law, [and] give itself its own government'. Within the limits imposed by natural law (impressed by God in the conscience of human beings), the Attorney General maintained, 'one must recognise that the primary constituent power resides in the people, and that the constituent power established in the Constitution is secondary and follows the primary one'. Judgment 2188-2189-2196, Supreme Court of Justice of Colombia (28 November 1957) 438. See also Leopoldo Uprimny, '¿Puede una Reforma de la Constitución ser Inconstitucional?' *Revista de la Academia Colombiana de Jurisprudencia* 174 (1957) 22, who relying on the famous 1951 *obiter* of the German Federal Constitutional Court , describing natural law as binding on the maker of the constitution, referred to 'the fundamental principles of justice' as potentially posing limits on the power of constitutional reform. See *Southwest Case*, 1 BVerfGE 14 (1951). The *Lisbon Case*, where the same court ruled on several issues surrounding the adoption of the Treaty of Lisbon, offers a more recent example. In that case, the court stated that 'the constituent power of the Germans which gave itself the Basic Law wanted to set an insurmountable boundary to any future political development' through an eternity clause that 'prevents a constitution-amending legislature' from affecting the principles laid down in Article 1 and Article 20. The court then added the following *obiter* statement: '[i]t may remain open whether, due to the universal nature of dignity, freedom and equality alone, this commitment even applies to the constituent power, i.e. to the case that the German people, in free self-determination, but in a continuity of legality to the rule of the Basic Law, gives itself a new constitution'. *Lisbon Case*, BVerfG,2 BvE 2/08 from 30 June 2009, paras 216–217. In a 2006 case, the Supreme Tribunal of Justice of Venezuela expressed a view similar to that of its German counterpart. In a judgment concerning the eligibility to office of certain state officials, the court stated in passing that the people's constituent power is subject, like any political power, to limits that arise 'from the rights inherent to all human persons and derived from their own dignity'. Supreme Tribunal of Justice of Venezuela, Constitutional Chamber, Expediente No. 06-0747, 28 July 2006, (Part IV). This type of language also appeared in the document that established the framework under which the Venezuelan National Constituent Assembly of 1999 was elected, which stated that the assembly would 'have as limits the values and principles of our republican history, as well as the compliance with international treaties, agreements . . . [and] the progressive character of the fundamental rights of men and democratic guarantees'. 'Bases Comiciales para el referéndum consultivo sobre la convocatoria de la Asamblea Nacional Constituyente a celebrarse el 25 de abril de 1999', Resolution No. 990323-71 (23 March 1999). In a 1999 case, one of the dissenting judges at the Supreme Court of Justice stated that those limits played the same function as natural law in the thought of Sieyès. Judgment

V. Conclusion

This chapter was about the limits posed by, and about those that that apply to, constituent power according to a number of 19th-century constitutional theorists. Constituent power, when conceived as the exclusive jurisdiction of an extra-legal entity, creates limits on ordinary and extra-ordinary institutions. For instance, despite the rejection of the imperative mandate in the late 18th and early 19th centuries, we saw that authors like Pradier-Foderé and Laboulaye understood the constitution as a *general* binding mandate, and members of legislatures and constituent assemblies as mandataires who could not go beyond their commission (i.e. legislatures could not change or adopt statutes contrary to the established constitution, and constituent assemblies could not exercise ordinary governmental powers). In those writings, the extra-legal constituent subject was associated more with the political limits it serves to justify than with the making of novel constitutions. For some authors, such as for Thouret and Hello, this was true even if the constitution lacked an amendment rule. Indeed, for Lumbreras, it made more sense for a constitution to lack an amendment rule than to have a rule of constitutional change that authorizes a legislature (even if subject to special thresholds) to alter the constitutional text.

Some 19th-century authors went beyond the traditional Sieyèsian approach to the extent that they saw actual citizens, as opposed to an abstract entity such as the nation, as the holders of constituent power. Accordingly, we begin to see works such as that of Quimper, Orban, and Fernández Concha, who sometimes willingly and sometimes reluctantly, saw periodically elected constituent assemblies, popular initiatives to trigger exercises of constituent power, and elected assemblies subject to the imperative mandate, as potentially justificable institutions. Other authors, like Pinzón, came closer to the idea of the constituent power of the people and the principle of popular participation by focusing on a defence of universal suffrage and in the institution of voting as the mechanism through which the entire community imposed limits on the exercise of political power. This kind of approach tended to move closer to a Rousseauian conception of constituent authority and at times even involved referendums (e.g. the cases of Pinzón and Laboulaye) for the ratification of new constitutions, a practice that, since 1793, had by then not been repeated

No. 1110, Supreme Court of Justice of Venezuela (14 October 1999) in *Bases Jurisprudenciales de la Supraconstitucionalidad* (Caracas: Supreme Court of Justice, 2002) 57. The court itself recognized natural law as a limit to constituent power. ibid. 47.

anywhere in the world outside the context of the Napoleonic plebiscites in the 19th century.

Finally, some authors, such as Durán y Bas, Taparelli, and Mellado, argued that constituent power itself may be subject to substantive limits. If this view is accepted, even the attribution of constituent power to parliament does not create an all-powerful constitution-making legislature. For them, the exercise of constituent power came accompanied by natural law obligations that advance some conception of the common good. In a way, the authors discussed in this chapter seem to embrace the theory of constituent power *because* of the legal and institutional limits that emerge from it. In the next chapter, we will consider the work of a group of authors and political actors who denied the idea that the recognition of an extra-legal constituent power would successfully promote limited political institutions. This is the view reflected in the work of a group of liberal thinkers generally identified as the doctrinaires and in the doctrine of the historical constitution. The ideas of the authors associated with these conceptions will be considered, firstly, at the level of theory and, secondly, in terms of their effects in the constitutional practice.

7

Rejecting Constituent Power

The theory of constituent power, we saw in the previous chapter, was understood by some 19th-century constitutional theorists to require a sharp separation between the constituent and the ordinary legislative authority. This separation, which can be traced back to Jean Jacques Rousseau and Emmanuel Sieyès,[1] involves two main types of limits: a negation of the ordinary legislature's power of constitutional change and a negation of the power of constituent assemblies to produce ordinary governmental acts. The separation between the constituent and the constituted powers rests on the idea that a constitution is a human creation, that a constitutional order can be *made*. The constituent subject, in this formulation, appears as the extra-legal holder of an ultimate constitution-making faculty. It is this idea that, for some authors, leads to the limitation of ordinary and extraordinary assemblies: the first of these entities is not authorized to engage in constituent activity, and the second is only called upon to revise or replace a constitution *on behalf* of the true constituent subject. In this chapter, I will examine two related traditions of thought that reject the existence of an extra-legal constituent power or, perhaps more accurately, deprive it of some of its main features. This rejection, it will be seen, was sometimes fuelled by a desire to restore an ancient constitutional order and sometimes by a fear of potentially uncontrolled exercises of political power.

The first of these traditions of thought, the doctrine of the *historical* or *internal* constitution, presented a direct challenge to the theory of constituent power. In Spain, the main exponent of this doctrine during the 19th century was Gaspar Melchor de Jovellanos, an influential figure during the creation of the Constitution of 1812. Jovellanos held that rather than the result of an act of will, constitutions emerged through long historical processes and could not be simply created and recreated. Of course, human beings can assemble and adopt a new constitutional text, but if they fail to respect the essential content of the historical constitution, they would not be able to create a stable legal system. The doctrine of the historical constitution is thus radically inconsistent with Rousseau's and Sieyès' constitutional thought and, indeed, was rejected

[1] See Chapters 2 and 3 of this book.

Constituent Power and the Law. Joel Colón-Ríos, Oxford University Press (2020). © Joel Colón-Ríos.
DOI: 10.1093/oso/9780198785989.001.0001

in France during the early stages of the Revolution.[2] But the doctrine did not entail the passive acceptance of an abusive government. It came accompanied by a theory of resistance which drew on the ideas of George Lawson and John Locke. A second (and related) line of attack against the concept of constituent power during the 19th century came from the French and Spanish doctrinaires. The doctrinaires rejected the idea that the people (or any other individual or group) had a right to create new constitutional orders. For them, sovereign authority belonged to reason itself, not to the monarch or the community.

These two traditions of thought, I will argue, while highlighting the risks of the always present threat of a popular extra-legal power, end up defending a de facto unlimited government. Put differently, while the authors discussed in Chapter 6 embraced the concept of constituent power in order to limit the law-making authority, the authors discussed in this chapter reject it in order to explain the reason why the Crown-in-Parliament should be conceived as a sovereign law-maker. I will proceed as follows. Part I will outline Lawson and Locke's theories of resistance. The purpose will be to highlight the differences between the right of resistance and the theory of constituent power and explain how proponents of the doctrine of the historical constitution could accept the former while negating the latter. Part II considers the origins and main features of the doctrine of the historical constitution, with a focus on Jovellanos and his followers at the Constituent Parliament in Cadiz. Part III focuses on the doctrinaire school of thought. It argues that the doctrinaire rejection of the theory of constituent power not only leads to the recognition of a sovereign law-making authority, but to the always present possibility of extra-legal exercises of unlimited political power during times of emergency. In Part IV, I examine the practical implications of these ideas by exploring the debates that took place during the adoption of the Spanish Constitution of 1845.

I. Between the Right of Resistance and Constituent Power

The authors who embraced the theory of constituent power after the French Revolution (both in continental Europe and Latin America) were to a large degree the heirs of Sieyès. There were some, however, who followed a different path. They rejected the theory of constituent power, defended some form of parliamentary sovereignty, and recognized the community's right of resistance to tyrannical government. An important example is that of Jovellanos, who

[2] See Chapters 2 to 4 of this book.

was among a group of 19th-century Spanish politicians heavily influenced by certain aspects of English constitutional thought.[3] An avid reader of Locke,[4] Jovellanos defended the right of resistance, although unlike many proponents of this right, he rejected the notions of the state of nature and the social contract as unnecessary fictions.[5] The right of resistance has a strong relationship with the theory of constituent power but it is possible to reject the former and defend the latter. In this section, I will explain why through a discussion of Lawson's and Locke's writings on the topic. By advancing a version of the right of resistance, Jovellanos and his followers were able to justify an extraordinary meeting of the *Cortes* (i.e. parliament) and, at the same time, negate this entity a full constitution-making authority.

a. Lawson and Locke

In his *Politica Sacra et Civilis*,[6] published in 1657, Lawson argued that once a commonwealth is established, individuals become subject to the power of those invested with the faculty of law-making. However, this law-making power was limited in important ways by the obligations imposed by the social contract, particularly the protection of individuals' liberty and property. Breaching them involved the risk of awakening the real sovereign, which was always the community. The 'power to constitute, abolish, alter, [and] reform forms of government', which Lawson identified as 'real majesty', was inalienable and different from the ordinary power of government, which he called 'personal majesty'.[7] Personal majesty included the power to adopt ordinary statutes. It was 'the power of a commonwealth already constituted', and it was

[3] Indeed, Lord Holland once wrote to Jovellanos that there were 'many, many people' in England who thought like him 'Carta de Lord Holland a Jovellanos' (Cádiz, 12 April 1809) in *Obras Completas* (Oviedo: Centro de Estudios del Siglo CVIII, 1986) vol. 5, 104. For an interesting discussion on the influence of English constitutional thought on Jovellanos, see Ignacio Fernández Sarasola, '"So you want us to be Englishmen . . . ": Jovellanos and British Influence on Spain's First Modern Parliament (1808-1810)', 4(1) *Comparative Legal History* 51 (2016).

[4] For a discussion, see John H. R. Polt, 'Jovellanos and his English Sources: Economic, Philosophical, and Political Writings', 54(7) *Transactions of the American Philosophical Society* 1, 7 (1964).

[5] Gaspar Melchor de Jovellanos, *Memoria sobre Educación Pública, o sea Tratado Teórico Práctico de Enseñanza* in *Obras Públicas e Inéditas* (Madrid: Biblioteca de Autores Españoles, 1858) vol. 1, 253. See also Adam Ferguson, *An Essay on the History of Civil Society* (Philadelphia, 1819) 3.

[6] George Lawson, *Political Sacra et Civilis* (Cambridge: Cambridge University Press, 1992).

[7] Ibid. 316. Lawson attributes the distinction between personal and real majesty to Christopher Besold, *De magistrate in genere* (Strasburg, 1625). Nevertheless Julian Franklin traces its origin to Hermann Kirchner, *Respublica* (1608). Julian Franklin, 'Sovereignty and the Mixed Constitution: Bodin and his Critics' in J. H. Burns (ed.) *The Cambridge history of Political Thought, 1450-1700*, (Cambridge University Press, 1991). See also Brian Tierney, *Religion and the Growth of Constitutional Thought 1150-1650* (Cambridge: Cambridge University Press, 1982) 98–99.

exercised in England by the two houses of Parliament and the King.[8] In cases of extreme governmental abuse, the community's original right to constitute a Commonwealth could be exercised again.[9] Operating by the then common idea about the divine nature of the ultimate political power, he added that when certain governmental abuses 'offend God', He might stir up the people to rebel and exercise their original rights.[10]

Importantly, although Lawson attributed the community with real majesty, he limited the possibilities of actually exercising it to instances in which government abused its law-making faculties. '[A]s the community hath the power of constitution', he wrote, 'so it hath of dissolution, *when there shall be a just and necessary cause*'.[11] Not surprisingly, he denounced the ideas of the French author of *Vindiciae Contra Tyrannos*, who in 1579 had suggested 'that those who may constitute may set aside', that is, that the community had the power to create a new government whenever it wished. According to Lawson, a multitude could not simply get together and alter or abolish the constitution for, as subjects, individuals had the duty to obey the 'laws once made, or suffer'.[12] It is only when the conditions on which personal majesty is held are transgressed, such as cases of 'negligence, imprudence, injustice, oppression, and other such like sins',[13] that the obligation to obey terminates and all authority reverts back to the community.[14]

Moreover, Lawson maintained that those attributed with personal majesty cannot 'meddle with the fundamental laws of the constitution'.[15] In this, he agreed with Sir Roger Owen, who thought that there were things even parliament could not do, such as changing the form of the polity from a monarchy to a democracy.[16] 'The form of government', Lawson maintained, 'was first constituted by the community of England, not by the parliament. For the community and people of England gave both king and parliament their being: and if they meddle with the constitution to alter it, they destroy themselves . . .'[17]

[8] Lawson (n. 6) 47.
[9] Similar views were advanced by other commentators during the 17th century. See, for example, William Bridge, *The Wounded Conscience Cured* (B. Allen, 1642).
[10] Lawson (n. 6) 69.
[11] ibid. (emphasis added).
[12] ibid. 52.
[13] ibid. 69.
[14] ibid. 68. See also Julian H. Franklin, *John Locke and the Theory of Sovereignty: Mixed Monarchy and the Right of Resistance in the Political Thought of the English Revolution* (Cambridge: Cambridge University Press, 1978) 72.
[15] Lawson (n. 6) 48
[16] ibid. 107.
[17] ibid.

Anticipating the Convention Parliament of 1689 (and the constitutional conventions of the 18th century in the territory later named the United States), Lawson maintained that once government was dissolved, the community could make use of the existing parliament to exercise its real majesty, 'but this cannot be as a parliament, but considered under another notion, as an immediate representative of a community, not of a commonwealth.'[18] Locke followed Lawson in most of this. He thought that 'the people alone can appoint the form of the commonwealth, which is by constituting the legislative and appointing in whose hands that shall be'.[19] But once a constitutional order is in place, it is only if the community is confronted by a 'long train of [governmental] abuses' that such a power could be exercised again. In such a situation, government dissolves and power 'devolves to the people who have a right to resume their original liberty'.[20]

Lawson and Locke (in contrast to Rousseau and Sieyès), were at pains to show that even if it is true that the people as a whole is the real supreme power, it cannot be considered as such 'under any Form of Government,' because 'this power of the people can never take place till the government be dissolved'.[21] During normal times parliament is supreme, for it has a superior power to adopt laws that bind all subjects.[22] But the community, Locke maintained, 'perpetually retains a supreme power of saving themselves from the attempts and

[18] ibid. 47. Consistent with that view, the Convention Parliament that met in 1689 without having been summoned by James II and which invited William and Mary to reign jointly—while seen by many as an inferior and legally irregular body—was depicted by others 'as something greater, and of greater power than Parliament'. Gordon Wood, *The Creation of the American Republic, 1776-1787* (University of North Carolina Press, 1998) 319. Although comprised by the Commons and Lords that would usually sit in Parliament, the Convention Parliament was elected specifically to bring the country to a settlement regarding the monarchy and presented William and Mary a Bill of Rights that sought to limit the powers of the Crown. For a discussion, see Steve Pincus, *1688: The First Modern Revolution* (New Haven: Yale University Press, 2009) 282–284. Not surprisingly, years later, James Otis suggested that the Convention Parliament of 1689 had 'created the government anew' and in that sense was something more than an ordinary Parliament. Wood (n. 18).

[19] Lawson (n. 6) 69John Locke, *Two Treatises of Government: A Critical Edition with an Introduction an Apparatus Criticus* (Peter Laslett ed.) (Cambridge: Cambridge University Press, 1967) para. 141.

[20] Locke, *Two Treatises* (n. 19) paras 222, 225, 233.

[21] ibid. para. 149. Nevertheless, and providing the community with an important role in determining whether it could exercise its constituent power, Locke maintained that whenever there was a question of whether the legislative or the executive have acted against the people's trust and therefore government should dissolve, 'the people shall be judge'. ibid. 245, para. 240. This passage can be taken to suggest that, after all, for Locke it is the people who decides whether a certain situation merits the dissolution of government, and therefore justifies the exercise of the power to create a new constitutional order. See also Algernon Sidney, *Discourses Concerning Government* (Indianapolis: Liberty Fund, 1990 [1698]) at 21. Such an interpretation would give force to the idea that Locke was advancing a theory of constituent power not very different from that of Sieyès. However, the very requisite of the occurrence of a set of governmental abuses in order for the exercise of constituent power to be morally justified, signals a fundamental distinction between Locke's approach and the theory of constituent power advanced by its French counterpart.

[22] Locke (n. 19) para. 155.

designs of anybody, even their legislators, whenever they shall be so foolish or so wicked as to lay and carry on designs against the liberties and properties of the subject.'[23]

Lawson's and Locke's conception of the people's faculty of exercising constituent power as depending on a set of previous governmental abuses later became part of the founding document of the American Revolution: '[W]henever any Form of Government becomes destructive of these ends ['that all men are created equal, that they are endowed by their Creator with certain unalienable Rights'] it is the Right of the People to alter or to abolish it, and to institute new Government.'[24] Echoing Locke's literal words, the same document established: '[W]hen a long train of abuses and usurpations, pursuing invariably the same Object evinces a design to reduce [the people] under absolute Despotism, it is their right, it is their duty, to throw off such Government . . .'[25] This limitation on the exercise of the constitution-making power was later expressed by Benjamin Rush in 1787: 'It is often said that "the sovereign and all other power is seated *in* the people". This idea is unhappily expressed. It should be—"all power is derived *from* the people". They possess it only on the days of their elections. After this, it is the property of their rulers, nor can they exercise or resume it, unless it is abused.'[26] Constituent power was thus to be only exercised in states of necessity, when an emergency gave the community no option but to try and save itself.

II. Jovellanos and the Doctrine of the Historical Constitution

In Spain, more than a century later, the right of resistance, as formulated by Lawson and Locke, was defended by Jovellanos, an Asturian jurist who became one of the main figures of the Spanish resistance government during the French occupation of Spain. Jovellanos was at times very critical of Locke (once describing him, together with Rousseau, Gabriel Bonnot de Mably, and John Milton, as someone 'who had not done more than rave on politics'), but embraced his thought on different issues.[27] In this section, I will outline some of

[23] ibid. para. 149.
[24] *Declaration of Independence* (1776).
[25] Locke (n. 19) para. 149.
[26] Benjamin Rush, 'Address to the People of the United States' (1787), *The Documentary History of the Ratification of the Constitution* (Wisconsin Historical Society Press, 2008) vol. 13, 46. This conception has some similarities to the source/exercise distinction, briefly discussed in Chapter 5: the sovereignty *exercised by government* comes from the people, but it is not exercised by the people.
[27] Polt (n. 4) 62, 64.

the main tenets of Jovellanos' thought, which were rejected by the drafters of the Spanish Constitution of 1812 but embraced by parliament in 1845. As explained in Chapter 5, the creation of the Constitution of 1812 was the result of the French invasion of Spain in 1808. Resistance to the French occupiers led to the convocation of a Constituent Parliament that, as we saw, was eventually dominated by liberals who assumed the jurisdiction to adopt a new constitution. The liberals' main opponents were a group of royalists who, largely following the thought of Jovellanos, insisted that the Constituent Parliament was bound to respect the essence of Spain's 'historical' constitution.[28] Not surprisingly, before his death in 1811, Jovellanos rejected the Constituent Parliament's embracement of national sovereignty, which he called a 'political heresy'.[29]

Of course, Jovellanos wrote, in the absence of any form of government, sovereignty rests in the community: sovereignty in that context is simply 'the absolute, independent, and supreme power that rests in any association of men'.[30] But political sovereignty, the type of sovereignty that exists once an association of human beings constitutes a form of government, is held by 'the agent or agents to which the constitution attributes the exercise of power'.[31] Political sovereignty always supposes an instance of empire and obedience; someone who orders and *someone else* who is ordered. No individual or people could be said to be sovereign over itself.[32] It is true that a nation has the power to direct society and constitute a form of government. But once that happens, the nation 'abdicates forever' this primitive right,[33] a fact that could be most clearly observed in those countries which, like Spain, were constituted as monarchies. Interestingly, Jovellanos maintained that it was in the executive power, and not in the legislative authority, where sovereignty resides: the executive power is the one that really rules.[34] When a nation abdicates its sovereignty, it would

[28] The third main group in the Constituent Parliament were the deputies from Spanish America, who rejected both the French and English models, and seemed to favour a federal arrangement as the one then present in the United States. For a discussion, see Joaquín Varela Suanzes-Carpegna, 'Las Cortes de Cádiz y la Constitución de 1812 (Una Visión de Conjunto)', 26 *Corts. Anuario de Derecho Parlamentario* 191 (2010) 195.

[29] Gaspar Melchor de Jovellanos, *Memoria en Defensa de la Junta Central*, vol. 5, 580. See also Joaquín Varela Suanzes-Carpegna, *Doctrina de la Constitución Histórica de España* (Alicante, 2013) 51.

[30] Jovellanos, *Memoria* (n. 29) 576

[31] ibid. 577.

[32] ibid. 576.

[33] ibid. 578.

[34] ibid. 578. Locke did not identify the executive as sovereign, but he did identify it as 'supreme' in certain contexts (he normally reserved the adjective 'supreme' to the legislative power and, in the context of his theory of resistance, to the community): 'In some commonwealths, where the legislative is not always in being, and the executive is vested in a single person who has also a share in the legislative, there that single person in a very tolerable sense may also be called supreme; not that he has in himself all the supreme power which is that of law-making; but because he has in him the supreme execution from whom all inferior magistrates derive all their several subordinate powers, or at least the greatest part of them. Having also no legislative superior to him, there being no law to be made without his consent

understandably do so by placing some limits on the exercise of political power. In a monarchy like that of Spain, those limits revolved around the idea that the nation had the right to participate in the legislative power and to require the king to respect this custom.[35]

Like Lawson and Locke, Jovellanos thought that in cases of serious governmental abuse, the nation had the right to resist sovereign power and assume its primitive rights.[36] He also called this right of resistance the '*supreme* power'. This was 'a power superior to any other power derived from the constitution . . . [it is an] original, and primitive power, immediately derived from nature itself'.[37] Its purpose, as he told Lord Holland in 1809, was no other than to 'preserve and defend the constitution' and, in that respect, it was not the same thing as sovereignty.[38] This supreme power was the one the Spanish Nation exercised during the French occupation, when it was left without a legitimate king. Jovellanos' version of the right of resistance, like Lawson's and Locke's, shares some important features with Sieyès' constituent power: it is extra-legal, inalienable, and superior to any constitution.[39] But Jovellanos' thought is directly inconsistent with Sieyès' theory of constituent power in the following sense: when a nation exercises its supreme power, its task is not to create a new constitution but—akin to someone who has been tasked to deal with an emergency—to restore the one that has been violated by government. A nation could always defend and even improve its constitution but could never 'alter it and destroy it to create a new one'.[40]

To a large extent, this was a result of Jovellanos' concept of constitution, which was similar to that defended in pre-revolutionary France by supporters of the traditional monarchy.[41] 'What is a constitution', he wrote, but the 'fundamental laws that fix the rights of the sovereign and the subjects,

which cannot be expected should ever subject him to the other part of the legislative, he is properly enough, in this sense, supreme.' Locke (n. 19) para. 151.

[35] Jovellanos, *Memoria* (n. 29) 580.
[36] ibid. 580–581.
[37] ibid. 582.
[38] ibid. 583.
[39] For the influence of Locke on this aspect of Jovellano's thought, see Antonio Elorza, 'La Formación del Liberalismo en España' in *Historia de la Política, vol. III: Ilustración, Liberalismo y Nacionalismo* (Fernando Vallespín ed.) (Madrid: Editorial Alianza, 1991) 411–412.
[40] Jovellanos, *Memoria* (n. 29) 584.
[41] See Chapter 3 of this book. It was also defended by other 18th- and 19th-century commentators in Spain. For a discussion, see José Manuel Nieto Soria, *Medievo Constitucional: Historia y Mito Político en los Orígenes de la España Contemporánea (ca. 1750-1814)* (Akal, 2007). It was also the conception of constitution defended by G. W. F. Hegel in his *Philosophy of Right*. For Hegel, the question 'Who shall frame the constitution?' was 'meaningless': 'To think of giving a people a constitution *à priori* is a whim, overlooking precisely that element which renders a constitution something more than a product of thought. Every nation, therefore, has the constitution which suits it and belongs to it . . . A constitution is not a mere manufacture, but the work of centuries.' The

and the healthy means of preserving both?'[42] These fundamental laws, which he called the 'effective or historical'[43] constitution were to be found in 'our old codes, in our ancient chronicles, in our depreciated manuscripts and dusty archives'.[44] Since the historical constitution was formed slowly through the ages, '[t]o think that a constitution can be made just in the same way that someone creates a play or a novel is a great insanity'.[45] The Spanish historical constitution prescribed that the king was the sovereign, and that the king's subjects had the right to be called to parliament. Accordingly, as Jean Bodin suggested some centuries earlier with respect to the absolute monarch, [46] Jovellanos insisted that not even the nation had the right to 'alter the form and the essence' of the 'received constitution'.[47] A constitution would lack stability if the very people who are supposed to defend it and respect it today can destroy it tomorrow.[48]

As we saw in Chapter 3, during the French Revolution, it was argued by Sieyès and others that France lacked a constitution; and as we saw in Chapter 6, some 19th century-theorists of constituent power (such as José María Quimper) claimed the same of England. What these theorists were missing, from Jovellanos' perspective, was that all those countries did have a historical constitution based on a set of fundamental laws according to which the king and his parliament shared sovereign power.[49] And this meant that the Spanish

last sentence forms part of the 'additions' to Hegel's original text. Georg Wilhelm Friedrich Hegel, *Philosophy of Right* (New York: Dover, 2005) 159–160.

[42] Jovellanos, *Memoria* (n. 29) vol. 2, 39.

[43] 'Diarios Inéditos de Jovellanos', cited in Ignacio Fernández Sarasola, *El Pensamiento Político de Jovellanos: Seis Estudios* (Oviedo, In Itinere, 2011) 43.

[44] Jovellanos, 'Carta a Antonio Fernández de Prado' (Gijón, 7 December 1795) in n. 3, vol. III, 179–180.

[45] 'Diarios Inéditos de Jovellanos', cited in Julio Somoza, *Las Amarguras de Jovellanos* (Gijón: Auseva, 1989) 178.

[46] Jean Bodin, *On Sovereignty: Four Chapters from the Six Books of the Commonwealth* (Julian Franklin ed.) (Cambridge: Cambridge University Press, 1992) 13, 18.

[47] Jovellanos, *Memoria* (n. 29) vol. 5, 585.

[48] ibid.

[49] The Spanish notion of fundamental laws is much older than Jovellanos' doctrine of the historical constitution. See Santos M. Coronas González, 'Las Leyes Fundamentales del Antiguo Régimen', 81 *Anuario de Historia del Derecho Español* 11 (2011). The notion of fundamental laws and the historical constitution also has an old history in England and in France. In these discussions, however, one needs to be aware that while the notion of 'fundamental law' frequently points to a historical or internal constitution that cannot be changed by an act of will, it sometimes points (as in Rousseau) to the kind of rule that can only be altered by the sovereign people (which is, in a way, exactly what the doctrine of the historical constitution negates). Oliver Cromwell, for example, seemed to embrace the former notion when writing that in 'every government there must be somewhat fundamental, somewhat like a Magna Charta, that should be standing and be unalterable', among which he included 'the government by a single person and a parliament'. In some cases, not even this distinction is entirely clear. Consider the following statement by Lawson: 'Fundamental laws in every state are those which concern the constitution; not fundamental, such as are made immediately to regulate the administration. The former are such as cannot be altered without taking asunder and disjointing the very frame

Parliament, even if convened extraordinarily and during an emergency (and even if acting together with the monarch), could not claim to be the bearer of a constituent power.[50] The fundamental laws of the realm had to be respected even by the nation. Nonetheless, Jovellanos (as Sieyès argued some years later) maintained that the convocation of the Constituent Parliament after the French occupation was more than justified by the historical constitution: 'If the nation should be consulted in difficult and serious cases, as for the imposition of taxes and the formation of new laws, I ask, can there be more serious cases . . . than that of providing the nation with security and independence?'[51]

Parliament, which had fallen into disuse in times of absolutism, was for Jovellanos an important part of the historical constitution. Unlike liberals, such as Lorenzo Calvo de Rozas, who argued for the convocation of a constituent entity, Jovellanos wanted to call a parliament representative of the three estates of the realm and to attribute it with limited functions. Such a parliament could reform anything that needed to be reformed and restore anything that needed restoring, but could not alter the country's fundamental laws.[52] Jovellanos' approach was defended in the Constituent Parliament by a number of royalist deputies, such as Pedro Inguanzo Rivero, who claimed that 'there are laws that because of their nature are unalterable in any event, and others that on the contrary, can and should be changed at different times and circumstances'. 'To the first type', he added, 'belong those laws that are called, and are truly, fundamental, which constitute the bases of the State, and if destroyed, the entire social edifice would fall. All the others belong to the second type'.[53] In fact, Inguanzo maintained that the fundamental laws should be formalized in a way that prevents them 'from ever being revoked'.[54] As will

and form of government; the latter may be altered, and yet the essential frame may stand. The former are the foundation of the state; the latter are but superstructions. The former determine the sovereign who he is, and what his power, and also define the bounds of liberty and subjection of the subject.' George Lawson, *An Examination of the Political Part of Mr Hobbs his Leviathan* (London, Printed by R. White, 1657) 108–109. For a historical examination of the concept of fundamental law in England, see J. W. Gough, *Fundamental Law in English Constitutional History* (Oxford: Clarendon Press, 1955). For France, see the discussion and sources cited in Chapter 3 of this book.

[50] Varela, *Doctrina* (n. 29) 54.

[51] Cited in Luis Sánchez Agesta, *Curso de Derecho Constitucional Comparado* (Madrid: Editora Nacional, 1963) 426. This time, however, the convocation of the Constituent Parliament would not involve a meeting of the different orders of the realm, but of national representatives. ibid. For Sieyès' argument, see Chapter 3 of this book.

[52] ibid. This approach did not prevail, and when Parliament was convened under the name of *Cortes Generales y Extraordinarias*, the term *extraordinarias* was quickly interpreted by liberals as meaning 'constituent'. See Ignacio Fernández Sarasola, *La Constitución de Cádiz: Orígen, Contenido y Proyección Internacional* (Madrid: Centro de Estudios Políticos y Constitucionales, 2011) 62.

[53] Varela, *Doctrina* (n. 29) 54.

[54] ibid. 57.

be seen in Part IV of this chapter, this type of discussion (reminiscent of contemporary debates about the material constitution and the doctrine of unconstitutional constitutional amendments) was also present during the creation of the Constitution of 1845.

Some aspects of Jovellanos' thought bear important similarities with that of Edmund Burke who, as we will see below, also influenced in important ways the French and Spanish doctrinaires.[55] Like Jovellanos, Burke rejected the very idea of constituent power. He expressed alarm that the French Constituent Assembly had 'no fundamental law' and that its members claimed to 'have the power to make a constitution which shall conform to their designs'.[56] For him, '[t]he very idea of the fabrication of a new government, is enough to fill us with disgust and horror'.[57] A constitution could of course be reformed, but only with attention to 'the principle of reference to antiquity'.[58] Like Jovellanos, Burke believed that 'the spirit of our constitution' was to be found 'in our histories, in our records, in our acts of parliament, and journals of parliament . . . '.[59] This did not necessarily mean that revolutions were never justified.[60] For example, the Glorious Revolution of 1688 had a clear justification, because it had the purpose of 'preserv[ing] our *antient* indisputable rights and liberties'.[61] But during the French Revolution, an assembly revolted against the French traditional institutions and against a monarch who attempted to protect them. Somewhat ironically, like Burke's doctrine of the ancient constitution, Jovellanos' doctrine of the historical constitution (as well as his rejection of the theory of constituent power) was entirely consistent with the institutionalization of a legally supreme parliament, a parliament with a legally unlimited constitution-making authority.[62]

[55] There is significant evidence of Burke's influence on Jovellanos. See Lioba Simon Schuhmache, 'Burke's Political and Aesthetic Ideas in Spain: A View from the Right' in *The Reception of Edmund Burke in Europe* (Martin Fitzpatrick and Peter Jones eds) (Bloomsbury, 2017).

[56] Edmund Burke, *Reflections on the Revolution in France* (Penguin Classics, 1986) 133.

[57] ibid. 117.

[58] ibid.

[59] ibid. For a discussion of the place of the doctrine of the ancient constitution in English constitutional history, see J. G. A. Pocock, 'Burke and the Ancient Constitution: A Problem in the History of Ideas', 111(2) *The Historical Journal* 125 (1960); J. W. F. Allison, *The English Historical Constitution: Continuity, Change and European Effects* (Cambridge University Press, 2007).

[60] For a discussion, see Martin Loughlin, 'Burke on Law, Revolution and Constitution', 29 *Journal of Constitutional History* 49 (2015) 53, 56.

[61] Burke (n. 56) 117

[62] The concept of the historical or ancient constitution was also present in 19th-century Latin American constitutional theory. There, it was sometimes presented in a negative light (as the legal foundation of Spanish colonialism). For a discussion of this and other uses of the concept of the ancient constitution in Latin American constitutional history, see José Carlos Chiaramonte, *Usos Políticos de la Historia: Lenguaje de Clases y Revisionismo Histórico* (Buenos Aires: Editorial Sudamericana, 2013) 190–196.

III. The Doctrinaires and the Sovereignty of Reason

In the previous chapter we saw that authors like Oscar Orban and Édouard Laboulaye argued in favour of the establishment of a legal framework for the exercise of constituent power so that its non-delegable character could be protected and the limits that emerge from it could be more easily identified. The same could be said about Rousseau, who defended the idea that in a legitimate state, constituent power was to be exercised according to law. However, in recognizing the nation's right to have any constitution it wanted, a conception that had a clear revolutionary potential emerged. The authors that will be discussed in this section, the doctrinaires, were particularly concerned with that revolutionary potential. The term 'doctrinaires' is normally used to refer to a group of politicians in 19th-century France and Spain who attempted to find a middle ground between the radicalism of the 1789 Revolution and the (then restored) monarchy. They were generally Anglophile, often influenced by the thought of Burke and, in Spain, also by that of Jovellanos. Some doctrinaires embraced the notion of the historical constitution and rejected the theory of the social contract, particularly in its Rousseauian version, as a dangerous imaginary construct. For them, as for some of the authors discussed in Chapter 6, society and government were co-original.[63]

Discarding the theory of constituent power and defending the 'sovereignty of reason' (as opposed to the sovereignty of any individual or entity), the doctrinaires held that human institutions could have de facto sovereignty, but never posses sovereignty by right. Moreover, as any political power, de facto sovereignty always had to be exercised according to the dictates of reason and justice. The doctrinaires rejected the appeals to a popular or monarchical constituent power that could be exercised outside ordinary government but recognized that constitutions sometimes need to change and accommodate to the evolution of society. Not surprisingly, their theory led to some version of parliamentary sovereignty.

This was the case of Antonio Alcalá Galiano, a Spanish politician exiled in England from 1823 to 1833, who later sat in the parliament where the Constitution of 1845 was adopted. Alcalá Galiano disagreed with those who 'found differences between the constituent and the constituted powers'.[64]

[63] See Aurelian Craiutu, 'Rethinking Political Power: The Case of the French Doctrinaires', 2(2) *European Journal of Political Theory* 125 (2003) 130. The idea that society and government was co-original, as we saw in Chapter 6, was very common among 19th-century constitutional theorists. See, for example, Rafael Fernández Concha, *Filosofía del Derecho, o Derecho Natural Dispuesto para Servir de Introducción a las Ciencias Legales*, vol. 2 (Barcelona, 1888) 177.

[64] Antonio Alcalá Galiano, *Lecciones de Derecho Político Constitucional* (Madrid, 1843) 416.

During the discussions that eventually led to the adoption of the Constitution of 1845, some of Alcalá Galiano's contemporaries insisted that the fact the then current Constitution of 1837 lacked an amendment formula meant that it only could be changed through an extraordinary constituent assembly, and not by parliament. For Alcalá Galiano, this was nonsense: the only thing that the legislative body acting together with the king could not do was to abdicate its own law-making jurisdiction, something that would amount to a revolution.[65]

Alcalá Galiano presented the doctrine of parliamentary sovereignty as an alternative to the distinction between constituent and constituted power by then well established in Spain and France.[66] Constituent power assumed that the law should recognize that there is a power outside of the constitutional order, and that this power was unregulated. For him and other doctrinaires, this approach unnecessarily subjected society to the permanent threat of an absolute power, a power that could be exercised in unjust or unreasonable ways.[67]

In France, the main exposition of this approach is found in the work of François Guizot. For Guizot (who served as Prime Minister for a short period after 1847), the notion of the sovereignty of the people falsely assumed that a numerical majority would 'know and want in every case what justice and reason' require.[68] No one had the right to adopt a law (constitutional law

[65] ibid. 423–424. Accordingly, he thought that the idea that the English Parliament lacked the authority of 'depriving English subjects, of the liberty of the press, or of the right to be tried by a jury' was mistaken. ibid. 424.

[66] English writers sometimes explicitly attributed constituent power to parliament. Before the turn of the century, in 1792, Thomas Oldfield stated that 'constituent power consists in every Englishman, from the prince to the peasant, and of whatever state, dignity, or quality, possessing the right of being present in parliament either in person or by procuration or attorney; and the consent of the parliament is understood to be every man's consent'. Thomas Hinton Burley Oldfield, *An Entire and Complete History, Political and Personal, of the Boroughs of Great Britain* (London: Printed for G. Riley 1792) vol. 1, 9.

[67] Alcalá Galiano had a theory of resistance and of 'just and necessary' revolutions reminiscent of that of Lawson and Locke. He defined revolutions as 'violent changes [*mudanzas*] in the form or in the spirit of the government of the states, resisted by a relatively numerous group'. Galiano (n. 64) 459. 'Just revolutions', he wrote, 'are those provoked by an unjust act that cannot be repaired without violence'. These revolutions occurred extra-legally but in a context where the law had already been violated by government. Revolutions were necessary when there was a profound inconsistency 'between the political and social state of a people, when the laws go in one direction, and opinion in another; and useful reforms do not arrive'. ibid. 462. Explicitly relying on Burke, Alcalá Galiano stated that just and necessary revolutions would normally come accompanied by serious harms, so they should be avoided as much as possible. Moreover, he noted that revolutions usually resulted in dictatorships, some of which could be as necessary as the revolution itself, provided their purpose was the 'conservation of the achievements of the revolution, putting an end to the excesses that were employed in order to succeed, and even combining the old with the modern'. ibid. 469. He thought that an example of a 'useful' dictatorship of that kind was that of Napoleon, who put an end to disorder and founded a government that combined the best of the past and the present. ibid. 469–470. In contrast, dictatorships that seek to simply bring back the state of things that preceded a revolution can be infinitely harmful and contradict the wishes and necessities of present generations. ibid.

[68] François Guizot, *Histoire des Origines du Gouvernement Représentatif en Europe* (Paris, 1851) 107. Guizot sometimes referred to the notion of a natural law binding on all individuals. For a discussion, see Aurelian Craiutu, 'Rethinking Political Power: The Case of the French Doctrinaires', 2(2) *European*

included) just because they wished it: 'the legitimacy of power rests in the consistency of its laws with eternal reason, not in the will of the man who exercises power nor in the will of the men over which power is exercised'.[69]

Representative government, for Guizot, was the best means to extract 'public reason' from society.[70] His conception of representative government involved a system where citizens are called to elect the 'most capable' deputies,[71] combined with a limited franchise and the limits imposed by the separation of powers. Such an arrangement would help to achieve the ultimate goal of government: 'the destruction of any permanent *de jure* sovereignty'.[72] Representative government was in this sense very different from democracy. The latter, like the theory of constituent power, rested on the sovereignty of numerical majorities.[73] Those radical democrats who proposed that constitutions should facilitate the exercise of an extra-legal power incorrectly assumed that revolutions could be properly channelled through law. 'One does not organise revolutions', Guizot wrote, 'nor give them a set of procedures'.[74] Under this approach, constituent power was better seen as a juridically irrelevant category, and the established constituted organs recognized as having the power to make ordinary and constitutional laws.[75] Indeed, Guizot maintained that even if an extra-legal constituent power had existed, it would have been exercised not by primary or extraordinary assemblies but by individuals or constituted entities acting during a crisis.

'I have seen, in my life time' Guizot wrote, 'three constituent powers: in the Year VIII, Napoleon; in 1814, Louis XVIII; in 1830, the Chamber of Deputies'.[76]

Journal of Political Theory 125 (2003) 140. See also Luis Diez del Corral, *El Liberalismo Doctrinario* (Madrid: Instituto de Estudios Políticos, 1973) 287.

[69] François Guizot, *Historia de los Orígenes del Gobierno Representativo en Europa* (KRK Ediciones, 2009) 668.

[70] ibid. 783, 671.

[71] ibid. 787. Guizot was a critic of the pyramidal system once defended by Sieyès; for him, small meetings of electors made the formation of factions more likely and affected the rationality of the vote. ibid.

[72] ibid. 842–844.

[73] Aurelian Craiutu, *Liberalism under Siege: The Political Thought of the French Doctrinaires* (Lexington Books, 2003) 115. See also Denis Serrigny, *Traité du Droit Public des Français* (Paris, 1846) 58.

[74] François Guizot, *Mémoires pour Servir a L'Histoire de mon Temps* (Paris, 1865) vol. 7, 26. Guizot thought that revolutions were not governed by human will but by what he called a 'greater master': when God determines that society must be reconstituted, he employs the most diverse means for such an event to take place. ibid. 26–27. For Salvador Cuesta, writing in 1887, the doctrinaires defended a fatally flawed approach: in the end, they had to assume 'that the people is the sovereign when it constitutes the state and the sovereign's subject after constituting it'. Salvador Cuesta, *Elementos de Derecho Político* (Salamanca, 1887) 172. In so doing, he added, they failed to explain what would count as a legitimate creation of the constituted powers.

[75] For a discussion, see also Douglas Johnson, *Guizot: Aspects of French History 1787-1874* (University of Toronto Press, 1963) 86.

[76] Guizot, *Mémoires* (n. 74) 27.

Denis Serrigny, a lawyer closely associated with the French doctrinaires, took this approach to its natural legal conclusion. The separation between the constituent and the constituted powers, which attributed absolute sovereignty to the former and a mandate subject to the limits established in the constitution to the latter, had no place in France.[77] Indeed, he maintained that by omitting an amendment formula, the French Charter of 1830 did 'not admit that distinction, radically contrary to the essential objective of the creation of political societies, which is to bring order to disorder'.[78] The fact that a constitution lacks an amendment rule should not lead one to appeal to a latent and disorganized power, but to the realization that the ordinary institutions of government possess a legally unlimited power of constitutional change (an approach unequivocally accepted by the Chamber of Deputies in 1842).[79] Such a power could be described as unlimited (in the sense that it was not subject to legal limits), but not as arbitrary because it would always be exercised 'consulting the right of reason'.[80]

Juan Donoso Cortés, pejoratively called *Guizotín* (little Guizot) by the Spanish press (even though he was often critical of Guizot),[81] shared with the French doctrinaires the emphasis on the sovereignty of reason (in his terminology, *la soberanía de la inteligencia*).[82] However, he did not abandon altogether the notion of constituent power, and attributed it to parliament in a somewhat more explicit way than Guizot.[83] Indeed, acting as Secretary of the Constitutional Commission that advised parliament on the reform of the Constitution of 1837, he wrote: 'there are some who see sovereignty coming

[77] Serrigny (n. 73) 57.

[78] ibid. 59. A similar view was exemplified by Jean-Étienne-Marie Portalis, one of the drafters of the French Civil Code, who complained in the early 1800s that people talked 'about constituent power as if it was always present, as if it were part of the constituted powers. This is an error: when the constitution of a people has been established, the constituent power disappears.' Jean-Étienne-Marie Portalis, *Discours, Rapports et Travaux Inédits sur le Code Civil* (Paris, 1844) 114. It is, he wrote, like 'the word of the creator that imposes a law that governs forever, it is his omnipotent hand that rests . . . after animating and giving life to all that exists.'

[79] For a brief discussion, see Chapter 6.

[80] Serrigny (n. 73) 76. Félix Berriat-Saint-Prix, in response to the doctrinaire's approach, maintained that the exercise of any right was subject to 'the lights of reason'. But that did not mean that the exercise of de facto sovereignty should be put in the hands of a political elite. Félix Berriat-Saint-Prix, *Théorie du Droit Constitutionnel Français: Esprit des Constitutions de 1848 et de 1852 et des Sénatus-Consultes Organiques Précédé d'un Essai sur le Pouvoir Constituant* (Paris, 1851) 8, 9, 12.

[81] See Diez del Corral (n. 68) 573. For Donoso's critique of Guizot and of doctrinaire's thought in general, see his 'Polémica con Rossi' in *Obras Completas de Juan Donoso Cortés* (Madrid: Biblioteca de Autores Cristianos, 1970) 496–499.

[82] One of the best cases of the 'sovereignty of intelligence', he said, was Napoleon. See Diez del Corral (n. 68) 565.

[83] Juan Donoso Cortés, *Obras* (Madrid: Imprenta de Tejado, 1954) 196, 198. cf. Juan Donoso Cortés, 'Polémica con el Doctor Rossi y Juicio Crítico acerca de los Doctrinarios', 3 *El Correo Nacional* 441 (1838). See also Rodrigo Fernández Carvajal, 'Las Constantes de Donoso', 95 *Revista de Estudios Políticos* 75 (1957) 85.

from the Heavens and place it in the Crown, and there are some who see it coming from the people, and place it in a popular assembly'.[84] Whenever any of these two maxims have prevailed, he continued, 'power has become tyranny'.[85] Moving away from what he considered to be two extremes, Donoso maintained that the 'constituent power (*potestad constituyente*) does not lie anywhere but in the constituted authority (*potestad constituida*), and in Spain this means in the Parliament acting together with the King'.[86]Donoso despised the idea of a constituent subject who, after performing its functions, fell into an 'indolent idleness'.[87] While in normal times the constitution-making authority lies in the Crown-in-Parliament, Donoso (like Guizot) maintained that in times of emergency, any entity (be it the people, the king, or any other group) capable of bringing society back to order can exercise 'a legitimate constituent power'.[88]

The relationship between the exercise of constituent power and times of emergency is key to the doctrinaire approach. During those critical times, their rejection of any form of sovereign power moved into the background. As we will see in Part IV, some members of the parliament that adopted the Constitution of 1845 relied on this view in their attempt to block the replacement of the constitutional order. For them, the exercise of constituent power was only justified in times of a serious crisis and Spain was not undergoing one. This idea was of course not only common to the doctrinaires. Constituent power is the kind of power that according to Jovellanos and his followers is exercised in the context of the right of resistance, in situations where the community finds itself in a state of necessity with relation to an oppressive government.[89]

Francisco Joaquín Pacheco, a close friend of Donoso's during their law studies in Sevilla, developed the doctrinaire approach in interesting ways while

[84] Juan Donoso Cortés, *Dictámen de la Comisión de la Reforma de la Constitución de 1837* (5 November 1844) in *Obras de Don Juan Donoso Cortés* (Marqués de Valdegamas ed.) (Madrid, 1854) 62. It is possible that Donoso was merely presenting the views of the commission, while being opposed to them. For a critique of the views reflected in the report and of Donoso's role in it, see Jaime Balmés, 'Sobre el Dictámen de la Comisión del Congreso' 41 *El Pensamiento de la Nación: Periódico Religioso, Político y Literario* 641–645 (13 November 1844).

[85] Donoso, *Dictámen* (n. 84) 62.

[86] ibid. 63. As noted in Chapter 1, Donoso's rejection of popular sovereignty, of the people's constituent power, led him to describe Rousseau as an author whose words launched 'thunderbolts against all constituted powers and social eminences'. Juan Donoso Cortés, *Obras* (Madrid, Imprenta de Tejado, 1954) 135.

[87] See Diez del Corral (n. 68) 576.

[88] Donoso, *Obras* (n. 83) 201, n. 1. The relation between Donoso's and Carl Schmitt's conception of dictatorship will be considered in Chapter 9 of this book.

[89] For a similar conception, see the discussion of Hauriou in Chapter 8 of this book.

also relying on the language of constituent power.[90] Pacheco thought that there was no logical relation between a popular, majoritarian act, and a decision that is in the interests of society (i.e. a rational decision).[91] While 'the will is human' he wrote, 'reason is independent of men'.[92] He believed that even though recognizing the constituent power of the nation may allow one to argue that no individual or faction could claim a right to alter the fundamental laws, such a view (which Pacheco associated with Benjamin Constant), was inconsistent with the very idea of sovereignty: the sovereign is someone who has actual power, not an entity that never acts, that always remains dormant and simply serves to limit the scope of the government's jurisdiction.[93] The idea that 'the constituent power belongs to the person or institution in which the constituted powers reside' was for Pacheco much closer to the truth. It was 'neither based in a philosophical delirium, like national sovereignty, nor in a mysterious and pseudo-theocratic principle, like the sovereignty of kings'.[94] Rather, it rested on the realization that the purpose of the constituted powers is to procure the well-being of societies. Accordingly, whenever the existing circumstances require, the constituted powers should have the right of altering the constitution.[95]

Like Guizot, Pacheco defended the sovereignty of the ordinary law-maker. The ability of the constituted powers to alter the constitutional order, he wrote, should not be subject to limits or exceptions.[96] This approach would be exemplified by a constitution that explicitly attributes the constituted institutions with the authority to alter the constitutional text in any way they consider desirable.[97] But what if a constitution explicitly prohibits the constituted powers from engaging in constituent activity and attributes to an extraordinary organ the exclusive power of constitutional change? Unlike Guizot, who would have probably seen that approach as a dangerous attempt to domesticate revolution, Pacheco invited his readers to look at it from a very formal point of view: it would simply amount to a situation where 'the constituent power would have been placed by law in a constituted power. Not in an ordinary

[90] Joaquín Francisco Pacheco, *Lecciones de Derecho Político Constitucional* (Madrid, 1845) 70–71. Pacheco briefly served as Spanish Prime Minister in 1847.
[91] Pacheco (n. 90) 77.
[92] ibid.
[93] ibid. 78–79. For a discussion of this aspect of Constant's thought, see Jeremy Jennings, 'Constitutional Liberalism in France: From Benjamin Constant to Alexis de Tocqueville' in *The Cambridge History of Nineteenth-Century Political Thought* (Gareth Stedman Jones and Gregory Claeys eds) (Cambridge University Press, 2011) 354–360.
[94] Pacheco (n. 90) 84.
[95] ibid.
[96] ibid. 85.
[97] ibid.

constituted power, but in an extraordinary one'.[98] If, however, the law denies to the ordinary constituted authorities the power of constitutional change while being silent about who has it, it would be absurd to say that no one can engage in constituent activity even if a change is needed.[99] Indeed, in such a case one could even say that the law itself is *ultra vires*: 'the law has no right to deprive society of what it absolutely needs'.[100] This was why, in contrast to Thouret and some of the authors discussed in Chapter 6, Pacheco would insist that the French legislature had the power to alter the Charter of 1830, just as the Spanish Parliament would not do anything inappropriate by amending the Constitution of 1837.[101]

Pacheco not only maintained that constituent power belonged to the constituted powers, but like other doctrinaires he thought that in tumultuous times, where governments are unable to fulfil their duties, the constituent power belongs to whoever can bring society to order.[102] This is why he held that during the 18th Brumaire, 'Bonaparte was the sovereign, was the legislator, was the constituent power' of France.[103] In this sense, like Donoso and Guizot, Pacheco ultimately accepted the inevitability of an extra-legal constituent power in times of emergency. This was a right of resistance of sorts, one not necessarily exercised by the community itself or by the community's representatives. But that kind of power played a very different role than in the theories discussed earlier. It is simply an expression of the view that order is better than disorder and that, when there are no other options, returning to order may demand the acceptance of exceptional measures. In that respect, Charles Guillaume Hello may have been right to claim that the doctrinaires failed to see that constituent power's function was to limit political power and to guarantee rights. [104] At the same time, by implicitly or explicitly insisting in parliament's constituent power, the doctrinaires, like Rousseau, saw no contradiction in the idea of a constitution-making power that is channelled through law.[105]

[98] ibid. 86.
[99] ibid. 87.
[100] ibid.
[101] ibid. 89.
[102] ibid. 93.
[103] ibid. 90, 92. A power that he could legitimately exercise in virtue of his 'intelligence and resolution'. ibid.
[104] Charles Guillaume Hello, *Du Régime Constitutionnel* (Paris, 1848) 16, 25–27. For a discussion, see Chapter 6 of this book
[105] Like the doctrinaires, Rousseau thought that in moments of emergency, 'a supreme ruler [should be authorized] to silence the laws'. Jean-Jacques Rousseau, *The Social Contract and The Discourses* (Everyman's Library, 1973) 290.

IV. The Doctrinaires and the Adoption of the Constitution of 1845

The writings of the doctrinaires sometimes reflected the tradition of the historical constitution. For example, during the process that led to the replacement of the Constitution of 1837, Donoso argued that any change to that document had to respect certain principles: 'The Courts and the King are the source of legitimate things; their power extends to everything, except those fundamental laws (*leyes primoriales*) against which nothing can be attempted that is not entirely null (*nulo de toda nulidad*) . . . '[106] Not surprisingly, the constitution that resulted from this process stated in its preamble (drafted by Donoso): 'Being our will [that of Queen Isabel II] and that of the Courts of the Reign [i.e. Parliament] to regularize and make consistent with the actual needs of the State the ancient laws (*antiguos fueros*) and freedom of these Kingdoms . . .' The Constitution of 1845 was adopted by the ordinary legislature, acting without explicit authoriszation from the then established constitutional text.[107]

The debates that took place during its adoption show the extent of the influence of the notion of the historical constitution among Spanish doctrinaires, and exemplify the practical implications of the rejection of the theory of constituent power by both traditions of thought. One of the most interesting discussions revolved around whether the Constitution of 1837 could be reformed by Parliament. Not surprisingly, the doctrinaires answered that question in the affirmative. For example, against those who referred to a power that lay outside of Parliament, Manuel Seijas Lozano asked: 'In a constituted society, in a society that has laws, that has institutions as ancient as society itself, it is not possible that we recognise that bastard power [i.e. the constituent power].'[108] But if that was true, then how could Parliament's constituent power be conceived in a way that did not extend to Spain's fundamental laws, to the historical constitution according to which sovereign power was shared between the legislative assembly and the Monarch?

Seijas' answer was that constitutional texts (*cartas constitucionales*) could be reformed, because 'they are nothing but an abbreviated, written formula,

[106] Diez del Corral (n. 68) 576. Donoso also maintained that: 'History teaches us that societies always tend to give themselves the forms that are proper to it and the Constitution they need, so they are able to rest in a consistent and harmonious whole.' Juan Donoso Cortés, *Consideraciones sobre la Diplomacia* (Madrid, 1834) 49, fn (d).

[107] For a discussion, see Alberto Pérez Calvo, *El Estado Constitucional Español* (Madrid, 2014). Not surprisingly, unlike the Constitution of 1837, which recognized the sovereignty of the nation (although only in the preamble), the Constitution of 1845 does not even mention the word 'sovereignty' and established a power-sharing scheme between the Crown and the legislative chambers.

[108] 'Diario de las Sesiones de las Cortes' (2 November 1844) 198, 199.

of those relationships that serve as the basis of a state'. 'Our competence', he added, 'is limited to establishing a formula that represents the history of the country' and cannot be used to alter 'the fundamental bases of society'.[109] Since the majority of the deputies had concluded that the Constitution of 1837 'did not represent the history of the country, they have the duty, based on a public necessity' of revising it. The types of provisions identified as problematic related, for instance, to the powers given to the municipalities, something that was seen as negatively affecting the decision-making authority of the central government.[110] Alcalá Galiano, now in his capacity as deputy, added that 'what can be reformed are some laws that are included in the constitution, but that are not the constitution'.[111] Isla Fernández agreed, postulating that their role was to 'bring together and secure (*fijar*) the fundamental laws . . . which have not been made by men but by time, by previous generations, by the state, circumstances, interests, and necessities of the people . . .'[112] He went further and described in some detail what he considered to be 'the fundamental laws of the Nation', which included Catholicism, the monarchy, the right to property, and the powers of (and the relationship between) the monarch and parliament.[113]

Those who opposed the reform, like Nicomedes Pastor Díaz, pointed towards the risks involved in changing an arguably functioning constitution. Pastor Díaz recognized parliament's legal power to alter any law (even the constitutional laws that some called 'fundamental' as opposed to merely 'reglamentary'), but for him the important question was whether the fact that parliament possessed constituent power meant that it should change or replace the existing constitutional text whenever it wished.[114] He accepted that from a legal perspective, parliament could adopt any constitution it wanted, because 'constituent power cannot be judged in any tribunal, and there is no force that can command it'.[115] But that was the very reason why such a power should be exercised with extreme care: the same things that those in the parliamentary majority may do today (i.e. replace a constitution), could be done to them

[109] ibid. 198.

[110] ibid. 201. This negative view of decentralization was heavily criticized by Enrique Vera y González, who years later maintained that once one accepts that the nation is the source of all law, 'even more [so are] its constituent elements: the regions, the towns, and the individuals'. Vera y González characterized the Spanish doctrinaires of the 1840s as suffering from 'an incomplete study of English institutions or, more frequently, of French constitutionalism'. Enrique Vera y González, *Pi y Margall y la Política Contemporánea: La Democracia Federal, su Origen, su Historia, sus Destinos Medio Siglo de Doctrinarismo en España; la Política de Programa y la Política Real* (Barcelona, 1886) 266.

[111] 'Diario' (n. 108) 212.

[112] ibid. 424.

[113] ibid.

[114] ibid. (30 October 1844) 141.

[115] ibid. 142.

tomorrow.[116] The Constitution of 1837 was 'the representation of the Spanish society' with all its virtues and defects, and could only be legitimately amended or replaced by the 'constituent powers in cases of extreme necessity'.[117]

Pedro José Pidal, who shared the doctrinaire's defence of parliamentary sovereignty, disagreed with most of this. He did not see anything wrong in amending those parts of the Constitution of 1837 that did not have a fundamental character.

One of those non-fundamental aspects, he argued, was 'the principle expressed in the preamble, national sovereignty, a principle rejected by many men, ridiculed by others, and which no political party has ever been able to put into practice'.[118] By recognizing national sovereignty, 'the preamble implicitly accepts the existence of a power capable of abolishing the established state powers'.[119] As we saw in the previous chapter, that is not the only way in which national sovereignty was understood. José Posada Herrera, a deputy who shared the approach to national sovereignty discussed in Chapter 5, did not see the preamble as attributing sovereignty to the masses, as some deputies insisted.[120] What 'we call Nation', he wrote, is a 'moral body' with 'an intelligence and will that can be represented by government'.[121] He thus rejected any association of his views with the notion of a constituent power that has no legal existence, an 'always fearsome, always dangerous' power 'that exposes the country to serious disorders'.[122] If removing the reference to national sovereignty was equivalent to denying the existence of such a power, then it would be a positive development; but if it meant that parliament acting together with the monarch would then become able to adopt a new constitution at will, without 'the social causes that justify it, without an evident necessity', the constitutional order would be subject to similar dangers.[123]

Diaz Cid, who had a much more positive view of parliament as a constitution-maker, replied that what the new preamble would do was to affirm 'the principle of parliamentary omnipotence, or more correctly, the principle that the Courts with the King are the only constituent power that could give ordinary and fundamental laws to the Nation'.[124] 'We are being told', Seijas had already noted a few days earlier, 'that there exists a constituent power, an indivisible

[116] ibid. 141.
[117] ibid. 142–143, 144, 152.
[118] ibid. 149.
[119] ibid. 150.
[120] ibid. (12 November 1844) 405.
[121] ibid. 405–406.
[122] ibid. 406.
[123] ibid.
[124] ibid. 409.

power, that no one knows where it is, to which no one can point to . . . Where is that power, sirs? Outside the law, there is no power'.[125] Indeed, Seijas denounced those deputies who deployed the idea of constituent power to block the possibility of constitutional change. While often recognizing parliament's constituent power, they limited its exercise to cases of extreme necessity.[126] But in so doing, argued Seijas, they made its exercise so difficult that it would in practice require a 'coup d'état or a revolution'.[127] And it would be irresponsible for parliament to wait until the necessity of constitutional change is expressed 'in the streets through riots and revolutions that the government is unable to contain'.[128] Parliament had the duty to 'save society' and to rationally determine when there was a need to replace a constitution.[129] That was consistent with what had happened. Indeed, Alcalá Galiano recognized that the demand for this reform had not come from the electors but from parliamentarians themselves.[130]

These debates reflected the doctrinaire's defence of parliamentary sovereignty as well as their reliance on the doctrine of the historical or internal constitution.[131] They also exemplify the ways in which opponents of the reform attempted to deploy the concept of constituent power, and in some cases the principle of national sovereignty, in order to block parliament's constitution-making faculty, the exercise of which they would only allow in cases of extreme necessity. One interesting characteristic of these debates (and, more generally, of most 19th-century discussions on constituent power and constitutional change), is the relative inattention given to the process through which constitutions are originally adopted. It is not that the nature of the initial constitution-making process was unimportant, but that what mattered was not how the existing constitution was adopted but *who* could change it. In fact, in one of his speeches in parliament, Alcalá Galiano expressed: 'I do not look at the origins of constitutions. There is in Spain a constitution that has the more pure and

[125] ibid. 198.
[126] During one of his interventions in the debate, Alcalá Galiano noted that there were no deputies arguing that constituent power needed to be exercised by an extraordinary assembly. ibid. 212–213.
[127] ibid.
[128] ibid. 199.
[129] ibid.
[130] A fact that, he added, made irrelevant the question of any imperative mandate being disobeyed. ibid. 214.
[131] This view was highly influential during the creation of the Spanish Constitution of 1876. For instance, the preamble of the Royal Decree that called for the election of the parliament that would draft the new constitution, written by Antonio Cánovas del Castillo, maintained that: 'The internal constitution . . . is without doubt contained in the monarchical principle.' The Constitution of 1876 also lacked an amendment rule and was also understood as been modifiable through the ordinary law-making process. For a discussion, see Varela, Doctrina (n. 29) 345, 354.

noble origin, that of 1812. Despite the pure, noble, and legitimate origins of that constitution, I would not advise that it is reinstated.'[132] Pastor Díaz, who disagreed with Alcalá Galiano on the question of constitutional reform, had a similar view on this point: 'I have said that I do not go to the origin of the constitution. A man can be the fruit of a crime, of adultery, of incest . . . The life of that man can be precious.'[133]

V. Conclusion

The traditions of thought discussed in this chapter did not reject constituent power in its entirety, but rather one or more of its main features. The doctrinaires argued against the idea that someone could have a right to be sovereign and against the existence of an extra-legal constituent power except in times of emergency, where the exercise of such a power became necessary to save society. Proponents of the historical constitution argued that no one, not even the entity attributed with constituent power, can change a country's fundamental laws, which may or not be contained in a written document. Unlike authors who embraced the theory of constituent power as a means of limiting the power of the ordinary institutions of government (such as the ones discussed in Chapter 6), the doctrine of the historical constitution and the teachings of the doctrinaires led to the establishment of de facto sovereign parliaments, parliaments *with* constituent power. It is in this sense not surprising that both of these traditions frequently relied on English constitutional thought. At the same time, the debates examined in this chapter provide us with a key insight into the legal functions of the concept of constituent power. That is to say, constituent power can serve to limit the scope of the jurisdiction of the ordinary institutions of government, but also to justify the complete overhaul of a juridical order.

Consider, for example, those deputies who (like Inguanzo Rivero) opposed the creation of the Constitution of 1812 by negating the existence of constituent power and defending the permanence of the historical constitution. In their view, constituent power was irrelevant from a legal perspective. But they failed to prevail against those delegates (whose ideas were discussed in Chapter 5) who argued that *because* it was the bearer of the constituent power, the Constituent Parliament could adopt an entirely new constitution based on

132 'Diario' (n. 108) 213.
133 ibid. 142.

the sovereignty of the nation, even if that act violated the fundamental laws of the Spanish realm. In that situation, the concept of constituent power was used to defend the unlimited constitution-making jurisdiction of a constitution-making body. In contrast, as we saw above, the concept was (unsuccessfully) deployed in 1845 to block the replacement of the Constitution of 1837. This raises the important question of whether a concept that can be used in such different ways (i.e. sometimes to limit, sometimes to justify, the exercise of political power) can actually be said to have legal functions. The answer, I think, lies in the fact that, in the political terrain, a concept or theory can only be used to persuade an official enjoying full discretion to make a particular decision. If the concept were to be deployed by courts, as has occurred in the context of the doctrine of unconstitutional constitutional amendments, one would enter into a different scenario. There, the possibility of constituent power becoming a juridical principle that has a decisive role in an authoritative legal decision that becomes binding on current and future officials, would emerge.[134]

In the next chapter, I will focus on the notion of the constitution in the material sense, mostly found in the work of 20th-century constitutional theorists, which makes such juridical functions possible. The material constitution, we will see, was understood by some constitutional theorists as posing limits on the ordinary power of constitutional reform, but not on the constituent subject. In that sense, it presupposed a distinction between ordinary amendments and changes that touched the material constitution. As we saw in Chapter 6, this distinction was not common in 18th- and 19th-century constitutional theory, where commentators usually described the very act of changing a constitution as a type of act in which only the constituent power could engage. It was nevertheless present in the doctrine of the historical constitution and, to some extent, in the writings and speeches of some doctrinaires: even though proponents of the historical constitution attributed to parliament a legally unlimited constitution-making faculty, they identified a fundamental core that could not be modified. Parliament could *amend* the constitutional text, but no one had the right to recreate the fundamental laws.

Thus authors indirectly accepted the distinction between amendment and replacement, but did not see the former as falling under the jurisdiction of the ordinary institutions of government and the latter as the exclusive domain of

[134] The doctrine of unconstitutional constitutional amendments has now been extensively discussed in the literature. See Yaniv Roznai, *Unconstitutional Constitutional Amendments: The Limits of Amendment Powers* (Oxford University Press, 2017). My discussion of the relationship between constituent power and the protection of the material constitution in the next chapter is, in a certain way, about the theoretical foundations of that doctrine.

the constituent subject. Rather, they believed that beyond the faculty of altering the constitutional text according to law, there was nothing else. The constituent subject was taken out of its usual terrain (that of fundamental constitutional change) and moved to the constituted order as a limited power of constitutional creation. The doctrine of the material constitution has important similarities with this kind of approach, but without any necessary animosity towards the idea of constitutional replacement by an extra-parliamentary entity. This is an idea that was not entirely absent in the 19th century, and that was sometimes expressed by political actors. For example, in his 1852 proclamation, Louis-Napoleon Bonaparte stated that 'the Senate can, with the agreement of the government, modify anything in the constitution that is not fundamental', but that changes in fundamental provisions needed to be submitted to the people.[135] Leaving aside the problematic nature of an 'appeal to the people' in Napoleon III's France, it is precisely this notion (the idea that fundamental constitutional changes require the direct participation of the people), that drives an important part of contemporary judicial engagement with the theory of constituent power.

[135] Cited in Paul Foderé Pradier, *Principes Généraux de Droit, de Politique et de Législation* (Paris, 1869) 210, fn 2.

8
The Material Constitution

The doctrine of the historical or internal constitution, examined in the previous chapter, is a manifestation of a basic idea of modern legal thought: that there are some norms that, because of their content, have a fundamental character and should be treated as such by the legal system. In the age of written constitutions, these norms are more often than not positivized in constitutional texts and thus protected from formal change. Nowadays, the doctrine of the historical constitution has been largely left behind,[1] but similar ideas are expressed by contemporary lawyers through different concepts. The better known of these is the concept of the constitution in the material sense, generally understood as including the norms that establish the basic structure of the state and that regulate the legal relations between state and citizens. More than six decades ago, Luis Sánchez Agesta noted the similarities between the historical/internal constitution and the material one, maintaining that 'the *internal* constitution is a fact that is prior to any formal juridical declaration; it is what we would today call the *material* constitution, using the unhappy term with which we have replaced the suggestive one invented by the Spaniards of the 19th century'.[2]

There is, nevertheless, a key difference between these two notions. The recognition of a constitution-*making* power is radically inconsistent with the

[1] There are of course some exceptions. See, for example, Article R(3) of the Constitution of Hungary (2011): 'The provisions of the Fundamental Law shall be interpreted in accordance with their purposes, the National Avowal and the achievements of our historical constitution.' For a discussion, see Ferenc Hörcher, 'Is the Historical Constitution of Hungary Still a Living Tradition? A Proposal for Reinterpretation' in *The Concept of Constitution in the History of Political Thought* (Arkadiusz Górnisiewicz and Bogdan Szlachta eds) (De Gruyter, 2017). See also Law No. 27600 (16 December 2001) of the the Republic of Peru, which mandated a constitutional reform that took into account the country's 'historical constitution'. The constitutionality of that law was challenged (for the reason of attributing to Congress constituent functions). In its decision, the Peruvian Constitutional Tribunal identified tha main content of the historical constitution in the provisions of the constitutional text that recognized popular sovereignty, the republican and representative form of government and the protection of fundamental rights. Among the arguments presented in support of the constitutionality of the law, it was stated to the extent that it require Congress to respect the historical constitution, the law would not allow that body to create an entirely new constitutional order (i.e. to invade the jurisdiction of the constituent power). Judgment No. 014-2002-AI/TC, Peruvian Constitutional Tribunal, paras. 37, 129.

[2] Luis Sánchez Agesta, *Los Principios del Constitucionalismo Español: Soberanía Nacional y Constitución Interna* (Granada: Universidad de Granada, 1953–1953) 29.

Constituent Power and the Law. Joel Colón-Ríos, Oxford University Press (2020). © Joel Colón-Ríos.
DOI: 10.1093/oso/9780198785989.001.0001

idea that the fundamental content of a country's constitution is a result of history and not of an act of will. The material constitution, by contrast, is entirely consistent with, and in certain formulations presupposes, an extra-legal constituent power. In fact, as will be seen below, one of the main juridical functions of the concept of constituent power is that of protecting the material constitution from the ordinary institutions of government, including the institutions authorized to amend the constitutional text. In this chapter, I will explore the notion of the material constitution in the work of Maurice Hauriou, Hans Kelsen, Carl Schmitt, Hermann Heller, and Costantino Mortati. The objective will not be to summarize the constitutional thought of these authors but to show the way in which they understood the relationship between the material constitution and constituent power, and how that understanding affected their views about the legal limits of the ordinary power of constitutional reform.

These conceptions, to different extents, reflected an important change in modern constitutionalism, one which went beyond the two main approaches to constituent power presented by 19th-century authors. Under the first approach, discussed in Chapter 6, constituent power is exercised every time a constitutional text changes; the ordinary institutions of government cannot be attributed with constituent jurisdiction.[3] Under the second approach, discussed in Chapter 7, there is no legal power outside of the established law-making authorities and the entire constitutional text is within its jurisdiction. There are limits imposed by reason or history but these are solely moral or political. When understood from a normative perspective (the type of perspective that, I will argue below, characterizes Hauriou and Schmitt), the notion of the material constitution is inconsistent with both approaches. The idea is that not all constitutional rules are the same, and that while some of them can certainly be amendable by the ordinary institutions of government acting through special procedures, this does not apply to a constitution's truly material content. That content lays outside the scope of the amending authority.

The view that the legally regulated amending power and the power to create a new constitution are not the same thing was present during the French Revolution,[4] but it was perhaps more clearly expressed in early North American constitutional thought. It is now exemplified by constitutions that contain eternity clauses which implicitly distinguish between amendment and

[3] Among the authors discussed in Chapter 6, of course, are some exceptions. See, for example, Paul Pradier-Fodéré, *Principes Généraux de Droit, de Politique et de Legislation* (Paris, 1869) 209.

[4] See Chapter 4 of this book, particularly the note (n. 11) about Frochot's proposed amendment rule.

replacement and, in some cases, by those constitutions with tiered amendment rules. Once that type of distinction is accepted, the logic behind the previously mentioned legal function of the concept of constituent power is brought to the surface: if the entity authorized to amend a constitutional text is not the constituent subject, there must be limits to its power of constitutional change. Those limits are found in the material constitution. Constituent power, by virtue of its relationship to the material content of the constitution, can thus serve the function of protecting certain types of constitutional norms.[5] In contrast, when the notion of the material constitution does not come accompanied by the recognition of an extra-legal constituent subject and the exclusive attribution to it of the authority to create material constitutional content, the idea of a limited power of constitutional reform becomes harder to justify. As we will see below, this is more clearly exemplified in Kelsen and, to lesser degrees, in Heller and Mortati.

The chapter has been organized in the following way. Part I begins with a brief examination of the development of the distinction between the amending and the constituent power. I will contrast the conception developed in early North American constitutional thought with the 19th-century approaches to constitutional change mentioned above. The objective will be to demonstrate how aspects of those two approaches are reflected in the increasingly prevailing view: that not all positive constitutional law has a material character, and that what is not material can be altered by an ordinary amending authority that can be placed in the hands of the constituted powers. In Part II, I will examine the place of the concept of super-legality (*superlégalité constitutionnel*) in Hauriou's work. For this author, constitutional super-legality includes not only the content of a written constitution protected by a special rule of change, but also the fundamental (and sometimes unwritten) principles that stand above the constitution itself. Importantly, his concept of super-legality came accompanied by a natural law conception of constituent power as a power that operates under a form of law which precedes the state and continues to exist besides it. These views, it will be seen, are consistent with those conceptions of the material constitution which present it as a limit to the ordinary amendment authority.

[5] This notion was implicit, for example, in Rousseau's distinction between sovereignty and government, discussed at length in Chapter 2 of this book. When embraced by the state (and particularly by judges), it involves the recognition, by *law*, of a power that, when *properly* summoned, can overcome any limits applicable to the amending authority. For some examples, see Part IV of this chapter. See also Yaniv Roznai, *Unconstitutional Constitutional Amendments: The Limits of Amendment Powers* (Oxford University Press, 2017).

Part III introduces Kelsen's conception of the material constitution which, unlike Hauriou's, is fully compatible with the idea of an unlimited amendment power, one which cannot ultimately be bound by eternity clauses and much less by implicit principles. Kelsen understood the material constitution in procedural terms and did not attribute any legal functions to an extra-legal constituent subject. In Part IV, this 'descriptive' approach will be contrasted to that of Schmitt, for whom the very notion of the material constitution depends on the recognition of a constituent subject *unbound* by legal forms. Somewhat counter-intuitively, under Schmitt's approach, the frequent appeal to an unlimited and unmediated constituent subject leads to the attribution of *limited* competences to the amending authority. Then, in Part V, I will show how Heller's conception of the material constitution, although at first sight appearing as a successful synthesis of Kelsen and Schmitt, provides no clear basis for justifying the protection of the material constitution through the *legal* appeal to an extra-legal constituent authority. Finally, I examine some aspects of Costantino Mortati's constitutional thought. Mortati provided a juridical explanation of the material constitution that sought to include the real social forces that influence its creation and development. The price of advancing such a realist conception, I will argue, is a difficulty in justifying the imposition of legally enforceable limits on the amending authority.

I. The Disaggregation of the Constituent and the Amending Power

In the previous chapter, we saw that defenders of the doctrine of the historical constitution, such as Gaspar Melchor de Jovellanos, attributed to the Crown-in-Parliament the power of altering the constitutional text, but at the same time maintained that no one had the right to alter the fundamental laws of the realm. The fundamental laws had been developed over time and could not be recreated at will. This conception, I noted, negated the very notion of constituent power: no one had the right to create a constitutional order anew. I examined a very different approach in Chapter 6, presented by authors such as Charles Guillaume Hello and Édouard Laboulaye, one which insisted that the jurisdiction to alter the constitution was an exclusive one: it belonged to the constituent subject, which was usually identified as the nation. Accordingly, legislatures (or any constituted institution) did not have the authority to amend the constitutional text, even in cases where the constitution lacked an amendment rule. The main thrust of this idea can be traced back to the American

Revolution.[6] For example, in 1768, Samuel Adams maintained 'that in all free States the Constitution is fixed; and as the supreme Legislative derives its Power and Authority from the Constitution, it cannot overleap the Bounds of it without destroying its own foundation'.[7]

This view was reflected in a number of North American constitutions, particularly in that of Pennsylvania (1776), which stated that the House of Representatives 'shall have no power to add to, alter, abolish, or infringe any part of this constitution'.[8] The Pennsylvania Constitution of 1776 established that the amending power could only be exercised by a convention called by an elected 'Council of Censors' convened every seven years.[9] The convention could only be called in light of an 'absolute necessity of amending any article of the constitution which may be defective . . . and of adding such as are necessary for the preservation of the rights and happiness of the people'. The changes (originally proposed by the Council of Censors) would then 'be promulgated at least six months before the day appointed for the election of such convention, for the previous consideration of the people, that they may have an opportunity of instructing their delegates on the subject'.[10] In the convention that drafted the constitutional text, some went as far as suggesting that if a legislature is given the power to 'alter one punctillio' of a constitution, legislators would become 'as absolute masters of the lives and fortunes of their constituents in Pennsylvania as their now are in Great Britain'.[11]

The idea, as put by James Burgh in 1775, was that the constitution could only be altered by the people, 'acting by and from *themselves*, without, or even in opposition to their *representatives*, if necessary'.[12] Attributing the legislature with the power of altering the constitution was, for many, no different than allowing its violation by the very entity it was supposed to limit.[13] Only special

[6] According to James Wilford Garner, '[o]f the twenty-five eighteenth century State constitutions, nine contained no provisions whatever for their own amendment although the bills of rights of most of them recognized the "inalienable and indefeasible right of the people to alter, amend or abolish their form of government" whenever they should deem it necessary to their safety and happiness'. James Wilford Harner, 'Amendment of State Constitutions', 1(2) *American Political Science Review* 213, 215 (1907).

[7] Samuel Adams, 'Massachusetts Circular Letter to the Colonial Legislatures' (11 February 1768).

[8] Constitution of Pennsylvania (1776), Section 9. For an additional example, among others, see the Constitution of Vermont (1777), Chapter 2, Section VIII.

[9] Constitution of Pennsylvania (1776), Section 47. The Council of Censors also had the duty to 'recommend to the legislature the repealing of such laws as appear to them to have been enacted contrary to the principles of the constitution'. It has some similarities with the Permanent Deputation of the Parliament under the Spanish Constitution of 1812 (briefly discussed in Chapter 5).

[10] ibid.

[11] As quoted in Gordon S. Wood, *The Creation of the American Republic 1776-1787* (Chapel Hill: University of North Carolina Press, 1998) 338–339.

[12] James Burgh, *Political disquisitions: Or, An Enquiry into Public Errors, Defects, and Abuses* (Philadelphia, 1775) 6 (Book 3).

[13] See Wood (n. 11) 272–273.

assemblies elected for the specific purpose of constitution-making (which, in a Rousseaninan/Jeffersonian fashion, were periodically convened by law in some states)[14] could alter the constitutional text.[15] As in the work of most of the authors discussed in Chapter 6, this approach saw the entire constitutional text as a fundamental law. Consequently, it did not distinguish between the amending and the constituent power: changing the text of a constitution involved, by definition, constituent activity.[16] But there were also glimpses of an alternative view elsewhere in North America, one that later became an almost standard feature of modern constitutionalism. This view involved a distinction between the power to amend and the power to replace, reflected in a statement by Roger Sherman at the US Congress of 1789: 'The Constitution is the act of the people, and ought to remain entire. But the amendments will be the act of the State Governments.'[17]

The institutional implications of that idea could already be seen years earlier in Article 30 of the Constitution of Delaware (1776). The first sentence of that provision contained an eternity clause that read as follows: 'No article of the declaration of rights and fundamental rules of this State, agreed to by this convention . . . ought ever to be violated on any pretence whatever.'[18] The second sentence of Article 30 attributed to the legislative branch of government a limited amendment power: 'No other part of this constitution shall be altered, changed, or diminished without the consent of five parts in seven of

[14] See, for example, the Massachusetts Constitution of 1780, which (in a way reminiscent of the French Constitution of 1793 and of the Girondin Draft Constitution, particularly in terms of the role given to primary assemblies) stated in Chapter VI, Article X: 'Art. X. In order the more effectually to adhere to the principles of the constitution, and to correct those violations which by any means may be made therein, as well as to form such alterations as from experience shall be found necessary, the general court [the legislative body] which shall be in the year of our Lord [1795] shall issue precepts to the selectmen of the several towns, and to the assessors of the unincorporated plantations, directing them to convene the qualified voters of their respective towns and plantations, for the purpose of collecting their sentiments on the necessity or expediency of revising the constitution in order to amendments. And if it shall appear, by the returns made, that two-thirds of the qualified voters throughout the State, who shall assemble and vote in consequence of the said precepts, are in favour of such revision or amendment, the general court shall issue precepts, or direct them to be issued from the secretary's office, to the several towns to elect or direct them to be issued from the secretary's office, to the several towns to elect delegates to meet in convention for the purpose aforesaid. And said delegates to be chosen in the same manner and proportion as their representatives in the second branch of the legislature are by this constitution to be chosen.'

[15] This idea was not accepted by all. For example, the New Jersey legislature was not shy to alter the constitutional text through the ordinary law-making process in 1777. For a discussion, see Wood (n. 11) 274.

[16] Article 30 of the current Constitution of Argentina, originally adopted in 1853, still reflects this approach: 'The Constitution may be totally or partially amended. The necessity of reform must be declared by Congress with the vote of at least two thirds of the members; but it shall not be carried out except by a convention summoned to that effect.'

[17] Annals of Congress, House of Representatives (August 13, 1789) 735.

[18] This provision reflects the view mentioned above, to amend the constitution was a way of violating it.

the assembly, and seven members of the legislative council.' Those provisions that were outside the scope of the amending power could only be changed by the people through a constitutional convention. This was true even though Delaware's Constitution of 1776, unlike the Constitution of Pennsylvania of the same year, did include a provision for the calling of a constitutional convention. Nonetheless, the view eventually accepted in Delaware and, according to some commentators, 'well settled' in American law by the 20th century, was that 'the legislature may, whether or not authorized by the constitution, provide by law for the calling of a convention to revise the constitution'.[19]

Indeed, Delaware replaced its constitution in 1792 through a Constitutional Convention that assumed sovereign powers, not limiting itself to drafting a constitution but also engaging in the exercise of ordinary legislative authority.[20] This approach was supported by a number of judicial opinions.[21] In *Wells v Bain*,[22] the Supreme Court of Pennsylvania associated it with the people's right to abolish or create a new government: 'The people, having reserved the right to alter or abolish their form of government, have, in the same declaration of their rights, reserved the means of procuring a law as the instrumental process of so doing.'[23] Even the Supreme Court of Massachusetts, while determining that the constitution could only be altered according to its established amendment rule, suggested that its decision was not about 'the natural right of the people in cases of great emergency or upon the obvious failure of their existing constitution to accomplish the objects for which it was designed to provide for the amendment or alteration of their fundamental laws'.[24] As some deputies in the assembly that adopted the Spanish Constitution of 1845 (discussed in Chapter 7), the court associated the justification of major constitutional change with states of necessity/emergency.

What we see here is a view inconsistent both with the notion that the fundamental laws cannot be changed (i.e. the doctrine of the historical constitution) *and*, at the same time, with the idea that the entire constitution is a fundamental law that can only be altered by the constituent

[19] Thomas Raeburn White, 'Amendment and Revision of State Constitutions', 100 *University of Pennsylvania Law Review* 1132 (1952) 1134. During the late 19th and early 20th centuries, contrasting views about the legality of constitutional conventions not authorized by the constitutional text were famously put forward by John Alexander Jameson (against their legality) and Roger Sherman Hoar (in their defence). John Alexander Jameson, *A Treatise on Constitutional Conventions: Their History, Powers, and Modes of Proceeding* (Chicago: Callaghan & Company, 1887); Roger Sherman Hoar, *Constitutional Conventions: Their Nature, Powers, and Limitations* [1917] (Kessinger Publishing LLC, 2004).

[20] For a discussion, see Wood (n. 11) 333.

[21] For a discussion, see Raeborn White (n. 19) 1135.

[22] 75 Pa. 39 (1874).

[23] ibid. 47.

[24] 6 Cushing 573 (Mass. 1833).

power.[25] That is to say, under this approach, not all of a constitution's content is of a fundamental nature or, at the very least, so fundamental that it should be placed outside the jurisdiction of the ordinary institutions of government even if subject to higher thresholds. The truly fundamental content, in contrast, should be open to change solely by an extra-legislative body that is closer to the original constituent authority. Nowadays, this conception is exemplified in contemporary constitutions with tiered-amendment rules that distinguish between mere amendments and revisions. Consider, for example, the Venezuelan Constitution of 1999 which, after establishing two processes for altering the constitutional text (each of them subject to different substantive limits),[26] states in Article 347: 'The original constituent power rests with the people of Venezuela. This power may be exercised by calling a National Constituent Assembly for the purpose of transforming the State, creating a new juridical order and drawing up a new Constitution.' It is exemplified, too, in constitutions that contain eternity clauses, but in which those clauses are understood as being only enforceable against the ordinary amending authority.[27]

Although this kind of arrangement can be understood as the modern alternative both to the 'permanently unalterable fundamental content' approach and the one that sees the entire constitution as fundamental, it is not universally held. During the 20th century, as I explained in the introductory chapter, the theory of constituent power was developed by some jurists in a way that blurred the distinction between the amending and the constituent authority. The idea, in a nutshell, was that while a constitution is created by the original constituent power, the entity formally authorized to amend it possesses a derived constituent jurisdiction that can perform the same function as the original one: producing any constitutional content. Under this approach, the amending authority, as a derived constituent power (or, as sometimes put, as the secondary or constituted/instituted constituent power), is attributed

[25] Garner provides the following helpful summary of the development of the notion of the amending power in early to 19th century-US constitutional thought: 'From these facts several conclusions may be drawn: first, that the policy of making no provision for amendment belongs to the eighteenth century; second, that the policy of effecting amendments through the agency of the convention only, belongs, roughly, to the first half of the nineteenth century; third, that amendment through legislative initiative and popular ratification only, was characteristic of the period immediately preceding and following the Civil War; and, fourth, that the double mode of amendment belongs to the present. Thus, the trend of development has shown a growing tendency toward the legislative mode, as against revision through the agency of the constituent assembly, and a preference for the double method over both.' Garner (n. 6) 220.

[26] Constitution of Venezuela (1999), Articles 340–346. For further discussion, see Chapter 10 of this book.

[27] For a discussion of this approach, see Yaniv Roznai (n. 5) 125; See also Richard Albert, *Constitutional Amendments: Making, Breaking, and Changing Constitutions* (Oxford University Press, 2019).).

a nature similar to that of a sovereign parliament. And just like a sovereign parliament, it can legally get rid of any attempt to limit the scope of its own jurisdiction. As has been widely discussed in the literature, some contemporary courts, while accepting a version of the original/derived distinction, have determined that the material constitution (understood as equivalent to the constitution's fundamental content) falls outside the competence of the derived constituent power.[28]

II. Constitutional Super-Legality and Constituent Power

The notion of the material constitution played an important role in the work of early 20th-century constitutional theorists. These works brought to the surface some of the possible juridical implications of assuming the existence of an extra-legal constituent subject. In what follows, I will examine Maurice Hauriou's constitutional thought, where one finds the main contours of the idea of the constitution in the material sense advanced by latter authors. An important part of Hauriou's constitutional thought is found in his *Précis de Droit Constitutionnel*, originally published in 1923. In that book, Hauriou compared a national constitution to the statute of a corporation, but one established by a constituent body 'in the name of the sovereign nation'.[29] Noting that not all constitutions exist in the same written and rigid form that characterizes most national charters, Hauriou also provided a more general description of the types of rules that would normally be considered part of a constitution. The first type referred to 'the essential social organisation, that is . . . to individual liberties'.[30] The second referred to norms about 'the political organisation and the functioning of government'.[31] Both types could exist as unwritten fundamental laws, as ordinary laws that regulate constitutional issues (what Hauriou called 'constitutional legality'[32]), or be contained in a rigid constitution. In the latter case, they would be part of what Hauriou called a 'constitutional super-legality' created by an exercise of constituent power.[33]

[28] See, for example, the cases discussed in Part IV of this chapter.
[29] Maurice Hauriou, *Précis de Droit Constitutionnel*, 2nd ed. (Paris: Recueil Sirey, 1929) 242. In what follows, I will generally refer to the Spanish translation of this work: Maurice Hauriou, *Principios de Derecho Público y Constitucional* (Carlos Ruiz del Castillo trans.) (Granada: Editorial Comares, 2003). For Hauriou's conception of national sovereignty, see Maurice Hauriou, *La Soberanía Nacional* (Madrid: Marcial Pons, 2013).
[30] Hauriou, *Derecho Público* (n. 29) 326.
[31] ibid.
[32] ibid.
[33] ibid. 326, 336.

One of the main aspects of constitutional super-legality involved the regulation of constitutional matters by laws that assume a special form and that are considered superior to ordinary laws.[34] Constitutional super-legality came accompanied by the acceptance of the separation between the constituent and the constituted power.[35] It also involved the presence of a legally regulated process of constitutional amendment and the possibility of constitutional review of ordinary legislation.[36] Hauriou associated the emergence of this first aspect of constitutional super-legality with two developments: the idea of the fundamental laws of the realm present in monarchical states and the idea of the state as a sort of corporation that can be regulated by a special statute.[37] While the identity of the constituent subject who creates these special statutes may change (from king, to people, to nation), the basic features of a constitutional order remain the same. This is even true of constitutions like the French Charters of 1814 and 1830.[38] That is to say, although under the Charter of 1814 constituent power rested in the king and under the Charter of 1830 it was shared between the Crown and the nation, these documents operated in practice as constitutions.[39]

This aspect of constitutional super-legality required, as suggested earlier, a separation between a constituent power and the power of revising a constitution according to a set of established procedures. Nonetheless, he believed that both types of power entailed, in the end, *constituent* processes. In fact, he maintained that although constitutional change was often revolutionary from a formal perspective, it was *always* so from a substantive point of view.[40] By this, he meant that even when a constitution is altered according to the established rules of change, there is an appeal (even if implicit) to the primitive or revolutionary right to political liberty of the majority of the individuals in a society.[41] A constituent process carried out following a set of pre-established rules would be valid in relation to state law; one that took place during a revolution where individuals exercise a right of legitimate defence against a state unable to protect them, would also be valid by virtue of their 'primitive' right to political liberty.[42] This right, the right to reconstitute government, precedes

[34] ibid.
[35] A distinction that, for Hauriou, was absent in the United Kingdom, where sovereignty belonged 'to parliament more than to the nation'. ibid. 332.
[36] ibid. 341.
[37] ibid. 336.
[38] For a discussion of these documents, see Chapters 5 and 6 of this book.
[39] ibid. 337–339; Hauriou, *Précis* (n. 29) 243.
[40] Hauriou, *Derecho Público* (n. 29) 341–342.
[41] ibid. 342.
[42] ibid.

the state and did not disappear with its creation.[43] The nation, for Hauriou, was 'in a permanent state of legitimate defence' against the minoritarian power of the state.[44] Constituent power, as we have saw earlier, was associated here with emergencies and states of necessity.

For Hauriou, constituent power has three main features. First, it is a kind of special legislative power, since a formal constitution is a type of legislation.[45] Second, it belongs to the nation it, but the nation is not its source (at least not fully), since in the past it almost invariably belonged to a monarch.[46] Third, unlike the ordinary legislative authority, it does not have a constituted nature. Even if exercised by representatives according to an established rule of change, individuals called to engage in constituent activity represent the nation—seen as a social group independent of political forms—and not the state. In contrast, according to Hauriou, ordinary representatives are closer to the state than to the nation: they operate under the assumption that the state has already been constituted and do not see themselves as exercising the natural liberties of individuals.[47] Hauriou noted that the exercise of constituent power has traditionally taken place through special assemblies.[48] Importantly, he maintained that these entities would be exercising an extraordinary (legislative) jurisdiction but would remain 'subordinated to the principle of the separation of powers' in the sense that they could not engage in ordinary legislative, judicial, or executive acts.[49]

Hauriou sometimes called the power to revise a constitution according to pre-established rules, 'governmental constituent power' (*le pouvoir constituant gouvernemental*), as opposed to the 'popular constituent power', understood as a revolutionary right of the nation exercised by special assemblies.[50] A written constitution, he maintained, could protect itself against both popular and governmental constituent processes by an amendment rule that establishes limits on the relevant organ. For example, the French Constitution of 1875 had been interpreted by some as allowing the legislative chambers, prior to meeting as an Assembly of Revision, to determine the specific subject(s) of the change(s) to be made.[51] But in order for the constituent power to respect any limits, one

[43] ibid. 343.
[44] ibid. 228–229.
[45] ibid. 348–349, fn 13; Hauriou, *Précis* (n. 29) 254.
[46] Hauriou, *Derecho Público* (n. 29) 349–350, 222.
[47] ibid. 350.
[48] ibid. 344.
[49] ibid. 348–349, fn 13; Hauriou, *Précis* (n. 29) 254. This point will be developed further in Chapter 9.
[50] Hauriou, *Derecho Público* (n. 29) 354, 271, fn 41; Hauriou, *Précis* (n. 29) 254. This distinction anticipates the dichotomy between the derived and the original constituent power, discussed in the introduction and also present in the next two chapters.
[51] Hauriou, *Derecho Público* (n. 29) 356.

has to be careful not to make constitutional change through established rules too difficult.[52] And even with those precautions, he thought that when constitutional change takes place during a period of 'political and electoral' agitation it is difficult to expect an exercise of the popular constituent power through a legally convened constituent assembly to act behave as bound by a mandate of the constituted authorities.[53] The governmental constituent power, in contrast, is much more likely to abide by the relevant constitutional norms.[54] In this sense, 'the progressive consolidation' of the principle of piecemeal amendments could be understood as 'a result, in the last analysis, of the progressive recoil of the popular constituent power'.[55]

More importantly for our purposes here, a constituent process was subject to a more general kind of limit, one that emerged from a proper understanding of the concept of constitutional super-legality. Constitutional super-legality 'did not refer only to what appears in the constitutional text, but also comprises all the fundamental principles of a regime', which Hauriou divided into those related to individual liberties and those related to the structure of the state.[56] These principles amounted to a sort of 'constitutional legitimacy' sitting above the written constitution.[57] An example of that aspect of constitutional super-legality was provided by the addition, in 1884, of an eternity clause to the Constitution of 1875.[58] That eternity clause placed the republican form of government outside the scope of the constitution's rule of change. But that kind of principle did not need to be explicitly mentioned

[52] ibid. 357.
[53] ibid.
[54] ibid.
[55] ibid. Hauriou maintained that in democratic contexts, processes of constitutional change were frequently combined with the popular ratification of the draft prepared by the relevant entity, an approach that reached its 'perfection' when constitutional changes can be presented by popular initiative. ibid. 352. These types of arrangements were being nonetheless overtaken by 'a reaction against the popular constituent power'. ibid. 353. Nowadays, particular institutions were attributed constituent functions (including that of replacing the entire constitutional text) without the need for popular intervention and, at the same time, the notion of piecemeal amendment was displacing the idea of total revision. 'In virtue of a secret logic', he wrote, 'rules of constitutional change tend to remove from constituent processes the salient role of majorities and put it as much as possible in the hands of the minoritarian governmental power', that is, a power that 'belongs to a small minority' of individuals. ibid. 344, 194, 211, 222; Hauriou, *Précis* (n. 29) 117. Under this increasingly prevailing conception, constituent processes led by popularly elected assemblies were being 'replaced by the use of ordinary organs of the legislative power subject to special procedures when exercising constituent functions'. Hauriou, *Derecho Público* (n. 29). These comments should not be taken to mean that Hauriou was a supporter of frequent (and major) constitutional changes. Indeed, he maintained that the alteration of a constitution 'should only take place as a last resort, when a serious political crisis makes the urgency of the reform evident'. ibid. 355. Moreover, it was important that these changes were only advanced in cases where 'public opinion' shows interest and support in the reform, otherwise there is a risk of producing 'fictitious revisions which only satisfy particular political interests'. ibid. 354.
[56] ibid. 358
[57] ibid. 359
[58] ibid.

in the constitutional text.[59] For example, Hauriou thought that the individual liberties of the English common law could eventually be deployed by judges in the United States to 'declare the unconstitutionality of a constitutional amendment'.[60] A similar conclusion applied in France, where those liberties were not explicitly recognized by the Constitution of 1875 but still formed 'part of the constitutional super-legality that sits above the written constitution'.[61]

As suggested earlier, Hauriou thought that both the governmental and the popular constituent power are technically bound by law: 'no sovereign power, not even the constituent one, is to be understood as unbound by the rules of law'.[62] He nonetheless maintained that while all 'delegated sovereignty' is subject to limits, the nation possessed an unlimited sovereign power (*une souveraineté incontrôlable)*.[63] This statement needs to be understood in light of the fact that when exercised through a constituent assembly, national sovereignty is necessarily channelled by officials that never acquire the plenitude of the nation's jurisdiction. However, when the assembly's proposals are ratified in a referendum, the relevant decisions are arguably not subject to legal control.[64] This also seems to apply in the context of constitutional reform, even though Hauriou refers to the possibility of unconstitutional constitutional amendments (so invalidated by courts) on the basis of inconsistency with the implicit principles that form part of the constitutional super-legality. When an amendment contrary to those principles is ratified in a referendum, the relationship between constitutional super-legality and the national will (as in this case expressed by the electorate), would arguably be akin to that between a sovereign power and natural law. That is to say, the nation should respect the constitutional super-legality, but no one can enforce any principle against the sovereign will.[65]

The idea that Hauriou was expressing when referring to principles that are somehow superior to the constitutional text was a key aspect of the doctrine of the historical constitution and was later captured by the notion of the constitution in the material sense. Nonetheless, the material constitution is

[59] ibid. 359.
[60] ibid. 359–360.
[61] ibid.
[62] ibid. 357.
[63] Hauriou, *Précis* (n. 29) 266.
[64] Hauriou, *Derecho Público* (n. 29) 273.
[65] Hauriou, *Précis* (n. 29) 266. For a discussion of the relationship between referendums and constituent power, see Chapter 10 of this book.

frequently seen as connected to the fundamental decisions made by the constituent subject at the time of constitution-making, a subject that operates in an extra-legal terrain. As such, it is presented as unamendable by the constituted authorities, the amending power included. It can only be altered by an extra-ordinary manifestation of what Hauriou called the 'popular constituent power'. He, nonetheless, did not make the connection between the popular constituent power and the creation and recreation of constitutional superlegality as evident as those authors who saw the material constitution as a limit to the ordinary power of constitutional reform. When constitution-makers in late 18th-century North America identified certain constitutional content as amendable only by a special assembly (as was the case, e.g, of the Constitution of Delaware of 1776), they were pointing to what these other theorists would later call the material constitution. In the next section, I introduce the contemporary concept of the material constitution through an analysis of Hans Kelsen's work on the subject.

III. The Formal and the Material Constitution

Kelsen's work provides a good entry point into the notion of the constitution in the material sense even though, as will be seen shortly, his conception is not representative of the most common view of the subject. In fact, it is an example of the consequence of an understanding of the material constitution that does not attribute any legal function to the constituent subject. Kelsen's material constitution is connected in important ways to his theory of the basic norm. Kelsen, it is well known, thought that norms derive their validity from other norms. But since all constitutional orders are ultimately linked to a norm (e.g. a constitution) adopted in violation of the established legal rules of change or created in the absence of any legal rules (as in the case of a society that adopts its first ever constitution), the presupposition of a non-positive basic norm is necessary. Without it, no human action and no constitution-making act could be interpreted as giving rise to valid law.[66] The function of the basic norm is thus 'to confer law-creating power on the act of the first legislator and on all the other acts based on the first act'.[67] At one point in his *General Theory of Law*

[66] Hans Kelsen, *General Theory of Law and State* (Cambridge: Harvard University Press, 1949) 116.

[67] ibid. See also Hans Kelsen, 'The Function of a Constitution', in *Essays on Kelsen* (Richard Tur et al. eds) (Clarendon Press: Oxford, 1986) 115. Hans Kelsen, *Teoría Pura del Derecho* (Moisés Nilve trans.) (Eudeba: Buenos Aires, 2009) 113.

and the State, Kelsen offered the following formulation of a basic norm: '[O]ne ought to behave as the individual, or the individuals, who laid down the first constitution have ordained.'[68]

Kelsen did not see the basic norm as adding anything new to what lawyers always had known: he was simply making explicit a norm everyone had to assume when identifying a rule as a valid norm belonging to a particular legal order.[69] Although he did not have a theory of constituent power, what his basic norm does is to explain the reason why the constituent subject (i.e. the first legislator) is retrospectively understood as having created a valid positive norm, even when it acts in violation of the established rules of change.[70]

A new basic norm needs to be presupposed when a constitution is adopted in violation of the relevant amendment rules. Every time this happens, a new 'first legislator' exercises constitution-making powers not derived from positive law and a new 'first constitution' is adopted. Kelsen famously illustrated this point with the following example. Suppose that a group of individuals living under a monarchical constitution attempt to transform it, by force, into a republic.[71] If the new republican order becomes able to effectively regulate the behaviour of those to which it applies,[72] one would have to say that the old monarchical constitution has ceased to exist. At that very moment, the basic

[68] Kelsen, *General Theory* (n. 66) 115. By 'first constitution', Kelsen means the constitution (itself adopted illegally) to which the established laws are linked through a chain of validity. In a country with an unwritten constitution, the basic norm could be formulated as follows: 'One ought to behave in the manner recognised by legal officials as constitutional'. See also, Kelsen, *Teoría Pura* (n. 67) 113.

[69] Kelsen, *General Theory* (n. 66) 395.

[70] Spanish translators of Kelsen's work frequently use the term 'first constituent subject' (*primer constituyente*), as opposed to 'first legislator' (*primer legislador*). See Kelsen, *Teoría Pura* (n. 67) 112, 113, 116. It is worth noting, however, that Kelsen did refer to the concept of constituent power in *The General Theory of Law and the State*: 'If the State is created in a democratic way, the first constitution originates in a constituent assembly, what the French call *une constituante*.' Moreover, he maintained that when a constitution requires that all amendments take place in a constituent assembly, 'it is customary to distinguish between a constituent power and a legislative power, each being exercised according to different procedures'. Kelsen, *General Theory* (n. 66) 259. It is nevertheless unclear whether Kelsen means that if the constitution authorizes the ordinary legislature to amend the constitution through a special majority, such an entity would be exercising what he calls 'constituent power' or a special form of 'legislative power' (i.e. one that results in the adoption of constitution-amending legislation).

[71] What actually happened during a period of constituent activity was irrelevant from the perspective of the pure theory of law. It did not matter if a revolution 'is effected through a movement emanating from the mass of the people, or though action from those in government positions'. ibid. 118. From a juridical point of view, he wrote, 'the decisive criterion of a revolution is that the order in force is overthrown and replaced by a new order in a way that the former had not itself anticipated'. ibid. 117.

[72] The question of effectivity is discussed at length by Kelsen, but it is not necessary to delve into it here given the purposes of this chapter. Simply put, a legal order must be efficacious (in the sense that the individuals subject to it behave, by and large, in conformity with it) for there to be valid norms. However, an individual 'norm is not valid *because* it is efficacious; it is valid *if* the order to which it belongs is, on the whole, efficacious'. ibid. 42, 119.

norm that required individuals and government officials to behave 'according to the rules created by the monarch or her successors', would have been replaced by another basic norm that mandates compliance with the new, republican constitution.[73]

Put in a different way, when a legal revolution (i.e. a break in the chain of legality) takes place, the presupposition of a novel *Grundnorm* becomes necessary. This is where the distinction between the material and the formal constitution assumes a central role. When Kelsen refers to a constitution being authorized by a basic norm, he did not have in mind the formal constitution but the material one. For him, the constitution in the formal sense (or the 'constitution-*form*')[74] is a 'certain solemn document, a set of legal norms that may be changed only under the observation of special prescriptions, the purpose of which is to render the change of these norms more difficult'.[75] With the most notable exceptions being New Zealand and the United Kingdom, most countries nowadays have a formal constitution. But *all* countries in which there is a legal system have a constitution in the material sense. The material constitution (or 'the constitution' as opposed to the 'constitution-form')[76] consists of 'those rules which regulate the creation of the general legal norms, in particular the creation of statutes'.[77] In some cases, the material constitution will include rules that limit the content of future legislation, such as a constitutional prohibition against the adoption of certain types of laws.[78]

Unlike the formal constitution, which is always a written document, the material constitution may be written or unwritten. That is, it may appear in a special statute called 'constitution', or it may be based on convention. When it is contained within a written document, it will normally co-exist with a set of norms that do not have a material character. But the separation between Kelsen's material and formal constitution is not as sharp as it may otherwise appear. Consider a constitution that contains a provision stating: 'The legislature shall adopt statutes by the affirmative vote of the majority of the elected members of both legislative chambers.' This provision would be clearly material under Kelsen's perspective, as it regulates an aspect of the law-making procedure. If those chambers were abolished by the government and replaced

73 ibid. 118.
74 Kelsen, 'The Function of a Constitution' (n. 67) 114.
75 Kelsen, *General Theory* (n. 66) 124.
76 Kelsen, 'The Function of a Constitution' (n. 67) 114.
77 ibid.
78 Kelsen, *General Theory* (n. 66) 125.

with an individual law-maker in violation of the constitution's amendment rule, a legal revolution would have clearly taken place. This would be what Kelsen described as an instance in which 'those in government positions [create a] new order in a way that the former had not itself anticipated'.[79] A material aspect of the constitution would have been illegally replaced and the presupposition of a new basic norm would become necessary. But this approach has the potential of being over-inclusive. Some aspects of Kelsen's material constitution, while important, are probably not as fundamental as requiring the conclusion that their illegal replacement amounts to the revolutionary creation of a new constitutional order. For example, would illegally raising—for relatively uncontroversial reasons—the majority required for the enactment of legislation from 50 per cent + 1 to 50 per cent + 2—amount to the creation of a new constitution?

At the same time, there might be aspects of the material constitution that are so fundamental that, even if replaced according to the established amendment rule, it could be argued that a new constitutional order has been created.[80] This problem is exemplified by Kelsen's comments about the possibility of making certain material content legally unamendable. He maintained that an eternity clause could establish that 'the procedure of legislation must not be altered at all, or not in such a way as to alter the form of the state'.[81] But regardless of how fundamental (or trivial) the protected content is, as long as the formal amendment rule is followed, it would be arguably admissible to alter the protected provision by first amending the eternity clause out of existence and then making the desired change. Indeed, Kelsen maintained that 'the unrepealable nature of a given norm does not mean that another norm conflicting with it cannot be posited and acquire validity'. Such a conflict would be solved by 'the repeal of the provision concerning the unrepealable nature of [the relevant] norm'.[82] For Kelsen, there is nothing *outside* of the law (i.e. nothing outside of the law that has actual juridical relevance) that could cause certain provisions to enjoy a heightened legal status. Put differently, the extra-legal constituent people that impacted the understanding of the nature of the amending power of some of the authors discussed in Chapter 6, as well as the drafters of early North American constitutions, was not in the picture painted by Kelsen.

[79] ibid. 117.
[80] Consider, for example, the 'legal' replacement of a sovereign monarch with a sovereign legislature.
[81] Kelsen, 'The Function of a Constitution' (n. 67) 114.
[82] Kelsen, *General Theory* (n. 66) 110–111.

IV. Towards a Normative Conception of the Material Constitution

If Kelsen had linked the exercise of constituent power to the alteration of the material constitution, he could have concluded that changes to material provisions, even in the absence of an eternity clause, *had* to take place through a procedure other than the ordinary amendment rule. Schmitt's conception of the distinction between 'constitutional laws' and 'constitution' provides support for that alternative approach. This distinction, it will be seen, is equivalent to that between the formal and material notions of the constitution, and between what Kelsen called 'constitution-*form*' and 'constitution'.[83] In *Constitutional Theory*, Schmitt argued that while the formal constitution could be changed through the ordinary amendment procedure, its material content (which, like Karl Loewenstein, he called 'the substance'[84] of the constitution or its 'substantive meaning'[85]) could only be altered by an extra-legal constituent subject.[86] Like Hauriou, Schmitt thought that the constitution in the formal sense did not exhaust what a constitution *is*. Authors who argued that 'the essential legal characteristic of constitutional laws lies exclusively in their enhanced formal legality',[87] such as George Jellinek, had missed this point. This resulted in theories that relativized the constitution by making the amendment rule its 'essential core and singular content', in the sense that the validity of *all* provisions would depend on whether they had not been the subject of a formal amendment.[88]

For Schmitt, that could not be true. The authority to adopt constitutional amendments, he maintained, 'does not include the power to establish a new constitution',[89] but only the ability to adopt, alter, or replace *constitutional laws*.[90] Constitutional laws, under Schmitt's terminology, are norms that have

[83] Kelsen, 'The Function of a Constitution' (n. 67) 114.
[84] Carl Schmitt, *Constitutional Theory* (Durham: Duke University Press, 2008) 87.
[85] ibid. 73.
[86] Karl Loewenstein, *Political Power and the Governmental Process* (Chicago: The University of Chicago Press, 1965) 128. Loewenstein refers to 'the differentiation between the substantive and the formal constitution, leading to the codification of the fundamental principles of the state society in a single written document . . .' ibid.
[87] Schmitt, *Constitutional Theory* (n. 84) 73. Jellinek's conception of constituent power will be briefly examined in Chapter 7.
[88] ibid. 74.
[89] Schmitt, *Constitutional Theory* (n. 84) 74.
[90] As the reader may note, this is a sophisticated formulation of the idea that the framers of some early North American constitution (as well as some French and English commentators) tapped into years or centuries earlier. The distinction between 'constitution' and 'constitutional laws' (or between material and formal constitution) is also reflected in Rousseau's distinction between 'laws' and 'decrees'. For a discussion of this aspect of Rousseau's work, see Chapter 2 of this book.

been included in the written constitution in order to protect them from ordinary parliamentary majorities.[91] One of the examples given by Schmitt of a constitutional law is Article 149 of the Weimar Constitution: 'Universities will maintain Faculties of Theology.' While important, this type of provision lacks a truly fundamental character and what distinguishes it from ordinary laws is only that it is subject to a special amendment rule.[92] In contrast, the *constitution* contained what Schmitt called 'the conscious decision' of the constituent subject about 'its peculiar form of political existence'.[93] He frequently referred to that decision (or decisions) as 'the constitution in the positive sense',[94] instead of using the more familiar notion of 'material constitution'.[95] In the context of the Weimar Republic, he maintained that the positive constitution was expressed, for example, in Article 1's adoption of democracy as a form of government and its rejection of monarchy,[96] in the adoption of a federal structure of government, of parliamentarism, and of the institutions of the '*bourgeois Rechtsstaat* with its principles, fundamental rights and the separation of powers'.[97] Those decisions constituted 'the substance of the constitution'.[98]

Since the constitution (as opposed to the constitutional laws) expressed the fundamental decisions of the constituent subject (i.e. the people in a democracy, and the king in a monarchy)[99] it could not be altered through the ordinary amendment rule. That is to say, unlike Kelsen, Schmitt thought that the distinction between constitutional laws and constitution (or between the formal

[91] Schmitt, *Constitutional Theory* (n. 84) 67.

[92] The problem of over inclusiveness identified above with respect to Kelsen's approach can be observed here. To the extent that Article 149 has implications for the content of future legislation (e.g. an ordinary law abolishing a Faculty of Theology would be unconstitutional), it would also form part of the material constitution. This is probably why, when referring to the material constitution as not only regulating the procedures for the creation of legislation but also their content, Kelsen usually inserted a qualification (e.g. 'The material constitution may determine not only the organs and the procedure of legislation, but also, *to some degree*, the contents of future laws'; Kelsen, *General Theory* (n. 66) 125.

[93] Schmitt, *Constitutional Theory* (n. 84) 75–76.

[94] ibid. 75.

[95] In fact, in his *Staatslehre*, when discussing Schmitt's conception of the material constitution, Hermann Heller wrote that 'for no reason', Schmitt used the term 'positive constitution' to refer to the constitution in the material sense. Hermann Heller, *Teoría del Estado* (Luis Tobío trans.) (Mexico: Fondo de Cultura Económica, 2012) 349.

[96] Schmitt, *Constitutional Theory* (n. 84) 77–78. Constitution of Germany (1919), Article 1: 'All state authority stems from the people' and 'The German Reich is a Republic'. This decision, Schmitt wrote, was also reflected in the preamble: 'The German people provided for itself this constitution.' Although the republican form of government (understood as a prohibition of the creation of a monarchy) and federalism are frequently mentioned as an example of a fundamental principle of the constitution or as part of the material constitution, some authors consider that this is no longer the case, and that the rights that derive from human dignity, democracy, and the separation of powers have now gained much more importance. See Peter Häberle, *El Estado Constitucional* (Buenos Aires: Editorial Astrea, 2007) 260.

[97] Schmitt, *Constitutional Theory* (n. 84) 77–78.

[98] ibid.

[99] ibid. 79.

and the material constitution) had legal implications. Schmitt had, for lack of a better term, a 'normative' conception of the material constitution as opposed to Kelsen's 'descriptive' one. Constitutional laws could be legally amended, but the modification of the fundamental political decisions contained in 'the constitution' could never be achieved through a fully regulated legal process.[100] The material constitution was the creation of an extra-legal constitution maker and could only be altered by it, through any type of procedure it considered appropriate. Accordingly, the suppression of Article 149 of the Weimar Constitution through the ordinary amendment procedure would be perfectly valid, while the substitution of Article 1 for a clause that reads: 'All power stems from the King' (regardless of how respectful one is of the amendment formula) would signify the annihilation[101] of the constitution and the revolutionary creation of a new one.[102]

Even in the context of those regimes that explicitly allow for the 'total revision'[103] of the constitutional text or that operate under the doctrine of parliamentary sovereignty[104], a change in the basic form of government lies beyond the competence of the constituted institutions.[105] 'The offices with jurisdiction over a decision on a constitution-amending statute', Schmitt wrote, 'do not thereby become the bearer or subject of the constitution-making power. They are also not commissioned with [its] ongoing exercise . . . They are not, for example, a latent, always present constitution-making national assembly with the powers of a sovereign dictatorship.'[106] They are, to put it in Rousseauian terminology, constitutional *magistrates* and not constituent legislators.[107] Not

[100] Moreover, Schmitt maintained that an alteration of Article 76 (the amendment procedure) would also amount to the elimination of the Constitution: the power to reform the constitution cannot modify the legal provision that regulates its existence and competences. ibid. 150.

[101] Once the constituent power of the people or the king is recognized, it will operate as 'a constitutional minimum' that must be respected. If the identity of the constituent subject changes, there would not only be a change in the positive or material constitution but its 'complete annihilation'. ibid. 142.

[102] ibid. In case of the French Constitutions of 1814 and 1830 (briefly examined in Chapters 6 and 7), which lacked an amendment rule, Schmitt sided with those who negated the amending power of the ordinary legislature: '[t]he correct answer is that the constitution as a *whole* can be eliminated through an act of the constitution-making power, while constitutional *law* changes are certainly prohibited'. ibid. 72.

[103] ibid. 152. See, for example, the Federal Constitution of the Swiss Confederation (1999), Article 193: 'A total revision of the Federal Constitution may be proposed by the People or by one of the Chambers, or may be decreed by the Federal Parliament.'

[104] For Schmitt, depictions of the Westminster Parliament as 'all powerful' were a cause of great confusion, since 'a majority decision of the English Parliament would not suffice to make England into a Soviet state.' ibid. 79–80. 'Only the direct, conscious will of the entire English people, not some parliamentary majority,' he added, 'would be able to institute such fundamental changes.' ibid.

[105] ibid. 152.

[106] ibid. 151.

[107] For the term 'constitutional magistrate' (*magistrate constitutionnel*) to refer to an entity that exercises the amending rather than the constituent power, see Olivier Beaud, *La Puissance de l'État* (PUF, 1994) 323.

even a citizenry entitled to act by a constitutional provision should be confused with the constituent subject. That is to say, when a constitution authorizes citizens to exercise direct political power through a referendum or popular initiative, it is not constituent power that is being exercised.[108] In those situations, citizens exercise 'competences in the context of the constitution that is already provided' and their power is not superior to that of the legislature.[109]

This also applied to entities like a convention called under Article V of the United States Constitution or an Assembly of Revision convened under the French Constitution of 1875: those were constitutionally regulated bodies that had the purpose of revising constitutional provisions, not of making new constitutions.[110] If any of those entities attempted to alter the material constitution, their actions could not be described as constitutional; they would be invading the terrain of the constituent subject. Under this approach, apart from their formal legal role, eternity clauses were confirmations of the distinction between constitutional change and constitutional elimination:[111] they made explicit the material content of a constitution, a content that was outside the scope of the amending power. Moreover, while the individual provisions of the constitution (constitutional laws) could be suspended during a state of emergency, the constitution itself is 'inviolable' even during those periods.[112] Of course, unlike the ordinary institutions of government, the constituent subject itself could alter and adopt any constitutional content. And unlike Hauriou, who thought that even the constituent authority was subject to the separation of powers,[113] Schmitt maintained that constituent power was the 'comprehensive foundation of all other "powers"and "division of powers"'.[114] It could, in that sense, engage not only in constitution-making but also in legislative, executive, or judicial action.[115]

[108] For a discussion, see Chapter 10 of this book.

[109] Schmitt, *Constitutional Theory* (n. 84) 146

[110] ibid. 148–149.

[111] For Schmitt, constitutional change refers to the alteration of the constitutional text while maintaining the material constitution intact, and 'constitutional elimination' to the alteration of the constitution's material content). ibid. 147.

[112] ibid. 80. Indeed, as we will see in Chapter 9, the very purpose of an emergency provision is to protect the material/positive constitution, to preserve the fundamental political decisions of the constituent subject. For example, Schmitt writes: 'Wide-ranging intrusions into the guaranteed basic rights are permitted via constitutional and statutory norms. But as soon as the basic right is *abolished*, the constitution itself is violated. In a bourgeois Rechtsstaat, such an elimination of rights may not be undertaken through a constitution-amending statute.' ibid. 81.

[113] Hauriou, *Derecho Público* (n. 29) 348–349, fn 13.

[114] Schmitt, *Constitutional Theory* (n. 84) 126. Indeed, he wrote that extraordinary representatives, that is, those 'who execute the *pouvoir constituant*', can have 'some arbitrary authority'. Carl Schmitt, *Dictatorship* (Cambridge: Polity Press, 2014) 125.

[115] This is the idea that will be challenged in Chapter 9 of this book.

In *Dictatorship*, Schmitt had similarly written that the constituent power was 'in principle unlimited and can do everything, because it is not subject to the constitution: it provides the foundation of the constitution itself'.[116] Importantly, constituent power was not exhausted in the act of constitutional creation, but rather continued to exist 'alongside and above the constitution'.[117] This meant that the presence of an eternity clause, or the recognition of implicit limits on the power of constitutional reform, did not amount to an unchangeable constitution. It just meant that such a content would need to be changed or replaced through a—procedurally unspecified—constituent exercise.[118] Although constituent power is often described by Schmitt as 'unmediated', 'above the constitution', and as 'not bound by legal forms and procedures', it ultimately plays an important legal function: protecting the positive constitution from the ordinary institutions of government, even if they act through the constitutional amendment rule or under an emergency provision.[119] At the same time, however, this conception has the potential of justifying unlimited acts of political power (as noted above, Schmitt placed the constituent subject outside the reach of the doctrine of the separation of powers), as long as they can be identified as expressing the will, or as having been done by or on behalf of, the constituent subject.

Schmitt, as we have seen, insisted in the invalidity of an ordinary amendment that contradicts or replaces a fundamental political decision. For him, 'constitutional laws are valid only on the basis and in the context of the constitution in the positive sense'.[120] However, he does not explain how that invalidity is to be enforced. One can infer from his work that he does not think judges should be attributed with the authority to invalidate unconstitutional constitutional amendments. In *Constitutional Theory*, Schmitt maintained that a court could be attributed with the authority to declare the invalidity of unconstitutional laws, and that the same reasoning could be applied to unconstitutional constitutional amendments.[121] Nonetheless, he did not think judicial review of legislation as, for example, understood in the United States, was a desirable

[116] Schmitt, *Dictatorship* (n. 114) 121.

[117] ibid. 126.

[118] While Schmitt described constituent power as 'prior and above every constitutional procedure', he nevertheless maintained that 'the execution and formulation of a political decision reached by the people in an unmediated form requires some organization, a procedure'. ibid. 132. In modern democracies, for example, the political decisions of the constituent subject were frequently executed by 'special commissioners, such as a so-called constitution making national assembly'. ibid. 140.

[119] ibid. 132, 126, 128.

[120] ibid. 144. Moreover, the constitution in the positive sense 'is valid only on the basis of the will of the constitution-making power'. ibid.

[121] Schmitt, *Constitutional Theory* (n. 84) 230–231.

institution. Moreover, he maintained that if judicial review is properly understood ('as the non-application of the ordinary statute to the concrete case at hand that occurs by virtue of an application of the constitutional statute'), the question of whether a court can invalidate a constitutional amendment does not even arise.[122] But as we know, multiple courts have now embraced the Schmittian approach to the limits of constitutional reform and declared themselves competent to enforce it.

For example,[123] the Colombian Constitutional Court has explicitly embraced Schmitt's definition of constituent authority, describing it as 'a commissioning power of the sovereign people'.[124] Although its predecessor once stated that it lacked the competence to review the constitutionality of 'the articles of the Constitution itself or the amendments introduced by the constituent power'[125] (choosing to treat the amending and the constituent power as equivalent), the Constitutional Court stated in a 2010 case that the 'power of constitutional reform, as a constituted power, is subject to material limits, since the ability to reform the Constitution does not involve the possibility of abrogating it, subverting it, or replacing it in its integrity'.[126] The Court has also maintained that if the amending power replaced the constitution with a new one, then it would have illegitimately become the 'originary constituent power'.[127] Given that the constitutional text (Constitution of 1991, Article 241) only authorizes the Court to engage in a procedural review of proposed changes to the constitutional text, the judges were at pains to show that in adopting the doctrine of unconstitutional constitutional amendments, they did not assess the material content of the relevant amendment, but the competence of the amending authority to produce it.[128] That is to say, those changes that, because of their

[122] See the English translation of the relevant sections of *Der Hüter der Verfassung* in Lars Vinx, *The Guardian of the Constitution: Hans Kelsen and Carl Schmitt on the Limits of Constitutional Law* (Cambridge University Press, 2015) 81, 83–84.

[123] This is a phenomenon (i.e. the judicial invalidation of constitutional amendments) that now has been widely discussed in the literature, and I will thus limit myself here to briefly illustrate it with some examples where the concept of constituent power has assumed a key role. For further analysis of the Colombian case, see Joel Colón-Ríos, 'Carl Schmitt and Constituent Power in Latin American Courts: The Cases of Venezuela and Colombia', 18(3) *Constellations* 365 (2011); Carlos Bernal Pulido, 'Unconstitutional Constitutional Amendments in the Case Study of Colombia: An Analysis of the Justification and Meaning of the Constitutional Replacement Doctrine', 11(2) *International Journal of Constitutional Law* 339 (2013).

[124] Judgment C-544/92, Colombian Constitutional Court, para. 10. The court approvingly refers to Schmitt's definition of constituent power in *Constitutional Theory*. Interestingly, the court also referred to Hermann Heller in support of the view that a constitution was more than a factual relation of domination and that its justification was to be found in 'ethical principles of the law'. ibid. para. 8.

[125] Judgment No. 2159, Supreme Court of Justice of Colombia (28 October 1955) 362; Judgment Nos 2163–2164, Supreme Court of Justice of Colombia (30 January 1956) 9.

[126] Judgment C-140/10, Colombian Constitutional Court para. 1.6.4.

[127] Judgment C-551/03, Colombian Constitutional Court, para. 40.

[128] ibid. para. 13

substance, involve the alteration of 'the constitution' (to use the Schmittian formulation) are only within the reach of the original constituent power.

A similar approach has been followed by courts in different regions. For example, in a case examining the constitutionality of several reforms to Article 96 (related to the public financing of political parties) of the Constitution of 1949, the Supreme Court of Justice of Costa Rica determined that if a constitutional change touches 'on essential aspects of the political, social, and economic life of the nation', it cannot be adopted through the ordinary amendment process. Such a course of action, the court stated, 'would represent an invasion to the exclusive attributions of the originary constituent power [*constituyente originario*] . . . and would thus be contrary to the Constitution and in need of invalidation'.[129] The now famous basic structure cases in India,[130] also exemplify a situation where a court decides to protect the fundamental principles of the constitution from the ordinary institutions of government, even if their alteration would require an exercise of constituent power not authorized by the constitutional regime. These cases include the invalidation of an amendment establishing that 'there shall be no limitation whatever on the constituent power of Parliament to amend by way of addition, variation or repeal the provisions of this Constitution under this article'.[131] In contrast to this approach, the Supreme Court of Mexico has attributed the amending authority with a 'permanent constituent power' (i.e. the type of constituent power that according to Felipe Tena Ramírez survives the adoption of a constitution)[132] that cannot be subject to legal limitation.[133]

V. Beyond Kelsen and Schmitt?

Hermann Heller, in his *Theory of the State* (1934), rejected both Schmitt's and Kelsen's conceptions of the material constitution.[134] The legal implications

[129] Judgment No. 2006-014632, Supreme Court of Justice of Costa Rica (4 October 2006).

[130] See, in particular, *Kesavananda Bharti Sripadagalvaru v State of Kerala*, 1973 (SUP) SCR 0001. For a discussion of the basic structure cases, see Sudhir Krishnaswamy, *Democracy and Constitutionalism in India: A Study of the Basic Structure Doctrine* (Oxford University Press, 2011). The Indian Supreme Court was influenced by the writings of Dietrich Conrad, who advanced a conception of constituent power very similar to that of Schmitt. See Dietrich Conrad, 'Limitation of Amendment Procedures and the Constituent Power', 15–16 *Indian Year Book of International Affairs* 347 (1970).

[131] *Minerva Mills v Union of India*, 1980 AIR 1789.

[132] See Felipe Tena Ramírez, *Derecho Constitucional Mexicano* (México: Editorial Porrúa, 1978). Tena Ramírez served as a justice of the Mexican Supreme Court from 1951 to 1970. For a discussion of the role of Tena's concept of the 'permanent constituent power' in Mexican jurisprudence, see Mariana Velasco-Rivera, 'On the Implications of a "Permanent" Constituent Power' (on file with authors).

[133] See, for example, *Acción de Inconstitucionalidad 168/2007*, 86.

[134] Heller, *Teoría del Estado* (n. 95).

of Heller's analysis, however, were ultimately Kelsenian: the material constitution had a largely descriptive nature: it did not create legal limits on the constitution-amending authority. Heller's argument is a complex one and his untimely death while exiled in Spain prevented him from completing the section on constituent power planned for the previously mentioned book.[135] I will thus attempt to briefly summarize *and* reconstruct his views on the subject. The point of departure will be his conception of the sovereignty of the people as presented in *Sovereignty*, published in 1927. In a key section of that book, Heller considered the way in which the notion of the sovereignty of the people had been often presented, either implicitly or explicitly, as consistent with that of monarchical sovereignty. G. W. F. Hegel provided a good example of that approach: he thought that 'the people, without their monarch, would be a formless mass and would not constitute a state',[136] and found a conciliation between popular and monarchical sovereignty in the notion of the 'sovereignty of the state'.[137] For Hegel, 'the state' was sovereign, but its power was exercised by the person to whom the crown belonged.

Heller explained that the notion of state sovereignty later became so influential that even anti-monarchists frequently attributed sovereignty not to the people but to an abstract state represented by different organs, the main ones of which were the legislature, the executive, and the courts.[138] These approaches, Heller argued, failed to confront the basic question of whether sovereignty came from the top (a monarch) or the bottom (the people, the nation).[139] This question was important because, in the last instance, identifying a concrete holder of sovereign power involved a choice between autocratic and democratic government, and it was clear that the former had to be rejected. Indeed, when properly understood, the very notion of the sovereignty of the state seemed to exclude that possibility: '[W]hen one affirms that the state is sovereign, what is meant is that the highest power of decision belongs to the state

[135] See the outline and Gerhart Niemeyer's editorial comments in *Theory of the State*. ibid. 358.

[136] Hermann Heller, *La Soberanía: Contribución a la Teoría del Derecho Estatal y el Derecho Internacional* (Mario de la Cueva trans.) (Mexico: UNAM, 1965) 160. An English translation of this book is now available: Hermann Heller, *Sovereignty: A Contribution to the Theory of Public and International Law* (David Dyzenhaus ed.) (Oxford University Press, 2019).

[137] ibid. 161. Georg Wilhelm Friedrich Hegel, *Philosophy of Right* (New York: Dover, 2005) 164. The notion of the sovereignty of the state was not surprisingly present in some 19th-century constitutions. One of the best examples are Articles 5 to 7 of the Constitution of Nicaragua (1838): 'Article 5: "Sovereignty is one, indivisible, inalienable and imprescriptible: it belongs to the State. None of its parts, and no individual, may assume its functions; Article 6: It is essential to the sovereign, and its main objective (*objeto*), the conservation of liberty, equality, security, and property; Article 7: The State, from which the [different] powers emanate, can only exercise them through delegates and in the form established by the Constitution.'

[138] ibid. 161–162.

[139] ibid. 159, 163.

as a corporation and not to an individual subject.'[140] But the question would then become whether 'the people' or 'the nation' (terms which Heller sometimes used interchangeably) could be understood as holders of the ultimate political power, as 'someone' to which political acts can be attributed to.[141] The main problem was that without a set of norms establishing their mode of action, a people can only be a 'human mass that cannot have either a will capable of making a decision nor a power capable of action, much less of authority'.[142]

Heller nonetheless thought that, through a combination of majority rule and representation, the people could in fact be understood as a political actor. Majority rule and representation were 'the technical means through which the people, as a unity, prevails over the people as a plurality'.[143] Since the acts of a majority in a representative assembly would have to be accepted as binding by the minority, Heller thought that the acceptance of something like Jean Jacques Rousseau's general will was necessary in order to allow the acts of a majority of representatives to enjoy authority over the minority.[144] Under such an arrangement, the constitutional system would be operating under what Heller called 'magisterial', as opposed to sovereign, representation: even though representatives are not subject to an imperative mandate, they have to act within the boundaries set by the constitution *and* in accordance with the general will, as opposed to simply listening to their own private consciences.[145] Only then would the minority have reasons to treat any legal norms as legitimate. Understood in this way, magisterial representation would allow one to speak of the sovereign state and the sovereign people interchangeably.[146] But what kind of power is sovereign power? And, more specifically for the purposes of this book, what is the relationship between sovereignty, constituent power, and the law?

In his notes (reorganized and included in *Staatlehre* after his death), Heller made the connection between these concepts explicit. Only where there is the possibility of exercising constituent power can there be a sovereign state: 'A state can only exist where the power over the social-territorial organisation belongs

[140] ibid. 164.
[141] Note here that, as in the source/exercise distinction mentioned in Chapter 5, being the holder of sovereignty is not the same as being able to exercise it directly.
[142] Heller, *Teoría del Estado* (n. 96) 352.
[143] Heller, *La Soberanía* (131) 166.
[144] ibid.
[145] ibid. 166–167. Heller maintained that it is the general will that a jurist has in mind when she refers to ideas such as 'the spirit of the constitution' or the 'will of the state'. ibid. 167. This is in fact very close to Rousseau's actual formulation. Jean Jacques Rousseau, 'A Discourse on Political Economy' in *The Social Contract and The Discourses* (Everyman's Library, 1973) 138.
[146] Heller, *La Soberanía* (131) 168.

to the organisation itself . . . , where the decision about the being and form of the organisation is located inside it.'[147] When acting 'as the constituent power', he wrote, the state becomes 'a social unity of power that technically cannot be limited'.[148] If the constitution is seen as the result of history and tradition, the idea of a constituent subject', wrote Heller, would understandably appear 'superfluous and fictitious'.[149] But in the modern state, where the fundamental governmental structure is *designed*, 'the existence of a real *pouvoir constituant*, with a capacity of action, had to be presupposed'.[150] The 'constituent power', he wrote echoing Schmitt, is the 'political will whose "power and authority" is able to determine the existence of the political unity in the whole'.[151] This power could rest in the people, but only in virtue of a norm.[152] In this sense, as in Rousseau,[153] Heller's constituent subject must act through law. And when the institution authorized by law to engage in constituent activity on behalf of the sovereign state/people (which Heller called the 'constitutional legislator'[154]) acts, it must do so guided by the general will, by interests that are common to both the majority and the minority.

a. Heller's Material Constitution and the Ethical Principles of Law

Heller's conception of sovereignty and constituent power came accompanied by a complex understanding of the notion of constitution. In addition to the distinction between the constitution in the formal and the material sense, he examined the concept of constitution from what he called a sociological

[147] Heller, *Teoría del Estado* (n. 95) 312. In a democracy, Heller wrote, the constituent power is said to come (like all other forms of political power) from the people even if in reality 'the electoral body is comprised by a small part of the population and there are individuals who, thanks for example to their economic superiority, are able to act as a counterweight to the power of the electorate'. ibid. 314. Moreover, even if one does not take into account those inequalities, in any large organization, actual power will have to be exercised by a small number of administrators, bureaucrats, and experts. ibid. Heller nonetheless thought that the idea of the sovereignty of the people was not a mere fiction, but a polemical principle that served the purpose of negating autocratic sovereignty. ibid. 315. Where such a principle is accepted, the people (or, more accurately, different segments of it) exercise various forms of control over political leaders. ibid.

[148] ibid.

[149] ibid. 351. This was the kind of view defended by proponents of the historical constitution, discussed in Chapter 7.

[150] ibid.

[151] ibid. 352.

[152] ibid.

[153] See Chapter 2 of this book.

[154] Heller, *Teoría del Estado* (n. 95) 347. As opposed to the 'historical constitutional legislator', that is, the one who originally created the constitution.

perspective.[155] For example, he described the 'real constitution' as referring neither to the norms contained in a particular document nor to those (written or unwritten) norms regulating the fundamental structure of the state and its relations to citizens, but to the actual 'relations of power present in a country'.[156] Following Ferdinand Lasalle,[157] Heller maintained that these relations went beyond the state, and included, for example, the army, the Church, public opinion, and the financial sector. Although ever changing, these relations resulted not in chaos but in some form of order and unity, and that order and unity was the real constitution of a state.[158] The real constitution was thus not captured either by the formal or material[159] concepts, which he presented through a critique of Schmitt's views.

Schmitt, as noted earlier, thought that the formal constitution relativized the fundamental decisions of the constituent power, making all the norms contained in a constitutional text equivalent. For Heller that notion was at least overstated, since there are no theoretical principles that could tell us exactly what counts as 'constitutional' from a material point of view. The formal concept of the constitution 'was scientifically necessary' in order to allow us to identify what counts as constitutional from a legal perspective.[160] After all, the material constitution, which he described as 'a content valued as fundamental',[161] could never be totally independent from the same type of considerations that determine the content of the formal one, that is, to issues of 'tradition, political convenience, power relations, and juridical conscience'.[162] For example, he wrote, 'one could question . . . whether the federal structure, as

[155] ibid.

[156] ibid. 317.

[157] See *infra* (n. 225).

[158] Heller, *Teoría del Estado* (n. 95) 317. In his *Law and the State in the National-Socialist Doctrine*, Roger Bonnard maintained that 'in the national-socialist doctrine, the word "constitution" has not been understood in its organic and formal sense, but only in a material sense, that is, in terms of its object and content. And, even in the material sense, [the national-socialist doctrine] goes beyond the common conception that limits the content of the constitution to the rules that organise the state, and extends that content to the rules of organisation of the community comprised by the people. Seen in this way, the constitution not only deals with political life strictly understood, but also contains orderings about the economic and cultural life; those orderings contribute to the organisation of the life of the people in a community.' Roger Bonnard, *El Derecho y el Estado en la Doctrina Nacional-Socialista* (José M. Pi Suñer trans.) (Barcelona, Bosch, 1950) 54, fn 1.

[159] Heller distinguished between the material constitution in the strict sense and the material constitution in the broad sense. The latter included the 'total juridical situation of the state, or, at least, the totality of the legal norms contained in the constitutional text together with all the other juridical precepts in the state order consistent with the Constitution', without distinguishing the ' "fundamental" from the "derived" precepts'. Heller, *Teoría del Estado* (n. 95) 348. In this section, my references to Heller's material constitution only refer to the material constitution in the strict sense.

[160] ibid. 317.

[161] ibid. 348.

[162] ibid. 317.

Schmitt thinks, is really a fundamental precept of the positive constitution of the Reich of 1919'.[163] Conversely, there is nothing that would prevent a 'constitutional legislator' to determine that a provision which Schmitt would consider a mere constitutional law is in fact as fundamental as one of those he would see as reflecting the fundamental political decisions of the constituent power.[164]

Nevertheless, Heller did agree with Schmitt that behind any constitution or ordinary law, one would always find 'a more or less political decision of the one who creates it'.[165] In that sense, he rejected Kelsen's 'pure normativism', which did not pay proper attention to the law-creating power of the constituent subject.[166] Although Kelsen saw the basic norm as the 'juridical hypothesis that establishes the constituent authority', the basic norm itself was only valid logically.[167] It was therefore powerless to confer binding force to a constitution. It is, Heller thought, the decision of the historical constituent subject what attributes juridical validity to new constitutional content.[168] This is why Schmitt had a point when he insisted that the validity of a constitution must rest in a decision and not on a logically presupposed norm. However, for Heller, this did not mean that the constitution could be properly understood as only expressing a decision (or several decisions) about, for example, the form of the state. The constitution also needed to be understood as involving a claim to authority, by the possibility that it will be considered binding even by those who disagree with it, something not captured by Schmitt's decisionism.[169] Only then would the constitution be able to guarantee over time the cooperation between the different actors in a political order.[170]

The realization of a constitution's authority depended in important ways on the extent to which it reflects what Heller called the ethical principles of law embedded in the relevant society. These principles are, to a large extent, the same kind of precepts associated by other authors with the notion of the material constitution. However, Heller eventually reached the same conclusion as Kelsen: the material constitution is subject to the decisions of the entity authorized to amend the constitutional text. As noted earlier, when acting 'as the constituent power', that is, when determining the 'nature and the form of the organisation itself', Heller thought that the will of the state could not be

[163] ibid.
[164] ibid. 349–350.
[165] ibid. 336.
[166] ibid. 350.
[167] ibid.
[168] ibid.
[169] ibid. 350, 320. For a discussion, see David Dyzenhaus, *Legality and Legitimacy: Carl Schmitt, Hans Kelsen and Hermann Heller in Weimar* (Oxford University Press, 2003) 181, 183–184.
[170] Heller, *Teoría del Estado* (n. 95) 336.

limited.[171] Nonetheless, as suggested above, he did maintain that the previously mentioned principles, which existed besides a constitution, had to be respected by all law-makers.[172] These juridical principles are sometimes contained in a bill of rights and are normally connected 'to the political structure, to the organisation of the family and to the property regime'.[173] For him, these were the only norms that are really embedded in the conscience of the great majority of the population, which has little sense of the specific content of the constitution or of the rest of the rules of the legal order.[174] If the constituent subject (e.g. the constitutional legislator who acts through the amendment rule) 'offers' the community a constitution inconsistent with those principles, it is unlikely to provide a stable basis for a juridical system.[175]

Although some authors interpret this idea as suggesting that 'the sovereign is legally bound to fundamental legal principles',[176] Heller probably had something less ambitious in mind. He thought that these principles constituted 'a sort of natural law dependent on culture' which, if transgressed, could give rise to popular resistance.[177] That is to say, in order to be more than a system of domination, the constitution needs to be justified under the ethical principles of law.[178] Indeed, Heller maintained that a constituent subject disconnected from the juridical principles that are common to society, and in that sense inseparable from the general will, would have neither power nor authority.[179] It would, he said, not even be able to exist.[180] The threat of popular resistance (or of the gradual loss of authority of the state as law-maker) could be enough to make certain constitutional changes unthinkable but would still fall short of formal legal enforceability. The state, acting as a constituent power, is from a *legal* point of view always akin to a dictatorial power 'not subject to any juridical limit', even if controlled by the 'effective power relations found in society'.[181] There is no constitutional mechanism, he reminded his readers,

[171] ibid. 310, 311–312. One must note that Heller never finished his *Theory of the State*, and many of his comments on constituent power are based on notes and unpublished manuscripts put together after his death.

[172] ibid. 325.

[173] Heller, *Soberanía* (n. 136) 179.

[174] Heller, *Teoría del Estado* (n. 95) 326.

[175] For a discussion of this point, see Jorge Vanossi, *Teoría Constitucional: Vol. 1—Teoría Constituyente: Poder Constituyente: Fundacional, Revolucionario, Reformador* (Buenos Aires: Ediciones Depalma, 2000) 111, 113, 116.

[176] Dyzenhaus (n. 169) 176.

[177] Heller, *Teoría del Estado* (n. 95) 326. Heller did say, however, that no one has been able to permanently violate those principles, which means that absolute sovereignty has never existed.

[178] ibid. 352.

[179] ibid. 353.

[180] ibid.

[181] ibid. 316.

that in a situation of crisis could effectively prevent the strongest power to make and enforce a political decision.[182]

VI. The Production of the Material Constitution

If my interpretation of Kelsen, Heller, and Hauriou is correct, it is, perhaps ironically, Schmitt's decisionism that most clearly provides the basis for a legal doctrine directed at the protection of the material content of the constitution. This is a conception that, like that advanced during the 19th century by defenders of the historical constitution, would seek to protect certain fundamental principles, but in which that protection has actual legal implications. It is, however, the notion of a constituent people or nation, as the extra-legal author of the constitution, what usually makes such a doctrine possible. An important part of the reason why this is so can be grasped through an examination of Costantino Mortati's concept of the material constitution.[183] Mortati's main work, *La Costituzione in Senso Materiale*, advances a notion of the material constitution which, like Schmitt's, rested on a political decision. Nonetheless, Mortati rejected the theory of constituent power as traditionally conceived. The result, as we will see below, is that the question of whether the limits posed by the material constitution on the amending power are to have actual legal implications (e.g. whether it would be possible for these limits to be enforced by courts) is left by and large open in Mortati's work. My discussion will begin with a brief examination of Mortati's critique of Kelsen's theory of the basic norm, and then move to his critique of Heller and Schmitt.

Mortati thought that, in the last instance, the function of a constitution is to provide a means of determining legal validity. A formal constitution, by itself, cannot offer those means, because it is ultimately the result of a fact and not of a valid norm. Kelsen's solution to this problem, as noted earlier, was to argue that below any constitution there is a constitution in the logical–juridical sense (i.e. the basic norm). Kelsen, Mortati maintained, wanted to exclude from his formulation of the basic norm any reference to the social relations of power existing in a determinate society and, at the same time, to deduct the basic norm from that very social reality. Thus, instead of positing the basic norm

[182] ibid. 329.

[183] For an illuminating account of Mortati's material constitution, as well as of its place in early 20th-century constitutional and political thought, see Chapter IV of Marco Goldoni and Mariano Croce, *Legacy of Pluralism: The Continental Jurisprudence of Santi Romano, Carl Schmitt, and Costantino Mortati* (Stanford: Stanford University Press, 2020).

as a generic formulation (e.g. one must obey whoever is the supreme organ of the state), Kelsen usually (although, one may add, not always) presented it with reference to the relevant juridical system (e.g. one must obey the king, one must obey the drafters of the republican constitution, and so on).[184] If a change in the *Grundnorm* only takes place when the formal constitution is altered in violation of the relevant amendment rule, then a formally correct replacement of a monarchy with a republic would leave the basic norm intact. But Mortati notes that that cannot be the case if the basic norm identifies the ultimate sovereign organ of the legal system (i.e. a king, a sovereign parliament, etc.) because that is precisely what is being changed in those cases.[185]

This ambiguity in Kelsen's theory was for Mortati symptomatic of a deeper problem. The social relations of power that Kelsen unsuccessfully tried to exclude from the basic norm are what confer not only efficacy but validity to the legal order. Put differently, the formal constitution is efficacious because the dominant social forces treat it as valid and apply it in a determinate territory. For Mortati, this means that the 'true specific concept of the constitution' must be fundamentally connected to those social forces. Kelsen's theory, for all its sophistication, does not provide a way of identifying the political subject from which the material constitution emanates. The most common attempt of identifying that subject, the theory of constituent power, insists in making reference to a collective will that gives society a constitution. Under the classical understanding of that theory, Mortati writes, there is a 'social unity' that appears 'as an active subject only during the instauration of [a new state form], that is, as a constituent power which acts intermittently'.[186] In more advanced formulations, the constituent power not only acts when a new state is constituted or its form changes but when the formal constitution is altered.[187] Moreover, under the prevailing view, the holder of the constituent power is the nation.[188]

For Mortati, this was highly unsatisfactory. The reason why locating the subject from which the material constitution arises is necessary is not to explain the legitimacy of a legal system or its origins—such questions, he wrote, are foreign to law—but to find 'the juridical foundation of a concrete positive system, its supreme source'.[189] That is to say, the source that is able to make it

184 Costantino Mortati, *La Constitución en el Sentido Material* (Almudena Bergareche Gros trans.) (Madrid: Centro de Estudios Políticos y Constitucionales, 2000) 30.
185 ibid. 30–31.
186 ibid. 43.
187 ibid. 44.
188 ibid.
189 ibid. 45.

a system of positive law. The nation, he said, cannot play that function. The nation can only act through individuals, and those individuals will have different interests and values. Mortati could not accept Heller's solution to this problem either: the notion of the general will is inconsistent with the reality that in every society there will be groups with irreconcilable fundamental aims. This means that some criteria will be needed to distinguish between the interests and values that will be advanced by the legal order and those which will not.[190] Since 'the nation' cannot provide that criteria itself, it will be left to the holders of state power, to 'those individuals who have been able to prevail over others', to do so.[191] In that sense, even if the existence of a homogenous community (i.e. a nation in the sociological sense) can facilitate the emergence of a state, it cannot determine its 'particular mode of being'.[192] The source of the material constitution, in this respect, cannot be a constituent nation.

Mortati rejected Schmitt's conception for similar reasons. That is to say, Schmitt's identification of the material constitution with the 'fundamental political decision' is promising, but in the end the identity of the decision-maker is unclear.[193] Schmitt seems to suggest that the fundamental political decision is made by the 'popular community'. But like the nation, Mortati thought that such an entity could only be given existence, could only act, through the structures provided by an already constituted state and often through a charismatic leader.[194] In the end, Mortati wrote, what Schmitt may have in mind is 'a concrete and particular decision that has as its carrier not the people, but forces that may vary through time'. Nonetheless, Schmitt did not inquire about the nature of these forces.[195] Another problem, Mortati maintained, is the content of the decision itself. The fundamental political decision, he wrote, cannot be *any* decision: it has to be a decision about an order that aspires to be valid through time.[196] And although Schmitt provides some clues about what would be the typical content of the fundamental political decision (i.e. the typical content of the material constitution) he does not provide the criteria to identify it.

Ultimately, for Mortati, the source of the material constitution could not be found in a unified social will, in a constituent nation, but in what he called the dominant social forces in a given society.[197] Those social forces advance a

[190] ibid.
[191] ibid. 45–46.
[192] ibid. 47.
[193] ibid. 51.
[194] ibid. 52, 70.
[195] ibid. 53.
[196] ibid.
[197] ibid. 72.

particular form of order, which can be expressed by notions such as 'the political regime' or 'the form of the state'. They establish the aim of the constitutional order and guarantee the legal validity of the formal constitution.[198] This aim should not be understood as the generic aim belonging to any state (i.e. the promotion of peace, order, etc.), but to the basic political idea that drives it.[199] To the extent that the social forces that establish the aims of the constitutional order also attribute it with *legal* validity, they should not be placed outside of the law (as with Schmitt's constituent power) or seem as part of a logical presupposition (as in Kelsen). They have a clear juridical character that fails to be captured by those perspectives.[200] Importantly, those social forces act through what Mortati called the 'political party', understood as referring 'only to those associations that, assuming as their own a general and comprehensive conception of the life of the state . . . tend towards transforming it to concrete state action, excluding any conflicting conceptions'.[201]

The political party, understood as the active expression of the social forces that bring about and sustain the constitutional order, seeks to realize a political idea, to create a form of state that will be guided by a determinate ideology.[202] In this context, the form of the state has at its core the 'value or the set of values of a determined social class and its party . . . around which the different state institutions are coordinated'.[203] The political party was accordingly identified by Mortati as the 'originary constitutive power of the state', as the subject from which the material constitution emerges.[204] As the source of the material constitution, the political party would have been able to go beyond being an

[198] ibid. 96.
[199] ibid. 103.
[200] ibid. 132, 137. The notion of the material constitution, as understood by Mortati and most of the authors discussed in this chapter, was also expressed by Georges Burdeau's 'idea of law' (*l'idée de droit)*. Georges Burdeau, *Derecho Constitucional e Instituciones Políticas* (Ramón Falcón Tello trans.) (Madrid: Editorial Nacional, 1981) 36. According to Burdeau, the idea of law expresses the prevalent view, in a particular community, about which are the basic rules of common life, rules that are needed for the maintenance of the desired types of social relations. ibid. 54. Burdeau talked, for example, about 'a liberal idea of law' and about a 'socialist idea of law'. Georges Burdeau, *Tratado de Ciencia Política: Presentación del Universo Político—El Orden Social y la Idea de Derecho* (Enrique Serna Elizondo trans.) (México: UNAM, 1982 [1949]) Title I, Vol. II, 97, 134. The essential character of the sovereign (which could be a monarch, an oligarchy, or the entire nation) 'is the possession of the constituent power', which is what ultimately makes it the 'absolute master' of the idea of law. Burdeau, *Derecho Constitucional* (n. 200) 46; Burdeau, *Tratado* (n. 199) 390, 392. Georges Burdeau, *Tratado de Ciencia Política: El Estado—La Formación del Estado* (Enrique Serna Elizondo trans.) (México: UNAM, 1982 [1949]) Title II, Vol. I, 382.
[201] Mortati (n. 183) 80. Under this conception, multiple political parties co-existing in a liberal constitutional order but sharing the same views about the direction of the state, may count as a single 'party'. ibid. 82. For a discussion, see Gustavo Zagrebelsky's epilogue to Mortati, ibid. 244–245.
[202] ibid. 81, 82.
[203] ibid. 214, 216.
[204] ibid. 76, 83, 84.

association of partial interests or common sentiments, becoming an authoritative institution 'organised for general aims and capable of achieving them'.[205] Those 'general aims', as suggested earlier, are not understood as equivalent to a general will, but as referring to those values and interests shared by the individuals and groups who comprise the political party. The political party may also facilitate the creation of a formal constitution with the objective of 'ensuring the stability and security of social relations, and of guaranteeing both party members and those foreign to it the development of state life in the forms and manners that are considered more suitable for the realisation of the juridical order's organising principle'.[206] In this respect, even in cases in which the formal and material constitutions are fully consistent with each other, the former one will always function as a means for the realization of the second.[207]

a. Mortati's Absolute Limits to Constitutional Change

The power of the social forces that have created the constitutional order, Mortati maintained, should not be described as the 'constituent power, if this concept is understood in the usual manner, that is, as the organ of constitutional reform'.[208] Theirs is rather a power that is not limited to formal constitutional change and that can alter the constitution, or affect the way it is understood, through unspecified procedures. Here, Mortati seems to be making a distinction similar to the one between the derived and the original constituent power: the derived constituent power is the one exercised by the organ authorized to formally amend the constitution; the original constituent power is the one held by the social forces that created the material constitution. But it is not clear if this is what Mortati actually had in mind. For example, while recognizing the possibility of unconstitutional constitutional amendments, he maintains that the power of constitutional reform is usually understood as 'not subject to restrictions in terms of the content of its activity'.[209] The other kind of power (i.e. what may be called the original constituent power, and which as we saw earlier Mortati at one point called the 'originary constitutive power of the state'),[210] on the contrary, carries with it 'a directive principle expressing

[205] ibid. 84. Those groups who represent ideologies and interests contrary to the ones reflected in the material constitution subject themselves to the established order not because they consider it legitimate (as in Heller), but simply because it is the strongest political force. ibid. 74.
[206] ibid. 127.
[207] ibid. 129.
[208] ibid. 132–133.
[209] ibid. 133.
[210] ibid. 76.

a constitutional super-legality, not founded [like in Hauriou] on natural law but connected to the ideological positions of the dominant political forces, that poses an absolute limit to its acts'.[211]

Under this view, the formal constitution can of course change. But as long as the 'substantial form of the state' remains the same, the ideological presuppositions mentioned above would have been respected.[212] Those presuppositions are a key component of the material constitution. According to Mortati, they can sometimes be found 'in the constitutional text itself, as a set of premises, or preambles, or declaration of principles'.[213] Like Schmitt, Mortati maintained that the juridical character of these declarations must not be denied, as long as it is possible to deduce from them 'an aim, a directive, a programme'.[214] Not surprisingly, Mortati rejected both major approaches to constitutional change (parliamentary sovereignty and a rigid constitution with a legally unlimited amendment power) since they would allow the replacement of the material constitution.[215] To the extent that the material constitution reflects the fundamental aims of the state, Mortati saw it as posing 'an absolute limit to constitutional change'. 'Its fall', he wrote, 'means the fall of the state itself'.[216] But the potential practical implications of that statement are not entirely clear. In what follows, I offer a possible way of understanding it.

It seems clear that for Mortati, the ordinary power of constitutional reform (the derived constituent power), has to respect the fundamental aims of the state.[217] When there is 'a lack of correspondence between the relevant activity and the aims that should have been followed and were not . . .',[218] the amending authority would have acted *ultra vires*.

[211] ibid. See also Costantino Mortati, *Studi sul Potere Costituente e sulla Riforma Costituzionale dello Stato* (Milan: Guiffré, 1971) 121: 'Each juridical order has its natural limit of action in the preservation of its own fundamental constitutive end, and at the very moment in which the insufficiency of that end is declared and a discussion about the will to find another one takes place, one goes beyond the limit and transcends the juridical order.'

[212] ibid. 213.

[213] ibid. 154.

[214] ibid. 154–155. In cases where it is not possible to identify the relevant ideological positions in the constitutional text, Mortati thought that one could instead look at different acts and documents of the party itself. ibid. 155.

[215] ibid. 202–203.

[216] ibid. 214. Mortati notes that the authors who maintain that there are absolute limits to constitutional change tend to defend the existence of implicit limits, or refer to the agreements that were the basis of the constitutional order, or point toward a 'totality' that needs to be respected. ibid. 215. These ideas, he suggests, can be better explained by reference to the social forces in which the validity of the constitutional system rests. But in order for any of these limits to be 'juridically relevant', one needs to show that 'the forces from which they emanate are juridical, because they become part of the law at the very moment they establish a constitutional order'. ibid. And Mortati thought that the social forces had a juridical character because it is from them were the legal validity of constitutional norms emanate.

[217] ibid. 105.

[218] ibid. 115.

Elsewhere in *The Constitution in the Material Sense*, Mortati writes that the absolute limits posed by the material constitution cannot be transgressed 'even by the activity of the constituent power itself'.[219] Mortati does not say whether this also applies to the dominant social forces. It could be that these forces, in setting the fundamental aims of the state, will always be limited by their own values and ideology. Even if those limits are understood as 'juridical' (in light of the fact that the dominant social forces have a juridical character), they would not be legally enforceable. They would be self-imposed limits, the type of internal limits that ultimately guide the conscience of the most absolute monarch, as Jean Bodin famously maintained. Since the dominant social forces are the holders of the original constituent power, it does make sense that they are only subject to internal limits. All this suggests that Mortati shares a normative conception of the material constitution, one similar to Schmitt's. That is to a certain extent correct, but there is an important difference.

As Gustavo Zagrebelski has noted, Mortati did not accompany his conception of the material constitution with the notion of a 'permanent "material constituent power"' that has to act through some extraordinary mechanism, such as a constituent assembly.[220] That is to say, the original constituent power of the political party always irradiates the constitutional order and may sometimes trigger formal constitutional change or simply alter the way in which the constitution is interpreted or applied. An important legal consequence of this approach is that the adoption of a norm contrary to the material constitution would not necessarily carry the sanction of invalidity; sometimes it would be impossible or too controversial to refer to a norm as void when it is has been adopted by institutions controlled by the very social forces in which the constitutional order rests.

In fact, Mortati maintained that 'there can be occasions in which it is more consistent with the public interest to . . . not apply the sanction of nullity in relation to an otherwise invalid act'.[221] The lack of such a formal sanction, he thought, did not take away from the juridical character of the limit at issue.[222] When applied to the context of formal constitutional change, this approach would entail the existence of juridical limits to the amending authority, but not necessarily their legal (or judicial) enforceability. In this respect, Mortati may be right in his critique of those approaches that, like Schmitt's, seek to identify the material constitution as a decision of a fictional

[219] ibid. 200.
[220] ibid. 255.
[221] ibid. 116.
[222] ibid.

constituent subject that somehow exists in an extra-legal terrain. But his attribution of a juridical character to the social forces that bring about and sustain the constitutional order does not seem sufficient to ground a legal doctrine that can limit the jurisdiction of the organs authorized to modify the constitutional text.

At a theoretical level, Mortati reaches a similar conclusion to that of Schmitt: there are limits to the power of constitutional reform. His reluctance to engage with the theory of constituent power allowed him to present a more realistic account of the forces that engender the material constitution. By providing a more accurate explanation of the source of the material constitution, Mortati's conception excludes the possibility of referring to an extra-legal constituent people as the author of the fundamental content of the constitutional order. In so doing, it makes the idea of legally enforceable limits to the power of constitutional reform harder to justify. That is to say, courts and government officials need to present the constitution as a reflection of the general will or of the will of the people, as a document that is supposedly 'neutral' in terms of what Mortati calls 'fundamental aims'. Conceiving an extra-legal constituent people as the author of the constitutional order is what allows legal officials to attribute a limited jurisdiction to the constituted amendment authorities, while at the same time keeping alive the idea that the most radical constitutional changes are possible as long as they are adopted through an exercise of constituent power.[223]

VII. Conclusion

This chapter examined the ways in which the concept of constituent power can play a role, at the level of theory, in justifying the idea of a limited power of constitutional reform. If the material constitution is seen as the creation of an extra-legal constituent subject, then it seems to follow that it can only be altered by it. The ordinary amending power can alter the constitutional text, but must always respect the material constitutional content. To put it in Rousseau's

[223] This is an idea that, in a Rousseauian tradition, some Latin American constitutions have attempted to put into practice through the facilitation of the exercise of constituent power by popular initiative. For example, see Article 444 of the Constitution of Ecuador, allowing 'the President of the Republic, two thirds of the National Assembly, or twelve percent (12%) of the persons registered on the voter registration list' to call a referendum asking the electorate whether it wants to convene a Constituent Assembly. For the relationship of that type of provision to the democratic legitimacy of a constitutional order, see Joel Colón-Ríos, *Weak Constitutionalism: Democratic Legitimacy and the Question of Constituent Power* (Routledge, 2012).

terminology, the material constitution is placed outside the terrain of the government or the administration.[224] An important problem with the notion of the material constitution, as Heller suggested, is that its content cannot be identified with precision. Most authors associate the material constitution with the norms that establish the structure of the state, but even this may be controversial. For example, the norms that establish a legislature have a material character, but what about those which establish an Electoral Commission? Moreover, some have argued that the material constitution not only govern political structures, but also economic ones.[225] These problems lead many jurists to reject the notion of the material constitution or to only attribute to it what I earlier called a descriptive nature. Contemporary courts which have embraced the doctrine of implicit limits to the power of constitutional reform are still grappling with them.

When courts deploy the theory of constituent power to justify their jurisdiction to invalidate (for substantive reasons) constitutional amendments, they implicitly or explicitly recognize not only the continuing existence of the material constitution, but also that of an extra-legal constituent subject.[226] It is the continuing existence of such a power that allows judges to understand the process of constitutional reform as having a juridical nature (as opposed to a merely political one) and at the same time defend the notion that certain changes can only be made through a different, and frequently not constitutionally specified, *constituent* process. Problematically, however, when a constituent process takes place outside the established amendment rule, courts, political actors, and commentators tend to understand it as a manifestation of sovereignty, as an incontrollable jurisdiction to transform any kind of will into law. In the next chapter, I will inquire deeper into the nature of constituent power and argue that constitutional theory needs to go beyond the identification of constituent power and sovereignty. Constituent power is an element of sovereignty, but it is not equivalent to it. A constituent assembly convened outside the rules of change in an already established

[224] For a discussion on Rousseau's concept of government or the administration, see Chapter 2 of this book.

[225] For the classic formulation of this approach, mentioned earlier, see Ferdinand Lasalle, 'On the Essence of Constitutions', 3(1) *Fourth International* 25 (1942) [1862]. For Lasalle the material constitution was 'nothing else but – *the actual relation of forces existing in a given society*'. For a recent and important contribution, see Marco Goldoni and Michael A. Wilkinson, 'The Material Constitution', 81(4) *Modern Law Review* 567 (2018). This notion was briefly considered (and not rejected) by the Supreme Court of Justice of Colombia, when it referred to those who saw the 'real factors of powers' not in the law but in the economy. Judgment No. 2397, Supreme Court of Justice, (5 May 1978) 105–106.

[226] For a discussion, see Pedro de Vega, *La Reforma Constitucional y la Problemática del Poder Constituyente* (Técnos, 1985) 71–76.

constitutional order will be normally subject to the separation of powers: it should be understood as unable to apply the very competences it is supposed to create. Those entities that, in different moments of crisis (or of an alleged crisis) have assumed constituted and constituent authority, are better understood simply as 'sovereign'.

9
Sovereignty and Dictatorship

This chapter develops distinction between sovereignty and constituent power. As we saw in Chapter 3, this distinction was already present in the writings of Emmanuel Sieyès. To say that sovereignty and constituent power are not the same thing is to say that the constituent subject, at least when it exercises constituent power, is not sovereign, that is, that there are certain things it cannot do. Some of the 19th-century authors discussed in Chapter 6 implicitly accepted the distinction between these concepts when, in one way or another, they identified constituent power as 'one of the elements' of sovereignty.[1] The distinction is also present in the idea, briefly considered in Chapter 5, that the nation is the *source* of sovereignty but that it cannot *exercise* it itself. If the nation cannot act, except by representatives, then there are arguably no instances in which a sovereign political power can be truly exercised. In this chapter, I will argue that when distinguished from constituent power, sovereignty appears not as a constitution-making force, but as the ability to create *any* legal content without being subject to the separation of powers. A sovereign, in this sense, is best understood as an individual or entity who enjoys an uncontrollable jurisdiction to transform its will into law. The exercise of constituent power, in contrast, only involves a constitution-making authority; it can only produce *constitutional* norms.

Put in a different way, an entity authorized to engage in constituent activity is like Jean Jacques Rousseau's sovereign: it cannot produce ordinary legislative, executive, or judicial acts.[2] I will present this argument in four main steps. In Part I, I will examine Georg Jellinek's conception of constituent power, which he developed in the context of his discussion of the theory of the organ. Although Jellinek sometimes used the concept of constituent power to refer to the legally regulated competence of constitutional reform, he mostly relied on it to explain the source of the separation of powers. In his work, constituent power usually appears as an extra-legal force, inseparable from the notion of an

[1] See, for example, Cerbeleón Pinzón, *Tratado de Ciencia Constitucional* (Bogotá, 1852) 4; Fernando Mellado, *Tratado Elemental de Derecho Político* (Madrid, 1891) 329, 331, 352.

[2] For a discussion on this aspect of Rousseau's thought, see Chapter 2 of this book. For a discussion on the ways in which different 19th-century authors defended a similar view, see Chapter 6.

Constituent Power and the Law. Joel Colón-Ríos, Oxford University Press (2020). © Joel Colón-Ríos.
DOI: 10.1093/oso/9780198785989.001.0001

omnipotent law-maker. For Jellinek, in an already existing regime, the supreme organ of the state possesses a similarly unlimited competence. In Part II, I contrast that conception with that of Raymond Carré de Malberg, who tried to avoid the risks of a constitution-maker attributed with the totality of political power by conceiving the nation as a sovereign entity that could only act and will through state organs which never enjoy sovereign authority. Nonetheless, aware that his legal theory was in the last instance unable to get rid of the idea of an extra-legal constituent power, he simply described it as irrelevant from a juridical perspective.

I will argue that the type of power that for Jellinek was the source of the separation of powers and that for Carré de Malberg was not within the realm of legal science is best understood simply as 'sovereignty'. A sovereign can produce constitutional laws and even engage in ordinary legislative or executive activity. It has an unlimited discretion to determine its own competences, it is the *Kompetenz-Kompetenz*. But when a specific entity, such as a constituent assembly, is authorized to adopt a new constitution, it does not become 'the sovereign'. Rather, it exercises a special jurisdiction which may be substantively unlimited (i.e. it can adopt any constitutional content) but that is still subject to a limited mandate: that of making a constitution.

That idea will be unpacked in Part III through a discussion of the relevant sections of Carl Schmitt's *Dictatorship*. When that book is read together with *Political Theology* and *Constitutional Theory*, what emerges is a distinction between sovereignty and constituent power (in Schmitt's terminology, between sovereignty and sovereign dictatorship) which has not been developed by jurists and has been largely ignored in constitutional practice. For Schmitt, sovereignty was the type of power held by absolute monarchs, a power exercised in the absence of a commission. The sovereign dictator, in contrast, ultimately acted on a commission from a sovereign who is unable (or unwilling) to exercise its unlimited political force directly.

Schmitt, however, did not take that distinction to its natural conclusion: the idea that even a constitution-making body convened outside a constitution's amendment rule does not hold the plenitude of political power. If constituent power is understood as a non-sovereign power, an important aspect of its juridical character surfaces. In contrast, when the distinction between sovereignty and constituent power is blurred, the scope of the jurisdiction of the latter tends to be exaggerated, sometimes in dangerous ways. In Part IV, I will consider examples of different individuals and entities that, in the 20th and 21st centuries, have assumed what I describe abobe as sovereignty and presented themselves as unbound by the separation of powers. The emphasis will be on the Colombian Constituent Assembly of 1991, which can be understood as the paradigmatic case of this phenomenon in a formally democratic context, and in the Venezuelan Constituent Assembly of 2017. These were elected (in the latter case, controversially) entities which, on the basis that they held constituent power, assumed a jurisdiction formally akin to that exercised by dictators and military juntas. While the exercise of that kind of power by a democratically elected assembly can in some cases result in the improvement of the constitutional order, the confusion between sovereignty and constituent power can also serve to justify important departures from democratic principles.

I. Between Sovereignty and Constituent Power

Some of the most interesting developments of the theory of constituent power during the early 20th century are found in the writings of German scholars. However, as Claude Klein has shown, the concept of constituent power had little or no presence in German constitutional theory in the 1800s.[3] This is well exemplified in the work of Paul Laband, who rejected the idea that a constitution should be attributed with an authority superior to that of ordinary laws.[4] The constitution, Laband maintained, was not to be seen as a sort of 'mystical power' sitting above the sovereign state. This approach was consistent with the idea of 'tacit' constitutional reforms that developed under the German Constitution of 1871 and continued during the Weimar period. Under that conception, the constitution (a general law) could be *implicitly* amended by an ordinary law (a special law) as long as the latter expressed in its preamble that it had been adopted by the same number of votes required by the applicable amendment rule (Article 78 of the Constitution of 1871; Article 76, of the Weimar Constitution).[5] For Klein, Laband's conception, as well as the notion

[3] Claude Klein, 'La Découverte de la Doctrine Française du Pouvoir Constituant en Allemagne: de l'Empire à la République Fédérale' in *La Science Juridique Française et la Science Juridique Allemande de 1870 à 1917* (Olivier Beaud and Patrick Wadesmann eds) (PUS 1997). Ewon Zweig's publication of *Die Lehre von Pouvoir Constituant* in 1909 was a key work in the dissemination of the theory in Germany. Egon Zwieg, *Die Lehre von Pouvoir Constituant- ein Beitrag zum Staatrecht der Französischen Revolution* (Tübingen, 1909). Duncan Kelly, 'Egon Zweig and the Intellectual History of Constituent Power' in *Constitutionalism, Legitimacy, and Power* (Kelly L. Grotke and Markus J. Prutsch eds) (Oxford University Press, 2014). The other main early work on constituent power published in early 20th-century Germany was Robert Redslob, *Die Staatstheorien der Französische Nationalversammlung* (Leipzig, 1912).

[4] Klein (n. 3) 137–138.

[5] ibid. 138, 144. For a discussion, see Karl Loewenstein, 'Constituciones y Derecho Constitucional en Oriente y Occidente', 164 *Revista de Estudios Políticos* 5 (1969) 30.

of tacit constitutional reforms, was at least an indirect consequence of a lack of engagement with the theory of constituent power.[6]

Such lack of engagement resulted in the augmentation of the power of constitutional change of the ordinary institutions of government, that is to say, in the legal validity of actions that could otherwise be seen as falling outside the scope of the constituted authorities.[7] The situation began to change early in the 20th century, as exemplified by Jellinek's *General Theory of the State*, published in 1903.[8] Relying on Laband, Jellinek maintained that to the extent there is no institution authorized to invalidate acts that contradict the literal meaning of a constitution (or to the extent that the relevant institution decides not to exercise that authority), those acts must be treated as valid.[9] But unlike Laband, Jellinek discussed the theory of constituent power at some length. Like Maurice Hauriou,[10] Jellinek saw constituent power as a natural law concept: the idea that human beings have a natural right to create a form of government.[11] This is why he maintained that its exercise took place outside of the realm of law and could only be 'juridically assessed' retrospectively: any legal norms against which its validity could be measured would only be in place after a constituent episode occurs.[12] Jellinek explained that the embracement of the theory of constituent power in some jurisdictions had led to the limitation of the power of the state.

As a state organ theorist, he understood the state as an abstraction; the state was sovereign, but it could only exist and act through different types of organs.[13] And in a system with a supreme constitution where the theory of constituent power is accepted, those state organs must only exercise their authority in accordance with the constitutional text. That, however, did not apply to what he called the 'supreme organ of the state', the one that has been attributed with constitution-amending faculties.[14] Indeed, Jellinek sometimes used the phrase 'constituent power' (*verfassunggebende Gewalt*)[15] to refer to the competence of the supreme state organ. At some points, Jellinek seemed to suggest that the supreme state organ was subject to legal limits, that it could not create any type of

[6] ibid. 145.
[7] As we saw in Chapter 8, a similar situation arises when the notion of the material constitution is presented without a recognition of an extra-legal constituent authority.
[8] Georg Jellinek, *Teoría General del Estado* (México: Fondo de Cultura Económica, 2012).
[9] ibid. 66–67, 343, 351.
[10] See Chapter 8.
[11] Jellinek, *Teoría* (n. 8) 332, 451, 627–628
[12] ibid. 272–273.
[13] ibid. 501. For a discussion, see Duncan Kelly, 'Revisiting the Rights of Man: Georg Jellinek on Rights and the State' 22(3) *Law and History Review* 493 (2004) 520.
[14] Jellinek, *Teoría* (n. 8) 343–344, 435.
[15] In the original, see Georg Jellinek, *Allgemeine Staatslehre* (Berlin, 1905) 354.

constitution. He wrote, for example, that if certain topics were placed outside of the jurisdiction of the 'constituent power', then the relevant change could be adopted by 'an act of force, but never by a legal act'.[16] He also argued that even in the absence of an eternity clause, there might be changes that are politically impossible, 'and what is factually impossible can never be understood as a juridical possibility'.[17] But these limits, as we will see below, do not pose an insuperable obstacle to a sovereign state.

This becomes evident when Jellinek considers the notion of constituent power as understood by most 19th-century authors: a political force that sits outside of the juridical order. He examined at some length the nature of constituent authority in that extra-legal variety in the context of a discussion about the separation of powers. In that discussion, one discovers that there is not much separating Jellinek's extra-legal constituent subject and his sovereign state. In a system that operates according to the doctrine of the separation of powers, Jellinek maintained, the power of the state was initially divided and limited by the constituent subject and attributed to different organs.[18] A defining feature of constituent power in this extra-legal variety is its original character, while a defining feature of the constituted powers is the fact that they 'derive their existence and competence' from the constitution.[19] In every constituted state, however, there will be an organ with the 'highest power of decision', including the 'power to decide, in a definitive way, about modifications to the juridical order'.[20] In a state organized as a democracy, that supreme organ is the people and, in a monarchy, the king.[21]

The existence of such an organ, for Jellinek, was a corollary of state sovereignty itself. Sovereignty, he maintained, is characterized by a capacity for internal and external self-determination. A state is sovereign to the extent that it can become subject to *self-imposed* limits without being bound by any other internal or external authority.[22] In this sense, in the context of an already constituted juridical order, the sovereign state is attributed with the same kind of

[16] Jellinek, *Teoría* (n. 8) 440.
[17] ibid.
[18] ibid. 453. This idea is already implicit in Montesquieu. That is, if powers are separated, they must at one point have existed in an unseparated form.
[19] ibid. 471, 473.
[20] ibid. 496.
[21] ibid. 496, 520–521. The latter was the case under the German Constitution of 1871, where the Bundesrat was generally conceived as a sort of collective monarch. For a discussion, see Peter Caldwell, *Popular Sovereignty and the Crisis of German Constitutional Law: The Theory and Practice of Weimar Constitutionalism* (Durham: Duke University Press, 1997) 26–27, 28. See also Philip Zorn, 'The Constitutional Position of the German Emperor', 14 *The Annals of the American Academy of Political and Social Science* 73 (1899).
[22] Jellinek, *Teoría* (n. 8) 433, 437.

law-creating force possessed by the original constituent subject. Put differently, in the exercise of its constituent power, the sovereign, acting through the supreme organ, has the discretion to determine its own competences. It can thus supersede any limits that it has previously imposed on itself, and as a result transform its will (regardless of whether it is a constitution-making, legislative, executive, or judicial will) into incontestable legal acts. When Jellinek spoke of eternity clauses as making certain changes juridically impossible, and when he insists that the sovereign power of the state is a 'juridical power and therefore bound by law',[23] he is not negating the possibility that the sovereign state may decide to free itself from those limits. If that happens, there will be no internal or external authority able to force it to conform to established law.

What the state *must* do, however, is to replace those limits with new ones: '[T]he state can free itself from any self-imposed limitation [which could, for example, take the form of a bill of rights or of obligations arising from international law], but only by creating, in the form of law, more limitations.'[24] This is why he wrote that even a sovereign is subject to a juridical limit: maintaining the existence of a legal order.[25] A state cannot 'make its own existence impossible'.[26] That is to say, the supreme organ of the state, in the exercise of its constituent authority 'can choose any constitution it wants, but it must necessarily choose one. Anarchy is a factual possibility, but not a possibility in the realm of law'.[27] In this respect, when Jellinek maintains that an eternity clause can only be superseded by 'an act of force',[28] he must mean by an act contrary to existing law. But acting contrary to established law is always within the reach of a sovereign state, that is, a state not subject to any internal or external authority able to negate the validity of its actions.[29]

Jellinek's supreme organ can thus theoretically expand its competences (or the competences of other state organs) in a way that blurs or eliminates the separation among the ordinary branches of government. It could also blur or eliminate the separation between those branches and the otherwise special constitution-making (or amending) jurisdiction. The conception that emerges from this approach is one in which whoever has the authority to alter the constitutional text (i.e. the supreme state organ) possesses a de facto unlimited law-making force. Whether that force is described as sovereignty or

[23] ibid. 438.
[24] ibid.
[25] ibid. 434.
[26] ibid.
[27] ibid. This is a limit that, as we saw in Chapter 3, was already present in Sieyès' work.
[28] ibid. 440.
[29] ibid. 438.

as constituent power (in either its original or derived variety) does not make a difference. True, Jellinek wrote that the supreme state organ, as a constituent subject, is bound by law and should never be conceived as an 'absolutely unlimited sovereign'.[30] Nonetheless, it can always free itself from *existing* law and act *as* an absolute unlimited sovereign, that is, one not even subject to the separation of powers.[31] This is the kind of view that needs to be superseded before constituent power can be distinguished from sovereignty. In what follows, I will consider Carré de Malberg's views about this subject, which will help us to move a bit closer to the desired distinction, although only in the context of legally convened extra-ordinary constitution-making bodies.

II. The State as the Nation

The conflation between sovereignty and constituent power is constantly reproduced in constitutional theory. One aspect of this conflation is the idea, exemplified above, that whoever has the power of constitutional reform (i.e. the derived constituent power) possesses a sovereign jurisdiction. In a 1960 lecture, Karl Loewenstein, apparently paraphrasing Schmitt's famous dictum, expressed this view succinctly: 'Sovereign is who, among the different powers, decides about the reform of the constitution.'[32] This approach, as discussed in Chapter 1, became highly influential among some constitutional theorists who thought that when a constitutional text establishes that amendments are to be adopted through a particular procedure (e.g. a legislative supermajority), it is giving a constituted institution the same power of constitutional change that was exercised when the constitution was originally created. If the constitution contains eternity clauses, the institution authorized to amend it can remove them and proceed to adopt any constitutional content.[33] As we saw in

[30] ibid.

[31] For a similar interpretation, see León Duguit, *Lecciones de Derecho Público General* (Madrid: Marcial Pons, 2011) 101–102.

[32] Cited in Klein (n. 3) 147–148.

[33] Put in a different way, eternity clauses are to the amending power as entrenched legislation is to a sovereign parliament. An interesting problem would arise if the relevant eternity clause is formally self-entrenched (As far as I am aware, no eternity clause contained in a national constitution is self-entrenched.) One could say that in such a situation, the question would be, as in the case of a sovereign parliament, whether the sovereignty of the amending power is continuing or self-embracing. However (unlike in the context of debates about the nature of parliamentary sovereignty), putting the question that way requires one to suppose that the amending power was sovereign when it 'created' the constitution (even though *that* amending power did not exist before the constitution was created). For an excellent discussion of these debates in the context of the theory of parliamentary sovereignty, see Jeffrey Goldsworthy, *Parliamentary Sovereignty: Contemporary Debates* (Cambridge University Press, 2010).

the previous discussion of Jellinek (as well as in Chapter 8), some authors attribute such a substantively unlimited power of constitutional change not to a sovereign nation or a sovereign people, but to a sovereign state acting through its supreme organ. Carré de Malberg, Laband's successor at the University of Strasbourg, attempted to make the state and the nation equivalent while at the same time getting rid of the very idea of a supreme state organ.[34]

Unlike Leon Duguit, who rejected the idea of national sovereignty and described it as a useless fiction,[35] Carré de Malberg proposed it as a solution to the undesirability of absolute monarchy and the impossibility of popular sovereignty.[36] Like Hermann Heller and Costantino Mortati, Carré de Malberg saw the nation itself as an amorphous mass that could not have a will of its own: the nation could only will through the state.[37] 'The State', he wrote, 'is nothing but the personification of the nation. The State and the nation, under two different names, are nothing but a single being'.[38] For Carré, unlike in monarchies and democracies, (where there is a supreme organ, i.e. the king in the former, the people in the latter) in a regime that operates in accordance with the principle of national sovereignty there is no entity authorized to exercise sovereign authority.[39] That is to say, the state and the nation are abstractions that can only act through different organs, none of those organs possessing the totality of sovereign power.[40] This was, for Carré, the correct interpretation of the provisions (Articles 1 and 2 of Title III) of the French Constitution of 1791

[34] In so doing, it has been argued, he attempted to bring together German state theory and the French constitutional tradition. Unlike some of his French contemporaries, who rejected the theory of the organ as a German invention not applicable to France, Carré de Malberg argued that this theory was already present in the concept of representation developed by the French Constituent Assembly in 1789. Under that conception, the nation could only will through another entity, and that entity is equivalent to which German constitutional theory called a 'state organ'. Raymond Carré de Malberg, *Teoría General del Estado* (México: Fondo de Cultura Económica, 1948) [1922] s. 377. For a discussion, see Olga Bashkina, 'Raymond Carré de Malberg and the Interpretation of Sovereignty in the Belgian Constitution', 35 *Journal of Constitutional History* 149 (2018) 152. For an account of the theory of the organ similar to Carré de Malberg's, see Martin Kriele, *Introducción a la Teoría del Estado: Fundamentos Históricos del Estado Constitucional Democrático* (Buenos Aires: Ediciones Depalma, 1980). For Kriele, 'within a constitutional state, there is no sovereign; no one has a sovereign power, not even a latent one . . . that could violate and create the law'. ibid. 150.

[35] León Duguit, *Manual de Derecho Constitucional* (Granada: Comares, 2005) 17–18.

[36] Carré de Malberg, *Teoría* (n. 34). For a brief discussion of Carré de Malberg's conception of national sovereignty, see Chapter 5.

[37] ibid. s 372, s 388.

[38] ibid. ss 373, 437, 379.

[39] See Bashkina (n. 34) 157.

[40] For the distinction between the *source* and the *exercise* of sovereignty, see Chapter 5 of this book. This distinction is reflected in a number of 19th- and 20th-century constitutions which, after identifying the people or nation as sovereign, explicitly or implicitly negate the possibility of its direct exercise. Consider, for example, Article 41 of the Constitution of Mexico of 1917: 'The people exercises its sovereignty through the Powers of the Union' (*El pueblo ejerce su soberanía por medio de los Poderes de la Unión*). As we will see in Chapter 10, there are some Latin American constitutions that explicitly recognize the possibility of the direct exercise of sovereignty by 'the people'.

which–after attributing it to the nation—described sovereignty as indivisible and inalienable and stated that it could not be exercised by any 'section of the people nor any individual'.

An important problem, however, was how to explain the ultimate origin of the different state organs.[41] This was seen by some authors as the great flaw of the theory of the organ: since state organs exist by virtue of the constitution, the constitution itself could not have been created by a state organ.[42] In other words, the constituent power must be prior and superior to the state. Carré de Malberg thought that this was only an apparent difficulty. The creation of a state occurs in a terrain of pure fact and is not susceptible of being explained through legal categories.[43] This meant that any attempt to assess the original constituent act in light of juridical principles (e.g. consent), such as Rousseau's *Social Contract*, was destined to fail. States exist because someone created them: a small community through a unanimous vote, a popular majority, or a powerful individual.[44] And such acts do not raise any juridical questions. Accordingly, Carré de Malberg wrote, the theory of the organ 'does not have anything to do with the creation of the first Constitution of the State'.[45] Outside of the state, he added, 'the constituent power will fall in the hands of the strongest'.[46]

However, the theory of the organ could perfectly explain 'the exercise of constituent power and of constitutional change in an already established State'.[47] This 'regular and pacific' constituent power would be exercised not by the sovereign but by the state organs so authorized by the constitution.[48] In a country that, like France, was organized according to the principle of national sovereignty, the exercise of constituent power by a single individual would be unthinkable.[49] The constituent organ could nevertheless take the form of an extraordinary assembly or of an ordinary legislature.[50] In some jurisdictions, it could appear as a citizenry acting directly through a referendum, although if seen as a direct exercise of sovereign power, such an approach would be inconsistent with the principle of national sovereignty. It would also be inconsistent

[41] Carré de Malberg, *Teoría* (n. 34) ss 451, 437.
[42] ibid. s. 438.
[43] ibid. s. 442.
[44] ibid.
[45] ibid. s. 443.
[46] ibid. s. 444.
[47] ibid. s. 443.
[48] ibid. s 445. In truth, he nevertheless maintained, in an already existing state, a 'constituent organ' is always 'constituted', as it derives its existence from the constitution. ibid.
[49] After all, the struggle for national sovereignty had precisely the purpose of excluding such a possibility. ibid. s. 447.
[50] ibid.

with the theory of the organ itself, that is, if exercising sovereignty directly, the people cannot be conceived as an (electoral) organ.[51]

Importantly, when a constitutional order denies the ordinary legislature the power to alter the constitutional text and attributes it to a special organ (e.g. an extraordinary assembly), a separation between constituent and constituted powers arises. One of the main practical advantages of that separation was 'to limit the power of the legislative organ, especially with respect to individual rights'.[52] The potential exercise of the constituent power thus served as a limit to the legislative one. Special constituent organs, however, involved several dangers. Carré de Malberg thought that this was particularly true of constituent assemblies. Since they are called to establish the competences of all state organs, these assemblies 'will naturally tend to form an exaggerated idea of their own power'.[53] This will usually be the case when the assembly is conceived as the means for the exercise of popular sovereignty and as able to create binding norms. In such a situation, the assembly may see itself as enjoying a popular mandate to act as if it was 'the nation', to exercise political power as if it was not a mere state organ acting on a commission but the source of the entire juridical order and of the separation of powers.[54] In those cases, he maintained, these assemblies may come to see themselves as omnipotent, abolish the separation of powers, and become 'supreme dictators', as the French National Convention did in 1793.[55]

At the same time, however, Carré de Malberg maintained that if understood in light of the principle of national sovereignty, the distinction between constituent and constituted powers offered 'important practical advantages in countries overwhelmed by a constituent mania'.[56] National sovereignty, to the extent that it negates the sovereignty of any particular state organ, means that there are certain things that a legally convened constituent assembly (an extraordinary state organ), properly understood, can do. Since there is no state organ with an authority superior to that of a constituent assembly, such an assembly is understandably identified by some as 'sovereign'.[57] But as any other

[51] For a discussion, see Bashkina (n. 34) 156, 158–159. See also Chapter 10 of this book, where I will consider Carré de Malberg's apparent defence of referendums and other mechanisms of direct democracy (as a means of negating parliamentary sovereignty) in later works.

[52] Carré de Malberg, *Teoría* (n. 34) s. 450. Carré de Malberg devotes some pages to demonstrate why there was no place in Rousseau's approach to a separation between constituent and constituted powers (even though, at some points, he suggests the possibility of a different interpretation). ibid. ss 450, 451, 452 (fn 19).

[53] ibid. s. 454.

[54] ibid.

[55] ibid. ss 454, 452.

[56] Ibid. s. 454.

[57] ibid. s. 456.

state organ, a constituent assembly can be attributed with important competences but never with full sovereign power. For Carré, as noted earlier, no state organ should be understood as truly supreme. In particular, given that it has the specific task of exercising constituent functions, a constituent assembly would be normally authorized to create constitutional forms without 'being able to apply any of the powers' it creates.[58] At the same time, under this conception, a constituent assembly, just like any other mechanism that forms part of a legally regulated amendment process, could be made subject to material limits, limits that, unlike Jellinek's, are not simply self-imposed. According to Carré, however, this was not the case of the special assembly contemplated by the French Constitution of 1875.[59]

The Constitution of 1875 contained an amendment formula (Article 8) according to which an absoliute majority of each of the legislative chambers had the authority to issue separate resolutions proposing constitutional amendments. The chambers would then meet together as a National Assembly (sometimes called an 'Assembly of Revision'), which could revise the constitution 'in whole or in part' through the vote of the absolute majority of its members. An amendment to Article 8 itself (adopted in 1884) established that 'the republican form of government shall not be the object of an amendment proposal.' Even in light of that eternity clause, some commentators, notably Duguit, maintained that the amending power of a National Assembly was unlimited: at most, the eternity clause prevented the legislative chambers from proposing a change to the republican form of government but, once the National Assembly was convened, it would have all the powers of a 'proper' constituent assembly, that is, 'a total and unlimited power of constitutional reform.'[60]

For Carré, by contrast, a technically correct interpretation of Article 8 would require one to conclude that the National Assembly's power of constitutional reform extended only to the proposals of the legislative chambers.[61]If the

[58] ibid. s. 456.

[59] Carré de Malberg, like Kelsen, had a descriptive notion of the material constitution (see Chapter 8 of this book): 'This distinction between two concepts, material and formal, of constitution, appears with frequency in public law treatises. It lacks, however, any value, at least from a juridical point of view. In law, the criterion that allows us to distinguish the constitutional from the ordinary laws is found only in a formal element, because the concept of constitution is purely formal.' ibid. s. 465.

[60] ibid. s. 469. Put in the terminology used in the United States, a National Assembly, once convened, could become a 'runaway' entity.

[61] In Argentina, a similar situation arose with respect to the changes adopted by a Constituent Convention according to Article 30 of the Constitution of 1853, which only allows amendments through that mechanism. Article 30 states that the Congress must express the necessity of a constitutional reform and call a convention that would carry it out. The 1994 Constituent Convention (sometimes called a Reforming Convention) adopted a number of constitutional amendments, including one related to the retirement age of judges that was not part of the reforms identified by Congress as necessary. That amendment was challenged on the basis that it exceeded the congressional mandate. In a

legislative chambers were unable to propose a change to the republican form of government, he thought that the National Assembly would also be unable to do so.[62] In other words, the National Assembly is not the *Kompetenz-Kompetenz*, it 'is not invested with a sovereign power to reform the constitution and to determine the scope of the reform. It only has the constituent competency that it receives' from the constitution.[63] Even if technically correct, however, Carré de Malberg recognized that this interpretation would lack practical force in France: Article 8 of the Constitution did not establish any mechanism that could be used to enforce those limits. As a result, its effectiveness would largely depend on the 'conscience of the members of the assembly'.[64] And tradition itself, he thought, was never enough to ultimately bind a legislature.[65] The National Assembly's power of constitutional change was thus not subject to material limits.

Granted, what national sovereignty requires in the context of constitution-making is that a constituent assembly is not attributed with the authority to execute the ordinary powers of government.[66] It is this additional power that would make the assembly *sovereign* and transform it into an entity not subject to the separation between the constituent and constituted powers. However,

1999 decision, the Supreme Court of Argentina agreed with the claimants, concluding that an Article 30 Convention was legally bound by the limits derived from the congressional decision to convene it. 'Caso Fayt', Judgment no 100/XXXV, Corte Suprema de la Nación (19 August 1999). In a subsequent decision, however, the court (even though describing the convention as a 'derived constituent power') departed from its previous reasoning, concluding that 'it is necessary to abandon the "Fayt" doctrine, and adopt a new control standard that shows deference and respect to the sovereign will of the people expressed by the Reforming Convention'. The court, however, maintained that it had jurisdiction to limit the actions of a convention in cases were there is an 'absolute incompatibility' between the congressional mandate and the reforms adopted by the convention, and in cases where the convention seeks to violate the republican system of government or fundamental human rights. 'Caso Schiffrin', Judgment 159/2012, Corte Suprema de la Nación (28 March 2017) 8–9, 13. This kind of 'mandate', given that it comes from a constituted power itself, is of a very different nature to that discussed further in Chapter 10.

[62] Carré de Malberg, *Teoría* (n. 34) s. 470–471, 473.
[63] ibid. s. 473.
[64] ibid. s. 478; Raymond Carré de Malberg, *La Ley, Expresión de la Voluntad General: Estudio sobre el Concepto de Ley en la Constitución de 1875* (Ignacio Massot Puey trans.) (Madrid: Marcel Pons, 2011). Carré de Malberg implicitly accepted the possibility of attributing courts with the power to invalidate unconstitutional constitutional amendments, but only if the relevant limits were found in positive law. Indeed, he rejected the idea that 'there are principles of a higher order, which are the same the doctrinaire school of thought, a century ago, saw as deriving their transcendent superiority from the highest of all sovereignties, that is, that of justice and reason, so that they would not only bind legislators, but would be above the constitution itself'. This would mean, he maintained, 'that courts would be tasked to make, through their judgments, the constitution we should actually have'. Carré de Malberg, *La Ley* (n. 64) 125. He also rejected those approaches, which he associated with the doctrinaires, according to which the legislative power was bound by 'principles which, even though not expressed in the Constitution . . . constitute the implicit basis of all our system of public law . . . such as the principle of the separation between administrative and judicial authorities . . . '. (at 125).
[65] Carré de Malberg, *Teoría* (n. 34) s. 478.
[66] ibid. s 479.

the problem was that in France, the members of a National Assembly were the very same individuals sitting in the constituted legislature.[67] Accordingly, the ordinary legislative chambers were 'practically the holders of the constituent power' and, in that respect, the legislative and constituent power were confused.[68] The French legislature was, therefore, just as sovereign as the Westminster Parliament.[69]

In a later work, published in 1930, Carré de Malberg maintained that this was partly a consequence of the adoption of Sieyès' claim that the legislature was called to express the 'general will' of the nation.[70] But the general will, and here Carré de Malberg sided with Rousseau, could not be represented.[71] 'The general will', Carré de Malberg wrote, 'is like sovereignty . . . [It] does not admit any superior power . . . Its influence extends both to fundamental questions about the organisation of state power and to any other topic that requires regulation'.[72] If the legislature is seen as representing the general will (rather than, for example, acting on an imperative mandate or on the general mandate of a constitution), there is no difference between it and a constituent assembly expressly authorized to adopt constitutional norms.[73]

Like Édouard Laboulaye, whose views on constituent power were discussed in the previous chapter, Carré de Malberg contrasted this situation with that of the United States, where he saw a clear distinction between the sovereign and the ordinary public authorities.[74] There, the entire citizenry was seen as 'the original sovereign and as the source and creator of all the constituted powers' who were in turn understood as unable to will for the people.[75] This made possible, for example, the recognition of the courts' ability to declare the invalidity of unconstitutional legislative acts and the corresponding inability of an ordinary legislative majority to override those declarations. In some US States, the people even reserved the right to approve, by referendum, changes to the constitutional text.[76] Carré de Malberg thus presents the US's system as

[67] The lack of effectiveness of Article 8 meant, for example, that even if a court was given the power to strike down unconstitutional legislation, parliament could simply use the amendment process to easily override that decision. Carré de Malberg, *La Ley* (n. 64) 129.
[68] Carré de Malberg (n. 34) s. 479.
[69] ibid. s 484.
[70] Carré de Malberg, *La Ley* (n. 64) 115.
[71] ibid. 119.
[72] ibid. 115.
[73] ibid. 122.
[74] Carré de Malberg, *Teoría* (n. 34) s 77, s. 455.
[75] ibid.
[76] Carré de Malberg maintained that in 1789 and 1875 constitution-making episodes in France, where the citizenry was not called to participate directly in the activity of constitutional reform, 'the people did not have constituent power'. ibid. s. 338.

superior to that of France and as coming very close to realizing an important aspect of the principle of national sovereignty: its incompatibility with any arrangement in which a state organ is understood as sovereign, as having the power to adopt any fundamental and ordinary laws, as well as that of executing them.[77]

Nonetheless, the theoretical 'outside' or extra-legal space that allows 'the people' in the United States to permanently influence legal validity is legally irrelevant under the approach presented in Carré de Malberg's *Theory of the State*.[78] Importantly, while his conception of national sovereignty and his theory of the organ allowed him to explain the reason why constituent assemblies convened according to a constitution's amendment rule (and only those kinds of constituent assemblies) were not sovereign and only had a constituent function, he treated the original constituent power more or less in the same way as Jellinek. Constituent power, when exercised outside of a constitution's amendment rule, is simply the source of the legal system, it is a matter of fact, not of law, and there is nothing preventing it from determining its own competence. In the next section, I will argue that Schmitt's distinction between sovereignty and sovereign dictatorship can serve as the basis for a solution of this problem.

III. Sovereignty vs Sovereign Dictatorship

In the previous sections, I explored some of the ways in which sovereignty and constituent power have been conflated, to different degrees, in key works of early 20th-century constitutional theory. In his first major work, *Dictatorship*,[79] written shortly after the Russian Revolution, Carl Schmitt engaged in a discussion about the relationship between constituent power and emergencies that not only contrasts with earlier understandings of constituent authority (including Jellinek's and Carré de Malberg's) but also allows us to reconsider some of the ideas associated with the doctrinaires (whose views on constituent power were examined in Chapter 7). The main theoretical contribution of *Dictatorship* is the development of the distinction between commissarial and sovereign dictatorship. This distinction was explained by Schmitt through a discussion of Book 4 of Rousseau's *Social Contract*. Rousseau, following the

[77] ibid.
[78] This is an approach that, as we will see in Chapter 10, Carré de Malberg partially abandoned later.
[79] Carl Schmitt, *Dictatorship* (Cambridge: Polity Press, 2014).

classic understanding of dictatorship, referred to it as 'a temporal suspension of the entire legal system'.[80] In such a situation, 'a supreme ruler' is nominated, 'who shall silence all the laws, and suspend for a moment the sovereign authority'.[81]

Largely following the Roman approach to this institution, Rousseau saw the purpose of dictatorship as that of preserving the existence of the state, of protecting it from those enemies who seek to destroy it.[82] Moreover, he maintained that the suspension of the sovereign legislative authority is not equivalent to its abolition: the dictator, 'the magistrate who silences [the legislative authority] cannot make it speak; he dominates it, but cannot represent it. He can do anything except make laws [i.e. constitutions].' [83] Rousseau's conception is an example of what Schmitt called commissarial, as opposed to sovereign, dictatorship. During a period of commissarial dictatorship the constitution remains valid, 'because its suspension only represents a *concrete exception*', that is to say, a situation different from the normal condition that the constitution presupposes and that the dictator is tasked to bring back.[84] Rousseau in fact described the dictator as acting on an 'important trust' (*une importante commission*), which like all commissions, was revocable by the commissar.[85]

A commissarial dictatorship is best exemplified by an executive who, according to a constitutional provision, is authorized to issue decrees that are valid even though contrary to one or more articles of the constitution. Article 48(2) of the Weimar Constitution provided an example: '[. . .] [t]he President can utilize the necessary measures to restore public security and order, if necessary with the aid of armed force. For this purpose, he may provisionally suspend, in whole or in part, the basic rights established in Articles [. . .].' In the approach presented in *Dictatorship*, that type of clause would make the exercise of extraordinary (dictatorial) powers by the President possible, but would not give her the power of constitutional change.[86]

While Rousseau's approach illustrates this institution in its traditional commissarial form, Schmitt argues that his Legislator provides important clues as to the nature of *sovereign* dictatorship. As we saw in Chapter 2, Rousseau

[80] ibid. 106. In *The Social Contract*; this discussion occurs in Chapter 6 of Book IV. Jean-Jacques Rousseau, *The Social Contract and The Discourses* (Everyman's Library, 1973) 290–291.
[81] ibid. 290.
[82] During a dictatorship the general will is respected because 'it is clear that the people's first intention is that the State shall not perish'. ibid. 290–291.
[83] ibid. 291. For a discussion of Rousseau's use of the term 'law' see Chapter 2 of this book.
[84] Schmitt, *Dictatorship* (n. 79) 118 (emphasis in the original).
[85] Rousseau (n. 80) 292; Schmitt, *Dictatorship* (n. 79) 107.
[86] Rousseau (n. 80) 208, 215, 176.

thought that the Legislator only had the power to propose a constitution: in order for its proposals to become law, they had to be ratified by the people. The Legislator is thus a constitution-drafter with no legal power.[87] But if one gives Rousseau's Legislator the power of his dictator (i.e. the power of producing conclusive legal acts), one gets sovereign dictatorship: a dictator authorized to replace the existing constitutional order.[88] The nature of a sovereign dictator, Schmitt maintained, is expressed in a concept that 'is a consequence of the *Contrat social*' but that Rousseau 'does not name as a separate power: *le pouvoir constituant*'.[89]

A sovereign dictator, for Schmitt, 'does not *suspend* an existing constitution through a law based on the constitution—a constitutional law; rather it seeks to create conditions in which a constitution—a constitution that it regards as the true one—is made possible. Therefore dictatorship does not appeal to an existing constitution, but to one that is still to come.'[90] While Schmitt's commissarial dictator is supposed, in the last instance, to protect the *material constitution*, the sovereign dictator, in contrast, is authorized to change it. Sovereign dictatorship would thus be exemplified by a monarch who has been authorized to replace the entire constitutional order, as well as by a democratically elected constituent assembly.[91] One of the main examples of a sovereign dictator provided by Schmitt was the French National Convention, which he described as 'a sovereign dictatorship of revolution', and as the 'extraordinary organ of a *pouvoir constituant*'.[92] In *Constitutional Theory*, published in 1928, Schmitt also noted that a constitution-making assembly 'which convenes after a revolutionary elimination of the pre-existing constitutional laws, is best designated a "sovereign dictator"'.[93]

The main reason is that such an entity 'has no jurisdiction, no competence in the actual sense, that is, in the sense of a sphere of office regulated and delimited in advance'.[94] 'The scope of its power resources and its empowerment' he added, 'stands entirely in its own discretion'.[95] Put in a different way, a sovereign dictator is not subject to the separation of powers: 'it can intervene arbitrarily—through legislation, through the administration of justice, or

87 Schmitt, *Dictatorship* (n. 79) 110.
88 ibid. 110–111.
89 ibid. 111.
90 ibid. 119.
91 It was also present in the notion of 'the dictatorship of a proletariat identified with the people at large, in transition to an economic situation in which the state is "withering away"'. ibid. 179.
92 ibid. 96, 127.
93 Carl Schmitt, *Constitutional Theory* (Durham: Duke University Press, 2008) 109.
94 ibid. 110.
95 ibid.

simply through concrete acts'.[96] Once the constitution is adopted, not only does sovereign dictatorship end, but it ceases to exist as a legal possibility: 'A sovereign dictatorship is irreconcilable with a constitutional form of government.'[97] As suggested by Jellinek, the separation of powers presupposes an instance of ultimate, unified power, where the initial separation is drawn; at first sight, sovereign dictatorship seems to be that instance.

Schmitt nevertheless maintained that, in the end, all forms of dictatorship, even the sovereign one, are based on a commission.[98] In a democratic regime, for example, a constituent assembly 'is not the sovereign, but instead acts always in the name of and under commission from the people', which (like Sieyès' nation), 'can at any time decommission its agents through a political act'.[99] From this perspective, being a *sovereign dictator* and a *sovereign* is not the same thing: the former is tasked to bring into existence a new constitutional order; the latter 'does not depend on the accomplishment of a specific task'.[100] For instance, the Constitution of 1793, as noted in Chapter 3, was itself suspended by an emergency decree issued by the National Convention. By going beyond its task (i.e. by remaining assembled after adopting a constitution), the assembly entered the terrain of pure sovereignty. A sovereign, in this sense, is more than a sovereign dictator. It is an entity that, like an absolute prince or a sovereign people, can arbitrarily exercise constituent *and* constituted powers in the absence of any commission.

However, Schmitt thought that an entity acting on a commission from the people would always lack a clear 'reference point for [its] dependence'.[101] That is to say, the will of the people is always 'unclear' and has to be 'shaped'.[102] Sieyès, Schmitt noted, understood this well when he insisted that the members of the constituent assembly (a sovereign dictatorship) were not subject to the imperative mandate and were therefore not 'messengers delivering' an already made decision.[103] They were tasked with the making of the decision themselves. In drawing up the will of the constituent people, a sovereign dictatorship is still subject to a mandate: the drafting of a constitution.[104] But given the ambiguous

[96] Schmitt, *Dictatorship* (n. 79) 123. This is in fact the 'standard definition' of dictatorship: 'a suspension of the separation of powers'. ibid. 129. This standard definition, however, failed to properly distinguish dictatorship from other types of arrangements in which the separation of powers is also absent, such as absolute monarchy. ibid. 116.
[97] ibid. 204.
[98] ibid. 119.
[99] Schmitt, *Constitutional Theory* (n. 93) 110.
[100] Schmitt, *Dictatorship* (n. 79) 119.
[101] ibid. 121.
[102] ibid. 124.
[103] ibid.
[104] ibid. 125.

character of the people's will, '[a]s long as such an assembly has not accomplished its work—the constitution—it possesses any imaginable authority'.[105] (This idea, as we will see in Part IV of this chapter, was reflected in the processes that led to the creation of the Colombian Constitution of 1991, as well as in the powers attributed to the Venezuelan Constituent Assembly of 2017.)

What those passages show is that Schmitt did not fully develop the more promising features of the distinction between a sovereign and a sovereign dictator. That is to say, if a constituent assembly, even if convened in violation of a constitution's amendment rule, is acting on a commission from the true sovereign (i.e. the people in a democracy), then it must be bound by the conditions of that commission. In some cases, those conditions would not have been (or could not have been) explicitly stated, as may be the case of a constituent assembly called after a civil war or a revolution. But in other cases, the nature and limits of the commission would be expressed in the process through which the assembly was convened.[106] This is the case, for example, where a constituent assembly is convened through a referendum in which the electorate is asked the following sort of question: 'Should a constituent assembly be convened to create a new constitution?'. Such a question is broad enough to result in different types of controversies and disagreements, but it seems clear that if the assembly has been convened for the creation of a new constitution, it has not been commissioned to adopt ordinary laws, or to carry out judicial or executive acts.[107]

In the absence of any more specific limits that can be derived from a referendum question, such an entity would, at the very least, be bound by two limits that are inherent in a commission to draft a constitution of behalf of the sovereign: the assembly has to actually draft a constitution (i.e. something that counts as a constitution in the society at issue) *and* respect the identity of the constituent subject (i.e. it cannot transform itself into a sovereign entity).[108] It could happen that the constituted powers are not allowing the assembly to perform its constitution-making function, and, in such a case, there might be a political justification for it to attempt to interfere in the exercise of the constituted powers in order to comply with its mandate.[109] But even in those

105 ibid. 204.

106 This point will be developed further in Chapter 10.

107 This is a view that, as we saw in Chapter 6, was already present in the 19th century. See, for example, Discours de M. Thouret, 'Député du Calvados' (4 October 1831); Édouard Laboulaye, *Del Poder Constituyente* (Guatemala, 1872).

108 The nature and legal implications of these limits will be further considered in Chapter 10 of this book.

109 In 19th-century United States, John Alexander Jameson made a similar point when maintaining that a constitutional convention was a 'mere committee, sitting for a specified purpose, under the express mandate of the sovereign, and possessed of such powers only as are expressly granted, *or as are*

exceptional situations, to describe the assembly as 'sovereign' as the sovereign people itself, and therefore as not subject to the separation of powers would be inaccurate.

Constituent power, from this perspective, is best understood as a special jurisdiction to issue constitutional norms; it is not the sovereign origin of the separation of powers but its creature. It can separate powers in novel ways but cannot engage in the exercise of constituted authority nor of the very powers it creates. It exists because these powers have already been divided and one can therefore speak about a special constitution-making jurisdiction different from the legislative power. If the exercise of constituent power violates the already established separation (by acting in an executive, ordinary legislative, or judicial capacity), it would be acting *ultra vires* the real sovereign; that is, *ultra vires* the commission that authorized its exercise in the first place.[110] In this sense, to identify a constituent assembly as authorized to exercise the original constituent power means that it is not bound by the material constitution, not that it is authorized to exercise the plenitude of political power. Of course, when power is concentrated in a single person or entity, that person is a sovereign, and the very distinction between constituted and constituent powers becomes inapplicable.[111]

necessary and proper for the execution of powers expressly granted' (emphasis added). John Alexander Jameson, *Constitutional Conventions* (Chicago: Callaghan and Co., 1887) 302.

[110] Moreover, since a supreme constitution presupposes a separation between the constituent and the constituted powers, the newly adopted constitution should arguably implement that separation This is one of the main meanings of the French Declaration of the Rights of Man of 1789, Article 16: 'A society . . . [were] the separation of powers [is not] defined, has no constitution at all'. For this argument, see Carlos Bernal Pulido, 'Prescindamos del Poder Constituyente en la Creación Constitucional: Los Límites Conceptuales del Poder para Reemplazar o Reformar una Constitución', 22 *Anuario Iberoamericano de Justicia Constitucional* 59 (2018).

[111] cf. Alessandro Pace, 'La Instauración de una Nueva Constitución: Perfiles de Teoría Constitucional', 97 *Revista de Estudios Políticos* 9 (1997) 18–20. Pace distinguishes sovereignty and constituent power but associates the idea of juridical limits with the former and not with the later. When Pace speaks about 'sovereignty', however, he is usually referring to sovereignty 'in the juridical sense', that is, what Dicey called 'legal sovereignty'. ibid. 18, fn 34, 40. Antonio Negri also distinguishes between sovereignty and constituent power, but the basis of the distinction is the radical potentiality of the latter. Sovereignty, he writes, 'is an accomplished finality, whereas constituent power is unfinalized; it implies a limited time and space, whereas constituent power implies a multidirectional plurality of times and spaces; it is a rigidified formal constitution, whereas constituent power is absolute process. Everything, in sum, sets constituent power and sovereignty in opposition, even the absolute character that both categories lay claim to: the absoluteness of sovereignty is a totalitarian concept, whereas that of constituent power is the absoluteness of democratic government.' Antonio Negri, *Insurgencies: Constituent Power and the Modern State* (Minneapolis: University of Minnesota Press, 1999) 13. See also Kriele (n. 34), who to a certain extent shares the conception advanced here, distinguishing between sovereignty and constituent power and arguing that the latter only holds an unlimited power 'in the sole act of *creating a constitution*'. Kriele (n. 34) 152 (emphasis in the original).

a. The Sovereign and the Exception

In *Dictatorship*, as in *Constitutional Theory*, Schmitt presented a straightforward account of dictatorship: while commissarial dictatorship is exercised according to whatever constitutional provisions apply in emergencies with the sole purpose of protecting the established constitution,[112] sovereign dictatorship amounts to the exercise of constituent power in virtue of a mandate from the true sovereign. Or, in Schmitt's words: 'The commissary dictator is the unconditional commissar of action of a *pouvoir constitué*, and sovereign dictatorship is the unconditional commission of action of a *pouvoir constituant*.'[113] In *Political Theology*, a famous collection of essays originally published in 1922 (i.e. after *Dictatorship* but before *Constitutional Theory*), Schmitt complicated things considerably. In the first of those essays, titled 'Definition of Sovereignty', he stated that 'Sovereign is he who decides on the exception', as well as on 'whether there is an emergency [and] what must be done to eliminate it'.[114] Given that Schmitt refers approvingly to *Dictatorship* in his 1922 collection, and to *Political Theology* in *Constitutional Theory*, it is worthwhile, even if briefly, to consider whether it is possible to reconcile these works. That reconciliation will serve to fully bring to the surface the distinction between sovereignty and constituent authority, and the idea that the latter, even if exercised outside the established amendment rule, can still be subject to the separation of powers.

The first point that needs to be stressed is that in *Political Theology* Schmitt does not mention the distinction between commissarial and sovereign dictatorship. He does talk about 'sovereignty', which in *Dictatorship* was understood as involving constituent faculties. At the same time, he said that the 'sovereign' 'must decide whether the constitution needs *to be suspended* in its entirety'.[115] There is also no explicit indication that the 'sovereign' who decides whether an emergency exists and suspends the constitutional order (to protect it from its enemies) has the power to create a new constitution. Schmitt also wrote that 'a self-governing body' can be the sovereign.[116] Some authors

[112] Since, according to Schmitt, any material limits to constitutional reform should not be judicially enforceable, commissarial dictatorship becomes the last means of protecting the material constitution. For a brief discussion of this point, see Chapter 8 of this book.

[113] Schmitt, *Dictatorship* (n. 79) 127.

[114] Carl Schmitt, *Political Theology: Four Chapters on the Concept of Sovereignty* (MIT Press, 1985) 5, 7.

[115] ibid. 7, 12 (emphasis added).

[116] ibid. 9–10. Interestingly, Hermann Heller maintained that to the extent that the German people could decide, through a popular petition, if a state of emergency should continue, it should be seen as 'the sovereign' of Schmitt's famous line: 'Sovereign is who decides on the state of exception.' Hermann

(including Hermann Heller) have taken these apparent contradictions to mean that in *Political Theology*, Schmitt moved beyond the commissarial/sovereign typology and embraced a decidedly anti-constitutionalist approach.[117] I nevertheless think that these three works present a coherent (even if objectionable) approach to the nature of dictatorship based on a particular understanding of the concept of constituent power.

What Schmitt is describing in the first chapter of *Political Theology* is a situation in which someone *becomes* sovereign during an emergency by protecting the established constitutional order. A sovereign, in that context, is an entity or individual who seeks to exercise the powers that in *Dictatorship* Schmitt associated with commissarial and sovereign dictators *by itself*, that is, in the absence (or in violation) of a commission. The French National Convention, for example, was a sovereign dictator that became a sovereign (or simply, a dictator) when it went beyond its commission and decided that the threat of counter-revolution required it to assume all powers of government (i.e. to abolish the separation of powers).[118] This is why, in *Dictatorship*, Schmitt wrote that the sovereign dictator 'is sovereign in a completely different sense from that in which the absolute monarch or a sovereign aristocracy can be said to be "sovereign"'.[119]

This is in fact consistent with Juan Donoso Cortés' conception of dictatorship, to which Schmitt frequently referred.[120] Donoso and other doctrinaires, it will be recalled from Chapter 7, maintained that—even though there is no such thing as de jure sovereignty—anyone able to save society from shipwreck could legitimately exercise sovereign authority. That type of situation did not involve a mere crisis, but referred to 'a case of extreme peril, a danger to the existence of the state, or the like'.[121] This approach was defended by Donoso in his 'Discourse on Dictatorship', given in Parliament in 1849, and which Schmitt once described as 'the grandest speech of world literature'.[122] There, Donoso

Heller, *La Soberanía: Contribución a la Teoría del Derecho Estatal y del Derecho* Internacional (Mario de la Cueva trans.) (Universidad Autónoma de México, 1965) 207.

[117] ibid. 155–156. See also John P. McComick, 'Dilemmas of Dictatorship: Carl Schmitt and Constitutional Emergency Powers' in *Law as Politics: Carl Schmitt's Critique of Liberalism* (David Dyzenhaus ed.) (Durham: Duke University Press, 1998); Schwab, *Challenge of the Exception*; David Dyzenhaus, *Legality and Legitimacy*.

[118] Schmitt, *Dictatorship* (n. 79) 128.

[119] ibid. 127.

[120] Schmitt, *Political Theology* (n. 115), Chapters 3 and 4; Schmitt, *Dictatorship* (n. 79) 276 n. 11, 297 n. 22. For a different approach, see Brian Fox, 'Schmitt's Use and Abuse of Donoso Cortés on Dictatorship', 23(2) *Intellectual History Review* 159 (2013).

[121] Schmitt, *Political Theology* (n. 115) 6.

[122] Letter to Ernst Jünger (13 November 1947) cited in Fox (n. 120) 170–171, n. 46.

argued that when legality was not enough to save society, dictatorship became necessary. Dictatorship, he maintained, was a strong word ('*una palabra tremenda*'), but not as strong as that of 'revolution'.[123] To live under a regime of freedom, he argued, was better than to live under a dictatorship, but given the choice between 'the dictatorship of insurrection and the dictatorship of government', he would always choose the latter.[124]

The purpose of Donoso's dictator was not to create new constitutional orders, but to protect the existing one from the revolutions that were sweeping Europe at the time of his speech. However, it was a dictator that would have all powers, even the constituent one: if the saving of society required the creation of a new constitution, then the sovereign has the power—and the duty—to create it.[125] This is perhaps why Donoso and other doctrinaires referred to the kind of power exercised during these periods as 'constituent', even though it was not specifically tasked to create new constitutions. Whoever exercised that power was a true sovereign entity acting free from any commission, an entity that *could* do anything. Schmitt, in *Political Theology*, simply called this power sovereignty; his sovereign dictator, in contrast, was all about the creation of new constitutional orders.

Schmitt's distinction between sovereignty and constituent power is thus best understood as leading to the conclusion that a constituent assembly authorized to adopt a new constitution is not *the sovereign*, but a sovereign dictator commissioned to exercise constituent power on behalf of the true sovereign. Sovereignty can in this sense be a de facto power; constituent authority is a de jure one to the extent that it rests on some form of mandate. If one takes this view one step further, it follows that such an entity would normally lack the competence to exercise ordinary or constituted authority (e.g. it is not allowed to carry out administrative or judicial acts unless it is explicitly mandated to do so). It must adopt a constitution and then disassemble. Schmitt nevertheless did not reach that conclusion and, as noted earlier, claimed that during the time the assembly has not adopted a constitution, it could exercise any 'imaginable authority'.[126] However, in distinguishing a 'sovereign' from a 'sovereign dictator', he implicitly separated sovereignty from constituent power.[127]

[123] Juan Donoso Cortés, 'Discurso sobre la Dictadura' (4 de enero de 1849) 34.

[124] ibid. 55.

[125] In fact, Donoso used the Westminster Parliament as an example of a dictatorship that existed not during an emergency, but in normal times: that 'Parliament has at all times, at all epochs, if it desires so, a dictatorial power', it can even 'replace the Constitution'. ibid. 37.

[126] Schmitt, *Dictatorship* (n. 79) 204.

[127] Note, for example, that Schmitt says that in a direct democracy the people are 'sovereign' and, as a result: '[T]hey can violate the entire system of constitutional norms and settle litigation like a prince in an absolute monarchy, who could resolve legal disputes before courts. The people are the highest judge, just as they are the highest legislator.' Schmitt, *Constitutional Theory* (n. 93) 300. In the context of

And this separation is of the outmost importance for understanding the nature and limits of constituent authority.[128]

IV. Of Omnipotent Things

The advantage of the distinction advanced in the previous sections is that the concept of constituent power can be reserved to describe instances of constitution-making by an entity (e.g. a constituent assembly) which is unable to engage in ordinary governmental acts. This is not a trivial advantage or one only relevant from the perspective of constitutional theory. Indeed, as we will see below, even in democratic contexts, constituent assemblies are frequently understood by courts and political actors as possessing, by virtue of an authorization to engage in constituent activity, an unlimited power. That is to say, a power similar to the one attributable to several military dictatorships during the 20th century. Consider, for example, the cases of Spain and Chile.[129]

In Spain, the formal authority of Francisco Franco rested in a decree issued in 1936 by the military junta. The decree stated that Franco would 'assume all the powers of the new State'.[130] Some year later, a 1939 law established that he had 'a supreme power to dictate juridical norms of a general character'.[131] For Luis Sánchez Agesta, these rules gave Franco the 'constituent power (*potestad constituyente*) for the establishment of a new juridical order'.[132] In describing Franco as able to exercise constituent authority, Sánchez Agesta attributed to him the qualities of a true sovereign: not only was he authorized to adopt a

a contemporary democracy, the people can only exercise one aspect of its sovereignty, the constituent power. As can be seen in Chapters 2, this idea was already expressed by Rousseau.

128 Maurice Hauriou, we saw in the previous chapter, advanced a distinction similar to the one presented here by conceiving constituent power as a kind of legislative power. Maurice Hauriou, *Principios de Derecho Público y Constitucional* (Carlos Ruiz del Castillo trans.) (Granada: Editorial Comares, 2003) 348–349, fn 13. Accordingly, he maintained, constituent power 'remains subordinated to the principle of the separation of powers', and the constituent, legislative, and executive powers cannot be accumulated. When such an accumulation takes place, he added, one could with the 'horrible experience of the constituent dictatorship of the National Convention'. ibid. 350, fn 13.

129 These cases have been widely discussed in the literature. See, for example, Renato Cristi, 'The Metaphysics of Constituent Power: Carl Schmitt and the Genesis of Chile's 1980 Constitution', 21 *Cardozo Law Review* 1749 (2000).

130 Decree Law No. 138 (29 September 1936), Article 1.

131 Law of 8 August 1939, Article 7.

132 Luis Sánchez Agesta, *Curso de Derecho Constitucional Comparado* (Madrid: Universidad de Madrid, 1963) 485. Franco, it was claimed, could legitimately exercise constituent power because he was leading an exercise of the right to rebel. A similar idea, we saw in Chapter 7, was put forward by Jovellanos and his followers in the 19th century. See also Manuel Durán y Bas, *Estudios Políticos y Económicos* (Barcelona: Imprenta de Antonio Brusi, 1856) 20, 23, 63.

constitution but also to create any norms he considered appropriate, and for the time he considered appropriate.[133] That type of power, as noted above, is more accurately described as 'sovereign' to the extent that it is free from any commission. And, as any sovereign power, it involves the discretion of determining its own competences.[134]

A similar type of power was assumed by a military junta in Chile. This was explicitly indicated in a decree issued on 12 November 1973: 'The Governing Junta has assumed, from 11 September 1973, the exercise of the Constituent, Legislative, and Executive Powers.'[135] Although there is evidence in the debates at the Constituent Commission that some understood that decree to refer to the 'constituent power' previously held by the then dissolved legislature (i.e. the ordinary amendment power),[136] in the end it was clear that the junta indeed claimed to hold an omnipotent law-making authority. This was best expressed by Jaime Guzmán in one of the Constituent Commission's sessions.[137]

[133] Sánchez Agesta, *Curso* (n. 132) 485.

[134] Sánchez Agesta operated under a conception of the material constitution that appealed to a historical conscience that could be in tension with the actual constitutional order (in this case, the republican constitution of 1931). In that sense his 'sovereign' did not necessarily have the task of protecting the material constitution of the day but, sometimes, that of bringing back the 'true' historical constitution. This is probably why Francisco Conde García (who had been Schmitt's distinguished disciple in Berlin a few years earlier), thought that in the exercise of his constituent power, Franco was called to create constitutional norms consistent with the historical, cultural, and social conditions reflected in the country's internal constitution. Francisco Javier Conde García, *Contribución a la Doctrina del Caudillaje* (Madrid: Ediciones de la Vicesecretaría de Educación Popular, 1952) 41. But Conde García was not simply attributing a fascist leader with the task of bringing back Spain's historical constitution (the same constitution that, as we saw in Chapter 7, Jovellanos wanted to restore). The *caudillo* was not to simply bring back an older constitution, but to 'realise the historical destiny' of the Spanish nation. Francisco Javier Conde, *Escritos y Fragmentos Políticos* (Madrid: Colección Ciencia Política, 1974) 357. In that respect, Conde García maintained, Franco was not a dictator in the traditional sense (someone called to defend the existing constitution), but a *caudillo* with full constitution-making powers: '[O]ne must not understand the concept of *caudillaje* as a commissarial dictatorship but interpret it as sovereign dictatorship, not subject to a time limit, or to the correction of an exceptional situation, or to the realisation of concrete objectives.' ibid. According to my interpretation of Schmitt, a *caudillo* of this type would be best described as a 'sovereign' plain and simple.

[135] Decree Law No. 128 (12 November 1973).

[136] For example, Enrique Evans de la Cuadra, the junta had assumed the Supreme Command (*Mando Supremo*) of the country and thus had all powers, including the constituent one (a view that was later expressed in Decree Law 128, ibid.). Eventually, Evans added, the 'original Constituent Power, that is to say the people, will sanction the new constitutional precepts'. Acta de Sesión No 13 (7 November 1973). Nonetheless, Evans considered it was important to make clear that the junta had no intention of 'replacing the people of Chile' as the constituent subject. Rather, what had happened was that, in the same way that the ordinary institutions of government could amend the constitutional text in the past (through the established amendment rule), the junta could do the same thing as it now enjoyed all the powers of government. Jaime Guzmán disagreed with his former constitutional law professor at the *Pontificia Universidad Católica de Chile*. For Guzmán, 'the first [power] that the Armed Forces gained when entering into power was the Constituent Power, and not by a consequence of holding the Executive and Legislative Powers'. Acta de Sesión no 13, ibid.

[137] Guzmán was a key figure in the drafting of the Constitution of 1980 and in the development of the official understanding of the junta's power. For Guzmán's role in this process, see Renato Cristi, *El Pensamiento Político de Jaime Guzmán: Autoridad y Libertad* (LOM Ediciones, 2000).

In response to a concern that a decision of the junta could be held unconstitutional, Guzmán maintained that that entity had 'assumed total power, so that it is responsible for its acts only before God and history'.[138]

The military junta, in short, was not acting under a commission, it was exercising political power as a sovereign. At one point, the junta even declared that any of its acts that contradicted the Constitution of 1925 should be understood as an exercise of constituent power that implicitly amended it.[139] Importantly, the assumption of sovereign powers is not exclusive to entities operating in authoritarian contexts. There are cases of constituent assemblies convened in formally democratic countries that, even though specifically authorized to enact (and in some cases only to draft) a constitution, have declared themselves sovereign. Accordingly, they have gone beyond the separation of powers and exercised—or interfered with the exercise of—the ordinary powers of government. The Colombian Constituent Assembly of 1991 provides a good example and will be considered below.[140] In addition to adopting a new constitution, this assembly dissolved the ordinary legislature and replaced it with a temporary legislative body and also interferred with the power of the ordinary courts.[141] The justification for the exercise of that seemingly unlimited jurisdiction was the notion that the assembly possessed constituent authority.

[138] Comisión Constituyente, Sesión 68 (5 September 1974).

[139] Decreto Ley No. 788, 2 December 1974, Article (c). The view expressed by some that a formal constitution can only be modified expressly, it was noted, simply had 'no validity during emergencies and much less in cases where, by the force of history [*por la fuerza de hechos históricos*] the exercise of the constituent and the legislative power are united in the same entity, without any formalities or requirements to distinguish them'. ibid., Article (h). Nonetheless, for the avoidance of doubt as to in which cases the junta intended to exercise its constituent jurisdiction, the decree stated in Article 3 that from then on, those Decree Laws inconsistent with the Constitution of 1925 would have the effect of modifying it only if they 'explicitly state that the Governing Junta is acting in the exercise of its constituent power [*Potestad Constituyente*]'. ibid. Article 3.

[140] For other discussions of this process, see, for example Andrew Arato, *The Adventure of the Constituent Power: Beyond Revolutions* (Cambridge University Press, 2017) 310–327 and the sources cited thereon. I have also examined it in Joel Colón-Ríos, *Weak Constitutionalism: Constituent Power and the Question of Democratic Legitimacy* (Routledge, 2012).

[141] For an in-depth discussion, see Nicolás Figueroa, *A Critique of Populist Jurisprudence: Courts, Democracy, and Constitutional Change in Colombia and Venezuela* (New School Doctoral Dissertation, 2006). For a discussion of the Venezuelan Constituent Assembly of 1999, where the intervention with the judiciary was significantly more intrusive than in Colombia, see Ricardo Combellas, 'El Proceso Constituyente y la Constitución de 1999', 30 *Politeia* 30 (2003). See also Laura Lousa, 'La Independencia del Poder Judicial a Partir de la Constitución de 1999', 38 *Politeia* 30 (2007). See also the cases contained in *Bases Jurisprudenciales de la Supraconstitucionalidad* (Caracas: Supreme Court of Justice, 2002), where the Venezuelan Supreme Tribunal of Justice attempted to provide a justification for the Constituent Assembly's interference with the constituted powers. This jurisprudence is briefly examined in Chapter 10.

a. Colombia, 1991

The Constituent Assembly of 1991 was convened under a state of emergency declared in 1984,[142] in light of the armed conflict prevalent in the country. The calling of such an entity was seen by key political actors as necessary to bring society to order. A key moment in the formal convocation of the assembly was a decree issued under special emergency powers by President Virgilio Barco on 3 May 1990.[143] The decree in question ordered that in the presidential elections of 27 May 1990, electors were asked the following question: 'In order to strengthen participatory democracy, do you vote in favour of the convocation of a Constitutional Assembly, with representation of the social, political, and regional forces of the Nation, democratically and popularly constituted, for the reform of the Political Constitution of Colombia?'. The constitutionality of that decree was challenged. It was argued that the decree had been adopted in violation of the amendment rule of the Constitution of 1886 and that the provisions regulating states of emergency had the purpose of protecting the constitutional regime, not of altering it.

The Supreme Court of Justice dismissed those arguments.The court expressed that the emergency provisions in the constitution did not attribute to the President absolute powers (these provisions, according to the court 'reject Carl Schmitt's affirmation according to which "the sovereign is that who decides on the State of Exception"').[144] However, those provisions did authorize the executive to take not merely repressive measures (e.g. the suspension of certain rights), but to adopt—or promote the adoption of—positive norms directed at overcoming a crisis. Asking the electorate about the convocation of a 'Constitutional Assembly' and counting the votes thereof constituted, for the court, a political act directed at the re-establishment of public order and did not involve a violation of any constitutional norm. After a positive vote in favour of the assembly's convocation, the newly elected President, Cesar Gaviria, issued another emergency decree where it was stated that 'the Nation, where sovereignty lies, has manifested, in the exercise of the constitutional function of the suffrage, the will of convening a Constitutional Assembly . . . with the

[142] Decree Law No. 1038 (1 May 1984).
[143] Decree Law No. 927 (3 May 1990).
[144] Judgment No. 59, Supreme Court of Jutice of Colombia (24 May 1990). The Colombian judgments cited in this section are contained in 'La Reforma Constitucional de 1991', *Gaceta Especial Sala Constitucional, Corte Suprema de Justicia, República de Colombia* (Santafé de Bogotá, D.C., 1993) vol. 1. The pagination of that collection will be used in any direct quotes.

purpose of strengthening participatory democracy'.[145] A new vote, where the assembly would be formally convened and its members elected, was called.

The premise of Gaviria's decree was the existence of a 'popular mandate' in favour of constitutional reform, which was said to be expressed through the informal ballot deposited by millions of citizens in the parliamentary elections of 11 March 1990.[146] In addition to referring to the strengthening of participatory democracy (a potential substantive limit on the assembly's constitution-making power), the decree included a long list of themes agreed to by different political and social groups.[147] It was also stated that the 'Assembly shall not consider issues different from the ones mentioned in the list ratified by the people, and shall not modify, in particular, the terms of officials elected this year, the commitments entered by the Colombian state through international treaties, and the republican form of government'.[148] The assembly was authorized to issue 'transitional provisions when it considers it necessary to guarantee the application of the reform'[149] and to adopt its own internal regulations.[150] The decree also stated that 'the Assembly shall adopt a single text of Constitutional Reform'.[151]

In ruling on the legality of the assembly's convocation, the Supreme Court of Justice removed those limits on the assembly's power. The substantive part of the court's decision begins with an analysis of Article 2 of the Constitution of 1886, which states that 'Sovereignty resides essentially and exclusively in the nation, from where public powers emanate . . .'.[152] Quoting approvingly from the work of José María Samper (who the reader will recall from Chapter 5), the court stated that Article 2 conceived sovereignty as 'one and indivisible' and that only its exercise could be divided. Whoever was called to exercise such a divided power, it was argued, was not the sovereign.[153] At the same time, the

[145] Decree Law No. 1926 (24 August 1990).

[146] Decree Law No. 927 (3 May 1990).

[147] The list included, for example, particular changes to the functions of the two houses of Congress, changes related to the democratisation of the public administration, the recognition of new rights, the establishment of the referendum as part of the process of constitutional reform, specific changes to the emergency provision, etc. These were presented in the decree as promoting the general purpose of improving participatory democracy.

[148] Decree No. 1926 (n. 145) Article 4.

[149] ibid. Article 20.

[150] ibid. Article 14.

[151] ibid. Article 15.

[152] Judgment No. 138, Supreme Court of Justice of Colombia (9 October 1990) 64.

[153] The court also attempted to make the principles of popular and national sovereignty consistent with each other—something that was criticized in the dissent. For the court, the nation was 'the people who inhabit our country', not merely the personification of the unitary state that succeeded the federation of 1863. ibid. 65. The dissenting judges maintained that the principle of national sovereignty defended by the court had the historical purpose, during the French Revolution, of excluding the actual people from the exercise of sovereign power. 'National sovereignty', the dissent notes, 'is an epiphenomenon extracted from the minds of politicians to attribute themselves with the power to define when and

court maintained that the 'Colombian nation is the primary constituent power, [and] can at any moment give itself a constitution different to the established one without abiding to its requirements'.[154] That right, the court stated quoting a 1957 judgment,[155] derived from the 'power of revolution, the state of necessity of reforming the constitution in which [a Nation] finds itself, and the exercise of the latent sovereignty of the people as constituent will'.[156] The action of the primary constituent power, the court added (again quoting approvingly from a previous judgment),[157] 'escapes any limits originating in the previous juridical order and, as a result, is free from any form of review that attempts to compare it with the precepts of that order'.[158]

Earlier I suggested that constituent power should be understood as an element of sovereignty, and that when a special assembly is authorized to engage in constituent activity it does not become sovereign. In its judgment, the Supreme Court of Justice did precisely the opposite. It not only treated those concepts as equivalent, but maintained that the 'National Constituent Assembly', *as the* 'Primary Constituent Power (*Constituyente Primario*)' had an unlimited competence.[159] This approach, in a certain way, was already present in an aspect of the process itself. The constitutional assembly was not only authorized to draft a constitution but to enact it: the constitution it created would not have to be popularly ratified in order to become valid law.[160] Put differently,

under what circumstances can sovereignty be exercised'. This conception, the dissenting judges argued, allowed Sieyès to defend a conception of constituent power where only certain types of citizens could directly participate in its exercise. ibid. 88. For a discussion on the distinction between national and popular sovereignty, and its relationship to the theory of constituent power, see Chapter 5 of this book.

[154] ibid.

[155] Judgment of 28 November 1957, Supreme Court of Justice of Colombia.

[156] ibid.

[157] Judgment No. 54, Supreme Court of Justice of Colombia (9 June 1987).

[158] ibid. 65–66.

[159] ibid. 67. It is worth noting that in 1992, after approvingly quoting Schmitt's definition of constituent power, the court referred to 'the National Constituent Assembly that adopted the new Political Constitution of Colombia as a commissary power [*poder comisionado*] of the sovereign people'. C-544/92, Colombian Constitutional Court, para. 10. In the preamble to the Constitution of 1991, it is stated that: 'The People of Colombia, in the exercise of their sovereign power, represented by their delegates to the National Constituent Assemby . . .'.

[160] The absence of a referendum to ratify (or reject) the constitutional text and the further acts of the assembly (particularly the dissolution of the then current parliament, discussed below), was perhaps more strongly criticized by Misael Pastrana Borrero, a conservative deputy who had previously served as Colombian President. For Pastrana, who eventually resigned his seat in the Constituent Assembly, 'simple logic indicates that the most important act that could be carried out by a group of spokesmen for the people in this century, that is, the drafting of a National Constitution, must be—within the spirit of a participatory democracy—the first one to be submitted to popular ratification'. This problem was accentuated by the low participation in the referendum where the assembly was convened. The need for a referendum was also defended by those who maintained that the assembly should be 'autonomous', but not 'sovereign'. Cited in Ricardo Zuluaga Gil, *De la Expectativa al Desconcierto: El Proceso Constituyente de 1991 Visto por sus Protagonistas* (Cali: Pontificia Universidad Javeriana, 2008). In the end, the view that the assembly had been authorized to adopt a new constitution without any mention of a further

once convened, the assembly (perhaps with one exception, noted below), would be able to act as if it was the sovereign, independently of the people who commissioned it. The consequences of this approach were clear. The limits contained in the previously mentioned decree (i.e. the clauses of the decree that limited the assembly to only consider certain topics and prevented it from engaging in particular constitutional changes, as well as the court's jurisdiction to review the consistency between the assembly's decisions and those limits) were declared invalid as they 'restricted the full exercise of the [assembly's] sovereignty'.[161] The court, however, determined that the more general limit applicable to the assembly, that is, the strengthening of participatory democracy, was valid. According to the court, that limit was part of the very reason why the constituent subject had convened the assembly, even though, one may add, was probably too general to act as a real constraint.[162]

As noted earlier, once convened, the assembly interfered in important ways with the legislative and judicial powers. In that respect, in describing the assembly as the primary constituent power, the court treated it as an entity which, even if based on a mandate (to improve participatory democracy) was not subject to the separation of powers. It could be argued, however, that such an unlimited jurisdiction was warranted in the context of a national emergency. That is to say, that the assembly assumed the sovereign authority that conservatives like Donoso and Schmitt thought was necessary to bring society to order precisely in this kind of situation. Indeed, although the decree that authorized the convocation of the assembly only referred to the 'reform' of the Constitution of 1886, the assembly not only adopted a new constitution (a course of action that was more than justified by the Supreme Court of Justice's decision describing it as the primary constituent power) but put itself above the separation of powers in an alleged attempt to guarantee a stable transition to the new constitutional regime.

This course of action was in a way suggested in the first resolution of the assembly. In that resolution, the assembly referred to itself as a 'National Constituent Assembly' (as opposed to 'Constitutional Assembly', the term used in the referendum and in the initial presidential decrees)[163] and stated: 'The

referendum (combined with some practical concerns about the holding of a new election) carried the day. ibid. 95.

[161] Judgment No. 54 (n. 157), 67–68.

[162] ibid. 66–67. The Constituent Assembly did consider itself bound by an additional limit: to produce a constitution within five months, the drafting period authorized by the electorate in the referendum. Zuluaga Gil (n. 160) 84.

[163] Early in the process, some groups insisted that the assembly should be named the 'Constituent Assembly'. For a brief discussion, see Zuluaga Gil (n. 160) 123. See also Humberto de la Calle, *Contra*

acts sanctioned and promulgated by the National Constituent Assembly are not subject to any type of jurisdictional control'.[164] These acts (which included the internal regulation of the assembly), it was stated in the preamble of the resolution, were 'not administrative but constituent acts'. In this way, the assembly made clear that it conceived itself as a sovereign entity: those statements were broad enough to cover more than the adoption of a new constitutional text. The National Constituent Assembly also decided to recall the mandate of the current legislators to call for early general elections.[165] The then current Congress objected to that course of action, issuing a resolution that stated that the assembly was subject to certain juridical limits that prevented it from interferring with the normal electoral cycle.[166] Until the new Congress was convened, the assembly determined that the existing one and its commissions would go into recess 'and will not have the authority to exercise any of its attributions neither by their own initiative nor by the decision of the President of the Republic'.[167]

The existing congress was then replaced by a Special Commission (popularly known as the *Congresito*) comprised of thirty-six members elected by the assembly itself. Half of these members could also be deputies to the Constituent Assembly, and many of them were. The President was also attributed with extraordinary powers to adopt certain laws by decree; one of the functions of the Congresito was to exercise a veto power over those norms. In this respect, during the transitional period, the National Constituent Assembly (acting through the

todas las Apuestas: Historia Íntima de la Constituyente de 1991 (Bogotá: Editorial Planeta, 2004) 88. During the first session of the assembly, some delegates referred to it as a 'Constitutional Assembly'. Nonetheless, the regulations of the assembly were discussed and approved, and the name given to the entity was 'National Constituent Assembly'. See 'Informe de Sesión Plenaria del Día 5 de febrero de 1999'. In the second session of the assembly, however, Delegate Zalamea stated that he was 'elected to a Constitutional Assembly' but that that entity had now become a Constituent Assembly. Delegate Nieto stated that it was true that in the past the terms 'constitutional' and 'constituent' had been used interchangeably, but that the name included in the assembly's internal regulations was 'National Constituent Assembly', and what mattered now was to continue using the term 'constituent'. 'Informe de Sesión Plenaria del Día 6 de febrero de 1999', 16. These interventions, however, seemed to be more concerned with matters of style and consistency. The Supreme Court of Justice, in its decision of the constitutionality of Decree no 1926 (n. 145), seemed to have attributed more importance to that terminological issue: 'There are some who present themselves as supporters of the convocation of a National Assembly that has a "constituent" character, and not merely the pretended "constitutional" one'. Judgment No. 138 (n. 153) 58. In the constituton-making process underway in Chile (which had just begun at the time of writing these lines), it was agreed to describe any modality of the assembly that would draft the constitution as 'constitutional' and not as 'constituent'. 'Acuerdo por la Paz Social y la Nueva Constitución' (15 November 2019). That decision provides an indication of the dangerous implications that describing an entity as 'constituent' has in the minds of some political actors.

164 Acto Constituyente No. 1 (9 May 1991), Article 2.
165 See 'Congreso: La Nuez del Revolcón', *El Tiempo*, 9 June 1991.
166 ibid. For a discussion, see Zuluaga Gil (n. 160) 100–112.
167 See transitional Articles 1 to 7 of the Colombian Constitution of 1991.

Congresito) and the Executive became ordinary law-makers not subject to any form of review. The assembly's self-attribution of unlimited jurisdiction (which was restated in transitional Article 59 of the Constitution of 1991) was challenged in the newly created Constitutional Court.[168] It was argued, for example, that what had been convened in 1990 was 'a constitutional assembly to reform the constitution, not a constituent assembly to abolish it'.[169] It was also maintained that by placing itself outside of the reach of a constitutional challenge through the transitional Article 59, the assembly was acting contrary to the ideal of participatory democracy, which it was required to respect.[170]

In its judgment, the court directly quoted Schmitt's definition of constituent power (i.e. constituent power as 'the political will, whose power or authority is capable of making the concrete, comprehensive decision of the type and form of its own political existence') and referred to the National Constituent Assembly as 'a commissioning power of the sovereign people'.[171] Nonetheless, instead of deriving from that conception a separation between the assembly and the sovereign that could be understood as posing limits on the former, the court determined that: 'The primary constituent power can be expressed directly through a referendum [*plebiscito*] or through a democratic National Constituent Assembly.'[172] In light of this conclusion, the claimants had no chance of prevailing. Though noting that the assembly was commissioned to adopt a new constitution that strengthened participatory democracy,[173] the court did not see that commission as constraining its power to engage in different kind of political acts and of producing legal norms of a varied nature. The assembly was, for all practical purposes, outside of the law and the separation of powers.

b. Venezuela, 2017

The idea that a constituent assembly, for the very reason of being 'constituent', can exercise sovereign power has also been exemplified in other jurisdictions.

[168] Judgment C-544/92, Colombian Constitutional Court.

[169] ibid. para. 3.1.

[170] ibid. para. 4.3.

[171] ibid. para. 10. For a discussion, see Chapter 8 of this book. See also Joel Colón-Ríos, 'Carl Schmitt and Constituent Power in Latin American Courts: The Cases of Venezuela and Colombia', 18(3) *Constellations* 365 (2011). The court also referred to Hermann Heller in support of the view that a constitution was more than a factual relation of domination and that its justification was to be found in the 'ethical principles of the law'. Judgment C-544/92 (n. 168) para. 8. For a discussion a brief discussion of this aspect of Heller's thought, see Chapter 8 of this book.

[172] ibid. para. 10.

[173] The court also referred to the temporal limit (150 days) contained in Decree No. 1926 (n. 145), which was complied with.

In addition to the Colombian example, we previously referred to that of the French National Convention of 1793. An extreme manifestation of this phenomenon, which clearly reflects the conflation between sovereignty and constituent power, is exemplified in the Venezuelan Constituent Assembly of 2017. This entity was controversially convened by the President of the Republic (i.e. with no authorizing referendum)[174] in a context of political violence and during a declared state of emergency.[175] In the very speech where the convocation of the assembly was announced, President Nicolás Maduro made clear that by calling a constituent assembly, he was convening a sovereign entity. 'In the use of my presidential attributions', he said in a speech on 1 May 2017, 'I convene the original constituent power . . . to achieve the peace that the Republic needs, to defeat the fascist attempts at a coup, and so that the people with its sovereignty imposes peace, harmony, and true national dialogue'. 'I am convening', he added, 'the totality of the motherland's power, above the Constituent Assembly there is no possible power!'

During Maduro's speech, there were mentions of the need for strengthening the Constitution of 1999, of transforming the state and particularly the National Assembly, and of constitutionalizing several social policies. The emphasis, however, was on the sovereign character of a constituent assembly and on its independence from the established institutions of government. In particular, he referred to Article 349 of the constitution, which maintains that '[t]he existing constituted powers shall not be permitted to obstruct the

[174] This mode of convocation was highly controversial and was eventually challenged in the Supreme Tribunal of Justice, where it was sanctioned. Judgment 2017-0519, Supreme Tribunal of Justice of Venezuela. It nonetheless seems directly inconsistent at least with the spirit, if not also with the letter, of the Venezuelan Constitution of 1999. The relevant provisions are the following. Article 347: 'The original constituent power rests with the people of Venezuela. This power may be exercised by calling a National Constituent Assembly for the purpose of transforming the State, creating a new juridical order and drawing up a new Constitution.' Article 348: 'The initiative for calling a National Constituent Assembly may emanate from the President of the Republic sitting with the Cabinet of Ministers; from the National Assembly, by a two-thirds vote of its members; from the Municipal Councils in open session [*cabildos*], by a two-thirds vote of their members; and from 15% of the voters registered with the Civil and Electoral Registry.' These provisions do not explicitly require a referendum for the convocation of a Constituent Assembly, as the Supreme Tribunal of Justice concluded. However, given the role that the referendum plays through the constitution as a whole (and in different aspects of the process of constitutional reform), the idea that a referendum requirement is implicit in those provisions seems particularly strong. It would also be strange that, in the same way that the President can unilaterally convene a constituent assembly, only 15 per cent of the registered voters can do so, without the need of a referendum. There was an interesting discussion about the role of the referendum in the convocation (and the approval of the work) of a future constituent assembly in one of the sessions of the entity that drafted the Constitution of 1999. See *Asamblea Nacional Constituyente*, Gaceta Constituyente: Agosto-Septiembre, Sesión Número 41 (Caracas: Imprenta del Congreso de la República, 1999) vol. 3.

[175] For a discussion of the process that led to the convocation of the assembly, see Ana Graciela Barrios Benatuil, Antonio González Plessmann, and Martha Lía Grajales Pineda, 'Constituyentes Venezolanas de 1999 y 2017: Contextos y Participación', 8(4) *Revista Direito e Práxis* 3144 (2017).

Constituent Assembly in any way'.[176] That same day, a presidential decree was issued, which referred to the 'severe internal and external threats' to which the country was subject and to the 'inescapable historical duty' to convene a National Constituent Assembly whose members (over 500) were eventually elected by popular vote in a process boycotted by the main opposition parties.[177] The decree also contained a number of 'proposals' that the assembly should adopt as objectives, including the constitutionalization of new forms of 'participatory and protagonic (*protagónica*) democracy' and the establishment of a new economic model. It also referred to the assembly's duty of respecting the Social State of Law and Justice (*Estado Social de Derecho y de Justicia*) and of 'channelling the popular clamour of those who insist that their rights, achievements, and conquests, are given constitutional status'.

In this sense, and unlike in Venezuela in 1999[178] (and Colombia in 1991), the constituent assembly's commission came from the President alone, that is, it did not arise from what can be identified as a constituent mandate.[179] Once convened, Maduro was invited to speak in the assembly's initial meeting. He stated that he was there 'to recognise [the assembly's] plenipotentiary, sovereign, original, and great powers, to determine the destiny of the Republic . . . As Head of State, I submit myself [*me subordino*] to the constituent powers of this National Constituent Assembly.'[180] In a set of rules adopted by the assembly which seek to regulate its relationship with the constituted powers,[181] the assembly also described itself as a 'sovereign power' (*postestad soberana*) that could 'issue decrees determining the competences, functioning, and organization of the organs of Public Power'. That jurisdiction, the document explained, came from the 'mandate of the sovereign people'. This mandate, it was claimed, was expressed through the elections of the assembly's members. The document also maintains that the 'Constitution of 1999 and the rest of the established

[176] 'Presidente Maduro Convoca al Poder Constituyente Originario del Pueblo' (https://www.youtube.com/watch?v=Q9lA0oeUAuI).
[177] Extraordinary Decree No. 6295 (1 May 2017). See also Barrios Benatuil et al. (n. 175) 3162.
[178] The relevant aspects of the 1999 process will be examined in the next chapter.
[179] For the notion of the constituent mandate, see Chapter 10 of this book.
[180] 'Maduro Reconoce Poder Plenipotenciario de la Asamblea Constituyente' (https://www.youtube.com/watch?v=lZq23Zq9v4U). There is a long tradition in Venezuela of the Executive Authority submitting itself to the decisions of a Constituent Assembly. See, for example, the message of José A. Páez (*Jefe Civil y Militar*) to the Venezuelan Constituent Congress of 1830 (30 April 1830), *Acta de Instalación del Congreso Constituyente de Venezuela* (6 May 1830). Much more recently, Hugo Chavez put his Presidency in the hands of the Constituent Assembly of 1999, which promptly ratified him as President of the Republic. Constituent Assembly of 1999 (Session of 8 August 1999). On 11 August 2017, the Constituent Assembly of 2017 did the same with Nicolás Maduro.
[181] 'Normas para Garantizar el Pleno Funcionamiento institucional de la Asamblea Nacional Constituyente en Armonía con los Poderes Públicos Constituidos', Gaceta Oficial No. 6323 (8 August 2017).

juridical order would continue to be valid in all of those aspects that are not inconsistent with the normative acts and decisions' of the assembly. However, it also notes that none of the acts of the assembly could contravene 'the progressive character of rights or the achievements of the Venezuelan people in social matters'.

Despite the previously mentioned reference to acting on a mandate of the people, it is undeniable that the National Constituent Assembly was conceived by the President of the Republic, and later by itself, as a sovereign entity. That is to say, as an entity that can determine its own competences and, by implication, the competences of any other public authority. In that respect, it did not act on a commission, at least not for any practical purposes. Indeed, shortly after it came into session, the assembly adopted a series of 'Constituent Acts' where it engaged in actions of a legislative,[182] executive,[183] and quasi-judicial[184] nature. At the time of writing, there are no clear indications of when the assembly will produce a draft constitution, if indeed a constitution is to be produced. From a theoretical point of view, there cannot be an objection to the powers claimed and exercised by this entity unless constituent power and sovereignty are properly distinguished. In fact, the conflation of these two concepts is what allowed President Maduro to convene an entity attributed with sovereign and plenipotentiary powers. The result is an assembly that—perhaps because it operates under a time of crisis—goes beyond the task of adopting a new constitution. In that sense, it should be understood not as a sovereign dictator but as a Schmittian or Donosian sovereign, like the French National Convention after the emergency declared on 10 October 1793.

V. Conclusion

This chapter sought to increase our understanding of the relationship between constituent power and the law by distinguishing the former from sovereignty. That distinction was developed through an examination of the work of Jellinek, Carré de Malberg, and Schmitt. Constituent power is the power to create novel constitutional orders and it is in that respect not bound by positive law. Nonetheless, I argued that the exercise of constituent power will always

[182] Gaceta Oficial No. 41274 (8 November 2017), enacting the Constitutional Law against Hate and for the Peaceful Coexistence and Tolerance.
[183] Gaceta Oficial No. 41265 (26 October 2017), convening early municipal elections.
[184] Gaceta Oficial, No 41272 (6 November 2017), removing parliamentary immunity and authorizing a judicial process against the Vice President of the National Assembly.

be based on, and limited by, a commission. Unlike a true sovereign, an entity authorized to exercise constituent power cannot transform any will into law, but only produce constitutional law. This is another way of saying that a constituent assembly authorized to draft (or even to enact) a new constitution will still be normally subject to the separation of powers and cannot exercise the ordinary powers of government. As I will argue further in the next chapter, this limit will usually be based on a constituent mandate contained in a referendum question, which would express the nature of the task given by the true sovereign (the people) to its commissioner (the constituent assembly). Nonetheless, this does not mean that a constituent assembly exercises only a derived constituent power. Such an entity should instead be understood as a *mechanism* for the exercise of the originary constituent power of the people. When only authorized to draft a constitution subject to popular ratification, it would be more like Rousseau's Legislator than like Schmitt's sovereign dictator.

I also considered examples of different individuals or entities that, at different moments during the 20th and 21st century, claimed to be sovereign *because* they were engaged in the exercise of constituent power.[185] All these individuals or entities operated under an emergency situation, in some cases an emergency created, or partly created, by themselves. It is precisely that type of context which provides a fertile ground for the confusion between sovereignty and constituent power. Even though the notion that in a profound political crisis a departure from the separation of powers may be politically justified (or presented as a justification), this notion can also serve to justify different

[185] The previous analysis should not be taken as an indication that in places where the theory of constituent power has not been as influential as it has in Latin America, similar phenomena have not taken place. Indeed, during the 19th century, the Constitutional Conventions in several US states were understood by different courts and political actors as sovereign, and frequently went beyond their mandate and engaged in the exercise of ordinary governmental powers (e.g. dismissing public servants, adopting particular ordinances, etc.). In his famous book on Constitutional Conventions, Roger Sherman Hoar showed that this was not only the case for conventions operating during the Revolutionary War and therefore governed by 'the law of extreme necessity', but also for conventions called according to the provisions of a constitution. Roger Sherman Hoar, *Constitutional Conventions: Their Nature, Power, and Limitations* (Kessinger Publishing, 1917) 153. For example, George M. Dallas—who in 1845 became Vice-President of the United States—maintained that once a Constitutional Convention assembled in Pennsylvania 'it will possess . . . every attribute of absolute sovereignty'. Cited in ibid. 156. Similarly, in the Illinois Convention of 1847, one of the delegates maintained: 'We are . . . the sovereignty of the State. We are what the people of the State would be, if they were congregated here in one mass meeting. We are what Louis XIV said he was, "We are the State".' Cited in ibid. 156–157. For the judicial sanction of that kind of approach, see *Frantz et al. v Autrey*, 18 Okla. 561 (1907). Of course, not everyone agreed with this view. For the view that constitutional conventions were mere committees of the people which only had the powers expressly or implicitly granted to them, see Allen Caperton Braxton, 'Power of Conventions', 7(2) The *Virginia Law Register* 79 (1901); Arthur N. Holcombe, *State government in the United States* (New York: MacMillan Company, 1916) 127; John Alexander Jameson, *Constitutional Conventions* (Chicago: Callaghan and Co., 1887); C. A. D., 'The Jurisdiction of a Court of Equity over Constitutional Conventions', 6(1) *Michigan Law Review* 70 (1906). *Ex parte Birmingham Ry*, 145 Ala. 514, 529 (1905); *State v Hunt*, 2 Hill (S. C.) 1, 270 (1834); *Plowman v Thornton*, 52 Ala. 559, 569 (1875).

forms of authoritarianism, as briefly exemplified through the cases of Chile and Spain. In any case, we should describe an entity operating during that kind of situation as a sovereign and reserve the concept of constituent power to constitution-making bodies who are only performing a specific task: the adoption of a constitution. That kind of entity, that is, a constituent assembly, would not be subject to substantive limits in terms of the constitutional content it can create, with the exceptions of any conditions imposed by the people (e.g. the adoption of a particular type of constitution) through its vote in a referendum. In the next chapter, I will develop this idea further and explore its connections to the institution of the imperative mandate and to what in Chapter 5 I called the 'constituent power of the people' approach.

10
The Juridical People

There are three distinctions that have been present, to different degrees, in the previous chapters of this book. The *first* one is that between constituent power as a necessarily extra-legal force and constituent power as susceptible of being exercised through law. Emmanuel Sieyès, as well as some of the authors discussed in Chapter 6, reflect the former approach. For them, it was not even necessary for a constitution to have an amendment rule. Whenever society needed to change its fundamental laws, something that would normally happen in a period of crisis or emergency, the constituent subject would find the way of manifesting itself. In contrast, Jean Jacques Rousseau and—for very different reasons—authors like Luis Sánchez Agesta and François Guizot, exemplify the latter approach. For them, there is nothing preventing the law from procedurally channelling a legally unlimited constitution-making jurisdiction. They would thus attribute to the ordinary power of constitutional reform the same function as the original constituent power. Under the Rousseauian version, however, any attempt to exercise constituent authority without the direct involvement of the people through a popular assembly or a set of primary assemblies would not only be illegal but illegitimate. Moreover, if resorting to a representative entity becomes necessary, its members must be subject to an imperative mandate.

The *second* distinction is that between the constituent power of the nation and the constituent power of the people. The main theoretical sources of this distinction are, once again, Sieyès and Rousseau. Under the Sieyesian approach, the individual members of a community do not appear as the holders of the constituent power. Rather, an abstract entity with a will of its own, a will that can depart, in any way considered necessary, from the actual preferences of the populace, becomes the constituent authority. This approach made the exercise of constituent power compatible with a limited franchise, with primary assemblies that can exercise no more than the *pouvoir commettant*, and with the absence of legally binding instructions. Under the Rousseauian approach, those forms of citizen involvement are necessary: the formal exclusion of parts of the citizenry from constituent activity would mean that the constituent subject has been illegitimately displaced. The constituent power of the

Constituent Power and the Law. Joel Colón-Ríos, Oxford University Press (2020). © Joel Colón-Ríos.
DOI: 10.1093/oso/9780198785989.001.0001

nation approach, as we saw in Chapter 5, was highly influential during the 19th century. Nowadays the idea of the nation as the constituent subject has been largely abandoned, and it is the people, frequently understood not in an abstract but in a Rousseauian sense, which is generally seen as the holder of constituent authority. Nevertheless, as I will argue later, the institutions associated with the constituent nation have for the most part stayed with us.

The *third* distinction, discussed at length in Chapter 9, is that between sovereignty and constituent power. Sovereignty, I argued, is the unlimited jurisdiction to transform any will into law; the sovereign is the source of, and is not subject to, the separation of powers. It can engage in executive, legislative, judicial, and constitution-making acts. The kind of uncontrolled law-making force attached to sovereign power is usually exercised during periods where a political actor (frequently an authoritarian one) becomes a de facto sovereign, usually under the pretext that society needs to be saved from a perceived emergency. Constituent power is an element of sovereignty. Accordingly, whoever is the source of the sovereign power also enjoys constituent authority. But unlike the exercise of sovereignty, the exercise of constituent power within an established constitutional order will always take place in virtue of a commission. To the extent that that commission only authorizes the relevant entity to engage in the task of drafting (or at most of enacting) a new constitution, it requires that in creating novel constitutional content, the entity commissioned with constituent authority respects the established separation of powers. That entity can, of course, propose a constitution that separates powers in novel ways, but cannot exercise the executive, judicial, legislative powers itself.

In this chapter, these three distinctions are brought together through an examination of the ways in which institutions associated with the 'constituent power of the people' approach are reflected (or not) in contemporary constitutional orders, as well as of the legal and institutional implications of that approach. Constitutions in which the constituent people, as opposed to the constituent nation, in some way assumes a real juridical presence are still relatively rare. Those constitutions would authorize the possibility of constitutional replacement under the premise that constituent authority can be channelled through law. They would normally deploy different legal techniques to allow citizens to directly participate in constitutional change. At the same time, since the entire citizenry, just as the entire nation, cannot be fully present in any assembly, such a mechanism would not be conceived as sovereign. A constitution-making body would, in that sense, always be acting on a mandate. Such a mandate could, for example, require the drafting of a constitution consistent with a set of principles or establish the maximum period during which a new constitution must be produced. It would normally be expressed through a referendum process. In practice, this means that, on the one hand, a constituent assembly will not be generally authorized to exercise the ordinary powers of government and, on the other, that it may be made subject to substantive limits.

I will proceed as follows. After briefly revisiting the connections between constituent instructions and constitutional change through a brief examination of early Anglo American constitutional practice, I consider, in Part I, the place of the imperative mandate in contemporary constitutional change. In Part II, I analyse the extent to which 'the people', understood in this context as a juridical entity, could be said to engage in constituent action through an electoral exercise. Before the electorate can be properly attributed with constituent functions, with the jurisdiction to issue constituent mandates that could legally bind a constitution-making body, the idea that in the context of constitutional change the electorate necessarily acts as a state organ (a view exemplified in the work of a number of constitutional theories as well as in some judicial decisions) needs to be left behind. I will do so by distinguishing between *constitutional* and *constituent* referendums. In Part III, I explore the process that led to the convocation of the Venezuelan Constituent Assembly of 1999. In that process, the court recognized the electorate's right to convene a constituent assembly through a referendum that took place outside of the established amendment rule. However, the constituent mandate contained in the referendum's question was transgressed by an assembly that assumed sovereign authority. The courts, relying on the theory of constituent power, later sanctioned that transgression.

I. The People as Co-Legislator

The institution of the imperative mandate is not always associated with constitutional change. On the contrary, to the extent that its basic idea is that representatives are legally bound by the instructions of their constituents, it seems particularly relevant in the context of ordinary law making. That is to say, a community elects their representative to the legislative chamber, somehow instructs her to vote in favour or against particular legislative proposals, and the representative (or perhaps more accurately, the delegate) is legally bound by that instruction. In the contemporary world, this idea is frequently associated with the institution of the recall. Consider, for example, the following statement found in a 2017 decision of the Supreme Tribunal of Justice of Venezuela: 'The Constitution of 1999 adopts the principle of popular sovereignty with the political consequences mentioned by Rousseau: the imperative mandate.' This is reflected in its Article 72, which states that all offices 'filled by popular vote are subject to recall . . .'[1] Of course, constitutional orders that simply allow the recall of national legislators only recognize the imperative mandate in a partial way.[2] There are no formal/express instructions from the electors, only the possibility of recalling those legislators who, for some reason, no longer enjoy the support of their constituents.[3]

The possibility of recalling ordinary legislators or other elected officials does not say much about the relationship between the imperative mandate and constituent power.[4] Nonetheless, as we saw in Chapter 4, for its Rousseauian supporters in revolutionary France, the imperative mandate was the means through which the entire community could participate in constitution-making. This was perhaps made more explicit in England, many decades before the French Revolution. Constituent instructions were frequently seen by English commentators and political actors as especially relevant not in the context of ordinary law making, but in that of fundamental constitutional change.[5]

[1] Judgment No. 2017-0519, Supreme Tribunal of Justice of Venezuela (Constitutional Chamber), Part V.

[2] In Latin American, the Constitutions of Ecuador (2008), Article 105 and Bolivia (2009), Article 240 also recognize the recall of national legislators (as well as of other elected officials, including the President) by popular initiative. The Constitution of Colombia recognizes the right of recall as one form of citizen participation, but it is limited to governors and mayors. See Articles 40, 103, and 259 of the Colombian Constitution (1991). See also C-179/02, Constitutional Court of Colombia, where the recall is identified as the 'most direct form of political control' established by the constitution. Other Latin American constitutions recognize the recall of legislators and other elected officials at a subnational level, as is also the case in the United States.

[3] In some US states, a recall election can only proceed if certain grounds (such as conviction of a felony, lack of fitness, neglect of duties, corruption) are present. See, for example, Article 1(33) of the Constitution of Washington (1889).

[4] Deputies sitting in a constituent assembly can also be made subject to popular recall. This was Lenin's approach in his 'Draft Decree on the Right of Recall' (19 November 1917), which stated: 'No elective institution or representative assembly can be regarded as being truly democratic and really representative of the people's will unless the electors' right to recall those elected is accepted and exercised. This fundamental principle of true democracy applies to all representative assemblies without exception, including the Constituent Assembly.' *Lenin's Collected Works* (Moscow: Progress Publishers, 1972) vol. 26, 336. The right of recall is also recognized in a number of socialist constitutions. See, for example, Article 68(a) of the Cuban Constitution of 2019: 'Representatives' mandate may be revoked at any moment in the form, for the causes, and according to the procedures established in the law.'

[5] See, for example, the 'Report of the Sub-Committee, appointed to enquire into the State of Representation in this Country, Free-Masons Tavern, March 19, 1780', *Morning Chronicle and London Advertiser*, Saturday 25 March 1780 (Issue 3386), which found that 'frequent parliaments were the fundamental constitution of the kingdom', and maintained that past alterations in the length of the parliamentary term 'were made without communication with the constituent body of the people, and have been continued without the sanction of their approbation'. See also Daniel Defoe, *A Collection of Original Papers Concerning the Union Between England and Scotland* (Printed for E. Curll: London, 1709) 21–22.

A similar phenomenon could be observed in North America. Indeed, Gordon Wood has explained that, by the 18th century, 'some Americans had come to believe that it was precisely on these 'great and leading questions of public policy', such as the formation of governments or the disestablishment of religion, rather than on the most parochial questions, that binding instructions were more necessary'.[6] Early commentators sometimes even suggested that a parliament that repeatedly ignored constituent instructions triggered the community's right of resistance and its ability to create a new government.[7]

Some 18th-century authors, such as Algernon Sidney, identified what seemed like an important obstacle to that conception. He maintained that members of parliament 'are not strictly and properly obliged to give account of their actions to any, unless the whole body of the Nation for which they serve, and who are equally concerned in their resolutions, could be assembled'.[8] Not surprisingly, there were attempts of designing mechanisms which would allow multiple counties and even the entire constituent body to try and force representatives to adopt particular views. One of the earliest examples in England is a document distributed among different constituencies in the context of the campaign for the Convention Parliament of 1660 (in the hope that the constituencies would then send it to the relevant candidates) which, among other things, would have 'require[d]' candidates to restore 'the ancient Constitution'.[9] The attempt at devising a system that would arguably allow the constituent will of the entire people to be expressed, we will see below, is exemplified in a number of contemporary constitutions. In this

[6] Gordon Wood, *The Creation of the American Republic: 1776-1787* (Chapel Hill and London: The University of North Carolina Press, 1998) 191. See also Robert Luce, *Legislative Principles: The History and Theory of Law Making by Representative Government* (Boston: Houghton Mifflin, 1930) 449. As an example, see 'Instructions of Anne Arundel County, Maryland (June 26, 1776)' in Peter Force, ed. *American Archives, 4th Series* (Washington, 1844) 1589, where the right to instruct the delegates that would later sit in the Continental Congress that eventually called independence was strongly asserted. For a discussion of the right to instruct representatives during the ratification of the US Constitution, see Pauline Maier, *Ratification: The Poele Debate the Constitution, 1787–1788* (New York: Simon & Schuster, 2010).

[7] *Junius: Stat Nominis Umbra*, vol. 2, Letter XXXII (3 April 1770) (London: Printed for Henry Sampson Woodfall, 1772) 18.

[8] Algernon Sidney, *Discourses Concerning Government*, vol. 2 (Edinburgh: Printed for G. Hamilton & J. Balfour, 1750) 370. For a more general discussion of this view, see Edmund Morgan, *Inventing the People: The Rise of Popular Sovereignty in England and America* (New York and London: W.W. Norton & Company, 1989) 101.

[9] The document is contained in its entirety as 'Appendix II' of Cecil S. Emden, *The People and the Constitution: Being a History of the Development of the People's Influence in British Government* (Oxford: Clarendon Press, 1956). Much later, at the beginning of the 20th century, Sir Frederick Pollock dismissed such an attempt as legally inconsequential, expressing that a resolution passed by every constituency would not have any legal effects. Frederick Pollock, *A First Book of Jurisprudence* (London: Macmillan, 1923) 274. For North American examples, see Wood (n. 6) 369.

respect, the imperative mandate, despite its explicit abolition in a number of jurisdictions, is still very much alive.

a. The Imperative Mandate Today

In England, the idea that the people had a right to instruct representatives and that representatives were bound by those instructions reached its climax in the 1774 election. Radical Whigs in London and Westminster sought to exact pledges from candidates that they would obey their constituents' mandates.[10] This attempt (which prompted Edmund Burke's famous letter)[11] failed: only a handful of candidates agreed to subscribe the pledge. But the explicit rejection of the imperative mandate was not exclusively a phenomenon of the 18th and 19th centuries (as our examination in Chapters 4 and 5 of early constitution-making episodes in France, Spain, Venezuela and Colombia may suggest).[12] There are, in fact, some contemporary constitutions that explicitly entrench the notion that representatives act on a free mandate and that expressly connect such a rejection with the principle of national sovereignty. Since in most contemporary constitutions representatives also play a key role in the formal amendment process, such prohibitions of the imperative mandate also have potential implications for constitutional change. Consider, for example, Article 67 of the current Italian Constitution (1947): 'Each Member of Parliament represents the Nation and carries out his duties without a binding mandate.' Article 94 of the Constitution of Peru (1993) similarly states: 'Congressmen represent the Nation. They are not subject to any binding mandate or interpellation.'[13]

[10] Morgan (n. 8) 215.

[11] Edmund Burke 'Speech to the Electors of Bristol' (3 November 1774), *The Works of the Right Honourable Edmund Burke*. 6 vols (London: Henry G. Bohn, 1854-1856) vol. 1, 446–448. For an example of this view in 18th-century North America, see Noah Webster, 'Government', 1 *American Magazine* (1787–1788) 205–209, where the idea that particular constituencies are unable to express the 'general interest' is discussed at some length.

[12] In the United States, the imperative mandate was implicitly abolished at a national level in the late 18th century. The practice of issuing instructions to representatives was so common in North America that some of the drafters of the US Constitution acted under instructions at the Philadelphia Convention it. But when a proposal was presented to insert into the First Amendment a provision declaring the right of the people 'to instruct their representatives', it was rejected. See Kris W. Kobach, 'May "We the People" Speak?: The Forgotten Role of Constituent Instructions in Amending the Constitution', 33 *U.C. Davis Law Review* 1 (1999) 55–58, 68.

[13] See also Article 38(1) of the German Basic Law (1949): '[Members of the Bundestag] . . . shall be representatives of the whole people, not bound by orders or instructions and responsible only to their conscience', and Article 152.3 of the Constitution of Portugal: 'Members shall represent the whole country and not the constituencies for which they are elected.'

The prohibition of the imperative mandate has become especially relevant in terms of the relationship between parliamentarians and their political parties.[14] For example, in a judgment that discussed the scope of the previously mentioned Article 67, the Italian Constitutional Court stated: 'The prohibition of the imperative mandate means that a member of parliament is free to vote in accordance with the directions [*indirizzi*] of its party, but it is also free to depart from them; no norm can legitimately result in negative consequences to the member of parliament that has voted against the directives of the party.'[15] A similar approach was accepted in a case that examined the legal implications of the constitutional oath that new members of parliament were required to take. The Spanish Constitutional Tribunal stated that: 'deputies are representatives of the Spanish people considered as a unity', and whatever commitments they have acquired from their political parties, have 'no relation with an obligation derived from an alleged imperative mandate'.[16] In the same vein, the French Constitution of 1958 notes in its Article 4 that 'political parties . . . shall respect the principles of national sovereignty and democracy' and in Article 27, that no member of parliament 'shall be elected with a binding mandate'.[17]

This type of provision notwithstanding, the right to instruct representatives has survived in several jurisdictions in the form of the previously mentioned mechanism of the recall election and, perhaps more importantly, through the popular initiative. The popular initiative, as the right to instruct representatives, rests on the idea that the people has a law-making authority that is not exhausted in the election of a representative assembly. It provides the 'constituent body' with the ability of bypassing the legislature and, as Oscar Orban noted in the late 19th century,[18] to bring into existence legal and constitutional

[14] For a discussion, see Francisco Fernández Segado, 'Partidos Políticos: Representación Parlamentaria e Interdicción del Mandato Imperativo', 2(2) *Revista Pensamiento Constitucional* 29 (1995).

[15] Judgment No. 14/1964, Constitutional Court of Italy,. The debate about the imperative mandate has become again relevant in Italy in light of the proposals of the *Cinque Stelle* movement about the relationship between electors and representatives. For a discussion, see Elena Falleti, 'La Democracia Directa y la Prohibición del Mandato Vinculante', 14(1) *Revista Jurídica Piélagus* 59 (2015).

[16] Judgment No. 119/1990, Spanish Constitutional Tribunal, 64. Article 67(2) of the Spanish Constitution (1978) states: 'Members of the *Cortes Generales* shall not be bound by any imperative mandate.' See also Judgment No. 10/1983, Spanish Constitutional Tribunal.

[17] A similar provision is found in Article 22 of the Constitution of Comoros (2001). The opposite approach is followed by the Constitution of Panama (1972, as amended), which in Article 151(2) explicitly authorizes political parties to 'revoke the mandate' of party members serving in the legislature for a number of reasons, including 'grave violations of the by-laws and of the ideological, political or general platform of the party'.

[18] For a discussion, see Chapter 6 of this book. See also Oscar Orban, 'Des Immunités Constitutionnelles' 3 *Revue du Droit Public et de la Science Politique en France et a L'étranger* 193 (1895) 213–214.

changes that state officials are not willing to adopt. [19] For example, the current Constitution of Ecuador (2008) states in Article 441 that amendments that 'do not alter the fundamental structure of the Constitution, the character and the constitutive elements of the state, that do not restrict rights and guarantees, and do not modify the process of constitutional reform', may be adopted 'by a referendum requested by . . . citizens with the support of at least eight percent of the persons registered in the electoral roll'. This kind of provision institutionalizes a contemporary form of the imperative mandate, one that functions at a national level and without primary assemblies.

That is to say, it attributes a legally binding character to an instruction from a group of citizens: public authorities must hold a referendum on whether an amendment proposal should be adopted, and if the majority of the electors answer 'yes' to that question, they must recognize that the constitutional text has formally changed. As suggested by the substantive limits mentioned in the previously mentioned Article 441 (which arguably identify the material content of the Constitution of Ecuador), popular initiatives of this sort are not generally understood as necessarily involving the expression of a full constitution-making authority. Indeed, they have frequently been subject to limits imposed by courts.[20] However, this kind of instruction is sometimes presented in the language of the original constituent power and directed at the production of major constitutional change. Consider the Constitution of Venezuela of 1999.[21] Its Article 347, mentioned in the previous chapter, states that: 'The original constituent power rests with the people of Venezuela. This power may

[19] See, for instance, the Constitution of Uruguay (1967), Article 331 and the Constitution of Switzerland (1874), Article 121. For an analysis of the role of citizens in constitution-making in Swiss Cantons, see Ana Tornic and Nina Massüger, 'Constituent assemblies in Swiss cantons' in *Patterns of Constitutional Design: The Role of Citizens and Elites in Constitution-Making* (Jonathan Wheatley and Fernando Mendez eds) (Farnham: Ashgate, 2013). Many US States's constitutions also allow constitutional amendments to be proposed by popular initiative and adopted by referendum. See, for example, Constitution of Maine (1820), Article IV, Section 18(2) ('The Legislative Power').

[20] This phenomenon will be considered in more detail later. An interesting example of it, in a US context, took place when a number of states engaged in a coordinated effort to bind their representatives in the US Congress to propose an amendment to the US Constitution. These initiatives were, one by one, struck down by the courts. For a detailed discussion, see Kobach (n. 12). See also *Morrissey v State*, 951 P. 2d 911, 916 (1998); *Miller v Moore*, 169 F.3d 1119 (8th Circuit) (1999) 1124.

[21] Similar provisions appear in the Constitution of Bolivia (2009), Article 411, the Constitution of Ecuador (2008), Article 444, and the Constitution of Panama (1972, as amended), Article 314. The Constitution of Panama is especially interesting, since it refers to a 'Parallel Constituent Assembly' ('parallel', because it would co-exist with the constituted powers), and states that 'the Parallel Constituent Assembly may reform the current Constitution totally or partially but in no case may adopt decisions with retroactive effects or alter the terms of office of elected or appointed officials who are exercising their functions at the moment when the new Constitution enters into force'. This entity implicitly differentiates between 'sovereignty' and 'constituent power', a distinction developed at length in Chapter 9. Compare that with Article 411 of the Bolivian Constitution, which refers to a 'originary and plenipotentiary' constituent assembly, but also attempts to regulate its internal decision-making rule.

be exercised by calling a National Constituent Assembly for the purpose of transforming the State, creating a new juridical order and drawing up a new Constitution.' The initiative to convene the assembly is then placed by Article 348 in '15% of the voters registered with the Civil and Electoral Registry' (as well as in the President, in the National Assembly acting through a two thirds vote and, interestingly, in the municipal *cabildos abiertos*,[22] also acting by a two-thirds vote of their members).[23]

What we see here is an attempt at channelling, through law, the exercise of the constituent power of the people. A popular initiative for the calling of a constituent assembly is, in the last instance, a binding mandate from a group of citizens that possess a part of the sovereign authority (as in Rousseau),[24] directed at the relevant public officials. Since it is regulated by the constitutional text, if such officials fail to abide by the relevant instruction they would be acting illegally and, if they are elected officials, they could also be subject to recall. This assumes that members of the electorate, when acting through the popular initiative or the referendum, at least in some contexts, can be understood as engaged in the exercise of sovereignty, as commissioning an entity with the exercise of a constituent authority that it is unable to exercise itself. If this interpretation is correct, the idea that the jurisdiction of a constituent assembly can be limited by the content of a referendum question (a practical implication of the distinction between sovereignty and constituent power, discussed in the previous chapter) naturally follows. If, on the contrary, the electorate is always understood as a state organ, as part of a regulated process of constitutional reform, then it becomes more difficult to justify the notion of

[22] Article 70 of the Venezuelan Constitution of 1999 states that the '*cabildo abierto* and the citizen assembly, which decisions will be binding' are means for the exercise of popular sovereignty. For a brief comment on the *cabildo abierto*, see n. 82 of Chapter 4 of this book and the sources cited there. For an interesting discussion at the National Constituent Assembly about the recognition of the historical institution of the *cabildo abierto*, see *Asamblea Nacional Constituyente*, Gaceta Constituyente: Agosto-Septiembre, Sesión de Número 23 (Caracas: Imprenta del Congreso de la República, 1999) vol. 2.

[23] Article 348 states: 'The initiative for calling a National Constituent Assembly may emanate from the President of the Republic sitting with the Cabinet of Ministers; from the National Assembly, by a two thirds vote of its members; from the Municipal Councils in open session [*cabildos abiertos*], by a two-thirds vote of their members; and from 15% of the voters registered with the Civil and Electoral Registry'. In the United States, the Constitution of Montana (1972), Article XIV, Section 2, also allows for the calling of a Constitutional Convention by popular initiative. Moreover, in a Rousseauian/Jeffersonian fashion, it states '[i]f the question of holding a convention is not otherwise submitted during any period of 20 years it shall be submitted as provided by law at the general election in the twentieth year following the last submission. ibid., Article XIV, Section 3. As we saw in Chapter 6, this kind of periodic assembly was also defended in the 19th century by authors like José María Quimper. J. M. Quimper, *Derecho Político General* (Lima, 1887) vol. 2, 137. For a history of the popular initiative in Montana, see Anthony Johnstone, 'The Constitutional Initiative in Montana', 71 *Montana Law Review* 325 (2010).

[24] See Chapter 5 of this book, where Rousseau's notion of popular sovereignty as shared among citizens is discussed.

a constituent assembly subject to substantive limits. In the next section I consider both possibilities.

II. Between Electorate and People

The notion of 'the people', as noted by some of the critics of the principle of popular sovereignty (such as Manuel Durán y Bas),[25] can be conceived as comprising all of the human beings living in a particular territory, including children, non-citizens, citizens not registered to vote, etc. The electorate, in contrast, is a juridical construct, it includes only those human beings who comply with the relevant criteria (e.g. requirements such as age, residency, and the completion of some administrative processes in order be included in the electoral registry). As Raymond Carré de Malberg noted, only the electorate, not the people, could have a formal role in an established constitutional order. And that role could not involve the exercise of a sovereign power. As we saw in Chapter 8, Carré de Malberg embraced the principle of national sovereignty and, with it, rejected the idea that there could be any means of exercising an unlimited jurisdiction in a state organized according to that principle. Under that conception, not only is the imperative mandate rejected, but citizens cannot be conceived as supreme law-makers. At most, citizens could have whatever limited 'electoral power' is conferred to them by the constitution.[26] In that capacity, they would normally function as an organ that participates in the creation of an elected assembly. Put differently, from a juridical perspective (and unlike in a direct democracy) the citizenry does not deliberate or engage in the making of substantive decisions, they only hold 'a pure electoral power'.[27]

Moreover, once elected, the legislature (or a constituent assembly) does not represent a pre-existing national will but expresses that will for the first time.[28] The electoral power was not, as in the work of Cerbeleón Pinzón[29], a constituent power, but a constituted one. Carré de Malberg's contemporary,

[25] See Chapter 6 of this book.
[26] A similar view is expressed in Sieyès' notion of the *pouvoir commettant*, discussed in Chapter 3 of this book.
[27] Raymond Carré de Malberg, *Teoría General del Estado* (México: Fondo de Cultura Económica, 1948) [1922] s. 371, 392.
[28] ibid. s. 371.
[29] For Pinzón, 'the constituent power, or the electoral power, has the task of constituting the representatives of the Nation for the exercise of public authority'. Cerbeleón Pinzón, *Tratado de Ciencia Constitucional*, 2nd ed. (Bogotá, 1852) 186. The work of Pinzón is discussed in Chapter 6. Consistent with Carré de Malberg's views, in 1872, a French commentator referred to the electoral power as the 'first constituted power' that the constituent body of the nation uses to select its representatives in the legislature. G. F. G, *Le Pouvoir Électoral* (Paris, 1872) 13–14.

Maurice Hauriou, offered a similar diagnostic of the status of the electorate vis à vis the sovereign, describing the former as the representative of the nation. 'The electoral body', Hauriou wrote, 'does not absorb the nation, it is nothing but its representative. In this sense, there is never a government that is an absolute direct democracy; government is always representative or semi-representative'.[30] Nonetheless, Carré de Malberg tended to qualify his rejection of the institutions and mechanisms associated with the principle of popular sovereignty.[31] In his *Contribution à la Théorie Générale de l'État,* there were already some indications of an uneasiness with how the principle of national sovereignty had been implemented in France.[32] He reflected that uneasiness further in his later work, where he moved closer to the notion of popular sovereignty and maintained 'that the idea of the sovereignty of the general will had been exploited with the purpose of giving rise to the sovereignty of parliament', and that as a result, the constituent power ultimately falls in the hands of ordinary representatives.[33]

Carré de Malberg seemed to have concluded that the best means of limiting the power of the ordinary legislature (and of creating a balance between parliament and the executive) was attributing the electorate with the possibility of making the final decision as to the content of the general will.[34] In such a system, the people would become a 'supreme organ' that acts through the mechanism of the referendum both in the context of ordinary law making and constitutional reform. In constitutional orders where the direct vote of the electorate was a constitutional possibility, Carré de Malberg maintained that popular decisions, unlike that of the legislature or the executive, would be considered 'sovereign and definitive'.[35] That approach, which he saw exemplified in Articles 73 and 76 of the Weimar Constitution, had the advantage of dismissing any attempt of making the will of the legislature equivalent to the general will, 'the expression of which the people reserves for itself'.[36] According to Carré de Malberg, the only French Constitution to follow a similar route was

[30] Maurice Hauriou, *Principios de Derecho Público y* Constitucional (Carlos Ruiz del Castillo trans.) (Granada: Editorial Comares, 2003) 553–554. For a discussion on this view, see León Duguit, *Manual de Derecho Constitucional* (Granada: Comares, 2005) 117–125.

[31] For a recent and illuminating discussion, see Olga Bashkina, 'Raymond Carré de Malberg and the Interpretation of Sovereignty in the Belgian Constitution', 35 *Journal of Constitutional History* 149 (2018) 160.

[32] For a discussion, see Chapter 9 of this book.

[33] Raymond Carré de Malberg, *La Ley, Expresión de la Voluntad General: Estudio sobre el Concepto de Ley en la Constitución de 1875* (Ignacio Massot Puey trans.) (Madrid: Marcel Pons, 2011) 199.

[34] ibid. 190.

[35] ibid. 192.

[36] ibid. 195.

the Constitution of 1793, which required the ratification of the laws by primary assemblies.[37] But the situation in France since 1789 had involved the 'limitation of popular influence to the power to elect representatives and to prohibit any kind of effective popular participation in the legislative power'.[38]

Making the people the ultimate supreme organ 'both in the constituent and in the legislative' context, would make clear that parliament is not the sovereign, that the legislature is 'a derived power and, accordingly, essentially subject to limitation'.[39] In attributing the electorate with the ability to express the general will, Carré de Malberg moved in the direction of the Rousseauian[40] principle of the constituent power of the people.[41] The electorate, it seemed, was neither a mere state organ performing the function of nominating members of the legislature or the nation's representative. It was the final arbiter of whether a proposed law or constitutional change was consistent with the general will. In other words, the electorate became the juridical personification of the people, the people in action within an established constitutional order. Note, however, that Carré de Malberg was operating here under the view that the amending power, when exercised by parliament or when it involves direct popular intervention, is not subject to substantive limits. That is to say, that, as we saw in Chapter 1, there can be an original and a derived constituent power, but only one constituent function. If, as suggested in Chapter 8, there is a difference between alterations in the constitutional text that can be achieved through the ordinary amendment power and material alterations that require an exercise of constituent authority, then Carré de Malberg's approach needs to be, once more, superseded.

[37] ibid. 199. But not in all cases. For a discussion, see Chapter 4 of this book.

[38] ibid. 200. Hauriou maintained in democratic contexts, processes of constitutional change were frequently combined with the popular ratification of the draft prepared by the relevant entity, an approach that reached its 'perfection' when constitutional changes can be presented by popular initiative. Hauriou (n. 30). These types of arrangements were being nonetheless overtaken by 'a reaction against the popular constituent power'. Carré de Malberg, *La Ley* (n. 33) 353. Nowadays, particular institutions were attributed constituent functions (including that of replacing the entire constitutional text) without the need of popular intervention and, at the same time, the notion of piecemeal amendment was displacing the idea of total revision. 'In virtue of a secret logic', he claimed, 'rules of constitutional change tend to remove from constituent processes the salient role of majorities and put it as much as possible in the hands of the minoritarian governmental power', that is, a power that 'belongs to a small minority' of individuals. ibid. 344, 194, 211, 222.

[39] ibid. 203

[40] In fact, while in his *Contribution* Carré de Malberg usually referred to the concept of the general will in a critical way (and mostly in discussions about Rousseau), he largely embraced it in *La Ley* (n. 33).

[41] This attempt to bring together national and popular sovereignty is reflected in Article 1(2) of the current Constitution of Spain (1978): 'National sovereignty belongs to the Spanish people, from which the powers of the State emanate'. It was also present in the Declaration of Rights of the French Constitution of 1793, Articles 23–25 (and in the Girondin Draft Constitution, Articles 25–27).

a. Of Constituent Referendums and Constituent Mandates

In considering whether the electorate, when it acts through a referendum (and, arguably, through a popular initiative), should be understood as exercising a sovereign power, as a juridical manifestation of the people, an important distinction needs to be made.[42] There are many constitutions with amendment rules that require popular ratification before a proposal to alter the constitutional text can become law. Some of those constitutions also require that the modification of fundamental principles takes place through a constituent assembly. Consider, for example, Article 411 of the Constitution of Bolivia (2019). That provision authorizes the *partial reform* of the constitution through a process that may be triggered by popular initiative (20 per cent of the electorate) or by a majority of the members of the legislative assembly, and that ends in popular approval or rejection in a referendum. The *total reform* of the constitution, defined as 'that which affects its fundamental premises, rights, duties, and guarantees, or the supremacy and reform of the Constitution, shall take place', according to the same provision, through an 'originary plenipotentiary Constituent Assembly'. The convening of the assembly must be authorized in a referendum which can be triggered by the President, by a two-thirds vote in the legislature, or by popular initiative (the same thresholds mentioned above apply here).

Under that approach, it seems clear that the *partial reform* process cannot be used to alter the material constitution. The constitution's material content can only be revised through the procedure of *total reform*. The first of these processes would involve the exercise of constituted authority; the second would involve the exercise of constituent power. Both, however, require the participation of the electorate through a referendum and, potentially, through popular initiative. Is it possible to say that in the first case, the electorate acts as a state organ and that, in the second, the same electorate acts as the sovereign? A number of constitutional theorists and courts have considered this question. Carl Schmitt, in contrast to Carré de Malberg, maintained that 'even the constitutional powers and competences of the 'people', which is to say the state citizens entitled to vote' (such as the referendum and the initiative under

[42] The importance attributed to referendums here should not be taken as an implicit dismissal of the academic critiques of that institution. It is rather an attempt at understanding the implications of the theory of constituent power assuming that the kinds of mechanisms that are now associated with its exercise will remain with us. For contemporary analyses of the problems and democratic potential of referendums, see Zoran Oklopcic, *Beyond the People: Social Imaginary and Constituent Imagination* (Oxford University Press, 2018); Stephen Tierney, *Constitutional Referendums: The Theory and Practice of Republican Deliberation* (Oxford University Press, 2012).

the previously mentioned Articles 73 and 76 of the Weimar Constitution), are not 'powers of the sovereign people, who give themselves a constitution and engage in acts of the constitution making power. They are, rather, competences in the context of the constitution that is already provided'.[43] In other words, the very fact that the referendum and the initiative are constitutionally regulated puts them in the terrain of constituted authority, an authority that is unable to touch the material constitution.

From the perspective of the theory of the organ, that conclusion also follows. As Pedro de Vega has explained, for an organ theorist, the participation of the electorate in constitutional reform can only be interpreted as an act of constituted power.[44] The reason is simple: in the context of those procedures, the people acts within the limits posed by the constitution itself; it does not act as an omnipotent political force, but as a non-sovereign state organ.[45] This would be the view that follows, for example, from Georg Jellinek's conception: the state, and not the electorate, is the sovereign.[46] Against that view (but reaching the same conclusion), de Vega argued that the referendum should be understood in its classical sense, that is, as an act of control. The referendum is 'an instrument of ratification of the act of a representative (an assembly) by the represented (the people), which is directly connected to the institution of the imperative mandate'.[47] To the extent that the referendum is an instrument of control, it cannot be understood as a means 'through which the power of constitutional reform—which is always a constituted power—becomes a sovereign constituent power'.[48]

This kind of view was also expressed in a series of judgments of the Colombian Constitutional Court. The Colombian court has stated that, in a

[43] Carl Schmitt, *Constitutional Theory* (Durham: Duke University Press, 2008) 145–146. See also Dietrich Conrad, 'Limitation of Amendment Procedures and the Constituent Power, 15–16 *Indian Year Book of International Affairs* (1966–1967), 405, who describes the referendum as best as 'an ultimate veto power'.

[44] Pedro de Vega, *La Reforma Constitucional y la Problemática del Poder Constituyente* (Madrid: Tecnos, 1985) 111.

[45] ibid.

[46] For a discussion of Jellinek's views, see Chapter 9 of this book. Jellinek noted that the idea that all powers of government are ultimately based on the will of the constituent subject sometimes affected the way in which the 'constituent power' of legislatures could be exercised: rather than authorizing a mere legislative supermajority to alter the constitutional text, many constitutions required a referendum, a dissolution of the legislature, or the convocation of a special assembly before an amendment could be adopted. Georg Jellinek, *Teoría General del Estado* (México: Fondo de Cultura Económica, 2012) 478.

[47] De Vega (n. 44) 113. De Vega notes that in the middle ages, the word 'referendum' was used to refer to communications between parliamentarians and their constituents on issues that were being discussed in an assembly, but that were not specifically included in the former's mandates. Representatives would express opinions on those issues, *ad referendum*, that is, subject to the subsequent ratification of their constituents. ibid.

[48] ibid. 114.

'participatory democracy, based on the principle of popular sovereignty', the people are not limited to act through their representatives (as would be the case in a system based on 'the principle of national sovereignty').[49] Rather, they are also able to engage in direct political acts. A democracy, the court has maintained, cannot be participatory unless the people can also appear as the bearer of the power of constitutional reform.[50] In Colombia, this was facilitated through what the court identified as the 'constitutional referendum', regulated by Articles 377 and 378 of the Constitution of 1991. Under Article 377, proposed constitutional changes that relate to the rights recognized in Chapter 1, Title II, to the procedures of popular participation or to Congress itself,[51] must be submitted to the electorate if requested by 5 per cent of the citizens who make up the electoral rolls. Under Article 378, upon a popular initiative presented in accordance with the procedure established in Article 155 or upon the initiative of Congress, any proposed change to the constitutional text must also be submitted to a referendum.[52]

Nevertheless, the court made sure to point out that the inclusion of the referendum as part of the mechanism of constitutional reform is not equivalent to the establishment of a 'pure direct democracy, not subject to judicial control'.[53] 'The power of constitutional reform, even when it includes a referendum', the court stated, 'is not the deed of neither the originary constituent power nor of the sovereign people, but an expression of a juridical competency organized by the Constitution itself'.[54] For that reason, the court maintained, such a power is always limited by the impossibility of replacing the constitution. Otherwise the power of constitutional reform would become the originary constituent

[49] Judgment C-551/03, Colombian Constitutional Court, para. 42. The court has also referred to the *cabildo abierto*, mentioned above, as a mechanism of democratic participation. Nonetheless, unlike in the Constitution of Venezuela (1999) (see nn 22 and 23, above), such mechanism is not attributed with a binding decision-making power. In a 1994 decision, the court stated that the legislature was free to attribute a binding character to the decisions made in *cabildo abierto*, and that such a mode of proceeding would be more consistent with that meeting of citizens through which the 'sovereign majesty of the people, as its original bearer, exercises it directly'. Judgment C-180/94, Colombian Constitutional Court, para. 1.8.

[50] Judgment C-551/03 (n. 49).

[51] This can be taken as an indication that those are the type of changes that alter the material core of the constitution. Note, however, that Title 1 of the Constitution of 1991, titled, 'Fundamental Principles', is excluded from the Article 377 procedure.

[52] The constitutional text can also be modified without a referendum under the procedure established in Article 375: 'The Government, ten (10) members of the Congress, twenty percent (20%) of councillors or deputies, or citizens totalling at least five percent (5%) of the electoral rolls in force may introduce legislative bills. The bill will be discussed in two (2) ordinary and consecutive session periods. After having been approved in the first period by a majority of those present, the bill will be published by the Government. In the second period, the approval will require the vote of the majority of the members of each Chamber. In this second period only initiatives presented in the first period may be discussed.'

[53] Judgment, C-551/03 (n. 49) para. 44.

[54] ibid. para. 40.

power.[55] Some years later, the court made the same point even more explicitly: 'The referendum as a mechanism of constitutional reform is, always, a manifestation of the derived constituent power and not even the intervention of the electorate . . . has sufficient juridical force to transform a referendum into a foundational, primary, or originary constituent act.'[56] The type of electoral act examined in those judgments can be identified, as suggested by the court itself, as a *constitutional referendum*. That is, a referendum through which a proposed constitutional change is approved as part of a procedure established by the constitutional amendment rule.

But not all referendums are like that. Indeed, the Colombian Constitutional Court has distinguished between situations 'where the citizenry acts as a constituted organ, and accordingly, as a limited one', and situations where the people, acting 'outside of any normative channel, decides to alter the constitution or give itself a new one', such as what occurred when the Colombian Constitution of 1991 was adopted (as seen in Chapter 9).[57] Only in the latter type of scenario, the people acts as the primary constituent power.[58] However, the court included within the former types of situations those cases in which, 'according to constitutional provisions, the people is convened to decide whether to call a national constituent assembly'.[59] Although the court's basic distinction is consistent with the view I will present shortly, the characterization of a referendum in which a constituent assembly is convened as a situation where the citizenry necessarily acts as a state organ is not. Such a referendum would be authorizing an entity to replace the existing constitution or to alter its material content. The fact that it takes place according to law cannot be enough to deprive it of a constituent

[55] ibid. For a rejection of this approach, see the 1962 decision of the French Constitutional Council determining that it lacked jurisdiction to assess the validity of a constitutional amendment ratified by a referendum in violation of the established amendment process. For the French Constitutional Council, as for Hauriou, a referendum was 'l'expression directe de la souveraineté nationale'. Constitutional Court Decision No. 62-20 DC (6 November 1962).

[56] Judgment C-141/10, Colombian Constitutional Court, para. 1.3. See also Judgment C-379/16, Colombian Constitutional Court, para. 4.4., where the court stated that 'it would be unconstitutional to restrict the fundamental rights of a minority through a constitutional referendum, since fundamental rights are not susceptible of being limited in their scope through mechanisms of citizen participation, because these rights constitute a limit to the exercise of political power both to that of the constituent and the constituted powers'. It is unclear if by making reference to the constituent power in the previous quote, the court was referring to the derived constituent power, or suggesting, as proponents of the natural law approach discussed in Chapter 6, that those limits are applicable to the constituent subject itself.

[57] Judgment C-140/10, Colombian Constitutional Court, para. 1.4. The same point was made in Judgment C-180/07, Colombian Constitutional Court, para. 2.2.2.2.1.

[58] Judgment C-140/10 (n. 57). The Peruvian Constitutional Court has also distinguished between the 'people as a constituted power and the people as the bearer of the Constituent Power'. Judgment No. 014-2002-AI/TC, Peruvian Constitutional Tribunal, para. 115.

[59] ibid.

nature, unless the entity called to produce a new constitution is conceived as superior to the people itself.

As Ernst-Wolfgang Böckenförde has stated, it is true that there can be a juridical distinction between the 'people as an organ and the people as sovereign; however, the two cannot be separated as though they were two distinct and real entities: in the final analysis, they are the same "people".'[60] '[A]nytime the people takes an active role as an organized entity', he added, 'the unorganised people of the *pouvoir constituant* is also involved and present in some way'.[61] In the case of a referendum calling a constituent assembly authorized to adopt a new constitution (within or outside the established amendment rule), the electorate is commissioning that entity (acting as a *pouvoir commettant* that is not only able to elect representatives who would act on a free mandate)[62] with the production of material constitutional content. That kind of situation is best understood as an instance in which the sovereign people acts through the electorate and sets the conditions to which the constituent assembly will be subject. Such conditions may include, for example, the creation of a specific form of constitutional content or the production of a new constitutional text within a certain period.[63] They may also require the submission of the new constitutional text to popular ratification. In that final act, the sovereign people, acting once again through the electorate, not only accepts or rejects a draft constitution, but also confirms that its commission has been respected.

As noted in Chapter 9, even a general authorization for the creation of a new constitution should be understood as accompanied by an implicit substantive

[60] Ernst-Wolfgang Böckenförde, Mirjam Künkler, and Tine Stein, *Constitutional and Political Theory: Selected Writings* (Oxford University Press, 2017) 179.

[61] ibid.

[62] For a discussion of Sieyès' conception of the *pouvoir commettant*, see Chapter 4 of this book.

[63] It is possible, even if objectionable, for a constituent referendum to expressly attribute a constituent assembly with the power to exercise both constituent and constituted power, that is to say, to place the assembly above the separation of powers. An example of this phenomenon is arguably that of the Ecuadorian referendum of 2007. The Ecuadorian Constitution of 1998 did not provide for the convocation of a constituent assembly, so the assembly was convened through a referendum, outside of the established amendment rule. In his first day in office, President Rafael Correa issued a decree which asked the electors whether they approved 'the convocation and installation of a Constituent Assembly of *plenary powers*, in conformity with the attached Electoral Statute, for the transformation of the institutional framework of the State and the creation of a new Constitution'. (Decreto Ejecutivo No. 2, 15 de enero de 2007, emphasis added). In its internal rules (*Reglamento de Funcionamiento de la Asamblea Constituyente*, 12 December 2007) the assembly was said to 'represent the popular sovereignty that resides in the people of Ecuador' and in the exercise of its 'plenary powers' it could not only propose a new constitution to the people, but also issue 'constituent mandates' (*mandatos constituyentes*) and ordinary laws (*Reglamento de Funcionamiento*, ibid. Articles 1 and 2). Its very first *mandato constituyente* stated that the assembly 'assumes and exercises the constituent power with plenary powers' (*Mandato Constituyente No. 1*, 29 de noviembre de 2007, Article 1). Perhaps more tellingly, in that *mandato constituyente* the Assembly also ratified Correa as President of the Republic and assumed 'the attributes and duties of the Legislative Function' (therefore suspending Congress until the results of the ratificatory referendum were announced) (*Mandato Constituyente*, Articles 6–7).

limit, that is, a prohibition of exercising the ordinary functions of government. Both authorizing and ratificatory referendums, as long as they involve the alteration of the material constitution, should be understood as *constituent* referendums, instances in which the sovereign exercises part of its power directly, that is, in the absence of a commission.[64] The legal implications of constituent referendums were indeed recognized in the process that led to the adoption of the Colombian Constitution of 1991, discussed in the previous chapter. There, the constitutional amendment rule did not include the possibility of convening a constituent assembly, and it was clear that the process through which that entity would be called was on its face illegal. However, the fact that such a process would involve the direct involvement of the people through a referendum was enough for the court to sanction the government's plan. For the court, when 'the Nation, in the exercise of its inalienable and sovereign power, decides to express itself about the constitutional charter that will rule its destinies, it is not and cannot be subject to the juridical normativity that predates its decision'.[65]

An expression of the electorate in favour of the convocation of a constituent assembly could not be declared invalid just because it failed to comply with positive law. As we will see in Part III below, some years later the Venezuelan Supreme Court of Justice reached a similar conclusion about the convocation of a constituent assembly through a referendum that took place outside the established amendment rule. In the end, however, the Venezuelan courts only recognized the binding character of the mandate contained in a referendum in a partial way. But it does not have to be like this, not even in the context of constituent assemblies convened outside a constitution's rules of change. In Chapter 6, we saw that some 19th-century authors, although operating under the idea that representatives act on a free mandate and therefore are not bound by citizen instructions, argued that they were mandataires with respect to the constitution itself.[66] That is to say, there were things that they could or not do because they had been authorized or deauthorized to do them by the constituent power that brought the constitution into existence. I have argued

[64] As Massimo Luciani has noted, '[i]t has never been claimed that the holder of sovereignty can only act in a sovereign capacity'. Massimo Luciani, 'El Referéndum: Cuestiones Teóricas y de la Experiencia Italiana', 37 *Revista Catalana de Dret Públic* 1 (2008) 11.

[65] Judgment No. 138, Supreme Court of Justice of Colombia (9 November 1990) in *Gaceta Especial Sala Constitucional, Corte Suprema de Justicia, República de Colombia* (Santafé de Bogotá, D.C., 1993) vol. 1, 65. The dissent, directly quoting from Carré de Malberg's work, maintained that the electorate only had the competence provided to it by the constitution, and that 'sovereignty cannot be reduced to the rude will of the citizens'. ibid. 101–102. See Raymond Carré de Malberg, *Teoría General del Estado* (México: Fondo de Cultura Económica, 1948) [1922], 1115.

[66] See, for example, Félix Berriat-Saint-Prix, *Théorie du Droit Constitutionnel Français: Esprit des Constitutions de 1848 et de 1852 et des Sénatus-Consultes Organiques Précédé d'un Essai sur le Pouvoir Constituant* (Paris, 1851) 45.

above that a popular initiative to amend the constitution or to convene a constituent assembly can be understood as an imperative mandate from the constituent body. The question that arises is whether the conditions expressed or implied in a constituent referendum through which a constituent assembly is convened[67] should also be understood as potentially imposing an imperative mandate on that constitution-making body.

The answer, as I have already suggested, must be in the affirmative, unless one is prepared to argue that during a constituent episode, the people ceases to be sovereign. This conception, of course, only makes sense once the 'constituent power of the nation' approach has been rejected.[68] What allows the electorate to issue constituent mandates is the (Rousseauian) notion that sovereignty lies in the multiplicity of individuals that comprise a political community and not in an abstract nation. But that sovereign power is only exercised when needed, that is, when the material content of the existing constitutional regime is to be replaced or modified. In such cases, the electorate acts as *if it* was the people. In situations where such an act takes place according to law (such as the technically lawful calling of a constituent assembly by popular initiative), the people is conceived as a *juridical entity* able to pose legally unsurpassable limits on a constitution-making body.[69] Whenever there is a constituent mandate, a ratificatory referendum would not only serve the purpose of approving or rejecting the proposed constitution, but of confirming that the relevant commission has been respected. In the next section, I will examine the process that led to the creation of the Constitution of Venezuela of 1999, where this approach was considered but—in my view incorrectly—rejected, by the courts.

III. Beyond Constituent Power in Venezuela, 1999

In Venezuela, the theory of constituent power was deployed by the courts in 1999 in a way that resulted in the attribution of sovereign powers to a constituent assembly. Unlike in Colombia,[70] the Venezuelan assembly was not

[67] The referendum would also normally call for a special election of the members of the assembly.

[68] Nevertheless, as noted in Chapter 5, the members of the council that drafted the Colombian Constitution of 1886 did not see themselves as subject to an imperative mandate from the electors but thought that the council itself was bound to a mandate from the nation to adopt a particular type of constitution.

[69] This is not a novel idea, it was even present in Article 117 of the French Constitution of 1793, which maintained that a National Convention could be limited in terms of the topics it was allowed to deliberate on. For a brief discussion, see Chapter 4 of this book.

[70] For a discussion of the Colombian process, see Chapter 9 of this book.

convened in the context of a declared state of emergency but at a time in which the traditional political forces were suffering from a profound crisis of legitimacy. Nonetheless, as in Colombia, the assembly was authorized to act by a referendum organized in violation of the amendment rule of the constitution then in place. Not surprisingly, the constitutionality of that mode of proceeding was tested at the Venezuelan Supreme Court of Justice. The court framed the issue before it as follows: 'The question that has been formulated is whether the Constitution should be reformed [through the ordinary amendment process], or if the convening of the constituent power, a sovereign power, is warranted'.[71] An important part of that decision consisted in an analysis of Article 4 of the Constitution of 1961, which established that 'Sovereignty rests with the people, who exercises it by voting, through the organs of public power'. For the court, it was necessary to determine whether this delegation of powers meant that sovereignty could not be exercised *directly* by the people, whether the people had permanently surrendered their sovereign force through the adoption of a constitution.

Embracing the theory of constituent power, the court abandoned the traditional interpretation of Article 4. That interpretation held that the objective of Article 4 was to protect the principle of representation and the old idea[72] that while sovereignty *rested* with the people (*la soberanía reside en el pueblo*), it had been delegated to government and could only be exercised by it.[73] The court rejected this interpretation by reasoning that whoever has a power and can delegate it can also exercise it herself.[74] The amendment rule contained in the Constitution of 1961 was an example of that type of delegation. Under this view, the requirements and limits established in the constitutional text regarding its modification only regulated the procedures through which *the legislature* could change the constitution. They could only be understood as limiting the constituted authorities' power of constitutional change and are not (and could not be) directed at the constituent people.[75] Indeed, the people

[71] Judgment No. 17, Supreme Court of Justice of Venezuela on the Referendum for Convening a Constituent Assembly (19 January 1999), 9. The original in Spanish reads: 'La pregunta que se formula es si procede convocar a una revisión de la Constitución o si procede la convocatoria a un Poder Constituyente, a un poder soberano.' This judgment is included in Allan R. Brewer-Carias, *Poder Constituyente Originario y Asamblea Nacional Constituyente* (Editorial Jurídica Venezolana, 1999) 35, and I am citing to that version of the case through this chapter. For a critical reading of this judgment (which nonetheless notes the relative independence of the Supreme Court of Justice from the President in 1999), see Alessandro Pace, 'Muerte de una Constitución', 57 *Revista Española de Derecho Constitucional* 271 (1999) 274.

[72] This is the distinction between the *source* and the *exercise* of sovereignty, briefly discussed in Chapter 5.

[73] Judgment No. 17 (n. 71) 35.

[74] ibid. 35.

[75] ibid. 39.

possessed a 'sovereign, unlimited, and principally originary' right to directly participate in the alteration of constitutional text.[76] The fact that such a right was not explicitly recognized only meant that it was one of the non-enumerated rights alluded to in Article 50 of the Constitution of 1961.

In a clear (though non-attributed) reference to Schmitt, the court expressed that constituent power 'presupposes the national life as a unity of existence and decision'.[77] In contrast to the constituted powers, the constituent one is not subject to any limits, it is 'prior and superior to the established juridical order'.[78] The people always retained its 'originary power' (*potestad originaria*) and this included the right to be consulted about the convocation of a constituent assembly for the adoption of a new constitution.[79] That right could be exercised through Article 181 of the Organic Law on Suffrage and Participation, which allowed the President of the Republic to call a referendum on issues of national importance.[80] When that right was exercised, the principle of constitutional supremacy had to give way to the principle of popular sovereignty.[81] Through the theory of constituent power, the Venezuelan Supreme Court of Justice was thus able to provide a justification for an exercise of political power not sanctioned (at least expressly) by the constitutional text, in a context of direct popular intervention. Importantly, the court did not explicitly refer to the constituent assembly as a sovereign entity.[82] Rather, it limited itself to describe the people as the sovereign or as the original constituent power and therefore as able to trigger the creation of a new constitution outside the established amendment rule.[83]

[76] ibid. 39.
[77] ibid. 38.
[78] ibid. 38.
[79] ibid. 36.
[80] ibid. 44.
[81] ibid. 34.
[82] For contrast, see the discussion of the Colombian constitution-making process in Chapter 9.
[83] This contrasted with the ways in which President Hugo Chávez and his followers had conceived the assembly from the beginning. Chávez, for example, frequently referred to the assembly as 'most sovereign' (*soberanísima*). See Ricardo Combellas, 'El Proceso Constituyente y la Constitución de 1999', 30 *Politeia* 183 (2003) 188. In the initial meeting of the assembly, there is a long and interesting discussion about its originary character. Luis Miquilina, President of the National Constituent Assembly, made his position clear early on: 'No one will diminish the sovereign character of this assembly, which will remain consagraged in the history of our motherland.' *Asamblea Nacional Constituyente*, Gaceta Constituyente: Agosto-Septiembre, Sesión de Instalación (Caracas: Imprenta del Congreso de la República, 1999) vol. I, 4. The attribution of 'sovereignty' to the assembly arguably had the purpose of underscoring its superiority over the constituted powers and was understood as consistent with the people being the ultimate sovereign. In Chapter X, Article 78 of the assembly's internal regulations (*Estatuto de Funcionamiento de la Asamblea Nacional Constituyente*), it is stated: 'The National Constituent Assembly will call for the active participation of the people and it is required to develop the necessary mechanisms to make a reality the involvement of the sovereign in the actual constituent process.'

The referendum on the convocation of the constituent assembly took place on 25 April 1999, and most of the electors answered 'yes' to the two questions that were posed to them. The first question read: 'Do you convoke a National Constituent Assembly with the purpose of transforming the State and creating a new juridical order that allows the effective functioning of a Social and Participatory Democracy?'. The second question asked the electors to ratify the regulations (*Bases Comiciales*)[84] issued by the National Electoral Council, which referred to the system by which the members of the assembly would be elected as well as to the nature of the assembly itself. The *Bases Comiciales* stated that the assembly would 'have as limits the values and principles of our republican history, as well as the compliance with international treaties, agreements . . . [and] the progressive character of the fundamental rights of men and democratic guarantees . . . '[85] Moreover, it stated that the 'National Constituent Assembly would function for a period of 180 days'. But in its Article 8, the National Electoral Council referred to the assembly as 'an originary power that comprises popular sovereignty [*poder originario que recoge la soberanía popular*]'. As we will see below, the Supreme Court of Justice found that description unacceptable.

a. The Assembly and the Courts

The assembly that was about to be convened, for the court, was bound 'by the spirit of the established Constitution'.[86] It was the Constitution of 1961, the court added, that would allow 'for the conservation of the rule of law' during the constituent period.[87] Consequently, the court ordered the National Electoral Council to publish a revised version of the *Bases Comiciales*, one without any reference to the constituent assembly as an 'originary power'.[88] Agreeing with that view, Allan Brewer-Carías (who sat in the assembly) maintained in 1999 that 'the Constituent Assembly cannot have any sovereign power whatsoever;

[84] 'Bases Comiciales para el referéndum consultivo sobre la convocatoria de la Asamblea Nacional Constituyente a celebrarse el 25 de abril de 1999', Resolution No. 990323-71 (23 March 1999). The second question originally asked the electorate whether it authorized the President to establish (after consultation with the political, economic, and social sectors) the system according to which the members of the assembly would be elected. That second question was declared invalid by the Supreme Court of Justice, on the basis that it did not ask citizens for their opinion about a determinate matter but instead would delegate in a single person the decision about it. That was determined to be contrary to the previously mentioned Article 181 Organic Law on Suffrage and Participation.

[85] ibid.

[86] Judgment No. 311 (13 April 1999). Included in Brewer-Carías (n. 71)197.

[87] ibid. 197.

[88] ibid. 198.

the sovereign is the people, as Originary Constituent Power, and it cannot transfer or delegate its sovereignty to an assembly'.[89] As my analysis in Chapter 9 would suggest, it is true that the assembly is not the originary constituent power, that such a power always lies with the people. But the assembly, unlike the Supreme Court of Justice and Brewer-Carías have suggested, is not a derived constituent power either, at least not if such a characterization is understood as necessarily involving a limited constitution-making jurisdiction.[90] For example, it would not be normally subject to an eternity clause contained in the very constitution it is called to replace, as argued by Brewer-Carías.[91] The assembly should instead be understood as a *mechanism* for the exercise of the originary constituent power of the people, as a means that is used for the exercise of that power in the absence of a better alternative.[92]

This means that the assembly is not subject to limits in terms of the constitutional content it can approve, with the exception of any conditions imposed by the sovereign people through its vote in a referendum. Being a mechanism for the exercise of the (original or primary) constituent power, as we saw in Chapter 9, is not the same thing as being sovereign, as being beyond the separation of powers. In this sense, there is some truth to the notion advanced by the court that the assembly was bound by the 'spirit' of the existing constitution, but only to the extent that that 'spirit' refers to the idea that ordinary political power has already been divided, and that an entity called to revise or replace the constitutional text is not implicitly authorized to exercise those ordinary powers. And this is exactly what the assembly did once convened, and it did so with the eventual sanction of the new Supreme Tribunal of Justice.

This was perhaps more clearly expressed in the internal regulations adopted by the assembly on 8 August 1999. Article 1 of that document stated that: 'The Assembly, in the exercise of the attributions that are inherent to itself, may limit or order the cessation of the activities of the authorities that comprise

[89] ibid. 154–155.

[90] ibid.; Judgment of 21 July 1999, Supreme Court of Justice of Venezuela, included in ibid. 252. Ricardo Combellas, who also sat in the Constituent Assembly, characterized the assembly as a derived constituent power, since 'democratic theory only recognises one Originary Constituent Power, the people, whose will is manifested through referendum'. Ricardo Combellas, *¿Qué es la Constituyente? Voz para el Futuro de Venezuela* (Caracas, 1998) 101. For a discussion, see also Roberto Viciano Pastor and Rubén Martínez Dalmau, *Cambio Político y Proceso Constituyente en Venezuela: 1998-2000* (Vadell Hermanos, 2001) 132–137.

[91] Brewer-Carías (n. 71) 163–164

[92] Constituent assemblies convened by referendum and comprised by elected deputies are now generally considered as the most democratic means of constitutional change. Other potentially more democratic mechanisms, such as primary assemblies, have now been left behind. For a proposal to include primary assemblies in contemporary processes of constitutional change, see Joel Colón-Ríos, 'Constituent Power, Primary Assemblies, and the Imperative Mandate', *Elgar Handbook of Comparative Constitution-Making* (Hanna Lerner and David Landau eds) (Edward Elgar, 2019).

the Public Power'.[93] Moreover, the same provision expressed that all the Public Powers (i.e. the ordinary institutions of government) were 'subordinated' to the assembly and required to abide (and ensure that others abide) by its decisions. Fully consolidating the assembly's status as a sovereign entity, the aforementioned provision also stated: 'The Constitution of 1961 and the rest of the established juridical order will continue in force in all aspects that do not collide or contradict with the juridical acts and other decisions of the National Constituent Assembly.'

Article 1 expressed the notion of sovereignty in the most dramatic way possible: from a formal perspective, the assembly had the power to transform any will into law. As noted in Chapter 9, this is the kind of power that authors like Donoso Cortés thought necessary in emergency situations. Although the Venezuelan assembly was not convened under a state of emergency, in one of its first sessions it proceeded to declare a 'National Emergency over the territory of the Republic', referring to a social, economic, and cultural crisis in the country.[94] In issuing such a declaration, the assembly was exercising a prerogative normally attributed to the constituted powers (Article 240 of the Constitution gave the President the authority to declare a state of emergency). At the same time, it was stated that in virtue of the state of emergency, the assembly would reorganise 'all of the organs of the Public Power' and make any decisions regarding the competences of those organs in order to overcome the crisis. At that moment and during the following weeks and months, the assembly engaged in the exercise of sovereign authority, transgressing the separation of powers in important ways and, arguably, the constitution-making mandate expressed through the referendum that convened it.

For example, on 19 August 1999, the assembly declared that the 'Judicial Power was in a state of emergency and reorganisation' and created a special commission with the power to order the suspension of judges and other judicial officers suspected of corruption. The commission could also remove judges from office (as well as other judicial officers) for a number of reasons, including having their judgments consistently reversed due to a manifest misunderstanding of the law, or enjoying a level of economic wealth which could not be explained.[95] Some days later, on 25 August 1999, the assembly adopted a decree which, among other things, identified the topics on which the Congress

93 'Estatuto de Funcionamiento de la Asamblea Nacional Constituyente', 8 August 1999.
94 'Decreto de Declaratoria de Emergencia Nacional', National Constituent Assembly (12 August 1999), Article 1.
95 'Reorganización del Poder Judicial y el Sistema Penitenciario', *Gaceta Oficial*, No. 36,805 (11 October 1999), Articles 6–7.

could legislate (in some cases those congressional acts would have to be ratified by the constituent assembly before they could be considered law) and attributed a general legislative power to the assembly itself.[96] But the greatest interference with the constituted powers occurred after the constitution was popularly ratified on 15 December 1999. Instead of dissolving itself, the constituent assembly continued in session, in an apparent violation of the mandate contained in the 25 April 1999 referendum, which only authorized it to create a new constitution and to operate for a period of six months.[97]

Such a mode of proceeding had the stated purpose of putting into practice a transitory regime that 'would allow for the immediate validity of the Constitution ratified by the people of Venezuela and proclaimed by the National Constituent Assembly'.[98] The assembly proceeded issue a decree on 27 December 1999 formally dissolving the Congress and replacing it with a special commission (*Comisión Legislativa Nacional*) whose members were appointed by the assembly itself (eleven deputies of the constituent assembly, and ten other citizens, comprised the commission).[99] This entity could 'legislate on matters of national competence and about the functioning of the different branches of the National Power'.[100] In its preamble, the decree maintained that the assembly was acting 'in the exercise of the originary constituent power conferred by the people through [the 25 April 1999] referendum'. The document also stated that it rested on the determination of the country's highest court recognizing 'the supra-constitutional character of the norms adopted by the National Constituent Assembly in representation of the originary constituent power'.[101] As part of the transitory regime, the assembly also issued a controversial decree on 30 January 2000 regulating the election of the new legislature created by the constitution.[102]

The Supreme Court of Justice (and later the new Supreme Tribunal of Justice, whose members where appointed by the constituent assembly during the transitory regime) developed the idea of supra-constitutionality in a series of decisions that challenged the constitutionality of the previously mentioned decrees.

[96] 'Regulación de las Funciones del Poder Legislativo' (25 August 1999).

[97] As we saw in Chapter 9, the Colombian assembly also continued in session after the constitutional text was completed.

[98] 'Régimen de Transición del Poder Público', Gaceta Oficial de la República de Venezuela, Decree No. 36,857, Article 1 (27 December 1999).

[99] ibid. Combellas (n. 83) 206.

[100] ibid. In that sense, it had more extensive powers than the Colombian *Congresito*. For a discussion, see Chapter 9 of this book.

[101] ibid. Judgment No. 1110, Supreme Court of Justice, (14 October 1999) 48.

[102] 'Estatuto Electoral del Poder Público', Gaceta Oficial de la República Bolivariana de Venezuela, no 36884 (3 February 2000). The Constitution of 1999 contains a number of transitory provisions, but they did not regulate the first elections that would take place under it.

The first of those decisions examined the validity of the 25 August 1999 decree (as well as that of another one issued some days later[103] which also reduced in important ways the powers of Congress).[104] The claimant, Henrique Capriles Radonski (then President of the Chamber of Deputies) argued, among other things, that the decree violated the terms of the 25 April 1999 referendum given that it involved the exercise of powers not explicitly given by the sovereign people. For the claimant, 'the National Constituent Assembly, by its very nature, should and must respect the established constitutional order as well as the limits imposed by the sovereign power through a referendum'.[105] Accordingly, it could neither act as a 'governmental organ of execution', nor limit the powers attributed by the Constitution of 1961 to the current Congress except through the drafting of a new constitution that would be subject to popular ratification.[106] Any 'transgression of those limits', the claimant argued, 'would violate the popular sovereignty expressed in the adoption of the *Bases Comiciales* through a referendum on 25 April 1999'.[107]

Moreover, the claimant maintained that the decree violated 'a fundamental principle, the column of the democratic system, as is the organic separation of powers . . . by concentrating in itself' key functions of the legislative and the judicial powers.[108] The majority of the Supreme Court of Justice disagreed with most of this. The limits approved by the electorate in the referendum, the court stated, did not bind the assembly to the constitutional order created in 1961 but only to the general principles mentioned in the *Bases Comiciales* (the principles of the country's republican tradition, the progressive character of human rights, and democratic guarantees, etc.). This meant that the National Constituent Assembly (despite the earlier decision of the Supreme Court of Justice where the removal of the phrase 'originary power' from the *Bases Comiciales* was ordered),[109] did not exercise a derived power, but an originary constituent one. This was the same kind of power, the court added, that the Colombian Constituent Assembly had exercised in 1991.[110] By maintaining that the assembly is unable to act as an 'organ of execution or replace the organs

[103] 'Reforma Parcial del Decreto de Regulación de las Funciones del Poder Legislativo', Gaceta Oficial de la República de Venezuela, No. 36,776 (31 August 1999).
[104] Judgment No. 1110 (n. 101) 39–41. This and the rest of the Venezuelan cases cited below have been collected in *Bases Jurisprudenciales de la Supraconstitucionalidad* (Caracas: Supreme Tribunal of Justice, 2002). I will use the pagination of that collection when quoting from the relevant judgments.
[105] ibid. 39.
[106] ibid. 40.
[107] ibid. 38.
[108] ibid. 40.
[109] ibid. 48.
[110] ibid. 48, 49.

of Public Power and transgress the principle of the division of powers', the court maintained, 'the claimant ignores that the Constituent Power is autonomous, unlimited and indivisible'.[111]

These passages make clear that the court understood the assembly as a sovereignty entity, implicitly rejecting the distinction developed in the previous chapter.[112] By so doing, the judges were able to justify a departure from the mandate contained in the authorizing referendum. Indeed, the court noted that in the exercise of the constituent power, the assembly was not limited 'to the creation of a new constitution, but also to act during the interregnum', that is, during the transition from the old to the new constitution.[113] This notion was further developed in a series of judgments authored by José M. Delgado Ocando at the new Supreme Tribunal of Justice. For example, in a case where the validity of the 30 January 2000 decree regulating the election of the new legislature was questioned, the court described the challenged norm as a constituent act that was part of 'a fundamental political decision' (explicitly referring to Schmitt's *Verfassungslehre*).[114] Such an act, the court continued, is not susceptible to being classified as unconstitutional *because* it was adopted by the National Constituent Assembly. Accordingly, it 'cannot be affected by the principle of the division of powers, and the categories that refer to the different competences of the branches of the constituted public power simply do not apply to it'.[115]

The norms adopted by the assembly were supra-constitutional with respect to the Constitution of 1961, as were the *Bases Comiciales* ratified by the people in the 25 April 1999 referendum.[116] The mandate that the people conferred to the National Constituent Assembly through that referendum, in turn, implied 'the validity of the constituent norms the assembly adopts, until the constituted powers have been designated or elected, that is, until the transition toward their institutionalisation has been completed'.[117] That is to say, even though

[111] ibid. 49.

[112] The dissenting judges attempted to counter that argument by unsuccessfully (and in my view incorrectly) describing this entity as derived from the established constitutional order and, as such, bound by the established governmental structure and its separation of powers. See, for example, the dissenting judgments of Hermes Harting, ibid. 52–3 and of Hildegard Rondón de Sansó, ibid. 55. Humberto J. La Roche, who authored the 19 January 1999 judgment (discussed above), issued a strong dissent which maintained that that earlier decision never 'made equivalent the notions of the Constituent Power and of the Constituent Assembly'. The former, he stated, belongs exclusively to the sovereign people, who can exercise it through an extraordinary assembly, but never gives it away. ibid. 66.

[113] ibid. 47, 49.

[114] Judgment No 179, Supreme Tribunal of Justice of Venezuela (28 March 2000) 76.

[115] ibid.

[116] ibid. 78.

[117] ibid. 80.

the assembly was acting outside of the six-month period established in the *Bases Comiciales*, it was nonetheless respecting the core element of its commission: the drafting of a constitution. Only a 'juridical fiction', the court stated, 'would allow one to distinguish between the nature of the [new constitution] and the rest of the norms sanctioned by the National Constituent Assembly'.[118] If a constituent assembly is sovereign, as this judgment suggests, both free from the separation of powers and from any kind of mandate. The entity that issued that mandate, that is, the electorate acting as the juridical people, would have transferred its sovereign jurisdiction by the very act of convening the assembly.

In reaching this conclusion, the court developed a seemingly coherent doctrine of the supra-constitutional nature of the acts of a constituent assembly. At the same time, however, it negated a key element of the notion of the constituent power of the people: the ability of citizens, acting together, of issuing binding instructions to a constitution-making body. This was the same notion the court had embraced in its earlier decision to authorize the convocation of a constituent assembly by referendum outside the established amendment rule. There is simply no escape from the fact that through the 25 April 1999 referendum, the National Constituent Assembly was only authorized to adopt a constitution, and to do so within a certain time limit. The assembly did produce a constitution but in so doing, interfered in important ways with the exercise of the ordinary public powers. Such a mode of proceeding could be politically justified in certain contexts, and perhaps the political crisis of the late 1990s in Venezuela was such a situation.[119] Nonetheless, as a matter of principle, the use of the concept of constituent power of the people to attribute sovereign jurisdiction to a constitution-making body in violation of a popularly ratified constituent mandate, lacks a proper justification.

IV. Constituent Referendums and Judicial Review

The previous paragraphs exemplify a situation, also present in the convocation of the Colombian Constituent Assembly in 1990 (discussed in Chapter 9), where a court sanctioned the convocation of an extraordinary constitution-making body in direct violation of the constitution's amendment rule. The judges relied on the concept of constituent power to justify a departure from

[118] ibid. 79.

[119] It could be argued that in the Venezuelan case, the final ratificatory referendum could have been understood as a retroactive authorization to go beyond the established separation of powers. However, the assembly continued in session after the ratificatory referendum.

established constitutional law. Such a justification needed to go beyond the simple description of the proposed extra-legal means of constitutional change as an exercise of constituent power. The court needed to show that the chosen mechanism—a constituent assembly convened by referendum—could be presented as a legitimate means for constituent activity. That is to say, the court (both in Venezuela and Colombia) emphasized the democratic/participatory character of the process at issue, particularly when compared with the established rules of change, which left the amending power in the exclusive hands of legislative supermajorities. In those cases, as in situations where courts rely on the concept of constituent power to justify the establishment of limits on the amending power,[120] constituent power assumed a clear legal function.

Nevertheless, in the context of sanctioning informal means of constitutional replacement, constituent power plays the role of justifying the exercise of a (potentially unlimited) political power, not that of limiting the jurisdiction of a constituted (amending) authority. This justifying function, as noted earlier, depends in important ways on the nature of the mechanism at issue. The court, as it were, engages in a balancing exercise between the possibility of a more or less democratic act of constitution-making power and the supremacy of the constitution. It tries to find a solution to what the Colombian Constitutional Court has identified as 'the tension between the sovereign people and constitutional supremacy'.[121] In this sense, constituent power could be understood as a juridical principle that, although not part of positive law, in some cases allows courts to determine what acts should be attributed with legal validity.[122] Under this approach, the more a constitution-making process realizes what in Chapter 5 was identified as the principle of participation, the more open a court would be to sanction a violation of the constitution's rule of change.[123] Constitutions that allow for the convocation of a constituent assembly through popular initiative would seem to rule out such kinds of departures from established legality. These constitutions attempt to channel the exercise of the original constituent

[120] For some examples, see Chapter 8 of this book.

[121] Judgment C-551/03, Colombian Constitutional Court, para. 40.

[122] The principles of federalism, parliamentary sovereignty, democracy, and the rule of law, although not being positive law, have directly informed the views of courts, governments, and citizens about legal validity (see, e.g., *Reference re Secession of Quebec* [1998] 2 SCR 217; *Jackson v Attorney General* [2005] UKHL 56).

[123] The same could apply in the context of the doctrine of unconstitutional constitutional amendments: the more participatory the process of constitutional change, the less justified the court would be in invalidating its acts. For approaches that point in that direction, see Yaniv Roznai, *Unconstitutional Constitutional Amendments: The Limits of Amendment Powers* (Oxford University Press, 2017) and Carlos Bernal Pulido, 'Unconstitutional Constitutional Amendments in the Case Study of Colombia: An Analysis of the Justification and Meaning of the Constitutional Replacement Doctrine', 11(2) *International Journal of Constitutional Law* 339 (2013).

power through what appear as highly participatory procedures according to the standards of modern constitutionalism.[124]

All this rests on the assumption that in a system where judges have among their functions the limiting of political power with the purpose of protecting the constitutional order (i.e. the *oeuvre* of the constituent subject), courts should be understood as having jurisdiction to regulate in some way the exercise of constituent authority. From this perspective, as I have suggested earlier, courts could also intervene where a lawfully or unlawfully convened constitution-making body attempts to go beyond the conditions that arise from a constituent referendum. As noted in Chapter 9, there are two limits inherent in a commission to draft a constitution on behalf of the sovereign: the assembly has to actually draft a constitution (i.e. something that counts as a constitution in the society at issue) and respect the identity of the constituent subject (i.e. it cannot transform itself into a sovereign entity). As for the first limit, the task of drafting *a constitution* in a contemporary society would normally involve the creation of a document that establishes a democratic form of government, that separates powers, and that recognizes rights.[125] But the meaning of 'constitution' would ideally not be derived from a philosophical or theoretical analysis to be applied by a court.[126] In the best scenario, it would rather be confirmed by the citizens themselves in a ratificatory referendum. This is partly why, despite the many defects of referendums, it is makes sense to condition the validity of draft constitutions to popular ratification even if only to provide the electorate with an ultimate veto power.[127]

[124] It is always possible, however, that a more popular form of constitution-making is developed and, in such a scenario, that even the constituent assembly convened from below would be seen as an obstacle to democratic constitution-making.

[125] The comments of the Peruvian Constitutional Tribunal are interesting in this respect. In a 2003 decision, the court maintained that the validity of a constitution does not depend on whether it has been 'adopted by an organ invested with such a power and according to a legally established procedure'. Judgment No. 014-2003-AI/TC, Tribunal Constitucional del Perú, s 4, para 17. In contrast, a constitution is 'the result of the exercise of the Constituent Power, whose bearer is the People. In fact, no formal limits can be imposed to the Constituent Power because it is beyond the positive law; and, being an *extra ordinem* power, its foundation is to be located in itself and in the dominant social views'. ibid. The court nonetheless stated that not any document can count as a constitution. Not only the constitution must have been 'adopted by the Constituent Power . . . in its text, as expressed in Article 16 of the French Declaration of the Rights of Man and the Citizen, must at least minimally recognise and guarantee the essential rights of man, as well as the separation of powers, which are the primary values of a Constitutional State'. ibid.

[126] See Bernal Pulido (n. 124).

[127] In the absence of a referendum, a court could be put in the difficult position of invalidating an entire draft constitution. For a case in which a court reviewed the validity of a draft constitution (this time as part of a multi-stage constitution-making process), see *Certification of the Constitution of the Republic of South Africa* [1996] ZACC 26. It is worth noting that the Venezuelan Constitution of 1999 does not explicitly state that a referendum is required for the ratification of the work of a constituent assembly convened under Articles 347 and 348. Given the fact that a referendum is required for ordinary amendments to the constitutional text, the most reasonable interpretation is that the same

The second limit is about a preventing the assembly from becoming a sovereign. This involves, on the one hand, a prohibition on going beyond the conditions established in the relevant mandate (e.g. the adoption of particular constitutional content) and, on the other, a prohibition on exercising the ordinary powers of government. These two prohibitions are interconnected: the exercise of the ordinary powers of government would normally constitute a violation of the constitution-making body's commission. If a court embarks on the (admittedly dangerous) business of enforcing these prohibitions, they would do so to limit the jurisdiction of a constitution-making body. In so doing, the court would not be limiting the constituent subject but rather protecting it; making sure its mandate has been respected.[128] This authority, much more than that of reviewing statutes or constitutional amendments, would have to be exercised with great care. The purpose is not to negate a constitution-making body's jurisdiction to alter the material constitution but to ensure that it abides by any substantive limits contained in a referendum question. Since it may take place in a context of crisis and operate within the very limits of the constitutional order, this kind of review would arguably takes place in an extra-legal terrain. It is about an institution that, given its role during ordinary times, becomes the obvious organ to challenge abuses of power during a constitution-making episode.

Precisely for that reason, it should only be exercised in rare situations, and with attention to the entire nature of the constitution-making process at issue. For example, there could be instances where the attempt to exercise the ordinary powers of government may be part of an effort to comply with the mandate of creating a new constitution, as when a legislature actively interferes with the activities of a constituent assembly. In that type of case, it could be argued that the constituent assembly's commission comes accompanied by an implicit

would apply to an entirely new or fundamentally transformed constitution. Nonetheless, in light of the recent decisions of the Supreme Tribunal of Justice about the convocation of the Constituent Assembly of 2017, it is not entirely clear that this would happen in practice. For a discussion, see Chapter 9 of this book.

[128] Even in situations where the established constitution seeks to limit the powers of a constituent assembly, the court should remember that those limits arise from the very entity (the constituent people) that is now commissioning the constitution-making body. That is to say, those kinds of limits (limits that a constitutional text it imposes on a future constituent assembly) should not be judicially enforceable if inconsistent with the commission arising from a referendum question. For a judicial statement against the possibility of a court reviewing the actions of a constituent assembly, see Judgment No. 0168/2010-R, Tribunal Constitucional de Bolivia, part III(4): 'In fact, the decisions of the organ tasked with the control of constitutionality and, in particular, the *ratios decidendis* of constitutional judgments, are binding on the constituted powers at least before the new constitutional order is in place; however, the constituent function, given its originary, autonomous, extraordinary and extra-juridical character, cannot find itself subject to the decisions of this organ.'

authorization to engage in any juridical act that is necessary in order to carry out its mandate.[129] The best course of action in this situation could be a judicial indication that a new referendum should take place.[130] There may also be cases were the court disagrees with the assembly's interpretation of the content of an explicit limitation arising from the constituent referendum. For example, does a mandate to create a constitution that establishes a bicameral legislature require that both chambers have equal powers? In these kinds of cases, the exercise of judicial authority should arguably be highly deferential as long as the disagreement is a reasonable one. Moreover, in constitution-making processes where the draft constitution is to be subject to popular ratification, courts should be especially careful: the question of whether the specific conditions set by a constituent referendum have been respected are sometimes better left to the electorate itself.

V. Conclusion

This chapter examined the connections between the imperative mandate and constituent power, and their relevance for the contemporary world. It built on the distinction between sovereignty and constituent power (developed in the previous chapter) and in the legal implications of what I have called the constituent power of the people approach. I have argued that in cases where a new constitution is being produced or the material content of the existing one is being altered, the participation of the electorate through a referendum assumes a constituent nature. When a referendum is combined with the convocation of a constituent assembly to alter the constitution in fundamental ways, a constituent mandate emerges. A constituent mandate of that sort could be issued extra-constitutionally (as in Venezuela in 1999 and in Colombia in 1991) or, for example, according to the provisions of a constitution that allows for the popular initiative to convene a constituent assembly. To the extent that that kind of procedure is legally regulated, it could be argued that it is of a 'derived'

[129] John Alexander Jameson maintained that a constitutional convention was a 'mere committee, sitting for a specified purpose, under the express mandate of the sovereign, and possessed of such powers only as are expressly granted, *or as are necessary and proper for the execution of powers expressly granted*' (emphasis added). John Alexander Jameson, *Constitutional Conventions* (Chicago: Callaghan and Co., 1887) 302.

[130] The idea that acts that exceed the authority given by a sovereign should be subject to ratification was already present in Jean Bodin, who maintained that if an official 'exceeds his authority his acts have no validity whatsoever unless approved and confirmed by him from whom he draws his authority'. Jean Bodin, 'Concerning Sovereignty' in *Six Books of the Commonwealth* (Book 1, Chapter VIII) (Blackwell [1576]).

nature. However, given that it can result in the establishment of an entirely new constitutional order, it is better understood as involving a true exercise of constituent power.

When a constituent assembly is bound by a constituent mandate and its actions require popular ratification, it would be even less powerful than Rousseau's Legislator.[131] That is to say, it would not only be limited to proposing a constitution, but could also be bound to produce certain constitutional content. This is the case of the provisions in various Latin American constitutions that, by allowing the convocation of a constituent assembly through popular initiative, authorize the exercise of constituent power through law. Nonetheless, if such mechanism is accompanied by a doctrine of supra-constitutionality akin to that developed by Venezuela's highest court, sovereignty and constituent power would be conflated. Such an approach would also fail to realize one of the main legal implications of the notion of the constituent power of the people, that is, the ability of the electorate, the juridical people, to issue binding mandates. If the constitutional system at issue empowers courts to assess the validity of political acts against the established constitutional order, such a mandate (which will normally include an implicit requirement to respect the established separation of powers) could be judicially enforceable. The reason would not be that the assembly is bound by the constitution that it is supposed to replace, but that it has only been commissioned by the sovereign to prepare a draft constitutional text. In other words, of the court would be enforcing the distinction between sovereignty and constituent power.

[131] For a discussion of Rousseau's Legislator see Chapters 2 and 9 of this book.

11
Conclusion

This book has examined the development of the theory of constituent power and its role in constitutional scholarship and practice since the French Revolution, with the objective of bringing to the surface its legal and institutional implications. Each chapter has considered an aspect of the theory of constituent power: its origins, its functions in discussions at different constitution-making bodies, its different roles in constitutional theory and in judicial and political discourse. I began the analysis with a close reading of Jean Jacques Rousseau and Emmanuel Sieyès. From there, I moved to a discussion of the role of primary assemblies in different constitution-making episodes and of the fate of the imperative mandate after its abolition in 18th-century France. I then examined the embracement of the concept of national (as opposed to popular) sovereignty if different jurisdictions, explored the reception of the theory of constituent power in 19th-century constitutional discourse, and its rejection by the doctrinaires and by defenders of the historical constitution. The doctrine of the material constitution and its relationship to the idea that certain constitutional changes can only be adopted by the constituent subject was then considered, and a distinction between sovereignty and constituent power developed. From that distinction, I derived the notions of constituent referendums and enforceable constituent mandates.

What emerged from this analysis was a notion of constituent power as an eminently juridical concept, one that has legal and institutional implications and that can play a role in determinations of legal validity. These juridical functions were identified in the debates of constitution-making bodies in 19th-century Spain, Venezuela, and Colombia, in the works of a number of 19th-century authors rarely examined in contemporary constitutional theory (e.g. Jovellanos, Durán y Bas, Fernández Concha, Hello, Quimper, Lumbreras, Taparelli, Mellado, Laboulaye, Guizot, and Donoso Cortés), through a discussion and re-interpretation of key 20th-century works that develop the theory of constituent power (e.g. Jellinek, Carré de Malberg, Schmitt, Kelsen, Heller, and Mortati), and through the examination of the ways in which many of these ideas and debates are reflected in recent processes of constitutional change (e.g. Colombia 1991 and Venezuela 1999, 2017). Constituent power, we have seen,

Constituent Power and the Law. Joel Colón-Ríos, Oxford University Press (2020). © Joel Colón-Ríos.
DOI: 10.1093/oso/9780198785989.001.0001

has been understood as requiring primary assemblies with the authority of issuing binding instructions, legislatures with no jurisdiction to alter the constitutional text, an amending power that finds the material constitution as an insuperable limit, and with the possibility of legally valid although informal episodes of constitutional change.

These juridical functions sometimes appeared in the context of political argumentation (e.g. when politicians deploy the concept of constituent power to explain the nature of the powers of a constituent assembly) and sometimes in judicial/legal analysis (e.g. when courts rule on the legality of informally convened constitution-making bodies). Building on these findings, in the final chapters of the book I advanced an argument about the limits of the jurisdiction of a constitution-making body. When I began writing this book, I had no plan to develop that idea. Indeed, once I began to unearth early discussions about constituent power (particularly its connections with the imperative mandate), the book acquired a life of its own and the analysis took me towards an unanticipated terrain.[1] Constituent assemblies, I argued, should be understood as bound by any conditions arising from what I called a constituent referendum. In actual constitutional practice, however, constitution-making bodies have been too frequently attributed with sovereign power, as we saw in the cases of Spain under Franco and Chile under Pinochet, as well as in the formally democratic contexts of Colombia in 1991 and Venezuela in 1999 (and arguably, in 2017). In what follows, I will consider in more detail what I think the main insights of the book are and offer some thoughts about future avenues of research.

I. Constituent Power through Time

An important part of the previous ten chapters was devoted to exploring the place of the concept of constituent power in constitutional history and in the history of constitutional thought. To the extent possible, I tried to respect the chronological order attached to the materials under examination, and as a general rule I did not consider ideas and arguments in light of developments that would be discussed in later chapters. In what follows, I will try to reconstruct

[1] The views advanced in this book are, nonetheless, consistent with my main argument in *Weak Constitutionalism*. There, I maintained that a democratically legitimate constitutional regime required an opening for constituent power to manifest from time to time, and that such an opening could take the form of constituent assemblies convened by popular initiative. See Joel Colón-Ríos, *Weak Constitutionalism: Democratic Legitimacy and the Question of Constituent Power* (Routledge, 2012).

key elements of the analysis considering the findings of the book as a whole. As the reader will remember, the book begins in the late 18th century, when the main elements of the theory of constituent power were developed by Rousseau and where commentators and politicians of a Rousseauian persuasion identified a key implication that followed from it: constituent power required the direct popular ratification of constitutional changes (through legally convened primary assemblies or referendums) and the ability of primary assemblies to issue binding instructions. But these ideas were successfully rejected by Sieyès and his followers, who denounced the imperative mandate often relying on the concept of constituent power itself. For them, constituent power did not belong to the people or to a collection of popular assemblies. It belonged to an abstract entity called 'the nation', and what mattered was to create institutions capable of identifying the national will.

Under that view, what constituent power required was not legally convened local assemblies that would issue instructions potentially contrary to the national will, but a separation between representatives called to exercise the ordinary powers of government and those called to engage in the making and remaking of constitutional norms on behalf of the nation. The Sieyèsian approach, we saw, was reflected in important ways in early constitution-making processes in France, Venezuela, Spain, and Colombia (1886). In those processes, the idea of the constituent power of the nation emerged triumphant, and what mattered was to design processes of constitution-making in a way that ensured that only those citizens capable of identifying the national will would be put in a position to exercise constituent authority. The rest of the active citizenry could only exercise the *pouvoir commettant*, the power of electing those that would speak for the constituent nation. The theoretical disagreements between Rousseau and Sieyès are still reflected in contemporary constitutional theory and practice. Although there is no doubt that the Sieyèsian approach has prevailed (indeed, in contemporary constitutional theory, Rousseau is seldom even seen as a theorist of constituent power), some constitutional developments suggest a partial return to the Rousseauian approach.

For example, as we saw in Chapter 10, some national constitutions in the Latin American region have found a place for the imperative mandate in the context of constitutional change: the popular initiative to convene a constituent assembly for the replacement of the constitutional order. This mechanism also puts into practice another key Rousseauian idea: that the exercise of constituent power can (and should) be facilitated by law, an idea that Sieyès and his supporters rejected in the French Constitution of 1791 (and that was partially reflected in the French Constitution of 1793 and in the Girondin

Draft Constitution). The separation between the constituent and the constituted authority was consolidated by 19th-century constitutional theorists. For some authors, such as Laboulaye, this separation required the attribution of an exclusive jurisdiction to the constituent and the constituted authorities: in the same way a legislature is unable to produce constitutional law, a constituent assembly should be understood as unable to engage in the exercise of the ordinary functions of government. As seen in Chapter 6, 19th-century commentators frequently operated under constitutions that lacked an amendment rule, such as the French Charter of 1830 and the Spanish Constitution of 1837. In that context, to say that the legislature is unable to engage in constituent activity meant that constitutional change required an extra-legal act. From a Sieyèsian perspective, this was entirely consistent with the theory of constituent power.

Although for somewhat different reasons, defenders of the historical constitution and the doctrinaires (whose views were discussed in Chapter 7) found that idea highly objectionable. For the former, fundamental constitutional principles were not the product of an act of will but of history and tradition: the very notion of an extra-legal power that could make and unmake constitutional orders was to be rejected. Societies always preserved a Lockean right of resistance, but that was very different from saying that constitutions could be created and re-created at will. For the latter, constituent power only appeared in situations of emergency, and it belonged to whoever could exercise it in order to bring society to order. The rejection of the theory of constituent power by Spanish and French doctrinaires (such as Donoso Cortés and Guizot), and by defenders of the historical constitution (such as Jovellanos) led, in both cases, to a defence of parliamentary sovereignty similar to that present in orthodox English constitutional thought. That is to say, during normal times, the Crown-in-Parliament can legally produce any constitutional content, even though it would be expected to respect fundamental principles of justice as well as the basic elements of the constitutional tradition.

Despite being presented above in the context of conceptions that rejected the theory of constituent power, these views are sometimes reflected in contemporary approaches which embrace it. They are, to a large extent, the kind of views that drive contemporary arguments in favour of a limited amending power. As we saw in Chapter 8, for this latter argument to emerge, a key idea needed to be accepted: the notion that at least some changes to the constitutional text could be adopted by the ordinary institutions of government acting through a legally regulated process. Once that happened and ordinary amendment rules became a standard feature of written constitutions, the potential legal and institutional implications of constituent power grew considerably. Perhaps paradoxically, it was the extra-legal notion of constituent authority, the original constituent power, that most often performed the function of limiting political power. As exemplified in the historical and theoretical discussions found in Chapters 5, 6, and 8, it is when constituent authority is understood in this legally unregulated variant that it has been mostly deployed to impose constraints in the exercise of power. For example, my analysis of the notion of the material constitution in a number of 20th-century works (including that of Mortati, Schmitt, and Heller) showed that if such conceptions do not come accompanied by the recognition of an extra-legal constitution-making force, they can hardly justify the imposition of legal limits on the amending authority.

That is to say, in the absence of a recognition of an extra-legal constitution-making force, the amending authority would rather appear, as we saw in Chapter 1, as a derived constituent power that, just as the original one, can produce any constitutional content.[2] The same applies in a judicial context: the recognition of the people as the bearer of a legally uncontrollable constitution-making force is what legally justifies the imposition of limits on the amending authority. Even members of constituent bodies, as we saw in the debates that led to the adoption of the Spanish Constitution of 1845 (discussed in Chapter 7), have attempted to curb the power of the entities in which they sit by appealing to a political outside in which the true sovereign operates. These are situations where the idea (as opposed to the exercise) of original constituent power is presented as an insuperable limit to political action. At the same time, as seen in Chapter 10, the notion of original constituent authority has been deployed by courts to legally justify exercises of seemingly unlimited political power. This has sometimes occurred with the aim of legitimizing what would otherwise be democratic—but constitutionally irregular—constitution-making acts. In those contexts, judges have usually been careful to stress the participatory character of the procedures at issue.

A very different scenario occurs when dictatorial regimes deploy the notion of original constituent power in order to justify illegal departures from the constitutional system. Perhaps those cases should be understood as situations in which the language of constituent power has been illegitimately usurped. In Chapter 9, I examined two of those type of scenarios (Chile under Pinochet,

[2] As the analysis in Chapter 10 suggests, this is highly problematic: the exercise of the derived constituent power is not necessarily based in a commission from the sovereign but can originate in the will of the ordinary institutions of government.

and Spain under Franco), presenting them as examples of the conflation between sovereignty and constituent authority. But when deployed in contexts where basic democratic principles are respected, the extra-legal notion of constituent power, despite pointing toward an unlimited constitution-making force, more often than not works as a legal principle: it provides officials and citizens with standards of juridically acceptable behaviour. In contrast, when constituent power is understood as regulated by law, as a derived power bound to respect certain procedural rules or as indistinguishable from the ordinary legislative authority, it has mostly played the role of justifying a substantively incontrollable law-making force. As suggested earlier, this is exemplified in the work of authors (who frequently advanced these arguments as members of legislative bodies) associated with the doctrinaire and historical constitution's schools of thought: the negation of an extra-legal space where a popular constituent subject operates serves to justify the sovereign law-making faculty of legislatures that, although procedurally regulated, can insert any content into a constitutional system.

The concept of derived constituent power, despite usually being presented as a successful domestication of an unruly popular political force, is in fact frequently deployed in order to justify the unlimited political power of the state. In constitutions consistent with what I called 'the constituent power of the people' approach , the limiting and enabling functions of constituent power seem to come together: the possibility of legally convening a constituent assembly appears as a means for the exercise of an otherwise extra-legal power *and* as a limit to the ordinary power of constitutional reform. In these scenarios, the democratic nature of constituent activity is built into the constitutional order and the ordinary institutions of government are excluded from participating in its exercise. What is missing from that kind of approach, I argued in Chapters 9 and 10, is a distinction between sovereignty and constituent power. By developing this distinction and building on the latter's relationship with the imperative mandate, I argued that a constituent assembly must respect the separation of powers and can be made subject to substantive limits. These limits would normally be expressed through what I called a constituent referendum, an act of the people acting in a juridical capacity, that is, as an electorate. Thus, in addition to the limiting functions played by the concept in the previously mentioned contexts, its very exercise can be understood as subject to limits. But those limits would not be grounded in an appeal to abstract reason or natural law (as in the work of some of the authors discussed in Chapter 6) but in political practice.

II. The Road Ahead

Although in the last few years the literature on constituent power has grown exponentially, constitutional theorists are yet to fully explore the juridical nature of this concept. The main objective of this book was to bring to the surface that juridical nature, sometimes by re-interpreting known texts and events, sometimes by unearthing forgotten ones. Through the analysis, I focused on key debates and theoretical works, but the possibilities of exploring the relationship between constituent power and the law in different jurisdictions, at different historical moments, and from different perspectives, are unlimited. Each of the main legal functions and institutional implications of the theory of constituent power discussed through the book (the defence—or rejection of—the imperative mandate, primary assemblies, limited amending authorities, the sanctioning of informal episodes of constitutional change, enforceable constituent commissions) is, in a certain way, a world of its own. Each of them can be explored further both from the perspective of constitutional history, as well as in terms of their nature and potential for contemporary constitutional practice. In what follows, I briefly revisit these functions and suggest future avenues of research. My suggestions are tentative and are the product of intuitions and questions that arose as I wrote the book. In that sense, they are in some ways canvassed, although not developed, in some of the preceding chapters.

a. Imperative Mandate

The imperative mandate was rejected early in the history of modern constitutional thought. The reasons for that rejection were clearly expressed during the French Revolution as well as in 18th-century English constitutional discourse. The recognition of the constituent power of the people (as opposed to that of the nation) was nevertheless understood by some as requiring a citizenry able to issue binding instructions, particularly in the context of constitutional change. Several contemporary constitutions have embraced some form of the imperative mandate in the context of constitutional change, as exemplified in the popular initiative to convene a constituent assembly. Ratificatory referendums, in a way, can also be understood as having a key connection to binding instructions: they are the means through which citizens confirm that their formal or informal mandate has been respected. To what extent the origins of the popular initiative and the ratificatory referendum are connected to attempts to keep the institution of the imperative mandate alive? Is there a place for more radical forms of the imperative mandate in constitution-making and constitutional change? What would those forms of the imperative mandate require in terms of the electoral systems used to elect the members of a constitution-making body, and what are their implications in the context of ordinary constitutional change?

b. Primary Assemblies

Primary assemblies have a strong connection with the imperative mandate: it was the election of deputies in a pyramidal system with primary assemblies at the bottom that made the issuing of instructions possible in the first place. Nowadays, these entities have largely disappeared from constitutional practice. There is an immense amount of work to be done on the type of political practices that developed in and around primary assemblies, and on the connections between primary assemblies and other local deliberating and decision-making entities, such as the *cabildo abierto* (which is now recognized as a mechanism of popular participation in some Latin American constitutions). Moreover, from the perspective of constitutional design, a key question is whether there is a place for primary assemblies in contemporary constitutional change.[3] Are the arguments against attributing primary assemblies decision-making authority on the basis that their local character makes them inappropriate sites for the discussion of matters affecting an entire country as convincing as they appeared to 18th- and early 19th-century politicians? To what extent can technological developments address the practical difficulties surrounding the convocation of possibly thousands of primary assemblies with the potential ability of issuing binding instructions, and what new challenges or problems can these developments create? Are the multiple informal 'people's assemblies' been convened in the midst of massive protests in countries like Chile and Puerto Rico a symptom of the need to institutionalize older forms of popular engagement?

c. Limited Amending Power

The idea that the existence of an extra-legal constituent subject leads to an amending power that finds its limits in the material constitution is present in

[3] I briefly explored this question in Joel Colón-Ríos, 'Constituent Power, Primary Assemblies, and the Imperative Mandate', *Elgar Handbook of Comparative Constitution-Making* (Hanna Lerner and David Landau eds) (Edward Elgar, 2019).

most contemporary judicial and academic discussions about the doctrine of unconstitutional constitutional amendments. But the notion that there are some constitutional changes that, because of their content, are under the exclusive jurisdiction of the people is much older than this doctrine. It is even implicit in Rousseau's conception of a government that can only adopt decrees that do not affect the fundamental laws, the latter being only alterable by the sovereign people. It was also reflected in debates in constitution-making bodies in 18th-and 19th-century France and Spain and, to a certain extent, in the limits that natural lawyers thought applicable to the constituent authority. Can the contemporary doctrine of unconstitutional constitutional amendments be traced back to those early developments, or do those earlier conceptions rest on fundamentally different premises? There are also theoretical and practical questions around the adoption of the doctrine of unconstitutional constitutional amendments. For example, is the adoption of the doctrine of unconstitutional constitutional amendments appropriate in a system where there are no mechanisms for the exercise of the original constituent power?[4] And, what should those mechanisms be?

d. Legality of Informal Democratic Constitution-Making Processes

The sanctioning by courts of otherwise illegal, although relatively democratic, constitution-making processes, is now well documented in the literature and was also considered in some detail in Chapter 10 of this book. In a certain way, a similar approach was implicit in the work of the constitutional theorists (examined in Chapter 6)[5] who thought that the fact that a constitution lacked an amendment process meant that it could only be amended by an informally convened (and arguably more democratic) constitution-making body. Are these isolated examples or manifestations of a rich and now forgotten tradition? That is to say, are there any other historical examples where public law attributes legal validity to informal but participatory episodes of constitutional change? There are also questions about the role of constituent power in contemporary judgments assessing legal challenges against the attempted departure from the established rule of change. One would imagine that the

[4] This is in a certain way one of the main questions I addressed in *Weak Constitutionalism* (n. 1).

[5] Some 19th-and 20th-century North American authors also thought that the calling of constitutional conventions was legal even if not explicitly authorized by the constitutional text. For an overview, see Roger Sherman Hoar, *Constitutional Conventions: Their Nature, Power, and Limitations* (Kessinger Publishing, 1917).

more participatory a constitution-making process is (i.e. the more than it can be understood as reproducing a constituent act) and the more stringent the establishment amendment rule, the more likely a court would be to sanction a departure from the latter. In such a scenario, as mentioned in Chapter 10, the court would seem to be balancing constituent power and constitutional supremacy. What elements inform, or should inform, such a balancing act? There are also questions about the relationship of this type of constituent exercise and the right to self-determination, questions that are only becoming more urgent in present times, as the recent events in Cataluña suggest.

e. Enforceable Constituent Mandates

Constituent mandates or commissions, as conceived in Chapter 10, are a form of imperative mandate without primary assemblies. As the imperative mandate, they are based on the notion that the electors (even if acting through a referendum that takes place outside of primary assemblies) and not their representatives in a constitution-making body, are the sovereign authority. This conclusion follows from the distinction between sovereignty and constituent power. It also depends on the acceptance of the idea that the electorate can sometimes act as a state organ, and sometimes as the sovereign. To what extent is this conception tenable in light of the deficiencies of the referendum as a mechanism of popular participation? In the cases I discussed in Chapter 10, courts did not adopt the previously mentioned distinction between constituent and sovereign authority, and ultimately attributed sovereignty to a constituent assembly. But these were also cases in which the relevant countries were experiencing serious political crises and situations of emergency. In such instances, the notion of a constituent commission may appear as a theoretical luxury rather than as a realistic or desirable legal limit on a constitution-making body. Is the exercise of constituent power so connected to emergency scenarios that any attempt to make it subject to substantive limits is destined to fail? How common is the exercise of constituent activity (understood as resulting in fundamental constitutional changes) outside the context of a political crisis?

III. Final Words: Constituent Power as Law?

The legal and institutional implications that emerged through the book suggest a conception of constituent power as an eminently juridical concept, one that can play a key role in determinations of legal validity and that places important demands on constitutional orders. The full extent and limits of that idea, as suggested above, will have to be explored in future works. Understanding constituent power as a juridical concept capable of placing limits on the constituent authorities opens the way for radical forms of political participation: if there are things that the ordinary institutions of government, even meeting special thresholds, cannot do, then it will be necessary to channel the exercise of constituent power through participatory mechanisms of constitutional change. At the same time, however, reconceiving constituent power as a juridical concept can arguably deprive it of its most contestatory elements: its connections to the right of resistance, to popular revolutions, and to the overthrow of unjust regimes. The approach presented in Chapter 10, which involves the imposition of substantive limits to constitution-making bodies, is susceptible to this critique. But rather than domesticate an otherwise revolutionary concept, this approach seeks to realize its radical democratic potential: that, as in Rousseau, it is the sovereign people, and not its representatives, who must determine the content of the fundamental laws. If those limits are not respected, the constitution-making body would, as Napoleon, be crowning itself as the true sovereign.

Bibliography

Abat i Ninet, A., 'The Messianic Thought of the Rule of Law', 47(3) *Philosophia* 733–755 (2019).

Adams, S., 'Massachusetts Circular Letter to the Colonial Legislatures' (11 February 1768).

Albert, R., *Constitutional Amendments: Making, Breaking, and Changing Constitutions* (Oxford: Oxford University Press, 2019).

Alcalá Galiano, A., *Lecciones de Derecho Político Constitucional* (Imp. de I. Boix: Madrid, 1843).

Allison, J. W. F., *The English Historical Constitution: Continuity, Change and European Effects* (Cambridge: Cambridge University Press, 2007).

Althusius, J., *Politica: Politics Methodically St Forth and Illustrated with Sacred and Profane Examples* (Indianapolis: Liberty Fund, 1995 [1614]).

'An Essay on Natural Liberty', *The London Magazine or, Gentleman's Monthly Intelligencer*, Vol. XXXVIII (1769).

Antraigues, E., Mémoire sur les Etats-généraux, leurs Droits, et la Manière de les Convoquer (1788).

Arango, R., 'La Construcción de la Nacionalidad' in *Miguel Antonio Caro y la Cultura de su Época* (Rubén Sierra Mejía ed.) (Bogotá: Universidad Nacional de Bogotá, 2002).

Arato, A., 'Conventions, Constituent Assemblies, and Round Tables: Models, Principles and Elements of Democratic Constitution-Making', 1(1) *Global Constitutionalism* 173–200 (2012).

Arato, A., *Adventures of the Constituent Power: Beyond Revolutions?* (Cambridge: Cambridge University Press, 2017).

Argüelles, A. G., *Discurso Preliminar a la Constitución de 1812* (24 December 1811) (Madrid: Centro de Estudios Políticos y Constitucionales, 2011).

Atria, F, *La Constitución Tramposa* (Santiago: LOM Ediciones, 2013).

Ayuso, M., 'El Problema Religioso y el Problema Político en la Historia Contemporánea de España (A Propósito de Luis de Trelles)', 4 *Anales de la Fundación Francisco Elías de Tejada* 79–97 (1998).

Baker, K. M., 'Constitution' in *The French Revolution: Recent Debates and New Controversies* (Gary Kates ed.), 2nd ed. (New York: Routledge, 2006).

Balmés, J., 'Sobre el Dictámen de la Comisión del Congreso', 41 *El Pensamiento de la Nación: Periódico Religioso, Político y Literario* 641–645 (13 November 1844).

Barrios Benatuil, A. G., González Plessmann, A., and Grajales Pineda, M. L., 'Constituyentes Venezolanas de 1999 y 2017: Contextos y Participación', 8(4) *Revista Direito e Práxis* 3144–3168 (2017).

Barthélémy, J., 'La Distinction des Lois Constitutionnelles et des Lois Ordinaires sous la Monarchie de Juillet', 26 *Revue de Droit Public* 7–47 (1909).

Bashkina, O., 'Raymond Carré de Malberg and the Interpretation of Sovereignty in the Belgian Constitution', 35 *Journal of Constitutional History* 149–166 (2018).

Beaud, O., *La Puissance de l'État* (Paris: PUF, 1994).

Bermejo Cabrero, J. L., 'La Junta de Protección de la Libertad de Imprenta durante el Trienio Liberal', 68 *Anuario de Historia del Derecho Español* 11–44 (1998).
Bernal Pulido, C., 'Unconstitutional Constitutional Amendments in the Case Study of Colombia: An Analysis of the Justification and Meaning of the Constitutional Replacement Doctrine', 11(2) *International Journal of Constitutional Law* 339–357 (2013).
Bernal Pulido, C., 'Prescindamos del Poder Constituyente en la Creación Constitucional: Los Límites Conceptuales del Poder para Reemplazar o Reformar una Constitución', 22 *Anuario Iberoamericano de Justicia Constitucional* 59–99 (2018).
Berriat-Saint-Prix, F., *Théorie du Droit Constitutionnel Français: Esprit des Constitutions de 1848 et de 1852 et des Sénatus-Consultes Organiques Précédé d'un Essai sur le Pouvoir Constituant* (Paris, 1851).
Bertram, C., 'Jean Jacques Rousseau', *Stanford Encyclopaedia of Philosophy* (2010).
Bertauld, C.-A., *Du Pouvoir Constituant de L'Assemblée Nationale* (Paris, 1871).
Böckenförde, E.-W., 'El Poder Constituyente del Pueblo: Un Concepto Límite del Derecho Constitucional' in *Estudios sobre el Estado de Derecho y la Democracia* (Madrid: Editorial Trotta, 2000).
Böckenförde, E.-W., Künkler, M., and Stein, T., *Constitutional and Political Theory: Selected Writings* (Oxford: Oxford University Press, 2017).
Bodin, J., 'Concerning Sovereignty' in *Six Books of the Commonwealth* (Book 1, Chapter VIII) (Blackwell [1576]).
Bodin, J., *On Sovereignty: Four Chapters from the Six Books of the Commonwealth* (Julian Franklin ed.) (Cambridge: Cambridge University Press, 1992).
Bonnard, R., *El Derecho y el Estado en la Doctrina Nacional-Socialista* (José M. Pi Suñer trans.) (Barcelona, Bosch, 1950).
Braxton, A. C., 'Power of Conventions', 7(2) The *Virginia Law Register* 79 (1901).
Brewer-Carías, A. R., *Poder Constituyente Originario y Asamblea Nacional Constituyente* (Caracas: Editorial Jurídica Venezolana, 1999).
Brewer-Carías, A. R., 'Sobre el Inicio del Constitucionalismo en América Hispana en 1811, antes de la Sanción de la Constitución de Cádiz de 1812', 17 *Pensamiento Constitucional* 45–78 (2012).
Brewer-Carías, A. R., *Historia Constitucional de Venezuela* (Caracas: Editorial Jurídica Venezolana, 2013).
Brewer-Carías, A. R., 'La Independencia de Venezuela y el Inicio del Constitucionalismo Hispanoamericano en 1810-1811, Como Obra de Civiles, y el Desarrollo del Militarismo a Partir de 1812 en Ausencia de Régimen Constitucional', 14 *Historia Constitucional* 405–424 (2013).
Bridge, W., *The Wounded Conscience Cured* (B. Allen, 1642).
Brissot, J.-P., 'Plan de Conduite pour les Députés du Peuple aux Etats-Généraux de 1789' (April 1789).
Brissot, J.-P., 'Le Patriote François', 5 *Journal Libre, Impartial et National* (1789).
Brookfield, F. M., 'Parliamentary Supremacy and Constitutional Entrenchment: A Jurisprudential Approach', 5 *Otago Law Review* 603–634 (1984).
Brunet, P., 'Les Contraintes de la Représentation en 1793: sur la Distinction des Lois et des Décrets et sa Justification' in *Théorie des Contraints Juridiques, Sous la Dir* (M. Troper, V. Champeil-Desplats eds) (Paris: Paris-Bruxelles, 2005).
Burdeau, G., *Derecho Constitucional e Instituciones Políticas* (Ramón Falcón Tello trans.) (Madrid: Editorial Nacional, 1981).

Burdeau, G., *Tratado de Ciencia Política: Presentación del Universo Político—El Orden Social y la Idea de Derecho* (Enrique Serna Elizondo trans.) (México: UNAM, 1982 [1949]) Title I, Vol. II.
Burdeau, G., *Tratado de Ciencia Política: El Estado—La Formación del Estado* (Enrique Serna Elizondo trans.) (México: UNAM, 1982 [1949]) Title II, Vol. I.
Burdeau, G., *Traité de Science Politique* (Paris: LDGJ, 1983) vol. IV.
Burgh, J., *Political disquisitions: Or, An Enquiry into Public Errors, Defects, and Abuses* (Philadelphia, 1775) (Book 3).
Burke, E., 'Speech to the Electors of Bristol' (3 November 1774), *The Works of the Right Honourable Edmund Burke*. 6 vols (London: Henry G. Bohn, 1854–1856).
Burke, E., *Reflections on the Revolution of France* (Penguin Classics, 1986).
Bushnell, D., *Las Elecciones en Colombia: Siglo XIX* (Credencial Historia, 1994).
C.A.D., 'The Jurisdiction of a Court of Equity over Constitutional Conventions', 6(1) *Michigan Law Review* 70–72 (1907).
Cadart, J., *Le Régime Électoral des États Généraux de 1789 et ses Origines (1302-1614)* (Paris, 1952).
Caldwell, P., *Popular Sovereignty and the Crisis of German Constitutional Law: The Theory and Practice of Weimar Constitutionalism* (Durham: Duke University Press, 1997).
Calvo, A. P., *El Estado Constitucional Español* (Madrid, 2014).
Cardona, P., and Céspedes, C., 'Cerbeleón Pinzón y la Paz Pública', 13–22*Revista Coherencia* 13 (2017).
Caro, M. A., *Escritos Políticos. Primera Serie* (Bogotá: Instituto Caro y Cuervo, 1990).
Carré de Malberg, R., *Contribución a la Teoría General del Estado* (Mexico: Fondo de Cultura Económica, 1948).
Carré de Malberg, R., *Teoría General del Estado* (México: Fondo de Cultura Económica, 1948).
Carré de Malberg, R., *La Ley, Expresión de la Voluntad General: Estudio sobre el Concepto de la Ley en la Constitución de 1875* (Madrid: Marcial Pons, 2011).
Casals Bergés, Q., 'El Proceso Electoral en España y Cataluña según la Constitución de 1812', 1(1) *Rúbrica Contemporánea* 5–28 (2012).
Casals Bergés, Q., 'Proceso Electoral y Prosopografía de los Diputados de las Cortes Extraordinarias de Cádiz (1810-1813)', 13 *Historia Constitucional* 193–231 (2012).
Casals Bergés, Q., 'Los Diputados Catalanes en las Cortes de Cádiz (1810-1813): Proceso Electoral y Prosopografía)', 31 *Manuscrits* 205–237 (2014).
Cebreiro Núñez, J. I., *La Administración Peiférica Provincial: Orígenes y Evolución al Final del Antiguo Régimen* (Madrid: Tirant, 2017).
Chavarri Sidera, P., *Las Elecciones de Diputados a las Cortes Generales y Extraordinarias (1810-1813)* (Madrid: Centro de Estudios Constitucionales, 1988).
Chiaramonte, J. C., *Usos Políticos de la Historia: Lenguaje de Clases y Revisionismo Histórico* (Buenos Aires: Editorial Sudamericana, 2013).
Cobban, A., 'The Political Ideas of Maximilien Robespierre during the Period of the Convention' 61 *English Historical Review* 45–80 (1946).
Cobban, A., *A History of Modern France—Volume 1: 1715-1799* (Penguin Books, 1963).
Cogollos Amaya, S. and Ramírez León, J., 'Perspectiva Histórica del Cabildo Abierto: Una Forma de Participación Ciudadana', 8(16) *Memoria y Sociedad* 41 (2004).
Cohen, J., *Rousseau: A Free Community of Equals* (Oxford: Oxford University Press, 2010).
Colegrove, M. *Distant Voices: Listening to the Leadership Lessons of the Past. Napoleon Bonaparte's Maxims, Quotes and Life in His Own Words*, 15 May 1804 (New York: iUniversity, 2005).

Colón-Ríos, J. I., 'Carl Schmitt and Constituent Power in Latin American Courts: The Cases of Venezuela and Colombia', 18(3) *Constellations* 365 (2011).
Colón-Ríos, J. I., *Weak Constitutionalism: Democratic Legitimacy and the Question of Constituent Power* (Routledge, 2012).
Colón-Ríos, J. I., 'Five Conceptions of Constituent Power', 130 *Law Quarterly Review* 306–336 (2014).
Colón-Ríos, J. I., 'Rousseau, Theorist of Constituent Power', 36(4) *Oxford Journal of Legal Studies* 885–908 (2016).
Colón-Ríos, J. I., 'Constitution-Making and Constituent Power' in *Comparative Constitutional in Latin America* (Dixon and Ginsburg eds) (Edward Elgar, 2017).
Colón-Ríos, J. I., 'Constituent Power, Primary Assemblies, and the Imperative Mandate' in *Handbook on Comparative Constitution-Making* (David Landau and Hannah Lerner eds) (Edward Elgar, 2019).
Combellas, R., *¿Qué es la Constituyente? Voz para el Futuro de Venezuela* (COPRE: Caracas, 1998).
Combellas, R., 'El Proceso Constituyente y la Constitución de 1999', 30 *Politeia* 183–208 (2003).
Conde García, F. J., *Contribución a la Doctrina del Caudillaje* (Madrid: Ediciones de la Vicesecretaría de Educación Popular, 1952).
Conde García, F. J., *Escritos y Fragmentos Políticos* (Madrid: Colección Ciencia Política, 1974).
Conrad, D., 'Limitation of Amendment Procedures and the Constituent Power', 15–16 *Indian Year Book of International Affairs* 347 (1970).
Coronas González, S. M., 'Las Leyes Fundamentales del Antiguo Régimen', 81 *Anuario de Historia del Derecho Español* 11–82 (2011).
Cottu, C., *De la Nécessité d'une Dictature* (Paris 1830).
Craiutu, A., *Liberalism under Siege: The Political Thought of the French Doctrinaires* (Maryland: Lexington Books, 2003).
Craiutu, A., 'Rethinking Political Power: The Case of the French Doctrinaires', 2(2) *European Journal of Political Theory* 125–155 (2003).
Cristi, R., *El Pensamiento Político de Jaime Guzmán: Autoridad y Libertad* (Santiago: LOM Ediciones, 2000).
Cristi, R., 'The Metaphysics of Constituent Power: Carl Schmitt and the Genesis of Chile's 1980 Constitution', 21 *Cardozo Law Review* 1749–1775 (2000).
Crook, M., *Elections in the French Revolution: An Apprenticeship in Democracy, 1789-1799* (Cambridge: Cambridge University Press, 1996).
Cuesta, S., *Elementos de Derecho Político* (Salamanca, 1887).
de la Calle, H., *Contra todas las Apuestas: Historia Íntima de la Constituyente de 1991* (Bogotá: Editorial Planeta, 2004).
de Vega, P., *La Reforma Constitucional y la Problemática del Poder Constituyente* (Madrid: Técnos, 1985).
Defoe, D., *The Original Power of the Collective Body of the People of England, Examined and Asserted* (London, 1702).
Defoe, D., *A Collection of Original Papers Concerning the Union Between England and Scotland* (Printed for E. Curll: London, 1709).
del Corral, L. D., *El Liberalismo Doctrinario* (Madrid: Instituto de Estudios Políticos, 1973).
Delarue, F., *Du Pouvoir Constituant et du Principe Souverain, d'après M. de Cormenin, au sujet de la Charte de 1830* (Paris: Levavasseur, 1831).

Dicey, A. V., *Introduction to the Study of the Law and the Constitution* (London: Macmillan, 1959).
Dicey, A. V., *Introduction to the Study of the Law of the Constitution* (Indianapolis: Liberty Classics, 1982).
Dixon, R., 'Constitutional Amendment Rules: A Comparative Perspective' in *Comparative Constitutional Law* (Tom Ginsburg and Rosalind Dixon eds.) (Cheltenham: Edward Elgar, 2011).
Donís, Ríos 'Los diputados de la provincia de Mérida al Supremo Congreso de Venezuela de 1811', 71 *ACTUAL Investigación* 119–149 (2012).
Donoso Cortés, J., *Consideraciones sobre la Diplomacia* (Madrid, 1834).
Donoso Cortés, J., 'Polémica con el Doctor Rossi y Juicio Crítico acerca de los Doctrinarios', 3 *El Correo Nacional*, vol. 3, 441(1838).
Donoso Cortés, J., 'Discurso sobre la Dictadura' (4 de enero de 1849).
Donoso Cortés, J., Dictámen de la Comisión de la Reforma de la Constitución de 1837 (5 November 1844) in *Obras de Don Juan Donoso Cortés* (Marqués de Valdegamas ed.) (Madrid, 1854).
Donoso Cortés, J., *Obras* (Madrid, Imprenta de Tejado, 1954).
Donoso Cortés, J., 'Polémica con Rossi' in *Obras Completas de Juan Donoso Cortés* (Madrid: Biblioteca de Autores Cristianos, 1970).
Doyle, W., *The Oxford History of the French Revolution* (Oxford: Oxford University Press, 2002).
Durán y Bas, M., *Estudios Políticos y Económicos* (Barcelona: Imprenta de Antonio Brusi, 1856).
Duvergier de Hauranne, P., *Histoire du Gouvernement Parlementaire en France: 1814-1848* (Paris 1871) vol. 10.
Duguit, L., *Manual de Derecho Constitucional* (Granada: Comares, 2005).
Duguit, L., *Lecciones de Derecho Público General* (Madrid: Marcial Pons, 2011).
Dyzenhaus, D, *Legality and Legitimacy: Carl Schmitt, Hans Kelsen and Hermann Heller in Weimar* (Oxford: Oxford University Press, 2003).
Edelstein, M., *The French Revolution and the Birth of Electoral Democracy* (Ashgate, 2014).
Elorza, A., 'La Formación del Liberalismo en España' in *Historia de la Política, vol. III: Ilustración, Liberalismo y Nacionalismo* (Fernando Vallespín ed.) (Madrid: Editorial Alianza, 1991).
Emden, C. S., *The People and the Constitution: Being a History of the Development of the People's Influence in British Government* (Oxford: Clarendon Press, 1956).
Escudero, J. A., 'Introducción. Las Cortes de Cádiz: Génesis, Constitución y Reformas' in *Cortes y Constitución de Cádiz 200 años* (José Antonio Escudero ed.) (Espasa: Madrid, 2011).
Falleti, E., 'La Democracia Directa y la Prohibición del Mandato Vinculante', 14(1) *Revista Jurídica Piélagus* 59–72 (2015).
Ferguson, A., *An Essay on the History of Civil Society* (Philadelphia, 1819).
Fernández-Carvajal, R., 'Las Constantes de Donoso', 95 *Revista de Estudios Políticos* 75 (1957).
Fernández Concha, R., *Filosofía del Derecho, o Derecho Natural Dispuesto para Servir de Introducción a las Ciencias Legales*, vol. 2 (Barcelona, 1888).
Fernández Sarasola, I., *El Pensamiento Político de Jovellanos: Seis Estudios* (Oviedo, In Itinere, 2011).
Fernández Sarasola, I., *La Constitución de Cádiz: Orígen, Contenido y Proyección Internacional* (Madrid: Centro de Estudios Políticos y Constitucionales, 2011).

Fernández Sarasola, I., '"Soyou want us to be Englishmen . . .": Jovellanos and British Influence on Spain's First Modern Parliament (1808-1810)', 4(1) *Comparative Legal History* 51–81 (2016).
Fernández Segado, F., 'Partidos Políticos: Representación Parlamentaria e Interdicción del Mandato Imperativo', 2(2) *Revista Pensamiento Constitucional* 29–57 (1995).
Figueroa, J. L., 'Apuntes para Servir a la Historia Contemporánea: La Legislatura de 1843', 3 *Revista de Madrid* 121–145 (1844).
Figueroa, N., *A Critique of Populist Jurisprudence: Courts, Democracy, and Constitutional Change in Colombia and Venezuela* (New York: New School Doctoral Dissertation, 2006).
Fonteneau, M., *Du Pouvoir Constituant en France et de la Révision Constitutionnelle dans les Constitutions Françaises depuis 1789* (Caen, 1900).
Forsyth, M., *Reason and Revolution: The Political Thought of Abbé Sieyes* (New York: Leicester University Press, 1987).
Fox, B., 'Schmitt's Use and Abuse of Donoso Cortés on Dictatorship', 23(2) *Intellectual History Review* 159–185 (2013).
Frank, J., *Constituent Moments: Enacting the People in Postrevolutionary America* (Durham: Duke University Press 2010).
Franklin, J. H., *John Locke and the Theory of Sovereignty: Mixed Monarchy and the Right of Resistance in the Political Thought of the English Revolution* (Cambridge: Cambridge University Press, 1978).
Franklin, J., 'Sovereignty and the Mixed Constitution: Bodin and his Critics' in J. H. Burns (ed.) *The Cambridge history of Political Thought, 1450-1700*, (Cambridge: Cambridge University Press, 1991).
Fridieff, M., *Les Origines du Referendum dans la Constitution de 1793* (Paris: Les Presses Universitaires de France, 1932).
Friedland, P., *Political Actors: Representative Bodoes & Theatricality in the Age of the French Revolution* (Cornell University Press, 2002).
Friedrich, C. J., *Constitutional Government and Democracy: Theory and Practice in Europe and America* (Blaisdell Publishing Company, 1968).
Fritz, C., *American Sovereigns: The People and America's Constitutional Tradition before the Civil War* (Cambridge: Cambridge University Press, 2001).
García, J.F. and Verdugo, S., 'Un Camino a la Constitución de 2020: Un Proceso Constituyente que Una y no Divida a los Chilenos' in La Solución Constitucional: Plebiscitos, Asambleas, Congresos, Sorteos y Mecanismos Híbridos (Claudio Fuentes and Alfredo Joignant eds) (Santiago de Chile: Catalonia, 2017).
García Gestoso, N., 'La Reforma de la Constitución de Cádiz: Algunas Consideraciones a Propósito de la Defensa de la Constitución', 29 *Civitas Europa* 53–77 (2012).
Gargarella, R., *Latin American Constitutionalism: 1810-2010: The Engine Room of the Constitution* (Oxford: Oxford University Press, 2013).
Garner, J. W., 'Amendment of State Constitutions', 1(2) *American Political Science Review* 213–247 (1907).
G.F.G, *Le Pouvoir Électoral* (Paris, 1872).
Gieysztorowa, I., 'Research into the Demographic History of Poland: A Provisional Summing-Up', 18 *Acta Polonia Historica* 5 (1963).
Goldoni, M. and Croce, M., *The Legacy of Pluralism: The Continental Jurisprudence of Santi Romano, Carl Schmitt, and Costantino Mortati*(Stanford: Stanford University Press, 2020).
Goldoni, M. and Wilkinson, M. A., 'The Material Constitution', 81(4) *Modern Law Review* 567 (2018).

Goldsworthy, J., *Parliamentary Sovereignty: Contemporary Debates* (Cambridge: Cambridge University Press, 2010).
Gómez Álvarez, C. and Tovar de Teresa G., *Censura y Revolución: Libros Prohibidos por la Inquisición de México* (1790-1819) (Trama Editorial y Consejo de la Crónica de la Ciudad de México, 2009).
Gómez Mampaso, M. V., 'La Convocatoria de las Cortes y los Diputados Presentes en la Sesión de Apertura el 24 de septiembre de 1810' in *Cortes y Constitución de Cádiz 200 años* (José Antonio Escudero ed.) (Espasa: Madrid, 2011).
Gough, J. W., *Fundamental Law in English Constitutional History* (Oxford: Clarendon Press, 1955).
Gözler, K., *Pouvoir Constituant* (Bursa: Ekin Kitabevi, 1999).
Gözler, K., *Pouvoir Constituant* (Bursa: Ekin Kitabevi, 2004).
Gueniffey, P., *La Revolución Francesa y las Elecciones: Democracia y Representación a Fines del Siglo XVIII* (México: Fondo de Cultura Económica, 2001).
Guizot, F., *Histoire des Origines du Gouvernement Représentatif en Europe* (Paris, 1851).
Guizot, F., *Mémoires pour Servir a L'Histoire de mon Temps* (Paris, 1865) vol. 7.
Guizot, F., *Historia de los Orígenes del Gobierno Representativo en Europa* (KRK Ediciones, 2009).
Guyomar, P., *Le Partisan de L'égalité Politique entre les Individus, ou Problème Très-Important de Légalité en Droits etde L'inégalité en Fait* (1793).
Häberle, P., *El Estado Constitucional* (Buenos Aires: Editorial Astrea, 2007).
Hauriou, M., *Précis de Droit Constitutionnel*, 2nd ed. (Paris: Recueil Sirey, 1929).
Hauriou, M., *Principios de Derecho Público y Constitucional* (Carlos Ruiz del Castillo trans.) (Granada: Editorial Comares, 2003).
Hauriou, M., *La Soberanía Nacional* (Madrid: Marcial Pons, 2013).
Hébrard, V., 'Opinión Pública y Representación en el Congreso Constituyente de Venezuela (1811-1812)' in *Los Espacios Públicos en Iberoamérica* (François-Xavier Guerra ed.) (Centro de Estudios Mexicanos y Centroamericanos, 2008).
Heller, H., *La Soberanía: Contribución a la Teoría del Derecho Estatal y el Derecho Internacional* (Mario de la Cueva trans.) (Mexico: UNAM, 1965).
Heller, H., *Teoría del Estado* (Luis Tobío trans.) (Mexico: Fondo de Cultura Económica, 2012).
Heller, H., *Sovereignty: A Contribution to the Theory of Public and International Law* (David Dyzenhaus, ed.) (Oxford: Oxford University Press, 2019).
Hello, C. G., *Du Régime Constitutionnel* (Paris, 1848) vol. 2.
Hermann González, S. J., 'Conversación sobre la Iglesia en la crisis del siglo XIX', 3(6) *Boletín CIHEV* 114 (1991).
Hoar, R. S., *Constitutional Conventions: Their Nature, Power, and Limitations* (Kessinger Publishing, 1917).
Hobbes, T., *Leviathan* (Penguin Books, 1985).
Holcombe, A. N., *State government in the United States* (New York: MacMillan Company, 1916).
Hörcher, F., 'Is the Historical Constitution of Hungary Still a Living Tradition? A Proposal for Reinterpretation' in *The Concept of Constitution in the History of Political Thought* (Arkadiusz Górnisiewicz and Bogdan Szlachta eds) (De Gruyter, 2017).
Inness, W. C., *Social Concern in Calvin's Geneva* (Pittsburgh Theological Monographs, 1983).
Jackson, V., 'The (Myth of the Un) Amendability of the US Constitution and the Democratic Component of Constitutionalism', 13(3) *International Journal of Constitutional Law* 575–605 (2015).

Jameson, J. A., *A Treatise on Constitutional Conventions: Their History, Powers, and Modes of Proceeding* (Chicago: Callaghan and Company, 1887).
Jameson, J. A., 'Constitutional Conventions' in *Cyclopaedia of Political Science, Political Economy, and of the Political History of the United States* (John J. Lalor ed.) (New York: Charles E. Meeril and Co., 1899) vol. 1.
Jefferson, T., *Writings* (Merrill Peterson ed.) (New York, Library of America, 1984).
Jellinek, G., *Allgemeine Staatslehre* (Berlin, 1905).
Jellinek, G., *Teoría General del Estado* (México: Fondo de Cultura Económica, 2012).
Jennings, J., 'Constitutional Liberalism in France: From Benjamin Constant to Alexis de Tocqueville' in *The Cambridge History of Nineteenth-Century Political Thought* (Gareth Stedman Jones and Gregory Claeys eds) (Cambridge: Cambridge University Press, 2011).
Johnson, D., *Guizot: Aspects of French History 1787-1874* (University of Toronto Press, 1963).
Johnstone, A., 'The Constitutional Initiative in Montana', 71 *Montana Law Review* 325–382 (2010).
Jones, C., *The Longman Companion to the French Revolution* (Routledge, 1998).
Jovellanos, G. M. D., *Memoria sobre Educación Pública, o sea Tratado Teórico Práctico de Enseñanza* in *Obras Públicas e Inéditas* (Madrid: Biblioteca de Autores Españoles, 1858) vol. 1.
Jovellanos, G. M. D., 'Carta a Antonio Fernández de Prado' (Gijón, 7 December 1795) in *Obras Completas* (Oviedo: Centro de Estudios del Siglo CVIII, 1986) vol. III.
Jovellanos, G. M. D., *Memoria en Defensa de la Junta Central*, vol. 5.
Kalyvas, A., 'Popular Sovereignty, Democracy, and the Constituent Power', 12(2) *Constellations* 223–244 (2005).
Kalyvas, A., *Democracy and the Politics of the Extraordinary: Max Weber, Carl Schmitt and Hannah Arendt* (Cambridge: Cambridge University Press, 2008).
Kalyvas, A., 'Constituent Power', *Political Concepts: A Critical Lexicon 3.1* (Winter 2013).
Kelly, C., " 'To Persuade without Convincing": The Language of Rousseau's Legislator', 31(2) *American Journal of Political Science* 321–335 (1987).
Kelly, D., 'Revisiting the Rights of Man: Georg Jellinek on Rights and the State', 22(3) *Law and History Review* 493–529 (2004).
Kelly, D., 'Egon Zweig and the Intellectual History of Constituent Power' in *Constitutionalism, Legitimacy, and Power* (Kelly L. Grotke and Markus J. Prutsch eds) (Oxford: Oxford University Press, 2014).
Kelsen, H., *General Theory of Law and State* (Harvard University Press, 1949).
Kelsen, H., 'The Function of a Constitution' in *Essays on Kelsen* (Richard Tur et al. eds) (Clarendon Press: Oxford, 1986).
Kelsen, H., *Teoría Pura del Derecho* (Moisés Nilve trans.) (Eudeba: Buenos Aires, 2009).
Klein, C., *Théorie et Pratique du Pouvoir Constituant* (PUF, 1996).
Klein, C., 'La Découverte de la Doctrine Française du Pouvoir Constituant en Allemagne: de l'Empire à la République Fédérale' in *La Science Juridique Française et la Science Juridique Allemande de 1870 à 1917* (Olivier Beaud and Patrick Wadesmann eds) (Strasbourg: PUS 1997).
Kobach, K. W., 'May 'We the People' Speak?: The Forgotten Role of Constituent Instructions in Amending the Constitution', 33 *U.C. Davis Law Review* 1–87 (1999).
Kriele, M., *Introducción a la Teoría del Estado: Fundamentos Históricos de la Legitimidad del Estado Constitucional Democrático* (Eugenio Bulygin trans.) (Buenos Aires: Ediciones Depalma, 1980).
Krishnaswamy, S., *Democracy and Constitutionalism in India: A Study of the Basic Structure Doctrine* (New Delhi:Oxford University Press, 2011).

Kwass, M., *Privilege and the Politics of Taxation in Eighteenth-Century France: Liberté, Egalité, Fiscalité* (Cambridge: Cambridge University Press, 2000).
Laboulaye, E., *Del Poder Constituyente* (Guatemala, 1872).
Laboulaye, E., 'De la Souveraineté' in *Questions Constitutionnelles* (Paris, 1872).
Landau, D., 'Constitution-Making Gone Wrong', 64 *Alabama Law Review* 923–980 (2013).
Larrère, C., 'Jean-Jacques Rousseau on Women and Citizenship', 37(2) *History of European Ideas* 218–222 (2011).
Lasalle, F., 'On the Essence of Constitutions', 3(1) *Fourth International* 25 (1942) [1862].
Lawson, G., *An Examination of the Political Part of Mr Hobbs his Leviathan* (1657).
Lawson, G., *Political Sacra et Civilis* (Cambridge: Cambridge University Press, 1992).
Lenin's Collected Works (Moscow: Progress Publishers, 1972) vol. 26.
Le Paige, L. A., *Lettres Historiques sur les Fonctions Essentielles du Parlement: sur le Droit des Pairs, et sur les Loix Fondamentales du Royaume* (1753).
Lousa, L., 'La Independencia del Poder Judicial a Partir de la Constitución de 1999', 30 *Politeia* 151–178 (2007).
Lefort, C., 'La Terreur Révolutionnarie' in *Essais sur le Politique* (Paris, 1986).
Levinson, S., *Our Undemocratic Constitution: Where the Constitution Goes Wrong (And How We the People Can Correct It)* (Oxford: Oxford University Press, 2008).
Lewes, G. H., *The Life of Maximilien Robespierre* (London, 1849).
Lindahl, H., 'Possibility, Actuality, Rupture: Constituent Power and the Ontology of Change', 22(2) *Constellations* 163–174 (2015).
Locke, J., *Two Treatises of Government: A Critical Edition with an Introduction an Apparatus Criticus* (Peter Laslett ed.) (Cambridge: Cambridge University Press, 1967).
Loewenstein, K., *Political Power and the Governmental Process* (Chicago: The University of Chicago Press, 1965).
Loewenstein, K., 'Constituciones y Derecho Constitucional en Oriente y Occidente', 164 *Revista de Estudios Políticos* 5–56 (1969).
López Boffil, H., 'Hubris, Constitutionalism, and "The indissoluble unity of the Spanish nation": The Repression of Catalan Secessionist Referenda in Spanish Constitutional Law', 17(3) *International Journal of Constitutional Law* 943–969 (2019).
Loughlin, M., 'Constituent Power Subverted: From English Constitutional Argument to British Constitutional Practice', in Martin Loughlin and Neil Walker (eds) *The Paradox of Constitutionalism* (Oxford: Oxford University Press, 2007).
Loughlin, M. and Walker, N. (eds), *The Paradox of Constitutionalism: Constituent Power and Constitutional Form* (Oxford: Oxford University Press, 2007).
Loughlin, M., *Foundations of Public Law* (Oxford: Oxford University Press, 2010).
Loughlin, M., 'The Concept of Constituent Power', 13(2) *European Journal of Political Theory* 218–237 (2013).
Loughlin, M., 'Burke on Law, Revolution and Constitution', 29 *Journal of Constitutional History* 49–60 (2015).
Luce, R., *Legislative Principles: The History and Theory of Law Making by Representative Government* (Boston: Houghton Mifflin, 1930).
Luciani, M., 'El Referéndum: Cuestiones Teóricas y de la Experiencia Italiana', 37 *Revista Catalana de Dret Públic* 1 (2008).
Lumbreras, J., *Lecciones de Doctrina Social* (Madrid, 1837).
Maistre, J. D., 'Etude sur la Souveraineté' in *Archives de la Révolution Française* (Oxford: Pergamon Press).
Máiz, R., 'Las Teorías de la Democracia en la Revolución Francesa', 6/7 *Política y Sociedad* 65–84 (1990).

Marini, F., 'Popular Sovereignty but Representative Government', 11(4) *Midwest Journal of Political Science* 451–470 (1967).

Marsilius of Padua, *The Defender of Peace: The Defensor Pacis* (Cambridge: Cambridge University Press, 2005).

Martínez Dalmau, R., 'Soberanía Popular, Poder Constituyente, Poder Constituido' 1 *Diritto Costituzionale* 71–94 (2018).

Marx, K. and Engels, F., *Manifesto of the Communist Party* (Moscow: Progress Publishers, 1969) vol. 1.

McCormick, J. P., 'Dilemmas of Dictatorship: Carl Schmitt and Constitutional Emergency Powers' in *Law as Politics: Carl Schmitt's Critique of Liberalism* (David Dyzenhaus ed.) (Durham: Duke University Press, 1998).

McCormick, J. P., 'Rousseau's Rome and the Repudiation of Populist Republicanism', 10(1) *Critical Review of International Social and Political Philosophy* 3–27 (2007).

McDonald, J., *Rousseau and the French Revolution 1762-1791* (University of London, 1965).

McLoughlin D., 'The fiction of sovereignty and the real state of exception: Giorgio Agamben's critique of Carl Schmitt', 12 *Law, Culture and the Humanities* 509 (2016).

Meckstroth, C., *The Struggle for Democracy: Paradoxes of Progress and the Politics of Change* (Oxford: Oxford University Press, 2015).

Mellado, F., *Tratado Elemental de Derecho Político* (Madrid, 1891).

Mercier, L.-S., *De J.J. Rousseau, Considéré comme l'un des Premiers Auteurs de la Révolution* (Paris, 1791).

Merlhiac, G. D., *La France, et son Roi* (1815).

Montesquieu, B. D., *The Spirit of the Laws* (New York: Hafner Press, 1949).

Morgan, E., *Inventing the People: The Rise of Popular Sovereignty in England and America* (New York: W.W. Norton and Company, 1988).

Mortati, C., *Studi sul Potere Costituente e sulla Riforma Costituzionale dello Stato* (Milan: Guiffré, 1971).

Mortati, C., *La Constitución en el Sentido Material* (Almudena Bergareche Gros trans.) (Madrid: Centro de Estudios Políticos y Constitucionales, 2000).

Negri, A., *Insurgencies: Constituent Power and the Modern* State (University of Minnesota Press, 1999).

Nieto Soria, J. M., *Medievo Constitucional: Historia y Mito Político en los Orígenes de la España Contemporánea (ca. 1750-1814)* (Madrid: Akal, 2007).

Nino, C. S., 'El Concepto de Poder Constituyente Originario y la Justificación Jurídica' in *El Lenguaje del Derecho: Homenaje a Genaro R. Carrió* (Eduardo Bulygin et al eds.) (Buenos Aires: Abeledo-Perrot, 1983).

Oakley, F., 'The Absolute and Ordained Power of God in Sixteenth- and Seventeenth-Century Theology', 59(3) *Journal of the History of Political Ideas* 437–461 (1998).

Ochoa Espejo, P., 'Paradoxes of Popular Sovereignty: A View From Spanish America' 74(4) *Journal of Politics* 1053–1065 (2012).

Oklopcic, Z., *Beyond the People: Social Imaginary and Constituent Imagination* (Oxford: Oxford University Press, 2018).

Oldfield, T. H. B., *An Entire and Complete History, Political and Personal, of the Boroughs of Great Britain* (London: Printed for G. Riley 1792) vol. 1.

Orban, O., 'Des Immunités Constitutionnelles' 3 *Revue du Droit Public et de la Science Politique en France et a L'étranger* 193–237 (1895).

Orlando Melo, J., 'La Constitución de 1886' in *Nueva Historia de Colombia* (Editorial Planeta, Bogotá, 1989) vol. 3.

O'Brian, J. B., *The Life and Character of Maximilien Robespierre* (London, 1837).
Pabón Cadavid, J. A., *De los Privilegios a la Propiedad Intelectual: La Protección en Colombia a las Obras Literarias, Artísticas y Científicas en el Siglo XIX* (Bogotá: Universidad Externado de Colombia, 2010).
Pace, A., 'La Instauración de una Nueva Constitución: Perfiles de Teoría Constitucional', 97 *Revista de Estudios Políticos* 9–44 (1997).
Pace, A., 'Muerte de una Constitución', 57 *Revista Española de Derecho Constitucional* 271–283 (1999).
Pacheco, J. F., *Lecciones de Derecho Político Constitucional* (Madrid, 1845).
Paine, T., *The Political Writings of Thomas Paine*, Vol. II (Charlestown: Printed by George Davidson, 1824).
Paine, T., 'The Rights of Man' in *Common Sense and other Writings* (The American Heritage Series, 1953).
Parker, H., *Observations upon Some of His Majesty's Late Answers and Expresses*, 2nd ed. (London, 1643).
Partlett, W., 'The American Tradition of Constituent Power', 15(4) *International Journal of Constitutional Law* 955–987 (2017).
Pasquino, P., 'Emmanuel Sieyes, Benjamin Constant et le 'Governement des Modernes', 37(2) *Revue Française de Science Politique* 214–229 (1987).
Pierson, W. W., 'Reflections on the Cabildo as an Institution', 5(4) *The Hispanic American Historical Review* 573–596 (1922).
Pincus, S., *1688: The First Modern Revolution* (New Haven: Yale University Press, 2009).
Pino Abad, M., 'El Consejo de Regencia y su Papel en la Convocatoria de las Cortes de Cadiz' in José Antonio Escudero (ed.) *Cortes y Constitución de Cádiz 200 años* (Espasa, Madrid, 2011).
Pinzón, C., *Tratado de Ciencia Constitucional*, 2nd ed. (Bogotá, 1852).
Plamenatz, J., 'The Sovereign People, the Law, and the Citizen' in *Machiavelli, Hobbes, and Rousseau* (John Plamenatz, Mark Philp, and Zbigniew Pelczynski eds) (Oxford: Oxford University Press, 2012).
Pocock, J. G. A., 'Burke and the Ancient Constitution: A Problem in the History of Ideas', 111(2) *The Historical Journal* 125–143 (1960).
Pollock, F., *A First Book of Jurisprudence* (London: Macmillan, 1923).
Polt, J. H. R., 'Jovellanos and his English Sources: Economic, Philosophical, and Political Writings', 54(7) *Transactions of the American Philosophical Society* 1-74 (1964).
Portalis, J.-E.-M., *Discours, Rapports et Travaux Inédits sur le Code Civil* (Paris, 1844).
Pou, V., *España en la Presente Crisis: Examen Razonado de la Causa de los Hombres que Pueden Salvar Aquella Nación* (Imp. de X. Jullien: Monpeller, 1842).
Pradier-Fodéré, P., *De Droit, De Politique et de Législation* (Paris, 1869).
Pradier-Fodéré, P., *Principes Généraux de Droit, de Politique et de Legislation* (Paris, 1869).
Putterman, E., 'Rousseau on Agenda-Setting and Majority Rule', 97(3) *American Political Science Review* 459 (2003).
Putterman, E., *Rousseau, Law and the Sovereignty of the People* (Cambridge: Cambridge University Press, 2010).
Quimper, J. M., *Derecho Político General* (Lima, 1887) vol. 2.
Raeborn White, T., 'Amendment and Revision of State Constitutions', 100 *University of Pennsylvania Law Review* 1132–1152 (1952).
Ramallo, J. M., 'Significado de la Revolución de Mayo', 103 *Revista Teología* 11–30 (2010).
Ramírez Cleves, G., *Limites a la Reforma Constitucional en Colombia* (Bogotá: Universidad Externado de Colombia, 2005).

Ratnapala, S., 'John Locke's Doctrine of the Separation of Powers: A Re-Evaluation', 38(1) *American Journal of Jurisprudence* 189–220 (1993).
Rausch, J. M., *La Educación durante el Federalismo. La Reforma Escolar de 1870* (Instituto Caro y Cuervo—Universidad Pedagógica Nacional, Santafé de Bogotá, 1993).
Redslob, R., *Die Staatstheorien der Französische Nationalversammlung* (Leipzig, 1912).
Roberts-Wray, K., *Commonwealth and Colonial Law* (F.A. Praeger, 1966).
Robespierre, M., 'Speech of 22 April 1791' in Keith M. Baker, 'Constitution' in *The French Revolution: Recent Debates and New Controversies* (Gary Kates ed.), 2nd ed. (New York: Routledge, 2006).
Robespierre, M., 'Robespierre on Constitutional Principles' (10 May 1793) in *The French Revolution* (Paul H. Beik ed.) (Macmillan, 1970).
Robespierre, M., 'Des Maux et des Ressources de l'Etat', in *Ouvres Completes* (Boloiseay, Lefebvre and Soboul eds) (Paris, 1958).
Roscio, J. G., *El Triunfo de la Libertad sobre el Despotismo: En la Confesión de un Pecador Arrepentido de sus Errores Políticos, y Dedicado a Desagraviar en esta Pate a la Religión Ofendida con el Sistema de la Tiranía* (Philadelphia, 1817).
Roscio, J. G., *Obras,* vol. 3 (Caracas, 1953).
Rosenblatt, H., *Rousseau and Geneva: From* the First Discourse *to* The Social Contract, *1749–1762* (Cambridge: Cambridge University Press, 1997).
Rossiter, C. ed., *The Federalist Papers* (New York: New American Library, 1961) no. 49.
Rousseau, J. J., *Letter à d'Alembert* (1758).
Rousseau, J. J., 'Considerations on the Government of Poland and on its Proposed Reformation', April 1772 (ISN ETH Zurich).
Rousseau, J. J., *The Social Contract and The Discourses* (Everyman's Library, 1973).
Rousseau, J. J., 'Letter to Mirabeau' in *The Social Contract and Other Latter Political Writings* (Voctor Gourevitch ed.) (Cambridge: Cambridge University Press, 1997).
Rousseau, J. J., *Letter to Beaumont, Letters written from the Mountain, and Related Writings* (Christopher Kelly and Eve Grace) (Hanover and London: University Press of New England, 2001).
Roznai, Y., *Unconstitutional Constitutional Amendments: The Limits of Amendment Powers* (Oxford: Oxford University Press, 2017).
Rubinelli, L.,'How to Think beyond Sovereignty: On Sieyes and Constituent Power', 18(1) *European Journal of Political Theory* 47–57(2019).
Rush, B., 'Address to the People of the United States' (1787), *The Documentary History of the Ratification of the Constitution* (Wisconsin Historical Society Press, 2008) vol. 13.
Rutherford, S., *The Due Right of Presbyteries or, A Peaceable Plea, For the Government of the Church of Scotland* (E. Griffin, 1644).
Rutherford, T., *Institutes of Natural law: Being the Substance of a Course of Lectures on Grotius De Jure Belli et Pacis* (Cambridge: Printed by J. Bentham, 1756).
Saige, G-J., *Catéquisme du Citoyen ou Éléments du Droit Public Française* (France, 1788) (originally published in 1775).
Samper, J. M., *Derecho Público Interno* (Biblioteca Popular de la Cultura Colombiana, Ministerio de Educación, Bogotá, 1951).
Sánchez Agesta, L., 'Los Principios del Constitucionalismo Español: Soberanía Nacional y Constitución Interna' in *Archivo de Derecho Público* (Universidad de Granada, 1953).
Sánchez Agesta, L., *Lecciones de Derecho Político* (Granada: Librería Prieto, 1959).
Sánchez Agesta, L., *Curso de Derecho Constitucional Comparado* (Madrid: Editora Nacional, 1963).
Sánchez Agesta, L., *Principios de Teoría Política* (Madrid: Editora Nacional, 1983).

Sánchez Viamonte, C., *El Poder Constituyente* (Buenos Aires: Bibliográfica Argentina, 1957).
Sánchez Viamonte, C., *Manual de Derecho Político: Los Problemas de la Democracia* (Editorial Bibliográfica Argentina, 1959).
Saranyana, J.I., *Teología en América Latina, Vol. II: De las Guerras de Independencia hasta Finales del Siglo XIV (1810-1899)* (Madrid: Iberoamericana Editorial Vervuert, 2008).
Sawyer, P., "Citizen Emperor': Political Ritual, Popular Sovereignty and the Coronation of Napoleon I', 100 *History: The Journal of the Historical Association* 40–57 (2015).
Schmitt, C., *Political Theology: Four Chapters on the Theory of Sovereignty* (University of Chicago Press, 1985).
Schmitt, C., *Constitutional Theory* (Durham: Duke University Press, 2007).
Schmitt, C., *Dictatorship: From the Origin of the Modern Concept of Sovereignty to Proletarian Class Struggle* (Polity, 2014).
Schneider, H., 'Patriotism and Nationalism' in *Concilium: Religion and Nationalism* (John Coleman and Miklós Tomka eds) (London: SCM, 1995).
Schuhmache, L. S., 'Burke's Political and Aesthetic Ideas in Spain: A View from the Right' in *The Reception of Edmund Burke in Europe* (Martin Fitzpatrick and Peter Jones eds) (Bloomsbury, 2017).
Schwartzberg, M., 'Rousseau on Fundamental Law', 51(1) *Political Studies* 387–403 (2003).
Scott, J. T., 'Rousseau's Anti-Agenda-Setting Agenda and Contemporary Democratic Theory', 99(1) *American Political Science Review* 137–144 (2005).
Seabra da Silva, J. D., *Deducción Chronológica y Analítica* (Madrid: Librería Francisco Fernandez, 1768).
Sealey, R., 'On the Athenian Concept of Law', 77(4) *The Classical Journal* 289–302 (1982).
Serrigny, D., *Traité du Droit Public des Français* (Paris, 1846).
Shapiro, G. and Markoff, J., *Revolutionary Demands: A Content Analysis of the Cahiers de Doléances of 1789* (Stanford University Press, 1998).
Shapiro, G. and Markoff, J., 'Officially Solicited Petitions: The *Cahiers de Doléances* as a Historical Source', 46 *IRSH* 79–106 (2001).
Shklar, J. N., *Men and Citizens: A Study of Rousseau's Social Theory* (Cambridge: Harvard University Press, 1969).
Sidney, A., *Discourses Concerning Government, Vol. 2* (Edinburgh: Hamilton & Balfour, 1750).
Sidney, A., *Discourses Concerning Government* (Indianapolis: Liberty Fund, 1990 [1698]).
Sieyès, E., *Dire de l'abbé Sieyès, sur la question du Veto royal* (7 September 1789).
Sieyès, E., *Préliminaires de la Constitution. Reconnoissance et Exposition Raisonnée des Droits de l'Homme et du Citoyen* (20–21 July 1789) (Versailles: Imprimeur ordinaire du Roi, 1789).Sieyès, E., *Vues sur les moyens d'execution don't les représentans de la France pourront disposer en 1789* (1789).
Sieyès, E., *Préliminaires de la Constitution* in *Écrits Politiques* (Roberto Zapperi ed.) (Paris 1985).
Sieyès, E., 'Bases de l'Ordre Social' in Pasquale Pasquino, *Sieyes et l'Invention de la Constitution en France* (Odile Jacobs, 1998).
Sieyès, E., 'What is the Third Estate' in *Political Writings: Including the Debate between Sieyès and Tom Paine in 1791* (Michael Sonenscher ed.) (Indianapolis: Hackett Publishing Company, 2003).
Sieyès, E., *Political Writings* (Hackett Publishing Company, 2003).
Sieyès, E., *The Essential Political Writings* (Leiden, 2014).
Sommerville, J. P., *Royalists & Patriots, Politics and Ideology in England 1603-1640* (London and New York: Longman, 1999).

Somoza, J., *Las Amarguras de Jovellanos* (Gijón: Auseva, 1989).

Sperber, J., *The European Revolutions, 1848–1851* (Cambridge: Cambridge University Press, 2005).

Suanzes-Carpegna, J. V., 'Las Cortes de Cádiz y la Constitución de 1812 (Una Visión de Conjunto)' 26 *Corts: Anuario de Derecho Parlamentario* 191–208 (2012).

Suanzes-Carpegna, J. V., *Doctrina de la Constitución Histórica de España* (Alicante, 2013).

Suarez, F., *Defensa de la Fe Católica y Apostólica Contra los Errores del Anglicanismo* (Instituto de Estudios Políticos, 1970 [1613]).

Taparelli, L., *Ensayo Teórico Apoyado en los Hechos* (Madrid, 1867).

Taparelli d'Azeglio, L., *Curso Elemental de Derecho Natural* (México, 1875).

Tapia, F. X., 'Algunas Notas sobre el Cabildo Abierto en Hispanoamérica', 11(1) *Journal of Inter-American Studies* 58 (1969).

Taylor, L. R., *Roman Voting Assemblies: From the Hannibalic War to the Dictatorship of Caesar* (Ann Arbor: University of Michigan Press, 1966).

Tena Ramírez, F., *Derecho Constitucional Mexicano* (México: Editorial Porrúa, 1978).

Thompson, E., *Popular Sovereignty and the French Constituent Assembly 1789-91* (Manchester University Press, 1952).

Thouret, M., 'Député du Calvados' (4 October 1831).

Tierney, B., *Religion and the Growth of Constitutional Thought 1150-1650* (Cambridge: Cambridge University Press, 1982).

Tierney, B., *The Idea of Natural Rights* (Scholars Press for Emory University, 1997).

Tierney, S., *Constitutional Referendums: The Theory and Practice of Republican Deliberation* (Oxford: Oxford University Press, 2012).

Tocqueville, A. D., *Democracy in America* (New York: New American Library, 1956).

Tocqueville, A. D., *Democracy in America* (Henry Reeve trans.) (Penn State Electronic Classics Series Publication, 2002) vol. 2.

Torres del Moral, A., 'La Soberanía Nacional en la Constitución de Cádiz', 82 *Revista de Derecho Político* 55–117 (2011).

Tornic, A., and Massüger, N., 'Constituent assemblies in Swiss cantons' in *Patterns of Constitutional Design: The Role of Citizens and Elites in Constitution-Making* (Jonathan Wheatley and Fernando Mendez eds) (Farnham: Ashgate, 2013).

Tuck, R., 'Democratic Sovereignty and Democratic Government: The Sleeping Sovereign' in *Popular Sovereignty in Historical Perspective* (Richard Bourke and Quentin Skinner eds) (Cambridge: Cambridge University Press, 2016).

Tuck, R., *The Sleeping Sovereign: The Invention of Modern Democracy* (Cambridge: Cambridge University Press, 2016).

Urbinati, N., 'Condorcet's Democratic Theory of Representative Government', 3(1) *European Journal of Political Theory* 53–75 (2004).

Uribe de Hincapié, M. T. and López Lopera, L. M., *Las Palabras de la Guerra: Un Estudio sobre las Guerras Civiles en Colombia* (Carreta Editores and Instituto de Estudios Políticos, Universidad de Antioquia, 2010).

Vanossi, J., *Teoría Constitucional: Vol. 1 – Teoría Constituyente: Poder Constituyente: Fundacional, Revolucionario, Reformador* (Buenos Aires: Ediciones Depalma, 2000).

Vassal Fox, H.R., 'Carta de Lord Holland a Jovellanos', in 5 *Obras Completas* (Cádiz, 12 April 1809).

Vatter, M., 'Political Ontology, Constituent Power, and Representation', 18(6) *Critical Review of International Social and Political Philosophy* 679 (2015).

Vaughan, C. E., 'Introduction', *The Political Writings of Jean Jacques Rousseau* (Oxford: Basil Blackwell, 1962).

Vedel, G., 'Schengen et Maastricht (à propos de la décision no 91-294 DC du Conseil constitutionnel du 25 julliet 1991', 8 *Revue Française de Droit Administratiff* 173–184 (1992).
Vedel, G., 'Souveraineté et Supraconstitutionalité', 67 *Pouvoirs* 79–97 (1993).
Vedel, G., *Manuel Élémentaire de Droit Constitutionnel* (Paris: Dalloz, 2002).
Veitch, G. S., *The Genesis of Parliamentary Reform* (Constable: London, 1913).
Velasco-Rivera, M., *The Political Construction of Amendment Difficulty* (SJD Thesis, Yale University, 2019).
Velasco-Rivera, M., and Colón-Ríos, J., 'On the Implications of a 'Permanent' Constituent Power' (on file with authors).
Vera y González, E., *Pi y Margall y la Política Contemporánea: La Democracia Federal, su Origen, su Historia, sus Destinos Medio Siglo de Doctrinarismo en España; la Política de Programa y la Política Real* (Barcelona, 1886).
Vergara Gonzalez, C., *Assembling the Plebeian Republic. Popular Institutions against Systemic Corruption and Oligarchic Domination* (PhD Thesis, Columbia University, 2019).
Viciano Pastor, R. and Martínez Dalmau, R., *Cambio Político y Proceso Constituyente en Venezuela: 1998-2000* (Vadell Hermanos, 2001).
Villar Borda, L., *Donoso Cortés y Carl Schmitt* (Bogotá: Universidad Externado de Colombia, 2006).
Vinx, L., *The Guardian of the Constitution: Hans Kelsen and Carl Schmitt on the Limits of Constitutional Law* (Cambridge: Cambridge University Press, 2015).
Waldron, J., 'Representative Lawmaking', 89 *Boston University Law Review* 335 (2009).
Wall, I. R., *Human Rights and Constituent Power: Without Model or Warranty* (Routledge, 2012).
Walzer, M., 'Philosophy and Democracy', 9(3) *Political Theory* 379–399 (1981).
Wenman, M., *Agonistic Democracy: Constituent Power in the Era of Globalisation* (Cambridge: Cambridge University Press, 2013).
Webster, N., 'Government', 1 *American Magazine* (1787–1788).
Williams, D. L., *Rousseau's Social Contract: An Introduction* (Cambridge: Cambridge University Press, 2014).
Wilson, J., 'James Wilson's Opening Address' in *Works of James Wilson* (James DeWitt Andrews ed.) (Chicago: Callaghan, 1896).
Wood, G. S., *The Creation of the American Republic 1776-1787* (Chapel Hill: University of North Carolina Press, 1998).
Zimmerman, J., *New England Town Meeting: Democracy in Action* (Westport, CT: Praeger, 1999).
Zorn, P., 'The Constitutional Position of the German Emperor', 14 *The Annals of the American Academy of Political and Social Science* 73–93 (1899).
Zuluaga Gil, R., *De la Expectativa al Desconcierto: El Proceso Constituyente de 1991 Visto por sus Protagonistas* (Cali: Pontificia Universidad Javeriana, 2008).
Zwieg, E., *Die Lehre von Pouvoir Constituant- ein Beitrag zum Staatrecht der Französischen Revolution* (Tübingen, 1909).

Index

Note: *For the benefit of digital users, indexed terms that span two pages (e.g., 52–53) may, on occasion, appear on only one of those pages.*